BOOK ONE   Fifth Edition

CENTURY 21

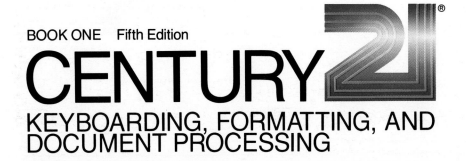

KEYBOARDING, FORMATTING, AND DOCUMENT PROCESSING

JERRY W. ROBINSON, Ed.D.
Senior Editor
South-Western Publishing Co.

JACK P. HOGGATT, Ed.D.
Professor of Business Education
and Administrative Management
University of Wisconsin,
Eau Claire

JON A. SHANK, Ed.D.
Professor of Administrative Management
and Business Education
Robert Morris College,
Coraopolis (PA)

ARNOLA C. OWNBY, Ed.D.
Professor of Office Administration
and Business Education
Southwest Missouri State University

LEE R. BEAUMONT, Ed.D.
Professor of Business, Emeritus
Indiana University of Pennsylvania

T. JAMES CRAWFORD, Ph.D.
Professor of Business/Education, Emeritus
Indiana University

LAWRENCE W. ERICKSON, Ed.D.
Professor of Education, Emeritus
University of California (LA)

 SOUTH-WESTERN PUBLISHING CO.

Contributing Author

Marilyn K. Popyk
Henry Ford Community College
Dearborn, Michigan

Photo Credits

COVER PHOTO:	© Geoff Gove/The IMAGE BANK
	© Steven Hunt/The IMAGE BANK
PHOTO, p. vi, top:	International Business Machines Corporation*
PHOTO, p. vi, bottom:	Brother
PHOTO, p. vii:	International Business Machines Corporation*
GLOSSARY PHOTOS, pp. xiii–xvi:	
"Disk"	Courtesy BASF Corporation Information Systems
"Facsimile"	Courtesy of AT&T
"Sheet feeder"	Photo Courtesy Xerox Corporation
PHOTO, p. ix:	Apple Computer, Inc.**
PHOTO, p. 128:	© Jose Carrillo, Ventura, CA
PHOTO, p. 167:	© Walter Hodges/West Light
PHOTO, p. RG13:	"Offset printer" Courtesy of A.B. Dick Company

* IBM is a registered trademark of International Business Machines Corporation.

** Apple and the Apple logo are registered trademarks of Apple Computer, Inc.

Any reference made to or use of any of these names or logos in this textbook refers to the foregoing credits.

Copyright © 1993
by SOUTH-WESTERN PUBLISHING CO.
Cincinnati, Ohio

ISBN: 0-538-60074-8
5 6 7 8 9 10 11 12 13 14 H 00 99 98 97 96
Printed in the United States of America

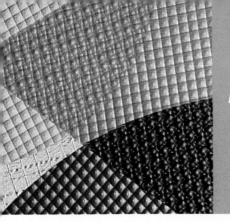

PREFACE

Keyboarding instruction is in a period of transition. Some schools still use predominantly electric typewriters for teaching/learning. Other schools have a mix of electric and electronic typewriters along with a few computers. Increasing numbers are moving almost exclusively to computers and word processors. The highest percentage of schools, however, have a mix of all these kinds of teaching/learning equipment.

Thus, this new Fifth Edition of *Century 21 Keyboarding, Formatting, and Document Processing,* Book 1, is designed and written to accommodate these differing configurations of learning conditions.

But whatever the equipment used for learning, instruction must center around the three historical thrusts of emphasis: *keyboarding* (the manipulative skills), *formatting* (the arrangement, placement, and spacing) of commonly used documents, and *document processing* (the production in quantity of documents of quality). This *Century 21* series of learning materials focuses heavily on these three fundamental components.

In addition to keyboarding, formatting, and document processing, two other components deserve and receive frequent emphasis: *language skills* (without which keyboard learning is of little consequence) and *familiarity with electronic word processing equipment* (without which keyboarding skill cannot be widely applied in the modern workplace).

Century 21 Keyboarding, Formatting, and Document Processing, Book 1, Fifth Edition, gives appropriate attention to each of these aspects of instruction at strategic times in its two cycles. Emphasis moves from the simplest and most basic toward the more complex and less often used. The amount of time and emphasis given to each facet of learning is carefully geared to the difficulty of the learning task and the level of skill required for effective job performance.

Basic Keyboarding Skills

Basic keyboarding skill consists of the fluent manipulation by "touch" (without looking) of the letter keys, the figure/symbol keys, and the basic service keys.

Mastery of keyboard operation is assured in this new edition by presenting just two keys in each practice session and by providing both intensive and extensive repetition of the reach-strokes to those keys.

The first phase of 25 lessons is devoted almost exclusively to alphabetic keyboarding skill development. Thereafter, emphasis on alphabetic keyboarding skill is provided mainly in periodic units of intensive skill-building practice.

Scientifically designed drills that are computer controlled are used to develop maximum skill in minimum time on the letter and figure/symbol keys. Some of these drills are best keyed without time pressure; others are best practiced under timed conditions. Still others are most effective when paced by teacher dictation, an audiocassette, or computer software.

Keyboarding skill on the top row is delayed until correct technique has been developed on the alphabetic keys and an essential level of keyboarding skill has been demonstrated.

For computer users, Appendix A (pp. A-2 to A-7) teaches the operation of the numeric keypad. These lessons should be used in addition to, not instead of, the figure-learning lessons of Unit 3.

During keyboard learning and skill development, this new edition places first emphasis on technique of keyboard operation (*without* time pressure) and second emphasis on speed of manipulative performance (*with* strategic timed writings). Then, when appropriate, it emphasizes accuracy of copy produced (with *restricted-speed* paced practice). This plan of emphasis is in harmony with generally accepted principles of skill learning and with a large body of keyboarding research findings.

(continued, p. iv)

combining of keyboarding and formatting skills with job-task planning, application of language skills, decision making, proofreading/correcting, materials handling, use of source materials, and efficient disposition of work produced.

Century 21 provides this integrative training through the steps of (1) format learning, (2) skill building, (3) sustained production, and (4) production measurement. In addition, this first-year course includes four realistic office job simulations during which students work independently and are responsible for the acceptability of all facets of the job tasks.

Basic Language Skills

Language skills are vital to the successful production of usable documents. *Century 21* begins language skills learning/review early and continues it frequently in manageable segments throughout the course. Beginning with rule-guided activities for punctuation, capitalization, number expression, and word division, the activities expand to include grammar, spelling, and word choice (commonly confused words). Using a study/learn/apply tactic, students get a thorough review of basic language skills. Periodic composing activities give students an opportunity to apply these learnings. In addition, many documents have embedded errors that students are expected to detect and correct.

Basic Computer Orientation

Word processing equipment and software have changed the language of keyboarding applications. *Century 21* uses the vocabulary of word processing and a simple set of abbreviations like computer operating commands in giving directions for practice activities. Further, many of its timed writings and documents are about computer and word processing applications and systems.

In these and additional ways, this Fifth Edition of *Century 21 Keyboarding, Formatting, and Document Processing* provides the best materials of the right amounts for this period of transition. Students who successfully complete the *Century 21* Book 1 activities will be well-prepared for entering the modern workplace.

Formatting Skills

Formatting includes arranging, placing, and spacing copy according to accepted conventions for specific documents (letters, memos, reports, tables, forms, and so on). It involves learning and following efficient, orderly steps for making machine adjustments, for making within-document decisions, and for evaluating final format acceptability.

Whether one learns to format on a typewriter, computer, or word processor, the concepts and principles are the same. What does differ are the machine-specific procedural steps for accomplishing the formatting task.

This Fifth Edition emphasizes those formats that can be completed with speed and ease, regardless of the equipment used. This new edition also includes many documents that permit the use of the time-saving features of word processing software. In Appendix B (pp. A-8 to A-24), students have an opportunity to practice automatic features and word processing functions of electronic equipment *before* attempting to use them in completing textbook documents.

Century 21 begins format learning with the simplest formats in the first cycle (block style letters, unbound reports, and simple tables with blocked columnar headings). Cycle 2 presents other letter and report formats and introduces the more complex formats for tables and other documents.

What is learned in Cycle 1 is reviewed and reinforced in Cycle 2 before new formats or variants of familiar ones are presented.

Formatting skill is built through special practice on those parts of documents that emphasize the format features (opening and closing lines of a letter style, for example).

Students work first from model typescript, then from semiarranged print, and later from handwritten and rough-draft copy. Each progression in difficulty of format features and source copy leads the learner increasingly nearer to the actual conditions of final performance.

Document Processing Skills

Document processing is the production of a series of usable documents over an extended period of time. It involves the

CONTENTS

■ ELECTRONIC (Brother EM-811fx)

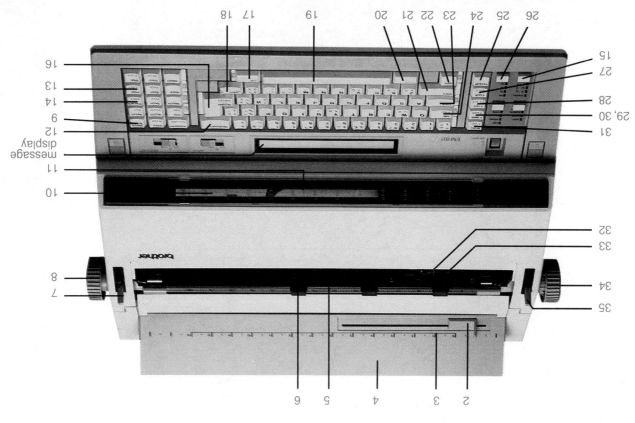

message display

■ ELECTRIC (IBM Selectric II)

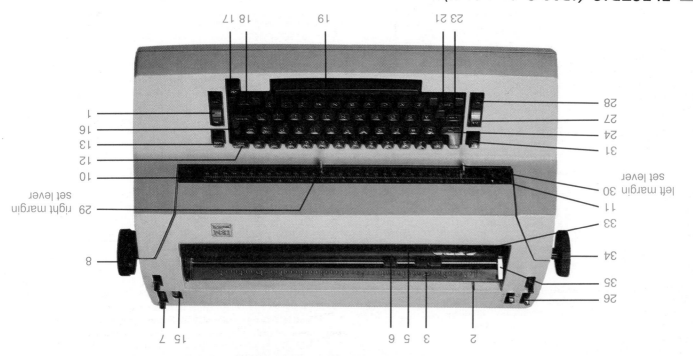

right margin set lever

left margin set lever

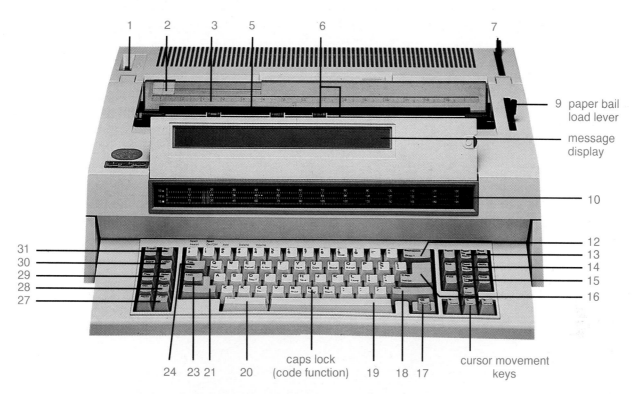

1   2   3   5   6   7

9 paper bail load lever

message display

10

31
30
29
28
27

12
13
14
15
16

24   23 21   20   caps lock (code function)   19   18 17   cursor movement keys

■ ELECTRONIC (IBM Wheelwriter 30 Series II)

The diagrams above show the parts of an electric and two electronic typewriters. Illustrated on pp. viii-ix is an array of microcomputers to which your keyboarding skills will transfer.

Since all typewriters have similar parts, you will probably be able to locate the parts on your machine using one of these diagrams. However, if you have the User's Manual that comes with your machine, use it to identify the exact location of each machine part, including special parts that may be on one machine but not on another.

1 ON/OFF control--used to turn machine on or off (not shown on Brother EM-811--under left platen knob)

2 paper guide--used to position paper for insertion

3 paper guide scale--used to set paper guide at desired position

4 paper support--used to support paper in machine (not on IBM Wheelwriter or Selectric)

5 platen--used to feed paper into machine and to provide a hard surface for daisy wheel or element to strike

6 paper bail and **paper bail rolls**--used to hold paper against platen

7 paper release lever--used to adjust position of paper after insertion

8 right platen knob--used to turn platen manually (not on IBM Wheelwriter)

9 paper insert key--used to feed paper into machine and advance paper to proper position for keying (not on Selectric); some machines also have an eject key

10 line-of-writing or **format scales**--used to plan margin settings and tab stops

11 print point indicator--used to position print carrier at desired point (on Selectric--red piece behind left margin set lever; not visible on IBM Wheelwriter)

12 backspace key--used to move print point to the left one space at a time

13 paper up key--used to advance paper one-half line at a time; can be used for paper insertion and ejection; also called **page up key** and **index key**

14 paper down key--used to retract paper one-half line at a time (not on Selectric); also called **page down key**

15 line space selector--used to select line spacing, such as single spacing or double spacing

16 return key--used to return print carrier to left margin and to advance paper up to next line of writing

17 correction key--used to erase ("lift off") characters

18 right shift key--used to key capital letters and symbols controlled by left hand

19 space bar--used to move print carrier to the right one space at a time

20 code key--used with selected character or service keys to key special characters or to perform certain operations (not on Selectric)

21 left shift key--used to key capital letters and symbols controlled by the right hand

22 caps lock key--used to lock shift mechanism for *alphabet characters only* (not on Selectric)

23 shift lock key--used to lock shift mechanism for *all* keyboard characters

24 tab key--used to move print carrier to tab stops

25 repeat key--used to repeat the previous keystroke (IBM Wheelwriter and Selectric have a feature that causes certain keys to repeat when held down)

26 pitch selector--used to select pitch (type size); some machines (like the IBM Wheelwriter) adjust pitch automatically depending upon the daisy wheel inserted

27 tab clear key--used to erase tab stops

28 tab set key--used to set tab stops

29 right margin key--used to set right margin

30 left margin key--used to set left margin

31 margin release key--used to move print carrier beyond margin settings

32 print carrier--used to carry ribbon cassette, daisy wheel or element, correction tape, and print mechanism to print point (not visible on IBM Wheelwriter or Selectric)

33 aligning scale--used to align copy that has been reinserted (not visible on IBM Wheelwriter)

34 left platen knob--used to feed paper manually; also **variable line spacer** on machines with platen knobs (not on IBM Wheelwriter)

35 paper bail lever--used to move paper bail forward when inserting paper manually (Selectric has one at each end of the paper bail)

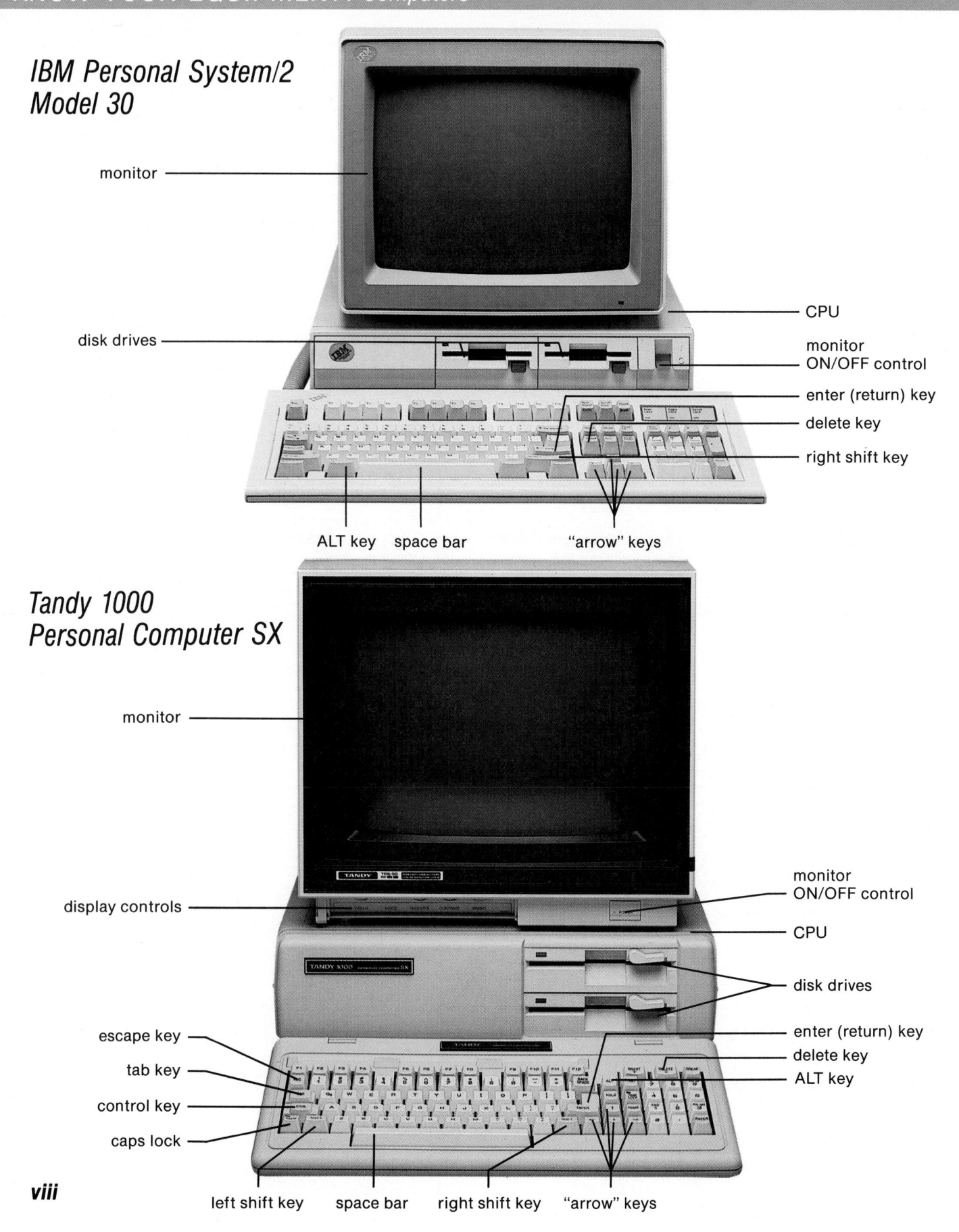

IBM Personal System/2 Model 30

monitor

CPU

disk drives

monitor ON/OFF control

enter (return) key

delete key

right shift key

ALT key   space bar   "arrow" keys

Tandy 1000 Personal Computer SX

monitor

monitor ON/OFF control

display controls

CPU

disk drives

enter (return) key

delete key

ALT key

escape key

tab key

control key

caps lock

left shift key   space bar   right shift key   "arrow" keys

Apple IIe

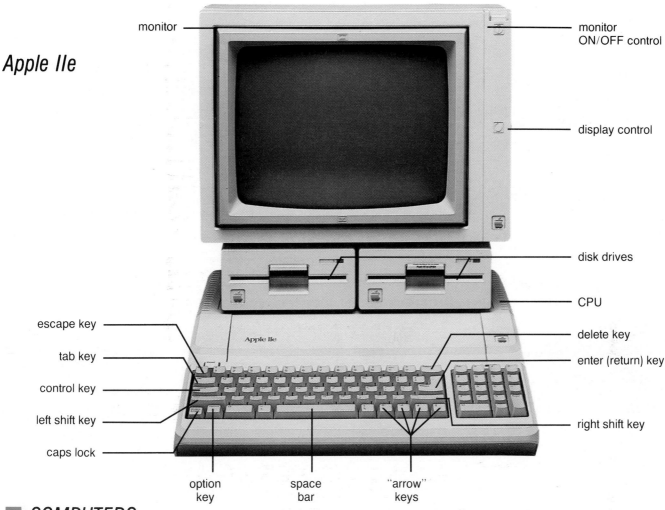

monitor

monitor ON/OFF control

display control

disk drives

CPU

escape key

tab key

control key

left shift key

caps lock

delete key

enter (return) key

right shift key

option key

space bar

"arrow" keys

■ COMPUTERS

The diagram above shows the parts of various microcomputers/ word processors with some examples of different types of machines.

Microcomputers/word processors have similar parts, though the names of these parts and their arrangement may differ. With the help of the User's Manual for your equipment, you should be able to identify each item labeled in the illustration above.

The particular word processing software that you use will determine the specific uses of so-called "function keys." Therefore, you must familiarize yourself with the User's Manual for your software as well as the one for your equipment.

The number in parentheses with some items in the alphabetized list at right refers to a comparable machine part on an electric or electronic typewriter (pp. vi-vii).

alternate (ALT) key--used with selected function keys to perform certain operations (called **option key** on Apple IIe)

"arrow" keys--used to move cursor in the direction of the arrow

caps lock key--used to lock shift mechanism for alphabet characters only (22)

control (CTRL) key--used with selected function keys to perform certain operations

CPU (Central Processing Unit)-- the piece of equipment that holds the hardware or "brain" of the computer

delete key--used to remove characters from the screen one by one

display control(s)--used to adjust contrast and brightness in display

disk drive--a device into which a disk is inserted so information can be either retrieved or recorded

enter (return) key--used to return cursor to left margin and down to the next line; also, to enter system commands (16)

escape (ESC) key--used to cancel a function or exit a program section

left shift key--used to key capital letters and symbols controlled by the right hand (21)

monitor--the piece of equipment used to display text, data, and graphic images on screen

ON/OFF control--used to "power up" or "power down" the system (1) (Apple IIe CPU control not shown--back of CPU, your left side)

right shift key--used to key capital letters and symbols controlled by the left hand (18)

space bar--used to move cursor to right one space at a time or to add space between characters (19)

tab key--used to move cursor to tab stops (24)

1 Insert Paper

Electronic Typewriters

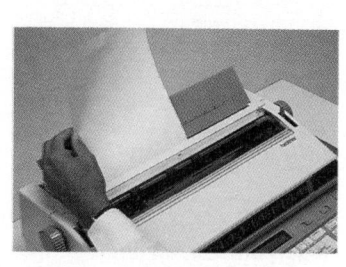

1. Align **paper guide** (2) with *0* (zero) on the **paper guide scale** (3). Turn typewriter on using **ON/OFF control** (1).

2. With your left hand, place paper on **paper support** (4), left edge against **paper guide.**

Electric Typewriters

1. Align **paper guide** (2) with *0* (zero) on the **paper guide scale** (3) or **line-of-writing** or **format scale** (10).

2. Pull **paper bail lever** (35) toward you (or upward on some machines).

3. With your right index finger, strike the **paper insert key** (9). Paper will feed to a preset point on the sheet.

4. If paper is not straight, pull **paper release lever** (7) toward you (or upward on some machines).

3. With your left hand, place paper on **paper support** (4), left edge against the **paper guide.**

4. With your right hand, turn the right **platen knob** (8) or strike the **index key** (13) until paper is about 1½" above the **aligning scale** (33).

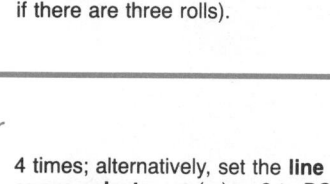

5. Straighten paper; then push **paper release lever** back.

6. Slide **paper bail rolls** (6) to divide paper into thirds (or fourths if there are three rolls).

5. If paper is not straight, pull **paper release lever** (7) toward you or upward, straighten paper, and push lever back.

6. Slide **paper bail rolls** (6) to divide paper into thirds (or fourths if there are three rolls).

2 Set Line Space Selector

Many machines offer 3 choices for line spacing--1, 1½, and 2--indicated by bars or numbers on the **line space selector** (15).

Set the **line space selector** as directed for lines to be keyed in Phase 1:

- on (−) or 1 to single-space (SS)
- on (=) or 2 to double-space (DS)

To quadruple space (QS), set the **line space selector** on (−) or 1 to SS and strike the **return key** 4 times; alternatively, set the **line space selector** on (=) or 2 to DS and strike the **return key** twice.

SPECIAL	PS
2	15
1½ 3	12
1	10
LINE	PITCH

1 Lines 1 and 2 are single-spaced (SS).
2 Lines 2 and 4 are double-spaced (DS).
3   1 blank line space
4 Lines 4 and 8 are quadruple-spaced (QS).
5
6   3 blank line spaces (2 DS)
7
8 Set the selector on "1" or "−" to SS.

③ *Plan Margin Settings*

A machine may have pica type (10-pitch type--10 spaces to a horizontal inch) or may have elite type (12-pitch type--12 spaces to a horizontal inch).

Machines have at least one **line-of-writing** or **format scale** (10) that reads as follows: from *0* to at least 90 for machines with *pica* type; from *0* to at least 110 for machines with *elite* type.

When 8½″ × 11″ paper is inserted into the machine (short side at top) with left edge of paper at *0* on the **line-of-writing** or **format scale**, the exact center point is 42½ for pica machines and 51 for elite machines. Use 42 for pica center and 51 for elite center.

To center lines of copy, set left and right margins the same number of spaces left and right from center point. Diagrams at right show margin settings for 50-, 60-, and 70-space lines. When you begin to use the warning bell, 5 or 6 spaces may be added to the right margin.

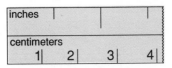

Pica, 10 keystrokes per inch
Elite, 12 keystrokes per inch

Pica center

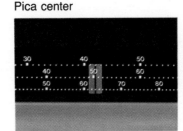

Elite center

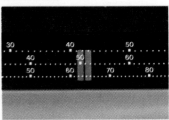

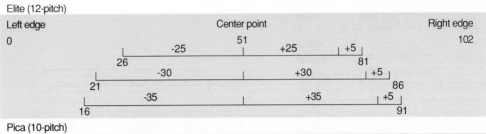

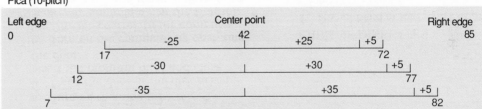

---

④ *Set Margins*

General information for setting margins on a typewriter is given here. The procedure for your particular model may be slightly different; therefore, consult the User's Manual or Operator's Guide for your machine.

Set left margin for a 50-space line for each lesson in Phase 1; set right margin position at right end of **line-of-writing** or **format scale** (10).

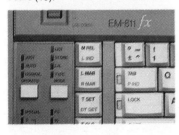

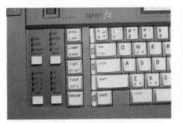

Electronic margin settings

1. Use the **space bar** (19) to move the **print carrier** (32) to the desired left margin position on the **line-of-writing** or **format scale**; strike the left **margin key** (30); on some models, depress the **code key** (20) at the same time.

2. Space to the desired right margin position and strike the **right margin key** (29) and the **code key**, if necessary.

Push-lever margin settings

1. Use the **space bar** (19) to move the **element** (32) to about the middle of the **line-of-writing** or **format scale**.

2. Push in on the **left margin set lever** (see diagram); slide it to the desired left margin position on the **line-of-writing** or **format scale**.

3. Repeat, using the **right margin set lever** (see diagram).

Key set margin settings

1. At current left margin position, depress the **margin set key** and simultaneously move the **carriage** to the desired left margin position; release the **margin set key**.

2. Using the **space bar** (19) or **tab key** (24), move the **carriage** to the current right margin position.

3. Depress the **margin set key** and simultaneously move the **carriage** to the desired right margin position; release the **margin set key**.

---

⑤ *Set Other Electronic Typewriter Options*

Mode select

Set the **mode select key** for ordinary keystroking. Later, you may choose to use other typewriter modes.

Operation/Auto select

Set the **operation select key** on "normal"; later, set it on "auto" when directed by your teacher to use automatic return.

Keyboard select

Set the **keyboard select switch** to correspond to the daisy wheel used (position 1 = standard).

Impact select

Set the **impact select switch** on "light" unless heavy, hard-surfaced paper is used.

Diskette care

Display control

Power switch

Diskette insertion

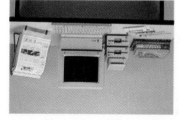

Computer work area

GET READY TO KEY

1. Position the keyboard so that the center of the alphabetic keyboard (the space between the G and H) is lined up with the center of your body. Position the front edge of the keyboard even with the front edge of the desk. If the keyboard is adjustable, adjust the angle so that the keyboard tilts slightly upward for ease of operation.

2. Turn the disk(s) you will use label-side up. Note the oval window at one edge. When directed to insert the disk, you will insert this edge into the slot of the disk drive.

3. Note whether you are using a single- or a dual-drive system. If there are two disk drives, you will use Drive 1. (Ask your teacher to identify the correct drive if drives are not numbered or are color-coded.)

4. Check that the power cords are plugged into a power source outlet.

5. Check that the monitor and keyboard are connected to the computer.

6. Locate the display controls (contrast and brightness) so that you may adjust them if nothing appears on the screen in Step 7.

7. Use one of the following "Power up" (turn on) procedures depending on the brand of equipment you are using.

For the Apple IIe, Apple IIc, and Apple IIGS computers, "Power up" as follows:

a. Turn on the monitor.

b. Open the door of the disk drive; insert the program disk; and close the door.

c. Turn on the computer by operating the ON/OFF control. (If the computer is already on, hold down the Control, "open apple," and Reset keys simultaneously.) The title screen will appear automatically.

d. Move from screen to screen by following the on-screen prompts.

For the IBM and Tandy 1000 computers, "Power up" as follows:

a. Insert the DOS disk into the disk drive and close the door.

b. Turn on the computer by operating the ON/OFF control. Make sure that the monitor (if separate) and printer (if one is connected to your computer) are also on. If the computer is already on, hold down the control (CTRL) and alternate (ALT) keys and strike the delete (DEL) key at the same time.

c. When the computer prompts you to enter the date, either do so or strike the enter key. When the computer prompts you to enter the time, either do so or strike the enter key.

d. The computer will display the message A). (If DOS has been installed on the program disk, go to Step 7f.)

e. Remove the DOS disk from Drive A and insert the appropriate program disk in the drive; then close the door.

f. Key the specific command for the software in use (see User's Manual).

g. Move from screen to screen by following the on-screen prompts.

CARE OF DISKETTES

1. Do not bend or fold a disk or attach a paper clip to it.

2. Keep disks away from direct sunlight, magnets, and x-ray devices.

3. Do not expose disks to extremely hot or cold temperatures.

4. Do not touch exposed areas of disks.

5. Use only felt-tipped pen when writing on disk labels.

6. Use care when inserting disks into and removing them from disk drives. Do so only when the disk drive light is off. If the door of the disk drive doesn't close easily, remove the disk and reinsert it. Never force the door to close.

7. Store each disk in its envelope when not in use.

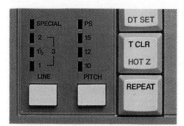

Character pitch

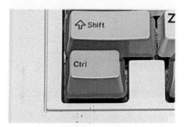

Continuous-feed paper

Control key (CTRL)

Cursor

Daisy wheel

ACCURACY degree of freedom from errors measured from zero--usually expressed as 1 error, 2 errors, etc.; sometimes as errors a minute (eam) or percent of error.

AUTOMATIC ADJUST a feature of automated equipment that automatically reformats the line endings to reflect changes caused by inserted/deleted text or margin changes.

AUTOMATIC CENTERING a formatting feature of automated equipment that places text at an equal distance from the right and left margin settings (equal copy on either side of the center point).

AUTOMATIC PAGE NUMBERING a formatting feature that automatically numbers the pages of a document as it is keyed and renumbers them during revision.

AUTOMATIC UNDERLINE a formatting feature that automatically underscores text.

AUTOMATIC WORD WRAP a formatting feature that places text on the next line without requiring the operator to strike the return key when the text reaches the right margin.

AUTOMATION the use of equipment and software programs to increase productivity and efficiency of procedures.

BACKSPACE to move the print carrier or print point (element, daisy wheel, or cursor) to the left one space at a time by striking the backspace ("back arrow") key once for each character or space.

BACKUP COPY a copy of an original storage medium such as a diskette.

BLOCK a word processing feature that defines a specific portion of text; used with the copy, move, and delete features.

BLOCK HEADING a column head that begins where the column begins.

BOILERPLATE stored text that can be merged with previously stored or new text to create new documents.

BOLD a formatting feature that prints the designated text darker than the rest of the copy to add emphasis.

BOOT to activate a central processing unit (CPU) by loading a disk operating system (DOS) into it.

CAPS LOCK a key that causes *all letters* to be CAPITALIZED without having to depress a shift key for each stroke; differs from the **SHIFT LOCK**, which causes *all shifted characters (letters and symbols)* to print.

CENTERED HEADING a heading that appears exactly centered over a column in a table or over document text.

CENTERING the placing of text so that half the copy is on each side of the center point.

CHARACTER PITCH type size expressed as the number (10, 12, or 15) of characters per horizontal inch: pica (10-pitch); elite (12-pitch); and 15-pitch. ("PS" for "Proportional Spacing" refers to a variable type size with a different number of characters per inch depending upon the particular characters.)

CONTINUOUS-FEED PAPER sheets of paper joined together for use in a printer but perforated for ease of separation.

CONTROL the power to cause the hands and fingers to make correct motions; also the ability to hold keystroking speed down so that errors (mistakes) are kept to an expected or acceptable number.

CONTROL KEY (CTRL) a special key that is pressed at the same time another key is struck, causing that key to perform a specific operation.

COPY a word processing feature that allows the operator to define text at one location and duplicate it in another location; also, material that has been or is to be keyed.

CPU (Central Processing Unit) the internal operating unit or "brains" of an electronic computer system.

CURSOR a lighted point on a display screen where the next character or space can be entered.

DAISY WHEEL a printing wheel shaped like a daisy used on some typewriters and electronic printers.

DECIMAL TAB a word processing feature that positions numbers in columns so that the decimal points are aligned (one under the other).

DEFAULT STANDARDS preset specifications in word processing software that control line length, tabs, etc.

DELETE to remove from text a segment of copy such as a character, a word, a line, a sentence, etc.; also, a word processing feature that allows the operator to eliminate a defined block of text.

DELETE EOL a word processing function that deletes text and codes from the cursor point to the end of the line.

DELETE WORD a word processing function that deletes the word at the cursor.

DESKTOP PUBLISHING using microcomputers, laser printers, and special software to create near typeset-quality documents.

GLOSSARY, continued

DIRECTORY a listing of documents filed on computer software.

DISK (DISKETTE) a magnetic, Mylar-coated record-like disk (encased in a pro-tective cover) used for recording, reading, and writing by a central processing unit (CPU). Common sizes are 5¼" and 3½".

Disk (diskette)

DISK DRIVE the unit into which a disk is inserted to be read or written on by the central processing unit (CPU).

DOCUMENT formatted information such as a letter, memo, report, table, or form.

DOS (Disk Operating System) a pro-gram recorded on a disk that causes a computer to operate or function.

Disk drive

DOUBLE-SPACE (DS) to use vertical line spacing that leaves one blank line space between printed lines of copy; equals 2 single-spaced lines.

EDIT to arrange, change, and correct existing text; editing includes proofreading but is not limited to it.

ELECTRONIC FILES information stored in machine-readable form.

ELECTRONIC MAIL information trans-mitted electronically from one computer to another without transmitting hard copy.

Element

ELEMENT a ball-shaped printing device on the print carrier of many electric and electronic typewriters.

ELITE a type size that prints 12 charac-ters per inch; see CHARACTER PITCH.

ENTER to input keystrokes; see KEY.

ENTER KEY see RETURN KEY.

ERROR any misstroke of a key; also any variation between source copy and dis-played or printed copy; departure from ac-ceptable format (arrangement, placement, and spacing).

ESCAPE KEY (ESC) a key that lets the user cancel a function or exit one segment of a program and go to another.

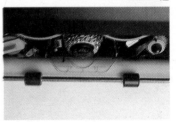

Facsimile

FACSIMILE the use of scanning devices and telephone lines to transfer text and im-ages; a copy of such text/images; commonly abbreviated "FAX."

FINAL COPY copy that is free of error and ready for use or distribution.

FLUSH RIGHT to key copy so that it ends even with the right margin.

FONT a set of characters of a named type style.

FOOTER see HEADER/FOOTER.

FORMAT the style (arrangement, place-ment, and spacing) of a document; also to arrange a document in proper form or style.

FORMATTING the process of arranging a document in proper form or style.

Function keys

FUNCTION KEYS special keys on com-puters and word processors that are used alone or in combination with other keys to perform special operations such as setting margins, centering copy, etc.

GWAM (Gross Words a Minute) a mea-sure of the rate of keyboarding speed; GWAM = total standard 5-stroke words keyed divided by the time required to key those words.

HANGING INDENT a word processing feature that positions the first line of a segment of text at the left margin or other point and indents the remaining lines a specific number of spaces to the right; frequently used with enumerations.

HARD COPY typewritten or printed copy.

HARD DISK high-capacity storage me-dium measured in megabytes (millions of characters).

HARD RETURN (REQUIRED RETURN) a manually entered return to the left mar-gin; used in letter addresses and closing lines and at the ends of paragraphs.

HARDWARE the physical equipment that makes up a computer or word processing system.

HEADER/FOOTER line(s) of copy keyed at the top (header) or bottom (footer) of each page of a multi-page document, usually the document title or chapter title and page number; also, a word processing feature for inserting header/footer lines automatically.

HELP SCREEN an on-screen list of in-structions for using the features of word processing software.

HIGHLIGHTING identifying on-screen text by changing the color or light intensity.

HYPHENATION a word processing fea-ture that overrides word wrap, allowing the operator to divide words at line breaks or to have words divided automatically.

INDENT to set copy farther to the right than the left margin; for example, the first line of a paragraph.

INFORMATION PROCESSING the task of putting text and data into usable form, as in letters, tables, and memos.

INPUT text and data that enter an infor-mation system; also the process of entering text and data.

INSERT (INSERTION) to add new text to existing text without rekeying the entire document; also the text that is added.

KEY to strike keys to print or display text and data; also called enter, key in, key-board, input, and type.

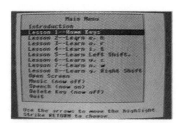
Menu

Monitor

Numeric keypad

Prompt

KEYBOARD an arrangement of keys on a "board" that is attached to a typewriter, computer, or word processor; also the act of keying or typing.

LOAD to retrieve a specified computer file or program.

MACRO a word processing feature that allows the operator to save a series of keystrokes--such as often-used phrases, paragraphs, and document formats--to be used repeatedly.

MARGINS specification of the number of spaces (or inches) at the left and right of printed lines; also the number of characters (inches) per line; also the number of line spaces above the page beginning (first line of type) or below the last line of type.

MEMORY data storage location in a computer, word processor, or electronic typewriter.

MENU a listing of available software options that appears on a display screen.

MERGE to assemble new documents from stored text such as form paragraphs; to combine stored text such as form letters with stored or newly keyed text (variables such as names and addresses).

MICROCOMPUTER a small-sized computer with a keyboard, screen, and auxiliary storage; its central processor is usually a single CPU chip.

MONITOR a TV-like screen used to display text, data, and graphic images; also called CRT, display screen, and video display terminal (VDT).

MOVE a word processing feature that allows the operator to define text at one location and shift it to another location.

NUMERIC KEYPAD an arrangement of figure keys and special keys, such as +, −, and =, to the right of most microcomputer keyboards; used for keying all-number copy and for calculations.

OPERATOR'S GUIDE (USER'S MANUAL) a set of instructions accompanying equipment or software that tells/shows how the hardware/software features are made to work.

ORPHAN the first line of a paragraph appearing alone at the bottom of a page; see **WIDOW/ORPHAN.**

OUTPUT data or documents that leave an information system, usually presented to the user as a screen display or a printout.

OVERSTRIKE a word processing feature that replaces existing text with newly keyed text; also, to key new text in place of existing text.

PAGINATION dividing text into segments that will print on a page; can be automatic or operator specified.

PICA a type size that prints 10 characters per inch; see **CHARACTER PITCH.**

POWER UP/DOWN to turn on/off a computer system by following established procedures for specific types of equipment.

PRINT to produce (using a printing device) a paper copy of information displayed on a screen or stored in computer, word processor, or typewriter memory.

PRINT COMMANDS software options for specifying the character pitch, margins, line spacing, justification, number of copies, page numbering, etc., of a document to be printed.

PRINTER a device attached to a computer or word processor that produces a paper (hard) copy of electronically stored text.

PRINTOUT the printed paper output of a computer, word processor, or electronic typewriter.

PROMPT a message displayed in the window of an electronic typewriter or on the screen of a computer or word processor telling the user that the machine is awaiting a specific response.

PROOFREAD to compare copy on a display screen or printout to the original or source copy and to correct errors (or mark them for correction); one of the steps in editing text.

PROOFREADER'S MARKS notations used to indicate changes and corrections needed to convert draft copy to final copy.

QUADRUPLE-SPACE (QS) to use vertical line spacing that leaves 3 blank line spaces between printed lines of copy; equals 4 single-spaced lines or 2 double-spaced lines.

RATE the speed of doing a task; keying or typing rate is usually expressed in gross words a minute (GWAM) or lines per hour.

RETRIEVE a software function that recovers information that has been stored (saved).

RETURN to strike the return or enter key to cause the print carrier or cursor to move to left margin and down to next line.

RETURN KEY (ENTER KEY) a key that when struck causes the print carrier or cursor to move to left margin and down to next line; also struck to enter system commands on word processors or computers.

RIGHT JUSTIFICATION a word processing feature that inserts extra spaces within and between words, causing printed copy to have an even right margin.

GLOSSARY, continued

SAVE (STORE) a software function that records keystrokes on a magnetic medium (disk) so that the data may be retrieved later; on some software, STORE records text and removes it from the screen while SAVE records and leaves it on the screen.

SEARCH a word processing feature that locates a specified series of characters or words in a document for editing purposes.

SEARCH AND REPLACE a word processing feature that locates a specific block of text and replaces it with new text. When an entire document is searched in this manner, the feature is called GLOBAL SEARCH AND REPLACE.

SHEET FEEDER a device attached to some printers that feeds separate 8½" × 11" sheets of paper into the printer.

SHIFT KEY a key that is depressed as another key is struck to make capital letters and certain symbols.

SHIFT LOCK see CAPS LOCK.

SINGLE-SPACE (SS) to use vertical line spacing that leaves no blank space between printed lines of copy.

SOFTWARE instructions, or programs, that tell a computer or word processor what to do; may be contained on a disk or on computer hardware.

SOURCE DOCUMENTS original papers (documents) from which information (data and/or text) is keyed.

SPACE BAR a long bar at the bottom of a keyboard used to move the print carrier or cursor to the right one space at a time; also used to add space between on-screen characters.

SPACING the number of blank line spaces between printed lines--usually indicated as SS (0), DS (1), or QS (3).

SPELLING VERIFICATION SOFTWARE a program that identifies misspelled words in a document generated on a computer, word processor, or electronic typewriter.

SPLIT SCREEN software capability that permits more than one file to be displayed on the screen at the same time.

STORE see SAVE.

SUBSCRIPT a word processing/printing feature that allows a character to print below the line of writing; also, the character itself.

SUPERSCRIPT a word processing/printing feature that allows a character to print above the line of writing; also, the character itself.

TAB KEY a key that when struck causes the print carrier or cursor to skip to a preset position; used to indent paragraphs or other document parts.

TECHNIQUE a keyboard operator's form or keying style.

TEMPLATE a disk on which only text files (documents) and/or document formats--but no program--are stored.

TEXT EDITOR automatic equipment that permits easy keying, revising, storing, and printing of information or documents.

TEXT (DATA) ENTRY the process of transferring text (data) from the writer's mind or from a written or voice record into a word processing system.

UNDELETE (UNDO) a word processing function that restores text to its state prior to deletion.

USER'S MANUAL see OPERATOR'S GUIDE.

VARIABLES information (such as names, addresses, or financial data) in prestored files that is inserted in standard documents to personalize messages; see MERGE.

VDT (Video Display Terminal) see MONITOR.

WIDOW the last line of a paragraph appearing alone at the top of a page; see WIDOW/ORPHAN.

WIDOW/ORPHAN a word processing feature that prevents the occurrence of widows and orphans (see definitions above) during automatic paging.

WORD PROCESSING the act of writing and storing letters, reports, and other documents on a computer, electronic typewriter, or word processor; may also include printing of the final document.

WORD WRAP a word processing feature that permits information to be keyed on successive lines without having to strike the return key at the end of each line.

ABBREVIATIONS YOU SHOULD KNOW

BM bottom margin
CH center horizontally
CS columnar spacing; space between columns
CV center vertically
DS double-space; double spacing
GWAM gross words a minute
LL line length
LM left margin
LP LabPac (workbook)
LS line spacing
N-PRAM net production rate a minute
PB page beginning
PI paragraph indent
QS quadruple-space; quadruple spacing
RM right margin
SM side margins
SS single-space; single spacing

User's Manual

Text (data) entry from a voice record

Source documents

Sheet feeder

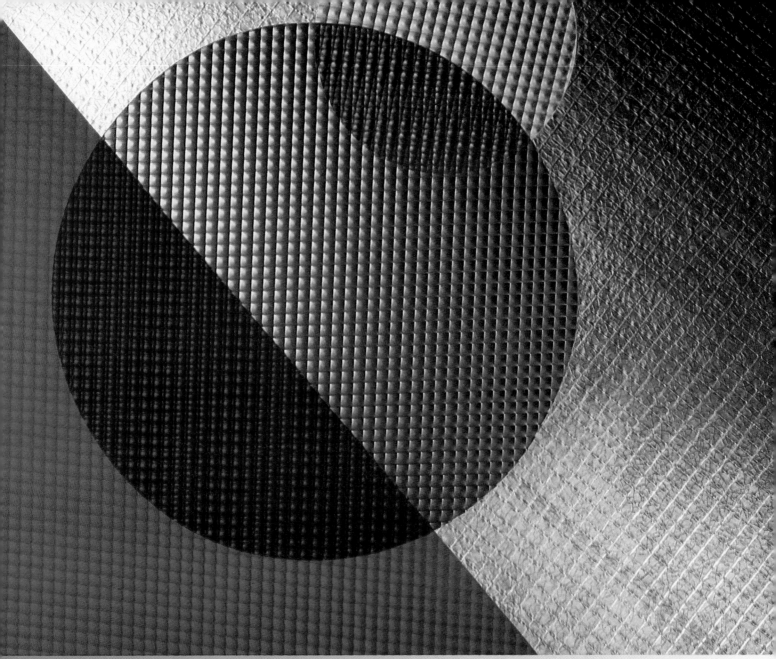

PHASE 1

LEARN ALPHABETIC KEYBOARDING TECHNIQUE

All professional and business offices in the modern workplace use a typewriter-like keyboard to enter data, retrieve information, and communicate facts and ideas. To achieve success in most careers today, you must be able to operate a keyboard with skill -- on a typewriter, computer, or word processor.

Fortunately, the alphabetic keyboards on these kinds of equipment have standard key locations. As a result, if you learn to key on one kind of machine, you can readily adapt to other keyboarding machines.

Your goal during the next few weeks is to learn to operate a letter keyboard with proper technique (good form) and at a reasonable level of keyboarding speed.

Phase 1 (Lessons 1-25) will help you learn:

1. To adjust (format) equipment for correct margins and vertical line spacing.

2. To operate the letter keyboard by touch (without looking at the keyboard).

3. To use basic service keys with skill: space bar, return/enter key, shift keys, caps lock, and tabulator.

4. To key words, sentences, and paragraphs with proper technique and without time-wasting pauses between letters and words.

5. To review/improve language skills.

Document 15

Travel Approval Request] ALL CAP & Center
QS

A travel approval request (Tar) form is to be used *utilized*

when requesting approval for any travel on company business,

whether is is paid in advance by the company or individual-
by the individual and reimbursed by the company
ly paid. Any travel over 300 miles one way requires a out-
long distance
of-state travel from completed and attached to the TAR
be
that

form. A Tar form should be completed as indicated below:
follows
DS

1. Date prepared: Enter the data on which the TAR is
SS
completed. (*in which the traveler works (example: Marketing)*)
DS

2. Department: Enter the name of the Department.
lc
DS

3. Destination: Enter the name of the metropolitin
DS   a
area--rather than specific address--which the traveler is
to   SS, etc.
going to (e.g. "Atlanta" instead of "Ben Hill, GA").
example:

4. Estimated costs: Enter approximate even-$ amounts
spell out
for transportation, lodging, and meals as follows

a. Public transportation: Estimate the cost of
DS
airfare, etc.   (Note: SS lettered enumerations
SS   and DS between them.)
DS

b. Company car: Enter the ititials "CC."
n

c. Personal car: Estimate total number of miles
roundtrip and multiply by 25.5 cents per mile.

d. Loging: Enter the room allowance ($75, $125,
d   *accommodation*
$175, $225) depending upon what area is visited (see list
the
of cities and rates on p. 44). *of Rascoe's Handbook for Employees*

e. Meals: Enter the meal allowance, including
gratiuty (Breakfast, $8; lunch, $12; dinner, $24) for meals
lc
to be taken during travel. Meals that traveler may pay for
buy
other parties, such as customers or suppliers, should not

be estimated on the TAR.

Learn Letter Keyboarding Technique

Learning Goals

1. To learn to operate letter keys and punctuation keys with correct technique.

2. To learn to operate service keys (SHIFT and RETURN/ENTER keys, SPACE BAR, CAPS LOCK, and TABULATOR) with correct technique.

3. To learn to operate letter, punctuation, and service keys by touch (without looking).

4. To learn to key sentences and paragraphs with correct technique and speed.

Format Guides

1. PAPER GUIDE at *0* (for typewriters).

2. Line length (LL): 50 spaces; see *Get Ready to Keyboard: Typewriters* (p. x) or *Computers* (p. xii).

3. Line spacing (LS): single-space (SS) drills; double-space (DS) paragraphs (¶s).

4. Page beginning (PB): line 6 or line 10, according to teacher directions.

Lesson 1 | **Home Keys (ASDF JKL;)** | Line length (LL): 50 spaces
Line spacing (LS): single (SS)

1a ▶
Get Ready to Keyboard

1. Arrange work area as shown at right.

Typewriter

- front frame of machine even with front edge of desk
- book at right of machine, top raised for easy reading
- paper at left of machine
- unneeded books and supplies placed out of the way

Computer

- keyboard directly in front of chair, front edge even with edge of table or desk
- monitor placed for easy viewing; disk drives placed for easy access
- diskette package within easy reach
- book at right of computer, top raised for easy reading
- unneeded books and supplies placed out of the way

2. Turn on equipment (ON/OFF control of typewriter or computer/monitor).

3. Make needed machine (format) adjustments (see pages x-xi, typewriter; page xii, computer).

4. Insert paper into typewriter (see page x). If using a computer printer, turn printer on and check paper supply and paper feed.

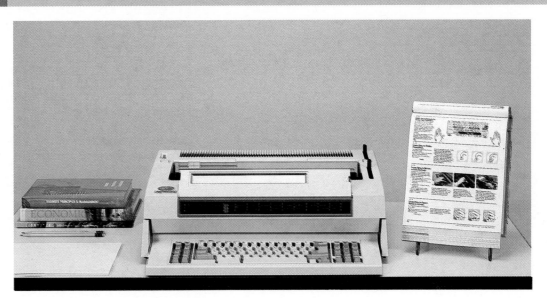

Properly arranged work area: typewriter

Properly arranged work area: computer

Document 13

WORK REQUEST FORM
Document: **F L M R T O**
Requested by: **RLR**
Date wanted: **May 1**
Addressee: ---
Address: ---
Subject: ---
Enclosures: ---
Copies: **2**
Envelopes: **0**
Special: **plain full sheet**

ITINERARY FOR ROBERT L. RASCOE
Center headings   May 3-5, 19--

Sunday, May 3 - Nashville to Philadelphia

1:16 p.m.   Leave Metropolitan Nashville Airport,
                   NorthStar Flight 730

4:36 p.m.   Arrive Philadelphia International Airport
                   (215-555-7700)

6 spaces   Confirmed reservation at Hotel Liberty,
                   118 East Meridian (215-555-3000)

7:00 p.m.   Briefing for conference presents in Salon D
                   (Bonnie Sen)

Monday, May 4 - In Philadelphia

11:00 a.m.   Present "Quality: Finding the Por of Gold
                   at the End of the Rainbow"--11:50 (Red
                   folder in brief case)

2:30 p.m.   Conduct workshop: "Start a Quality Program
                   in Your Organization--3:45 (Yellow folder)

Tuesday, May 5 - Philadelphia to Nashville

8:50 a.m.   Leave Philedelphia International Airport,
                   NorthStar Flight 639 (Exec Limo from hotel
                   lobby at 6:45)

9:15 a.m.   Arrive Metropolitan Nashville Airport
                   (615-555-2121)

Document 14

WORK REQUEST FORM
Document: **F L M R T O**
Requested by: **bmg**
Date wanted: **May 1**
Addressee: ---
Address: ---
Subject: ---
Enclosures: ---
Copies: **0**
Envelopes: **0**
Special: **plain full sheet;
   center up & down and
   across; use bold for top line
   and company name**

BUSINESS-EXPO SPRING '92
Area's Longest Running Business Show--Since 1958
A SHOWCASE OF BUSINESS PRODUCTS AND SERVICES
Attend Industrial Expo during your visit
Cosponsored by RASCOE ENTERPRISES
Daniel Boone Convention Center
West Hall
Tuesday, May 19, 1992--11 a.m.-5 p.m.
Wednesday, May 20, 1992--11 a.m.-7 p.m.   } SS these
Thursday, May 21, 1992--11 a.m.-4 p.m.   lines; DS above them

1b ▶ Take Keyboarding Position

Proper position is the same for typewriters and computers. The essential features of proper position are illustrated at right and listed below:

- fingers curved and upright over home keys
- wrists low, but not touching frame of machine or keyboard
- forearms parallel to slant of keyboard
- body erect, sitting back in chair
- feet on floor for balance

Proper position at typewriter

Proper position at computer

1c ▶ Place Your Fingers in Home-Key Position

1. Locate the home keys on the chart: **a s d f** for left hand and **j k l ;** for right hand.

2. Locate the home keys on your keyboard. Place left-hand fingers on **a s d f** and right-hand fingers on **j k l ;** *with your fingers well-curved and upright (not slanting).*

3. Remove your fingers from the keyboard; then place them in home-key position again, curving and holding them *lightly* on the keys.

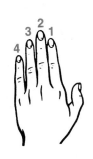

1d ▶ Learn How to Strike Home Keys and Space Bar

1. Read the keystroking technique statement and study the illustrations at right.

2. Read the spacing technique statement and study the illustrations at right.

3. Place your fingers in home-key position as directed in 1c, above.

4. Strike each letter key for the first group of letters in the line of type below the technique illustrations.

5. After striking **;** (semicolon), strike the SPACE BAR once.

6. Continue to key the line; strike the SPACE BAR once at the point of each color arrow.

Keystroking technique
Strike each key with a light tap with the tip of the finger, snapping the fingertip toward the palm of the hand.

Spacing technique
Strike the SPACE BAR with the right thumb; use a quick down-and-in motion (toward the palm). Avoid pauses before or after spacing.

Space once

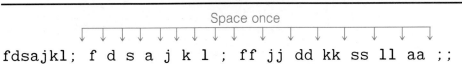

```
fdsajkl;  f d s a j k l ;  ff jj dd kk ss ll aa  ;;
```

Document 11

OFFICE SYSTEMS SEMINAR
MAY 26, 8:00-4:30
CONVENTION CENTER--PEARCE-FORD ROOM

8:00-8:30	Continental Breakfast, Opening Remarks
8:30-10:00	"Defining System Needs/Productivity Measures" Ronald W. LeForge, Jr., Sysco, Ltd.
10:00-10:15	Break
10:15-11:45	"Linking Business Goals and System Plans" Mark J. Laukus, I/O Corp.
12:00-1:00	Luncheon (Suite D)
1:15-2:45	"The Optimal Integrated Office System" Euphemia Leung, Liu Data, Inc.
2:45-3:00	Break
3:00-4:30	"Human Factors in Office Automation" Cheryl Land, Iona Life Insurance Co.

Document 12

Rascoe Enterprises always has been a leader in new and emerging technologies. To help Rascoe's administrative personnel keep up with advances in office automation, a one-day seminar has been scheduled for them on May 26.

Several current topics will be covered under the general topic "Office Systems." The attached agenda provides details. This event is important for all of us; please clear your calendar for the 26th of May.

1e ▶ Learn How to Return at Line Endings

Return the *printing point indicator* of a typewriter or the *cursor* of a computer to the left margin and move down to the next line as follows:

● Strike the RETURN key on electric and electronic typewriters.

● Strike the RETURN/ENTER key on computers.

Study the illustrations at right and return 4 times (quadruple-space) below the line you completed in 1d, page 3.

Typewriter return

Reach with the little finger of the right hand to the RETURN key, tap the key, and return the finger quickly to home-key position.

Computer return

Reach with the little finger of the right hand to the RETURN/ENTER key, tap the key, and return the finger quickly to home-key position.

1f ▶ Practice Home-Key Letters and Spacing

1. Place your hands in home-key position (left-hand fingers on **a s d f** and right-hand fingers on **j k l ;**).

2. Key the lines once as shown: single-spaced (SS) with a double-space (DS) between 2-line groups.

Do not key the line numbers.

Fingers curved and upright

Down-and-in spacing motion

Spacing hint

With the LINE SPACE SELECTOR set for single spacing, return twice at the end of the line to double-space (DS).

Strike SPACE BAR once to space

```
1 j jj f ff k kk d dd l ll s ss ; ;; a aa jkl; fdsa
2 j jj f ff k kk d dd l ll s ss ; ;; a aa jkl; fdsa
```
Strike the RETURN/ENTER key twice to double-space (DS)
```
3 a aa ; ;; s ss l ll d dd k kk f ff j jj fdsa jkl;
4 a aa ; ;; s ss l ll d dd k kk f ff j jj fdsa jkl;
```
DS
```
5 jf jf kd kd ls ls ;a ;a fj fj dk dk sl sl a; a; f
6 jf jf kd kd ls ls ;a ;a fj fj dk dk sl sl a; a; f
```
DS
```
7 a;fj a;sldkfj a;sldkfj a;sldkfj a;sldkfj a;sldkfj
8 a;fj a;sldkfj a;sldkfj a;sldkfj a;sldkfj a;sldkfj
```
Strike the RETURN/ENTER key 4 times to quadruple-space (QS)

1g ▶ Practice Return Technique

each line twice single-spaced (SS); double-space (DS) between 2-line groups

```
1 a;sldkfj a;sldkfj
```
DS
```
2 ff jj dd kk ss ll aa ;;
```
DS
```
3 fj fj dk dk sl sl a; a; asdf ;lkj
```
DS
```
4 fj dk sl a; jf kd ls ;a fdsa jkl; a;sldkfj
```
QS

Reach out with little finger; tap RETURN/ENTER key quickly; return finger to home key.

WORK REQUEST FORM

Document: **F L M R T O**
Requested by: **rlr**
Date wanted: **April 27**
Addressee: **List below**
Address: ---
Subject: ---
Enclosures: **Indicated in letter**
Copies: **1 each**
Envelopes: **1 each**
Special: **LP pp. 173-176; supply appropriate salutation; V = variable; variables and paragraphs shown on address list (below)**

{B1} Thank you for agreeing to participate in our Office Systems Seminar. The seminar will be held in the Pearce-Ford Room of the Convention Center in Bowling Green, Kentucky, on May 26.

{B2} Thank you for including our Office Systems Seminar in your busy schedule. We look forward to seeing you at the Convention Center on May 26.

{M1} Your talk, {V1}, is scheduled from {V2}. Within the 90 minutes, a question-and-answer session is optional. Also, please plan to join the group for the noon luncheon.

{M2} Your presentation, {V1}, is scheduled from {V2}. You mentioned a need for special equipment. Please use the enclosed form to specify equipment needs. I hope your travel arrangements will allow you to join us for lunch at noon.

{M3} The seminar schedule is final. You are slated to serve as recorder for a session titled {V1} from {V2}. The enclosed form provides pertinent information about the topic and the presenter. The form also should be helpful to you in recording the proceedings. Lunch will be served at noon; I hope you can join us for that part of the program, too.

{E1} An honorarium of {V3} will be provided; also, your mileage will be covered. Give a list of your expenses to me. A map of the area is enclosed. See you at the seminar.

{E2} Any expenses you incur in making this presentation should be forwarded to me. Please send the last copy of your airline ticket. In addition, an honorarium of {V3} will be provided. I look forward to your participation in this program.

Address List

	¶s	V1	V2	V3
Mr. Mark J. Laukus I/O Corp. 27 Long Ridge Road Glasgow, KY 42141-6922	B2 M1 E1	"Linking Business Goals and System Plans"	10:15 a.m. to 11:45 a.m.	$200
Ms. Euphemia Leung Liu Data, Inc. 5104 San Pueblo Avenue Oakland, CA 94612-9400	B1 M2 E2	"The Optimal Inte- grated Office System"	1:15 p.m. to 2:45 p.m.	$250

1h ▶ Key Letters, Words, and Phrases

1. Key the lines once as shown; strike the RETURN/ENTER key twice to double-space (DS) between lines.

2. If time permits, rekey the drill at a faster pace.

Fingers curved and upright

Spacing hint
Space once after ; used as punctuation.

Technique hint
Keep fingers curved and upright over home keys with right thumb just barely touching the SPACE BAR.

```
1  aa ;; ss ll dd kk ff jj a; sl dk fj jf kd ls ;a jf
                                                      DS
2  a a as as ad ad ask ask lad lad fad fad jak jak la
                                                      DS
3  all all fad fad jak jak add add ask ask ads ads as
                                                      DS
4  a lad; a jak; a lass; all ads; add all; ask a lass
                                                      DS
5  as a lad; a fall fad; ask all dads; as a fall fad;
```

1i ▶ End of Lesson

Standard typewriter

1. Raise PAPER BAIL or pull it toward you.

2. Pull PAPER RELEASE LEVER toward you.

3. Remove paper with your left hand. Push PAPER RELEASE LEVER back to its normal position.

4. Turn machine off.

Electronic typewriter

1. Press the PAPER UP (or EJECT) key to remove paper.

2. Turn machine off.

Computer

1. Remove diskette from disk drive and store it.

2. If directed to do so, turn equipment off.

Review Lesson 1	Home Keys (ASDF JKL;)	Line length (LL): 50 spaces Line spacing (LS): single (SS)

R1a ▶ Get Ready to Keyboard

Typewriters

1. Arrange your work area (see page 2).

2. Get to know your equipment (see pages vi-vii).

3. Make machine adjustments and insert paper into machine (see pages x-xi).

4. Take keyboarding position (see illustration at right and features of proper position on page 3).

Computer

1. Arrange your work area (see page 2).

2. Get to know your equipment (see pages viii-ix).

3. Make format adjustments unless you are using the built-in default margins and spacing (see page xii).

4. Take keyboarding position (see illustration at right and features of proper position on page 3).

WORK REQUEST FORM
Document: **F L M R T O**
Requested by: **Eduardo Munoz**
   Quality Control Manager
Date wanted: **April 26**
Addressee: **see file cards**
Address: **" " "**
Subject: ---
Enclosures: ---
Copies: **1 each**
Envelopes: **1 each**
Special: **LP pp. 169-172**

Nishida Rubber Products

Mr. Kumiko Oh
Nishida Rubber Products
312 Blane Drive
Glasgow, KY 42141-6163

Murrell Container Company

Mrs. Laura A. Baber
Production Manager
Murrell Container Company
1309 Ridgeway
New Albany, IN 47150-7523

¶ The future of Rascoe Carpet Division depends upon the quality carpets we produce and our performance. Rascoe Carpet Division is known as a source of high-quality carpets throughout the automotive industry, and our survival will be determined by our ability to maintain this reputation.

¶ Our primary buyer has established a quality-and-performance rating system. The MCN (Materials Complaint Notice) is the format used for this system that notifies Rascoe (the source) that discrepant materials have been received by National Motors (the buyer). Rascoe has been issued 12 MCNs so far this year.

¶ As a supplier of materials for carpets, you can easily understand our position. We must eliminate the MCNs and strive for the highest ratings. We know we can do it; but it requires that everyone, including our suppliers, help us meet this goal. Our future, and possibly yours, depends upon reducing the number of MCNs.

¶ Can we meet to discuss this issue and pinpoint problem areas. If possible, please call to schedule an appointment between May 8 (I'll be in and out in the meantime.) and May 22.

R1b ▶ Review Home-Key Position

1. Locate the home keys on the chart: **a s d f** for left hand and **j k l ;** for right hand.

2. Locate the home keys on your keyboard. Place left-hand fingers on **a s d f** and right-hand fingers on **j k l ;** *with fingers well-curved and upright (not slanting).*

3. Remove fingers from the keyboard; then place them in home-key position again, curving and holding them *lightly* on the keys.

R1c ▶ Review Keystroking, Spacing, and Return Technique

Keystroke

Curve left-hand fingers and place them over **a s d f** keys. Curve right-hand fingers and place them over **j k l ;** keys. Strike each key with a quick-snap stroke; release key quickly.

Space

To space after letters, words, and punctuation marks, strike the SPACE BAR with a quick down-and-in motion of the right thumb. Do not pause before or after spacing stroke.

Typewriter return

Reach the little finger of the right hand to the RETURN key, strike the key, and release it quickly.

Computer return

Reach the little finger of the right hand to the RETURN/ENTER key, strike the key, and release it quickly.

Key the lines once as shown: single-spaced (SS) with a double space (DS) between 2-line groups.

Do not key the line numbers.

Strike SPACE BAR once to space

```
1  f  ff  j  jj  d  dd  k  kk  s  ss  l  ll  a  aa  ;  ;;  fdsa  jkl;
2  f  ff  j  jj  d  dd  k  kk  s  ss  l  ll  a  aa  ;  ;;  fdsa  jkl;
```
Strike the RETURN key twice to double-space (DS)

```
3  j  jj  f  ff  k  kk  d  dd  l  ll  s  ss  ;  ;;  a  aa  asdf  ;lkj
4  j  jj  f  ff  k  kk  d  dd  l  ll  s  ss  ;  ;;  a  aa  asdf  ;lkj
```
DS

```
5  a;a  sls  dkd  fjf  ;a;  lsl  kdk  jfj  a;sldkfj  a;sldkfj
6  a;a  sls  dkd  fjf  ;a;  lsl  kdk  jfj  a;sldkfj  a;sldkfj
```
Strike the RETURN key 4 times to quadruple-space (QS)

> **Spacing hint**
> To DS when in SS mode, strike the RETURN/ENTER key twice at the end of the line.

R1d ▶ Improve Home-Key Stroking

1. Review the technique illustrations in R1c, above.

2. Key the lines once as shown: single-spaced (SS) with a double space (DS) between 2-line groups.

Goal: To improve keystroking, spacing, and return technique.

```
1  f  f  ff  j  j  jj  d  d  dd  k  k  kk  s  s  ss  l  l  ll  a  a  aa;
2  f  f  ff  j  j  jj  d  d  dd  k  k  kk  s  s  ss  l  l  ll  a  a  aa;
```
DS

```
3  fj  dk  sl  a;  jf  kd  ls  ;a  ds  kl  df  kj  sd  lk  sa  ;l  j
4  fj  dk  sl  a;  jf  kd  ls  ;a  ds  kl  df  kj  sd  lk  sa  ;l  j
```
DS

```
5  sa  as  ld  dl  af  fa  ls  sl  fl  lf  al  la  ja  aj  sk  ks  j
6  sa  as  ld  dl  af  fa  ls  sl  fl  lf  al  la  ja  aj  sk  ks  j
```
QS

Document 5

Here is the report you requested. It recommends initial training activities to help in implementing desktop publishing (DTP) within Rascoe Enterprises.

Training represents a big part of the budget for the DTP project. Unless several basic training decisions are made before software is purchased, we could find ourselves with everything we need (e.g., personal computer, mouse, page-composition software, laser printer) except personnel to use the equipment. The report identifies several matters that should be settled up front.

Document 6

Global Office Supplies		03204-705
Department 35		April 25, 19--
7515 Vanderbilt Place		2/10, n/30
Nashville, TN 37212-8967		UPS
5 Pad-Loks, 3 1/2"x4"(K7-05103)	14.95	74.75
3 Disk Cases, 3 1/2"(A945450)	3.95	11.85
12 Static Control Mouse Pads (A9-50940)	14.95	179.40
2 Laser Printer Workstations(A9-1900)	199.95	399.90
1 System Sweeper(K8-440)	39.95	39.95
		By Ron Bauer

R1e ▶ Improve Return Technique

each line twice single-spaced (SS); double-space (DS) between 2-line groups

Goals
- curved, upright fingers
- quick-snap keystrokes
- down-and-in spacing
- quick return without spacing at line ending

Return without moving your eyes from the copy.

Technique hint
Reach out with the little finger, not the hand; tap RETURN/ENTER key quickly; return finger to home key.

1 a;sldkfj a;sldkfj
                    DS
2 a ad ad a as as ask ask
                          DS
3 as as jak jak ads ads all all
                                DS
4 a jak; a lass; all fall; ask all dads
                                        DS
5 as a fad; add a jak; all fall ads; a sad lass
                                                 QS

R1f ▶ Key Home-Key Words and Phrases

each line twice single-spaced (SS); double-space (DS) between 2-line groups

Goals
- curved, upright fingers
- eyes on copy in book or on screen
- quick-snap keystrokes
- steady pace

Correct finger curvature

Correct finger alignment

Down-and-in spacing motion

1 a jak; a jak; ask dad; ask dad; as all; as all ads
                                         Return twice to DS
2 a fad; a fad; as a lad; as a lad; all ads; all ads
                                                      DS
3 as a fad; as a fad; a sad lass; a sad lass; a fall
                                                      DS
4 ask a lad; ask a lad; all jaks fall; all jaks fall
                                                      DS
5 a sad fall; a sad fall; all fall ads; all fall ads
                                                      DS
6 add a jak; a lad asks a lass; as a jak ad all fall

R1g ▶ End of Lesson

Standard typewriter
1. Raise PAPER BAIL or pull it toward you.
2. Pull PAPER RELEASE LEVER toward you.
3. Remove paper with your left hand. Push PAPER RELEASE LEVER back to its normal position.
4. Turn machine off.

Electronic typewriter
1. Press the PAPER UP (or EJECT) key to remove paper.
2. Turn machine off.

Computer
1. Remove diskette from disk drive and store it.
2. If directed to do so, turn equipment off.

What is the training "mix?" Will special training materials, seminars, etc, be required of all TDP users? Besides typical DTP programs, the market now offers stream-lined versions--"low-end" programs that canbe learned easily and quickly. Popyk (1990, p. 5) referred to these programs as "word publishing." Users of such programs should not require the same type of training as users of high-end DTP. The number of employees involved at each "end" remains to be determined.

Interim Recommendations

These recommendations are for the task force to include in the DTP implementation plan:

1. Classify all Rascoe documents in 1 of four categor-ies: word processing, word publishing, DTP, typesetter. (Do not assume that all publications will be published in-house within the future.)

2. Implement high-end and low-end software and offer seperate training paths for the users.

3. Lineup a consultant-instructor with art/design back-ground for design seminars. to conduct

4. Acquire DTP tutor programs for high-end users; acquire document templates for low-end users.

5. Subscribe now to at least one DTP journal and get on mailing lists for free newsletter.

REFERENCES

Hudson, Walter. "Training Packages for Ventura," *Ventura Professional*, April, 1990, pp. 27-31.

McMahon, Jennifer. "The EP&P Tutor: Learning Desktop/ Electronic Skills." *Electronic Publishing & Printing*, December, 1989, 40-44.

Popyek, Marilyn K. "If Gutenberg Could See Us Now: Teaching Desktop Publishing," *The Balance Sheet*, Spring, 1990, 5-9.

Rakow, Joel. "Skill-Based Training: The New Wave," *Elec-tronic Publishing & Printing*, December, 1989, pp. 46.

Read Before Beginning Lesson 2

Work area properly arranged

Standard Procedures for Getting Ready to Keyboard

DO at the beginning of each practice session:

Typewriter

1. Arrange work area as shown at left.
2. Adjust PAPER GUIDE to line up with *0* (zero) on the LINE-OF-WRITING or FORMAT SCALE. See page x.
3. Insert paper (long edge against the PAPER GUIDE). See page x.
4. Set the LINE SPACE SELECTOR to single-space (SS) your practice lines. See page x.
5. Set line length (LL) for a 50-space line: left margin (LM) at center −25; right margin (RM) at center +25 or at right end of LINE-OF-WRITING or FORMAT SCALE. See page xi.

Computer

1. Arrange work area as shown on page 2.
2. Check to see that the computer, display screen, and printer (if any) are properly plugged in.
3. Choose the appropriate diskette for your computer and for the lesson you are to complete.
4. "Power up" the computer, following the steps given in the User's Guide or the Operator's Manual for your computer.
5. Align the front of the keyboard with the front edge of the desk (table).

Standard Plan for Learning New Keys

All keys except the home keys (ASDF JKL;) require the fingers to reach in order to strike them. Follow these steps in learning the reach stroke for each new key:

1. **Find** the new key on the keyboard chart given with the new key introduction.
2. **Look** at your own keyboard and find the new key on it.
3. **Study** the reach-technique drawing at the left of the practice lines for the new key. (See page 9 for illustrations.) Read the printed instructions.

4. **Identify** the finger to be used to strike the new key.
5. **Curve** your fingers; place them in home-key position (over ASDF JKL;).
6. **Watch** your finger as you reach it to the new key and back to home position a few times (keep it curved).
7. **Refer** to the set of 3 drill lines at the right of the reach-technique drawing. Key each line twice single-spaced (SS):

• once *slowly*, to learn the new reach;
• once *faster*, to get a quick-snap stroke.

Double-space (DS) between 2-line groups.

Technique Emphasis During Practice

Of all the factors of proper position at the keyboard, the position of the hands and fingers is most important because they do the work.

Position the body in front of the keyboard so that you can place the fingers in a vertical (upright) position over the home keys with the fingertips just touching the faces of the keys. Move your chair forward or backward or your elbows in or out a bit to place your fingers in this upright position. Do not let your fingers lean over onto one another toward the little fingers.

Curve the fingers so that there is about a 90-degree angle at the second joint of the index fingers. In this position, the fingers can make quick, direct reaches to the keys and snap toward the palm as reaches are completed. A quick-snap stroke is essential for proper keystroking.

Place the thumbs *lightly* on the SPACE BAR with the tip of the right thumb pointing toward the *n* key; tuck the tip of the left thumb slightly into the palm to keep it out of the way. Strike the SPACE BAR with a quick down-and-in motion of the right thumb.

Fingers properly upright

Fingers properly curved

Thumb properly positioned

properly positioned

TRAINING RASCOE PERSONNEL FOR DESKTOP PUBLISHING (DTP)
by Jeanne C. McCarty, Trainer

Training of personnel is critical to implementing

desktop publishing (DTP). To reduce typesetting/printing

costs and maintain high-quality "publications," DTP users

must master the various component skills: ". . . the elec-

tronic designing, editing, laying out, and production of a

document using a personal computer and word processing,

graphics, and page-layout software" (Popyk, 1990, p. 5).

Training--not hardware or software--is the tool to maxi-

mize efectiveness of any operation, including DTP. (Rakow,

1989, p. 47). Therefore, DTP training is being considered.

The DTP training program will be guided by 2 facts: 1.

Most DTP users already have some of the requisite skills;

few now have all. 2. Optimum training prepares workers

only for tasks each performs regularly.

DTP Training Considerations

What type(s) of training materials should be used?

Commercially prepared training materials exist in seemingly

infinite variety: ". . . disk and/or book and/or tape

and/or work book and/or video" (Hudson, 1990, p. 27). In

addition, is the option of creating our own materials.

Should training consist of general principals or

specific skills? Most hardware/software training has em-

phasized program-specific skills. The trend is to ofer

seminars in principles of publication design (McMahon,

1989, p. 43). The trend has merged as organizations have

placed design responsibilities in the hands of empl

who lacks design experience or knowledge.

2a ▶ Get Ready to Keyboard

1. Arrange work area (see p. 2).

2. Adjust machine for 50-space line, single spacing (SS). (For typewriters, see pp. x-xi; for computer, see p. xii.)

3. Insert paper if necessary (see p. x) or check paper supply in printer.

Your teacher may guide you through the steps appropriate for your machine.

2b ▶ Review Home Keys

each line twice single-spaced (SS): once slowly; again, at a faster pace; double-space (DS) between 2-line groups

all keystrokes learned

```
1  a;sldkfj a; sl dk fj ff jj dd kk ss ll aa ;; fj a;

2  as as ad ad all all jak jak fad fad fall fall lass

3  a jak; a fad; as a lad; ask dad; a lass; a fall ad
```
Return 4 times to quadruple-space (QS) between lesson parts

2c ▶ Learn H and E

Use the *Standard Plan for Learning New Keys* (see p. 8) for each key to be learned. Study the plan now.

Relate each step of the plan to the drawings and copy at right and below. Then key each line twice SS; leave a DS between 2-line groups.

Reach technique for h

Reach to *left* with *right first* finger.

Reach technique for e

Reach *up* with *left second* finger.

Do not attempt to key the color verticals separating word groups in Line 7.

Learn **h**

```
1  j j hj hj ah ah ha ha had had has has ash ash hash

2  hj hj ha ha ah ah hah hah had had ash ash has hash

3  ah ha; had ash; has had; a hall; has a hall; ah ha
```
Return twice to double-space (DS) after you complete the set of lines

Learn **e**

```
4  d d ed ed el el led led eel eel eke eke ed fed fed

5  ed ed el el lee lee fed fed eke eke led led ale ed

6  a lake; a leek; a jade; a desk; a jade eel; a deed
```

Combine **h** and **e**

```
7  he he he|she she she|shed shed|heed heed|held held

8  a lash; a shed; he held; she has jade; held a sash

9  has fled; he has ash; she had jade; she had a sale
```
Return 4 times to quadruple-space (QS) between lesson parts

WORK REQUEST FORM
Document: **F L M R T O**
Requested by: **John Phipps**
Date wanted: **April 23**
Addressee: **All Personnel**
Address: **---**
Subject: **COMPANY POLICY ON ALCOHOL, DRUGS, AND NARCOTICS**
Enclosures: **0**
Copies: **1**
Envelopes: **0**
Special: **plain full sheet; key policy statement as a long quote**

Rascoe enterprises has a policy forbidding the use or possession of intoxicant beverages or narcotics by employees
on company grounds. Evidently the Policy is being vio-
lated. As we have done occasoinally in the past, wewant to
insure that all employes--those presently employed and new
employees hired, realize the possible consequences of a
violation. violating this policy.

Reporting for work under the influence of intoxicating
beverages, drugs, or narcotics or the use or possession
of such substances at any time on company property (including parking lots) may be just cause for dismissal.

Clearly, the individual who violates the policy jeopar-
dizes her or his future at Rasco Enterprises. Though Rascoe's 3-year-old Alcohol/Drug Dependency (ADD) program, we
give porfessional counselling for any employee desiring
help with a dependence problem. Alexandra Pinter, human
resources department, directs ADD. Call x424 to arrange an
apointment. Complete confidentaility is assured.

WORK REQUEST FORM
Document: **F L M R T O**
Requested by: **Ms. Gartin**
Date wanted: **April 24**
Addressee: **---**
Address: **---**
Subject: **---**
Enclosures: **---**
Copies: **12**
Envelopes: **---**
Special: **plain full sheet**

Summer-Fall
tentative holiday schedule--19--) all cap and Center

Division	July 4	September 3	November 22
Automotive Carpets	NS	NS	NS
Customer Service	S	NS	NS
Warehouse	S	NS	NS
Corporate offices	S	NS	NS
Radio Station Switchbaord	NS	S	NS
Hospitality Switchboard	S	S	S

NS - Not scheduled to work.   DS between notes

S - Scheduled to work. (salaried employees receive compensa-
tory time.)

Winter schedule to be issued June 15.

2d ▶ Improve Keyboarding Technique

1. Key the lines once as shown: SS with a DS between 2-line groups.

2. Key the lines again at a faster pace.

> Do not attempt to key the line identifications, line numbers, or color verticals separating word groups.

> Space once after ; used as punctuation.

Fingers curved

Fingers upright

| home row | 1 | ask ask│has has│lad lad│all all│jak jak│fall falls |
| | 2 | a jak; a lad; a sash; had all; has a jak; all fall |

DS

| h/e | 3 | he he│she she│led led│held held│jell jell│she shed |
| | 4 | he led; she had; she fell; a jade ad; a desk shelf |

DS

| all keys learned | 5 | elf elf│all all│ask ask│led led│jak jak│hall halls |
| | 6 | ask dad; he has jell; she has jade; he sells leeks |

DS

| all keys learned | 7 | he led; she has; a jak ad; a jade eel; a sled fell |
| | 8 | she asked a lad; he led all fall; she has a jak ad |

Time schedule

A time schedule for the parts of this lesson and lessons that follow is given as a guide for pacing your practice. The numeral following the triangle in the lesson part heading indicates the number of minutes suggested for the activity. If time permits, rekey selected lines from the various drills.

3a ▶ 5
Get Ready to Keyboard

Follow the steps on page 8.

3b ▶ 7
Conditioning Practice

each line twice SS; DS between 2-line groups

Goals

First time: Slow, easy pace, but strike and release each key quickly.

Second time: Faster pace, move from key to key quickly; keep element or cursor moving steadily.

> **Technique hints**
> **1.** Keep fingers upright and well-curved.
> **2.** Try to make each reach without moving hand or other fingers forward or downward.

| home keys | 1 | a;sldkfj a;sldkfj as jak ask fad all dad lads fall |

Return twice to DS

| h/e | 2 | hj hah has had sash hash ed led fed fled sled fell |

DS

| all keys learned | 3 | as he fled; ask a lass; she had jade; sell all jak |

Return 4 times to quadruple-space (QS) between lesson parts

WORK REQUEST FORM
Document: F L M R T O
Requested by: **Mr. Rascoe**
Date wanted: **April 23**
Addressee: **Shown**
Address: **Shown**
Subject: ---
Enclosures: **0**
Copies: **1**
Envelopes: **1**
Special: **plain full sheet**

Mr. James Powell
OSHA Representative—Southern Region
285 King Alfred Drive SW
Atlanta, GA 30331-2340
Dear Mr. Powell

The purpose of this letter is to request your presence at a meeting between Rascoe Enterprises and Local 485 of the Service Employees International Union (SEIU). The meeting has been set for June 10 at 9 a.m. and will be held in the Conference Room of our office building. The focus of the meeting will be problems associated with VDT usage. More specifically, the following issues will be addressed:

1. Right-to-know laws.
2. Issues related to VDT usage. *Letters align with first letter of copy above, as shown.*
   a. Number of uninterrupted hours a person may safely work at a VDT.
   b. The right of women to transfer to jobs that do not require the use of VDTs during pregnancy.
   c. The use of nonglare *display* screens and other ergonomic factors.

¶ Representing Rascoe Enterprises will be Mr. Howard Poindexter *, Director of Labor Relations,* and me. Union representatives will be Ms. Julie Priddy, President, and Mr. Virgil Price, Business Manager.

¶ I look forward to your assistance in answering specific questions regarding health and safety factors related to VDT usage. Please call me at 502-555-2118 by May 15 to confirm.

Sincerely

Robert L. Rascoe, President

3c ▶ 18
Learn I and R

1. Key each line twice SS (slowly, then faster); DS between 2-line groups.

2. If time permits, key each line once more.

Goals
- curved, upright fingers
- finger-action keystrokes
- quick return, eyes on textbook copy

Follow the *Standard Plan for Learning New Keys* outlined on page 8.

Reach technique for **i**

Reach *up* with *right second* finger.

Reach technique for **r**

Reach *up* with *left first* finger.

Learn **i**

```
1 k k ik ik is is if if did did aid aid kid kid hail
2 ik ik if if is is kid kid his his lie lie aid aide
3 a kid; a lie; if he; he did; his aide; if a kid is
                                                    DS
```

Learn **r**

```
4 f f rf rf jar jar her her are are ark ark jar jars
5 rf rf re re fr fr jar jar red red her her far fare
6 a jar; a rake; a lark; red jar; hear her; are dark
                                                    DS
```

Combine **i** and **r**

```
7 fir fir|rid rid|sir sir|ire ire|fire fire|air airs
8 a fir; if her; a fire; is fair; his ire; if she is
9 he is; if her; is far; red jar; his heir; her aide
```
Quadruple-space (QS) between lesson parts

3d ▶ 20 Improve Keyboarding Technique

R 9-98

1. Key the lines once as shown: SS with a DS between 2-line groups.

2. Key the lines again at a faster pace.

Goals
- curved, upright fingers
- finger-action keystrokes
- down-and-in spacing
- quick return, eyes on textbook copy

reach review

```
1 hj ed ik rf hj de ik fr hj ed ik rf jh de ki fr hj
2 he he if if all all fir fir jar jar rid rid as ask
                                                    DS
```

h/e
```
3 she she|elf elf|her her|hah hah|eel eel|shed|shelf
4 he has; had jak; her jar; had a shed; she has fled
                                                    DS
```

i/r
```
5 fir fir|rid rid|sir sir|kid kid|ire ire|fire fired
6 a fir; is rid; is red; his ire; her kid; has a fir
                                                    DS
```

all keys learned
```
7 if if|is is|he he|did did|fir fir|jak jak|all fall
8 a jak; he did; ask her; red jar; she fell; he fled
                                                    DS
```

all keys learned
```
9 if she is; he did ask; he led her; he is her aide;
10 she has had a jak sale; she said he had a red fir;
```

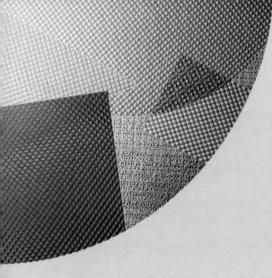

Simulation

Learning Goals

1. To transfer your keyboarding, formatting, and language skills to realistic job tasks.

2. To process documents according to standard procedures with minimum directions/assistance.

3. To improve your ability to work from script and rough-draft copy.

Documents Processed

1. Letters
2. Memos
3. Report
4. Purchase Order
5. Program
6. Form Letter with Variables
7. Itinerary

RASCOE ENTERPRISES
(An Office Job Simulation)

Before you start to process the documents on pp. 277-286, read the *Work Assignment* given at right. When processing documents, refer again to the *Standard Formatting Guides* on this page.

WORK REQUEST FORM

Document: **F L M R T O**
Requested by: **John Phipps**
Date wanted: **April 23**
Addressee: **Rebecca Crum**
Address: ---
Subject: ---
Enclosures: **1 attachment**
Copies: **1**
Envelopes: **0**
Special: **plain full sheet**

WORK ASSIGNMENT

Welcome to Rascoe Enterprises, a diversified corporation with corporate offices in Bowling Green, Kentucky. Rascoe consists of 3 divisions--Rascoe Carpets, Rascoe Hospitality, and Rascoe Communications (RasCom)--that operate independently, except for the Information Processing Center. In the center, information is processed for all 3 divisions.

You begin your career at Rascoe Enterprises as a Level 1 Document Processing Specialist. The persons who originate documents send them to the center with a Work Request Form attached. Miss Belinda M. Gartin, who supervises the Level 1 operators, selects those requests that you can fill and assigns them to you. Directions for processing each document are provided on the Work Request Form. An example of the form is shown at left.

The **M** indicates that a memo is requested; the remaining codes are Form, Letter, Report, Table, and Other. The name following *Requested by* indicates the originator--the person who will sign or initial the document if a signature is required.

The *Date wanted* indicates the assignment due date and the date that is to appear on forms, letters, and memos (if any). The name and address (for forms and letters) is also given on the Work Request Form. (When the sender's and receiver's position titles are shown on the form, key them on the document.)

The number of enclosures (letter) or attachments (memo) is given as a reminder to key the proper notation at the end of the document. The number of copies to be prepared is shown, also. (*Ask your teacher if you are actually to prepare the copies.*) The number of envelopes to be addressed (letters only) is noted. Space is also provided on the form for special instructions.

When Ms. Gartin introduced you to the *Standard Formatting Guides* used in the center, you found them very similar to formats in this textbook. You keep the guides handy for quick reference.

STANDARD FORMATTING GUIDES
Forms

1. Process purchase orders, etc., on preprinted Rascoe forms.

2. SS items in column; DS between items.

Letters/Envelopes

1. Process letters on Rascoe letterhead unless otherwise instructed; use block format/open punctuation.

2. Use a 60-space line (standard), regardless of letter length.

3. Place the date on line 16, regardless of letter length.

4. Use USPS style for envelope addresses.

Memos

Process memos on plain paper; use simplified format (1″ SM; date on line 10).

Reports

1. Process reports on plain paper; use unbound format (1″ SM).

2. Begin first page (PB) on line 10 (pica) or line 12 (elite), depending on type size; place page number (*except* page 1) on line 6 at RM.

3. DS between all lines of report, *but* QS below the main heading *and* SS enumerated items (block at paragraph indention).

4. Key REFERENCES on a separate sheet.

Tables

1. Process tables on full-sized plain paper.

2. Center tables vertically and horizontally; center column headings over the column entries; select appropriate (even number) column spacing.

3. DS all lines unless otherwise directed.

Other

1. Process other documents on full-sized plain paper.

2. Center announcements vertically and horizontally.

3. Format itineraries, etc., on a 60-space line; PB: line 10 (pica) or line 12 (elite); SS, DS, or QS as shown.

4a ▶ 3 Review
Get-Ready Procedures

1. Review the steps for arranging your work area (see p. 2).

2. Review the steps required to ready your machine for keyboarding (see pp. x-xi for typewriters; see p. xii for computers).

3. Review the steps for inserting paper into a typewriter (see p. x) or checking the paper supply in a printer (see p. xii).

4. Take good keyboarding position:

- fingers curved and upright
- wrists low, but not touching frame of machine
- forearms parallel to slant of keyboard
- body erect, sitting back in chair
- feet on floor for balance

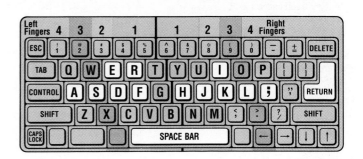

4b ▶ 5
Conditioning
Practice

each line twice SS; DS between 2-line groups; if time permits, rekey selected lines

all keystrokes learned

```
1  a;sldkfj fj dk sl a; jh de ki fr hj ed ik rf fj a;
2  a if is el he la as re led fir did she has jak jar
3  he has fir; she had a jak; a jade jar; a leek sale
```
QS

4c ▶ 10 Improve
Space-Bar Technique

1. Key each line twice SS; DS between 2-line groups. Space *immediately* after keying a word; make the space a part of the word it follows.

2. If time permits, rekey lines 1-3.

Use down-and-in motion

Short, easy words

```
1  if is ha la ah el as re id did sir fir die rid lie
2  ad lad lei rah jak had ask lid her led his kid has
3  hah all ire add iris hall fire keel sell jeer fall
```
DS

Short-word phrases

```
4  if he|he is|if he is|if she|she is|if she is|as is
5  as he is|if he led|if she has|if she did|had a jak
6  as if|a jar lid|all her ads|as he said|a jade fish
```
QS

4d ▶ 10 Improve
Return Technique

1. Key each line twice SS; DS between 2-line groups. Keep up your pace at the end of the line, return quickly, and begin the new line immediately.

2. If time permits, rekey the drill.

```
1  if he is;
2  as if she is;
3  he had a fir desk;
4  she has a red jell jar;
5  he has had a lead all fall;
6  she asked if he reads fall ads;
7  she said she reads all ads she sees;
8  his dad has had a sales lead as he said;
```
QS

Reach out and tap return

Skill-Enrichment Drill: Skill-Comparison

1. Key each line once SS as shown; DS between 3-line groups.

2. A 1' writing on each of lines 3, 6, and 9. Find *gwam* on each and compare rates.

3. Another 1' writing on each of the slowest two sentences.

Technique hint
fingers curved; upright

combination response

1 duty fare corn edge both text half rest coal vast turn wear body ready
2 to wear | is pink | do join | he sets | if ever | fix cars | key data | do join them
3 Pamela is to wear the pink gown to the union social at the civic hall.

adjacent keys

4 open were poor walk quit boil weak ruin says silk mere suit spot words
5 were open | news spot | silk suit | walk here | weak crew | open post | silk dress
6 We stopped asking the questions and quietly assisted the poor teacher.

long direct reaches

7 sun gym nut any sync many debt numb curb must verb gums stun guns sung
8 my debt|any herb|much fun|must curb|tiny lynx|many myths|stun my aunts
9 Brig sang three hymns on my TV show and received many musical praises.

| 1 | 2 | 3 | 4 | 5 | 6 | 7 | 8 | 9 | 10 | 11 | 12 | 13 | 14 |

Skill-Enrichment Timed Writing

1. A 1' writing on ¶ 1; find *gwam*. Add 2-4 words to set a new goal rate.

2. Two 1' writings on ¶ 1 at your new goal rate, guided by ¼' guide call.

3. Key ¶s 2 and 3 in the same way.

4. A 3' writing on ¶s 1-3 combined; find *gwam*; circle errors.

5. A 5' writing on ¶s 1-3 combined; find *gwam*; circle errors.

6. If time permits, take additional 1' writings on each ¶ for speed or control.

gwam	¼'	½'	¾'	1'
20	5	10	15	20
24	6	12	18	24
28	7	14	21	28
32	8	16	24	32
36	9	18	27	36
40	10	20	30	40
44	11	22	33	44
48	12	24	36	48
52	13	26	39	52
56	14	28	42	56

all letters used | A | 1.5 si | 5.7 awl | 80% hfw

gwam 3' | 5'

Our news media and editorial writers have made this idea well known: | 5 | 3 | 47
A high school education is not just important--it is almost essential. | 9 | 6 | 50
Most jobs now go to those men and women with the skills needed to run our | 14 | 9 | 53
electronic world of today, skills that almost always must be acquired in | 19 | 12 | 56
high school or college. Jobs for the unskilled dropout are dying out. | 24 | 14 | 59

Very few persons are in the position of not having to earn a living | 29 | 17 | 62
for themselves and their families. Moreover, many men and women who have | 34 | 20 | 64
enough sources of income still prefer to engage in a job of some kind. | 38 | 23 | 67
Your primary goal, therefore, should be to learn the skills necessary for | 43 | 26 | 70
a career that you would find both pleasant and profitable. | 47 | 28 | 73

We need to emphasize the merit of making our next goal that of | 51 | 31 | 75
learning how to be complete and fulfilled as a person. Students who | 56 | 34 | 78
make a concentrated effort can, by wisely and sensibly using their time, | 61 | 36 | 81
take not only technical classes but also courses that will help them to | 66 | 39 | 84
think, reason, inquire, evaluate, and enjoy. Indeed, not only their | 70 | 42 | 86
business lives but also their social lives can be enriched. | 74 | 44 | 89

gwam 3' | 1 | 2 | 3 | 4 | 5 |
5' | 1 | 2 | 3 |

4e ▶ 10
Build Keying Speed by Repeating Words

Each word in each line is shown twice. Practice a word the first time at an easy speed; repeat it at a faster speed.

1. Key each line once SS; DS after the third line. Use the plan suggested above.

2. Key each line again. Try to keep the printing point or cursor moving at a steady speed. QS at the end of the drill.

Technique hint
Think and say the word; key it with quick-snap strokes using the fingertips.

Goal: to speed up the combining of letters

```
1  is is│if if│ah ah│he he│el el│irk irk│aid aid│aide
2  as as│ask ask│ad ad│had had│re re│ire ire│are hare
3  if if│fir fir│id id│did did│el el│eel eel│jak jaks
                                                    QS
```

4f ▶ 12
Build Keying Speed by Repeating Phrases

1. Key each line once SS. Speed up the second keying of each phrase.

2. Key the lines once more to improve your speed.

Space with right thumb

Use down-and-in motion

Goal: to speed up spacing between words

```
1  ah ha│ah ha│if he│if he│as if│as if│as he│as he is
2  if a│if a│a fir│a fir│a jar│a jar│irk her│irks her
3  he did│he did│if all│if all│if she led│if she fled
4  a lad│a lad│if her│if her│as his aide│as his aides
```

Lesson 5	O and T	Line length (LL): 50 spaces Line spacing (LS): single (SS)

5a ▶ 8
Conditioning Practice

each line twice SS (slowly, then faster); DS between 2-line groups

In this lesson and the remaining lessons in this unit, the time for the *Conditioning Practice* is changed to 8 minutes. During this time you are to arrange your work area, ready your machine for keyboarding, and practice the lines of the *Conditioning Practice*.

Fingers curved

Fingers upright

```
home row  1  a sad fall; had a hall; a jak falls; as a fall ad;
3d row    2  if her aid; all he sees; he irks her; a jade fish;
all keys  3  as he fell; he sells fir desks; she had half a jar
learned                                                      QS
```

Skill-Enrichment Drill: Response Patterns

1. Key each line once SS as shown; DS between 3-line groups.

2. Take a 1' writing on each of lines 3, 6, and 9; find *gwam* on each.

3. Compare rates and identify the 2 slowest lines.

4. Key two 1' writings on each of the slowest lines to increase your speed.

letter response

1 in eat pin bad ink set you gas east milk debt pink safe join safe upon
2 act on |set in |was no |are you |act upon |car tags |milk ads |you were exact
3 Ed set up a few data base cards after a union started a wage tax case.

word response

4 tie fur fix dot cow lay cut bus rug oak worn pens owns iris laid vigor
5 pen name|lay down|map work|big risk|may fish|hand down|such good goals
6 They may all go to the auto firms to fix the panel signs if they wish.

combination response

7 map bag key few man car may act lay get owns join auto rest kept water
8 six ads |own age |tie pin |got him |bus tax |air bag |oak base |may join them
9 The six ads we did for the nylon gowns were paid for by the union man.

| 1 | 2 | 3 | 4 | 5 | 6 | 7 | 8 | 9 | 10 | 11 | 12 | 13 | 14 |

Skill-Enrichment Timed Writing

1. A 1' writing on ¶ 1; find *gwam*. Add 2-4 words to set a new goal rate.

2. Two 1' writings on ¶ 1 at your new goal rate, guided by ¼' guide call.

3. Key ¶s 2 and 3 in the same way.

4. A 3' writing on ¶s 1-3 combined; find *gwam*; circle errors.

5. A 5' writing on ¶s 1-3 combined; find *gwam*; circle errors.

6. If time permits, take additional 1' writings on each ¶ for speed or control.

gwam	¼'	½'	¾'	1'
20	5	10	15	20
24	6	12	18	24
28	7	14	21	28
32	8	16	24	32
36	9	18	27	36
40	10	20	30	40
44	11	22	33	44
48	12	24	36	48
52	13	26	39	52
56	14	28	42	56

all letters used A 1.5 si 5.7 awl 80% hfw

gwam 3' | 5'

Knowing that there are sixty seconds in every minute and sixty min- | 4 | 3 | 49
utes in each hour, we should be able to schedule our activities into the | 9 | 6 | 52
available time without difficulty. Why, then, do so many people end up | 14 | 8 | 55
rushing around in a frenzy, trying to meet deadlines? The answer is in | 19 | 11 | 58
the psychological nature of time. When we are enjoying ourselves, time | 24 | 14 | 61
seems to fly away; but time spent on tedious jobs seems endless. | 28 | 17 | 63

Do you ever "goof off" for an hour or more with a television pro- | 32 | 19 | 66
gram or a visit on the telephone and discover later that you haven't ac- | 37 | 22 | 69
tually enjoyed your leisure? Each nagging little vision of homework or | 42 | 25 | 72
chores to be completed always seems to result in taking the edge off your | 47 | 28 | 75
pleasure. And you still have to complete whatever you postponed--prob- | 52 | 31 | 78
ably in a hurry. | 53 | 32 | 78

If you fit the situation above, don't waste valuable time feeling | 57 | 34 | 81
guilty; for you have lots of company. What you should feel is cheated-- | 62 | 37 | 84
out of leisure that you didn't enjoy and study time that didn't produce | 67 | 40 | 87
results. Check with your companions who always seem ready for a good | 71 | 43 | 89
time but are also ready for unexpected quizzes. The secret is in the | 76 | 46 | 92
budgeting of your time. | 78 | 47 | 93

gwam 3' | 1 | 2 | 3 | 4 | 5 |
     5' | 1 | 2 | 3 |

5b ▶ 20
Learn O and T

each line twice SS (slowly, then faster); DS between 2-line groups; if time permits, key lines 7-9 again

Follow the *Standard Plan for Learning New Keys* outlined on page 8.

Reach technique for o

Reach *up* with *right third* finger.

Reach technique for t

Reach *up* with *left first* finger.

Learn O

1　l l l ol ol do do of of so so lo lo old old for fore
2　ol ol of of or or for for oak oak off off sol sole
3　do so; a doe; of old; of oak; old foe; of old oak;
DS

Learn t

4　f f tf tf it it at at tie tie the the fit fit lift
5　tf tf ft ft it it sit sit fit fit hit hit kit kite
6　if it; a fit; it fit; tie it; the fit; at the site
DS

Combine O and t

7　to to|too too|toe toe|dot dot|lot lot|hot hot|tort
8　a lot; to jot; too hot; odd lot; a fort; for a lot
9　of the; to rot; dot it; the lot; for the; for this
QS

5c ▶ 22 *Improve Keyboarding Technique*

1. Key the lines once as shown: SS with a DS between 2-line groups.

2. Key the lines again at a faster pace.

Goals
- curved, upright fingers
- quick-snap keystrokes
- down-and-in spacing
- quick return, eyes on textbook copy

Goal: quick-snap keystrokes; quiet hands

reach review
1　hj ed ik rf ol tf jh de ki fr lo ft hj ed ol rf tf
2　is led fro hit old fit let kit rod kid dot jak sit
DS

h/e
3　he he|she she|led led|had had|see see|has has|seek
4　he led|ask her|she held|has fled|had jade|he leads
DS

i/t
5　it it|fit fit|tie tie|sit sit|kit kit|its its|fits
6　a kit|a fit|a tie|lit it|it fits|it sits|it is fit
DS

o/r
7　or or|for for|ore ore|fro fro|oar oar|roe roe|rode
8　a rod|a door|a rose|or for|her or|he rode|or a rod
DS

space bar
9　of he or it is to if do el odd off too for she the
10　it is|if it|do so|if he|to do|or the|she is|of all
DS

all keys learned
11　if she is; ask a lad; to the lake; off the old jet
12　he or she; for a fit; if she left the; a jak salad

Skill-Enrichment Drill: Response Patterns

1. Key each line once SS as shown; DS between 3-line groups.

2. Take a 1' writing on each of lines 3, 6, and 9; find *gwam* on each.

3. Compare rates and identify the 2 slowest lines.

4. Key two 1' writings on each of the slowest lines to increase your speed.

letter response

1 in we on be no at up as my ad you are him was oil get ink few pin date
2 no card | in case | on base | in fact | join in | be aware | after him | saw him get
3 You based my case on a gas tax rebate; no tax rebate was ever awarded.

word response

4 with they them than when also such form then wish paid name held right
5 to keep | for them | when she | and paid | may form | the city | big town | own land
6 When he signs the form, title to all the lake land may go to the city.

combination response

7 if no do we is up to be it the are and you for him she ink aid oil pan
8 for him | and you | the oil | pay tax | may get | am safe | all data | he ate a plum
9 In case she signs the deed, the city may test the case with the state.

| 1 | 2 | 3 | 4 | 5 | 6 | 7 | 8 | 9 | 10 | 11 | 12 | 13 | 14 |

Skill-Enrichment Timed Writing

1. A 1' writing on ¶ 1; find *gwam*. Add 2-4 words to set a new goal rate (see chart on p. 272).

2. Two 1' writings on ¶ 1 at your new goal rate, guided by ¼' guide call.

3. Key ¶s 2 and 3 in the same way.

4. A 3' writing on ¶s 1-3 combined; find *gwam*; circle errors.

5. A 5' writing on ¶s 1-3 combined; find *gwam*; circle errors.

6. If time permits, take additional 1' writings on each ¶ for speed or control.

all letters used | A | 1.5 si | 5.7 awl | 80% hfw

	gwam 3'	5'
Although the path to success is usually lengthy, you can make it	4	3	46
shorter if you will start to develop two important skills at the begin-	9	5	49
ning of your business career. The first is the ability to see and to	14	8	52
solve problems; the second, the ability to gather facts and arrange them	19	11	55
in logical order, from which you can draw the correct conclusions.	23	14	58
Surely you can recall occasions when you devoted many hours, even	27	16	60
days, to striving unsuccessfully for a goal, and then you happened to see	32	19	63
the difficult problem from a new viewpoint. Perhaps you exclaimed to a	37	22	66
friend or yourself, "Now I see what the problem is." And once identi-	42	25	69
fied, the problem was easily solved. As you begin work on a project,	46	28	72
make your initial step that of seeing the actual problem.	50	30	74
To solve problems, use all effectual means to get the data that you	55	33	77
will need. Books and magazine articles give facts and expert opinions,	60	36	80
and a request by mail or phone may result in added aid. Enter the data	64	38	83
on cards, divide the cards into logical groups, review the work, and	69	41	85
apply common sense to reach conclusions that the data support.	73	44	88

gwam 3' | 1 | 2 | 3 | 4 | 5 |
5' | 1 | 2 | 3 |

6a ▶ 8
Conditioning Practice

each line twice SS (slowly, then faster); DS between 2-line groups

all letters learned

home row 1 has a jak; ask a lad; a fall fad; had a jak salad;

o/t 2 to do it; as a tot; do a lot; it is hot; to dot it

e/i/r 3 is a kid; it is far; a red jar; her skis; her aide
QS

6b ▶ 20
Learn N and G

each line twice SS (slowly, then faster); DS between 2-line groups; if time permits, key lines 7-9 again

Follow the *Standard Plan for Learning New Keys* outlined on page 8.

Reach technique for n

Reach *down* with *right first* finger.

Reach technique for g

Reach to *right* with *left first* finger.

Learn n

1 j j nj nj an an and and end end ant ant land lands

2 nj nj an an en en in in on on end end and and hand

3 an en; an end; an ant; no end; on land; a fine end
DS

Learn g

4 f f gf gf go go fog fog got got fig figs jogs jogs

5 gf gf go go got got dig dig jog jog logs logs golf

6 to go; he got; to jog; to jig; the fog; is to golf
DS

Combine n and g

7 go go|no no|nag nag|ago ago|gin gin|gone gone|long

8 go on; a nag; sign in; no gain; long ago; into fog

9 a fine gig; log in soon; a good sign; lend a hand;
QS

6c ▶ 5 Improve Return Technique

1. Key each line twice SS; DS between 2-line groups. Keep up your pace at the end of the line, return quickly, and begin new line promptly.

2. If time permits, rekey the drill.

1 she is gone;

2 he got an old dog;

3 she jogs in a dense fog;

4 she and he go to golf at nine;

5 he is a hand on a rig in the north;
QS

Reach out and tap return

Skill-Enrichment Drill: Machine Parts

1. Key the drill once SS as shown; DS between 3-line groups.
2. Key the lines again at a faster pace.

Technique hints
Lines 1-3: Fingers upright over home keys.

Lines 4-6: Fingers deeply curved; do not let hands move forward or downward.

Lines 7-12: Eyes on copy; do not pause before or after tab or return.

space bar

1 jam own man oak key eye lay pen pan worn turn duty busy firm form down
2 to form| when it| to sign| key firm| the busy| and then| turn down| with them
3 Both men may go to the city to work on the audit of the big soap firm.

shift keys and LOCK

4 Mrs. Pasley attended the NBEA convention in San Francisco, California.
5 The LVA convention will be in Little Rock; ABCA will convene in Omaha.
6 Please buy Kisha and Jo these books by Gore Vidal: LINCOLN and BURR.

tab and return

7 Tab————— (35 spaces) —————→Before you key a timed writing, tab
8 to the paragraph beginning.   As you key each line, maintain your
9 speed to the end of the line.   Return without pausing; then, begin
10 the new line quickly.   Pausing before or after the tab and
11 return reduces your speed.   If you use a word-wrap feature, you
12 should continue keying the next line.

Skill-Enrichment Timed Writing

1. A 1' writing on ¶ 1; find *gwam*. Add 2-4 words to set a new goal rate.
2. Two 1' writings on ¶ 1 at your new goal rate, guided by ¼' guide call.
3. Key ¶s 2 and 3 in the same way.
4. A 3' writing on ¶s 1-3 combined; find *gwam*; circle errors.
5. A 5' writing on ¶s 1-3 combined; find *gwam*; circle errors.
6. If time permits, take additional 1' writings on each ¶ for speed or control.

gwam	¼'	½'	¾'	1'
20	5	10	15	20
24	6	12	18	24
28	7	14	21	28
32	8	16	24	32
36	9	18	27	36
40	10	20	30	40
44	11	22	33	44
48	12	24	36	48
52	13	26	39	52
56	14	28	42	56

all letters used | A | 1.5 si | 5.7 awl | 80% hfw

			gwam 3'	5'

The most crucial aim of all of your keying practice now must be to de- 5 | 3 | 44
velop the highest skill possible. Regardless of whether you plan to apply 10 | 6 | 47
your skill at home, at school, or in the business world, the principal 14 | 9 | 50
goal of your efforts must be to attain top skill. The firmest assurance 19 | 11 | 53
of your eventual success is to build the best possible keying power now. 24 | 14 | 56

You must work hard to build high skill; it is not bestowed. No 28 | 17 | 59
magic plan or simple system will help you obtain maximum keyboarding 33 | 20 | 61
skill. To build a high skill, you must expend extra energy, devote many 38 | 23 | 64
hours to developing proper technique on copy containing ideas for growth, 42 | 25 | 67
and use the most effective work method each and every time you practice. 47 | 28 | 70

No single skill-building activity will supply the variety of ex- 51 | 29 | 73
periences that will yield maximum progress and skill. Sometimes the ob- 56 | 34 | 75
ject of practice is to reach for speed; at other times, the purpose may 61 | 37 | 78
be to practice at a slower rate to lower the number of errors. Learn 68 | 39 | 81
now to employ each kind of technique with equal zest. 69 | 42 | 83

gwam 3' | 1 | 2 | 3 | 4 | 5
5' | 1 | 2 | 3

6d ▶ 17 Improve Keyboarding Technique

1. Key the lines once as shown: SS with a DS between 2-line groups.

2. Key the lines again at a faster pace.

Goals
- curved, upright fingers
- quick-snap keystrokes
- down-and-in spacing
- quick return, eyes on textbook copy

reach review
1 a;sldkfj ed ol rf hj tf nj gf lo de jh ft nj fr a;
2 he jogs; an old ski; do a log for; she left a jar;
                                                    DS

n/g
3 an an|go go|in in|dig dig|and and|got got|end ends
4 go to; is an; log on; sign it; and golf; fine figs
                                                    DS

space bar
5 if if|an an|go go|of of|or or|he he|it it|is is|do
6 if it is|is to go|he or she|to do this|of the sign
                                                    DS

all keys learned
7 she had an old oak desk; a jell jar is at the side
8 he has left for the lake; she goes there at eight;
                                                    DS

all keys learned
9 she said he did it for her; he is to take the oars
10 sign the list on the desk; go right to the old jet

Left Shift and . (Period)

Line length (LL): 50 spaces
Line spacing (LS): single (SS)

Finger-action keystrokes

Down-and-in spacing

Quick out-and-tap return

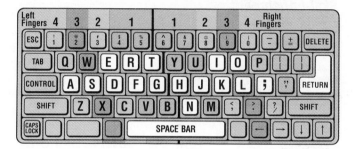

7a ▶ 8 Conditioning Practice

each line twice SS (slowly, then faster); DS between 2-line groups

reach review
1 ed ik rf ol gf hj tf nj de ki fr lo fg jh ft jn a;

space bar
2 or is to if an of el so it go id he do as in at on

all keys learned
3 he is; if an; or do; to go; a jak; an oak; of all;
                                                    QS

7b ▶ 5 Improve Space-Bar/Return Technique

1. Key each line once SS; return and start each new line quickly.

2. If time permits, rekey the drill at a faster pace.

1 the jet is hers;

2 she has gone to ski;

3 he asked her for one disk;

4 all the girls left for the lake;

5 she is to take this list to his desk;

6 he is at the lake to ski if the fog lifts;

7 he is to see her soon if the jet lands at nine;
                                                    QS

Skill-Enrichment Drill: Machine Parts

1. Key the drill once SS as shown; DS between 3-line groups.

2. Key the lines again at a faster pace.

Technique hints

Lines 1-3: Keep your fingers upright over the home keys.

Lines 4-6: Keep the fingers deeply curved; do not let the hands move forward or downward.

Lines 7-12: Keep your eyes on the source copy; do not pause before or after you tab or return.

space bar
1 Am an so he in she any and pan ran jam the pen cam for dim six map say
2 to say | he may | for us | by six | the map | if they | sign it | when she | if he can
3 She is to sign the form to pay the men for the work they did for them.

shift keys
4 Cap and I | March or April | Tuesday and Friday | Jane and Zoe | Epson & Jakes
5 Jan works for Paulsen & Sons in Boston; Max, for Appel Corp. in Salem.
6 Nan and Kat Epps sailed for London in April on the Queen Elizabeth II.

tab and return
7 Tab———————(35 spaces)———————→To save time and to increase speed,
8 tab and return quickly. To do this, keep your eyes fixed on
9 the source copy. Don't pause before or after you tab
10 or return; keep on keying. Think of the copy as one continuous
11 line of print. Think of the tab and return as mere
12 spaces between words.

Skill-Enrichment Timed Writing

1. A 1' writing on ¶ 1; find *gwam*. Add 2-4 words to set a new goal rate (see chart on p. 270).

2. Two 1' writings on ¶ 1 at your new goal rate, guided by ¼' guide call.

3. Key ¶s 2 and 3 in the same way.

4. A 3' writing on ¶s 1-3 combined; find *gwam*; circle errors.

5. A 5' writing on ¶s 1-3 combined; find *gwam*; circle errors.

6. If time permits, take additional 1' writings on each ¶ for speed or control.

all letters used	A	1.5 si	5.7 awl	80% hfw

	gwam 3'	5'
Human relations skills on the job are very critical in terms of	4	3 | 42
how you will be perceived by peers as well as by superiors. During	9	5 | 45
your early weeks at work, you will be sized up quickly by coworkers.	14	8 | 48
How they observe and evaluate you will help to determine whether your	18	11 | 51
work experience will be pleasant, successful, and valuable.	22	13 | 53
Be cautious at first and do not align yourself closely with any	26	16 | 56
of the cliques that often develop in the workplace. Show understand-	31	19 | 58
ing and be courteous to everybody, but don't take sides in a dispute	36	21 | 61
that may occur between members of any group of workers. Show that you	40	24 | 64
can think for yourself, but don't convey your ideas too freely.	45	27 | 66
Look, listen, and learn before you take an active part in the poli-	49	29 | 69
tics of the workplace. Let the older, experienced workers be the agents	54	32 | 72
of change. Study and learn from them and carefully notice what seems	59	35 | 75
to cause their successes or failures. As you develop on a job, all	63	38 | 78
positive human relations skills will be rewarded.	66	40 | 80

gwam 3' | 1 | 2 | 3 | 4 | 5 |
5' | 1 | 2 | 3 |

7c ▶ 20 Learn Left Shift Key and . (Period)

each line twice SS (slowly, then faster); DS between 2-line groups; if time permits, rekey each line

Spacing hints

Space *once* after . used at end of abbreviations and following letters in initials. *Do not* space after . *within* abbreviations.

Space *twice* after . at the end of a sentence except at line endings. There, return without spacing.

Control of LEFT SHIFT key

Reach *down* with *left little* finger; shift, strike, release.

Reach technique for . (period)

Reach *down* with *right third* finger; space twice after. at end of sentence.

Learn **Left Shift Key** (Shift; strike key; release both quickly.)

1 a a Ja Ja Ka Ka La La Hal Hal Kal Kal Jae Jae Lana
2 Kal rode; Kae did it; Hans has jade; Jan ate a fig
3 I see that Jake is to aid Kae at the Oak Lake sale
DS

Learn **.** (period)

4 l l .l .l fl. fl. ed. ed. ft. ft. rd. rd. hr. hrs.
5 .l .l fl. fl. hr. hr. e.g. e.g. i.e. i.e. in. ins.
6 fl. ft. hr. ed. rd. rt. off. fed. ord. alt. asstd.
DS

Combine **Left Shift** and **.**

7 I do. Ian is. Ola did. Jan does. Kent is gone.
8 Hal did it. I shall do it. Kate left on a train.
9 J. L. Han skis on Oak Lake; Lt. Haig also does so.
QS

7d ▶ 17 Improve Keyboarding Technique

1. Key the lines once as shown: SS with a DS between 2-line groups.
2. Key the lines again at a faster pace.

Goals
- curved, upright fingers
- finger-action keystrokes
- quiet hands and arms
- down-and-in spacing
- out-and-down shifting
- quick out-and-tap return

Technique hint: Eyes on copy except when you lose your place.

abbrev./initials
1 He said ft. for feet; rd. for road; fl. for floor.
2 Lt. Hahn let L. K. take the old gong to Lake Neil.
DS

3d row emphasis
3 Lars is to ask at the old store for a kite for Jo.
4 Ike said he is to take the old road to Lake Heidi.
DS

key words
5 a an or he to if do it of so is go for got old led
6 go the off aid dot end jar she fit oak and had rod
DS

key phrases
7 if so|it is|to do|if it|do so|to go|he is|to do it
8 to the|and do|is the|got it|if the|for the|ask for
DS

all letters learned
9 Ned asked her to send the log to an old ski lodge.
10 O. J. lost one of the sleds he took off the train.

Skill-Enrichment Drill: Double Letters, Adjacent-Key Combinations, and Long Direct Reaches

1. Key each line once SS as shown; DS between 3-line groups.

2. Take a 1′ writing on each of lines 3, 6, and 9; find *gwam* on each.

3. Compare rates; then take another 1′ writing on each of the slowest lines to increase your speed.

double letters

1 see too ebb inn all err zoo seen poor hall boot will soon bells little
2 all jazz | too soon | will see | good inn | pool hall | less room | call all rooms
3 A tall fellow in the pool hall stuffed his jeans into his muddy boots.

adjacent keys

4 as saw opt are mop was pod few ruin weak soil crew port went stop were
5 he saw | in ruin | you were | new coin | open pod | suit her | stop here | was where
6 Were they there when the popular soprano with the operatic voice sang?

long direct reaches

7 my ace ice gym any gun herb many brow must deck debt under brass penny
8 my face | any ice | my debt | many myths | tiny lynx | sun myself | nylon umbrella
9 The rainy day became sunny after we ate lunch under a bright umbrella.

| | 1 | 2 | 3 | 4 | 5 | 6 | 7 | 8 | 9 | 10 | 11 | 12 | 13 | 14 |

Skill-Enrichment Timed Writing

1. A 1′ writing on ¶ 1; find *gwam*. Add 2-4 words to set a new goal rate.

2. Two 1′ writings on ¶ 1 at your new goal rate, guided by ¼′ guide call.

3. Key ¶ 2 the same way.

4. A 3′ writing on ¶s 1-2 combined; find *gwam*; circle errors.

5. A 5′ writing on ¶s 1-2 combined; find *gwam*; circle errors.

6. If time permits, take additional 1′ writings on each ¶ for speed or control.

gwam	¼′	½′	¾′	1′
20	5	10	15	20
24	6	12	18	24
28	7	14	21	28
32	8	16	24	32
36	9	18	27	36
40	10	20	30	40
44	11	22	33	44
48	12	24	36	48
52	13	26	39	52
56	14	28	42	56

all letters used | A | 1.5 si | 5.7 awl | 80% hfw

gwam 3′ | 5′

Information is made up of words, numbers, and symbols that convey 4 | 3 | 41
knowledge that can be used in many ways. The mass of information we 9 | 5 | 44
have is expanding at a rapid rate, causing a paperwork explosion. One 14 | 8 | 47
of the major results is a revolution in the way information is processed 19 | 11 | 49
in the office. The most widely used term for such work is word process- 23 | 14 | 52
ing. It is a system that involves workers who are educated to use spe- 28 | 17 | 55
cific procedures and electronic equipment. 31 | 19 | 57

A word originator dictates or writes the input that a word process- 36 | 21 | 60
ing worker keys on electronic equipment. The input is then stored in the 40 | 24 | 63
system for later use. The system makes it easy to record, store, recall, 45 | 27 | 66
and revise information. For instance, name and address lists can be re- 50 | 30 | 68
called from a memory bank to be changed or used to send bills, fliers, 55 | 33 | 71
and other notices. As you can see, the sizable amount of information 60 | 36 | 74
that is stored in the system can be used in many different ways. 64 | 38 | 77

gwam 3′ | 1 | 2 | 3 | 4 | 5 |
5′ | 1 | 2 | 3 |

8a ▶ 8
Conditioning Practice

each line twice SS (slowly, then faster); DS between 2-line groups; if time permits, practice each line again

Space once

reach review   1 ik rf ol ed nj gf hj tf .l ft. ↓i.e. ↓e.g. ↓rt. ↓O. ↓J.

spacing   2 a an go is or to if he and got the for led kit lot

left shift   3 I got it. Hal has it. Jan led Nan. Kae is gone.
QS

8b ▶ 10 Improve Return Technique

1. Key each pair of lines once as shown: SS with a DS between 2-line groups.
2. Repeat the drill at a faster pace.

Return hint
Keep up your pace to the end of the line; return immediately; start the new line without pausing.

1 Nan has gone to ski;
2 she took a train at nine.
                          DS

3 Janet asked for the disk;
4 she is to take it to the lake.
                          DS

5 Karl said he left at the lake
6 a file that has the data she needs.
                          DS

7 Nadia said she felt ill as the ski
8 lift left to take the girls to the hill.
                          QS

Eyes on copy
as you return

8c ▶ 10 Build Keyboarding Skill: Space Bar/Left Shift

each line twice SS; DS between 2-line groups

Goals
- to reduce the pause between words
- to reduce the time taken to shift/strike key/release when making capital letters

Down-and-in spacing

Out-and-down shifting

Space bar (Space *immediately* after each word.)

1 if is an he go is or ah to of so it do el id la ti

2 an el|go to|if he|of it|is to|do the|for it|and so

3 if she is|it is the|all of it|go to the|for an oak
                                                    DS

Left shift key (Shift; strike key; release both quickly.)

4 Lt. Ho said he left the skiff at Ord Lake for her.

5 Jane or Hal is to go to Lake Head to see Kate Orr.

6 O. J. Halak is to ask for her at Jahn Hall at one.
                                                    QS

Skill-Enrichment Drill: Skill-Comparison Sentences

1. Take a 1' writing on line 1; find *gwam*.
2. Using the *gwam* on line 1 as a goal rate, take a 1' writing on each of lines 2-10; find *gwam* on each.
3. Identify the 5 lines on which you made your lowest speeds.
4. Take another 1' writing on each of the harder lines to increase your speed.

balanced hand	1 The girls cut and curl their hair when they visit their rich neighbor.
third row	2 He was quite prepared to wire our true report to Peter after the riot.
double letters	3 Hollis took his little book of excellent poems to his class at school.
combination	4 The only man awarded the extra six acres may look for reserves of oil.
adjacent keys	5 As sad as it may be, we were open for suit when he stated his opinion.
long reaches	6 Since the sun was bright, the umpire did not notice the runner swerve.
one-hand	7 Milo, in my opinion, treated a tax at my gas pump only as a state tax.
shift keys	8 Patsy and Sol Sparks are skiing in the Alps with May and Nan Appleton.
figures	9 I shall print 850 cards, 173 calendars, 96 leaflets, and 24 circulars.
symbols	10 Use Customer's I.D. #472903 on our Invoice #16582 (dated November 16).

| 1 | 2 | 3 | 4 | 5 | 6 | 7 | 8 | 9 | 10 | 11 | 12 | 13 | 14 |

Skill-Enrichment Timed Writing

1. A 1' writing on ¶ 1; find *gwam*. Add 2-4 words to set a new goal rate (see chart on p. 268).
2. Two 1' writings on ¶ 1 at your new goal rate, guided by ¼' guide call.
3. Key ¶ 2 in the same way.
4. A 3' writing on ¶s 1-2 combined; find *gwam*; circle errors.
5. A 5' writing on ¶s 1-2 combined; find *gwam*; circle errors.
6. If time permits, take additional 1' writings on each ¶ for speed or control.

all letters used | A | 1.5 si | 5.7 awl | 80% hfw

	gwam 3'	5'
A great many people alibi that if they could only stop the clock or	5	3 35
hold back the hands of time, they could accomplish whatever they desire.	9	6 38
Unfortunately, time marches on whether human beings do or not. The ques-	14	9 41
tion therefore becomes not how can we acquire more time for ourselves,	19	11 44
but how can we utilize more productively the time allotted us. Learning	24	14 47
to use time wisely is a major step toward success.	27	16 49
Time is a constant, for everyone has an equal amount of it. How we	32	19 51
use time, however, is a critical variable in the equation of excellence.	37	22 54
Thinking requires time, of course; but we can conserve our time by taking	42	25 57
time to plan before beginning our work. The likelihood of having to do	46	28 60
work over is decreased by thinking through all related problems and plan-	51	31 63
ning the project before getting started.	54	32 65

gwam 3' | 1 | 2 | 3 | 4 | 5 |
5' | 1 | 2 | 3 |

8d ▶ 22 *Improve Keyboarding Skill*

each line twice SS (slowly, then faster); DS between 2-line groups

Correct finger curvature

Correct finger alignment

Key words (*Think,* *say,* and *key* the words.)

1 an the did oak she for off tie got and led jar all
2 go end air her dog his aid rid sit and fir ask jet
3 talk side jell gold fled sign stir fork high shall
DS

Key phrases (*Think,* *say,* and *key* the phrases.)

4 to do|it is|of an|if he|is to|or do|to it|if he is
5 to aid|if she|he did|of the|to all|is for|is a tie
6 is to ask|is to aid|he or she|to rig it|if she did
DS

Easy sentences (Strike keys at a brisk, steady pace.)

7 Joan is to go to the lake to get her old red skis.
8 Les asked for a list of all the old gold she sold.
9 Laska said she left the old disk list on his desk.

Lesson 9	U and C	Line length (LL): 50 spaces
		Line spacing (LS): single (SS)

9a ▶ 8 *Conditioning Practice*

each line twice SS (slowly, then faster); DS between 2-line groups

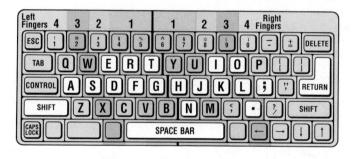

1 nj gf ol rf ik ed .l tf hj fr ki ft jn de lo fg l.
2 lo fir old rig lot fit gin fog left sign lend dike
3 Olga has the first slot; Jena is to skate for her.
QS

9b ▶ 5 *Build Keyboarding Skill: Space Bar/Left Shift*

Key the lines once as shown: SS with a DS between 3-line groups. Keep hand movement to a minimum.

space bar

1 Ken said he is to sign the list and take the disk.
2 It is right for her to take the lei if it is hers.
3 Jae has gone to see an old oaken desk at the sale.
DS

left shift

4 He said to enter Oh. for Ohio and Kan. for Kansas.
5 It is said that Lt. Li has an old jet at Lake Ida.
6 L. N. is at the King Hotel; Harl is at the Leland.
QS

This section of enrichment activities contains eight pages of skill-enrichment drills and timed writings.

Each page consists of a set of lines designed to review the keyboard, to improve technique, or to build speed and/or control. Each of these drills may be used as a warm-up before the timed writing.

Each skill-enrichment drill is followed by a paragraph timed writing of average difficulty, word counted for 1', 3', and 5' timings.

Each drill and timed writing is accompanied by a set of guides for effective practice. The materials may, however, be practiced in a variety of ways.

For drills use a 70-space line and SS; for timed writings use a 70-space line and a 5-space paragraph indent and DS.

Skill-Enrichment Drill: Alphabetic Sentences

each line twice SS (slowly, then faster); DS between 2-line groups

Technique hint
Quiet hands and arms; finger-action keystroking

1 Jan analyzed her quest for perfection by examining a few vital skills.

2 The judge observed as the expert workers quickly froze the boned meat.

3 Gomez jokes expertly with a friend but can be very shy and very quiet.

4 Louise Zabel worked five months on projects requiring expert analysis.

5 In January, six inches of snow very quickly paralyzed many big cities.

6 Jack Devlin may export white and azure flowers to big antique markets.

7 Ms. Varney, executor of the will, kept quizzing the judge about dates.

| 1 | 2 | 3 | 4 | 5 | 6 | 7 | 8 | 9 | 10 | 11 | 12 | 13 | 14 |

Skill-Enrichment Timed Writing

1. A 1' writing on ¶ 1; find *gwam*. Add 2-4 words to set a new goal rate.
2. Two 1' writings on ¶ 1 at new goal rate, guided by ¼' guide call.
3. Key ¶ 2 the same way.
4. A 3' writing on ¶s 1-2 combined; find *gwam*; circle errors.
5. A 5' writing on ¶s 1-2 combined; find *gwam*; circle errors.
6. If time permits, take more 1' writings on each ¶ for speed or control.

gwam	¼'	½'	¾'	1'
20	5	10	15	20
24	6	12	18	24
28	7	14	21	28
32	8	16	24	32
36	9	18	27	36
40	10	20	30	40
44	11	22	33	44
48	12	24	36	48
52	13	26	39	52
56	14	28	42	56

all letters used | A | 1.5 si | 5.7 awl | 80% hfw

	gwam 3'	5'
We live in a society of numbers. From the number of a birth cer-	4	3	35
tificate to the number of a death certificate, numbers play a vital	9	5	38
role in the daily life of each of us. Virtually all typed business and	14	8	41
personal papers contain figures. Quite often these documents contain	18	11	44
some commonly used symbols, also. Therefore, skill in keying on the top	23	14	47
row is critical to your future use of the machine.	27	16	49
Data arranged in table form shows a common use of figures and sym-	31	19	51
bols. Although some tables include no figures, the greatest percentage	36	21	54
of them do. Just as top skill on a letter keyboard may help you land a	41	24	57
well-paid job, expert skill on figure copy may land you a prized data	45	27	60
entry job that's even better. Workers in accounting and data processing	50	30	63
offices must know how to operate the number row with efficiency.	54	33	65

| gwam 3' | 1 | 2 | 3 | 4 | 5 |
| 5' | 1 | 2 | 3 |

9c ► 20
Learn U and C

each line twice SS (slowly, then faster); DS between 2-line groups; if time permits, repeat selected lines

Follow the *Standard Plan for Learning New Keys* outlined on page 8.

Reach technique for **u**

3-2-96

Reach *up* with *right first* finger.

Learn U ▼

1 j j uj uj us us us jug jug jut jut due due fur fur
2 uj uj jug jug sue sue lug lug use use lug lug dues
3 a jug; due us; the fur; use it; a fur rug; is just

DS

Reach technique for **c**

Reach *down* with *left second* finger.

Learn C ▼

4 d d cd cd cod cod cog cog tic tic cot cot can cans
5 cd cd cod cod ice ice can can code code dock docks
6 a cod; a cog; the ice; she can; the dock; the code

DS

Combine U and C

7 cud cud cut cuts cur curs cue cues duck ducks clue
8 a cud; a cur; to cut; the cue; the cure; for luck;
9 use a clue; a fur coat; take the cue; cut the cake

QS

9d ► 17 Improve Keyboarding Technique

1. Key the lines once as shown: SS with a DS between 2-line groups.

2. Key the lines again at a faster pace.

Technique goals
- reach *up* without moving hands away from you
- reach *down* without moving hands toward your body
- use quick-snap keystrokes

3d/1st rows
1 in cut nut ran cue can cot fun hen car urn den cog
2 Nan is cute; he is curt; turn a cog; he can use it

DS

l. shift and .
3 Kae had taken a lead. Jack then cut ahead of her.
4 I said to use Kan. for Kansas and Ore. for Oregon.

DS

key words
5 and cue for jut end kit led old fit just golf coed
6 an due cut such fuss rich lack turn dock turf curl

DS

key phrases
7 an urn|is due|to cut|for us|to use|cut off|such as
8 just in|code it|turn on|cure it|as such|is in luck

DS

all keys learned
9 Nida is to get the ice; Jacki is to call for cola.
10 Ira is sure that he can go there in an hour or so.

armed forces. The person holding the office is ~~also~~ 268

responsible for making treaties, appointing ambassadors, and 280

appointing judges of the Supreme Court. Additional respon- 292

sibilities of the President include giving The State of the 304

Union address, recieving foreign dignitaries, enforcing the 316

laws, and protecting the rights of the citizens of the 327

United States. 330

The role of the President has ~~been~~ *remained* about the same as 341

when the Constitution was written. However, Davis *(1987, 4)* states 355

that the responsibilities to fulfill that role have in- 366

creased. 368

No new ¶ *(1986, 14-15)* Koenig suggests that today's President has the respon- 381

sibility of dealing with 386

. . . survival problems in which the very future of the hu- 398
man race, is at stake; the threat of nuclear weapons tech- 409
nology; the persistence of war abroad; the remorseless 420
growth of population, production, and pollution, and their 432
endangering of the environment; grave unemployment and in- 444
flation; blighted cities and pervasive poverty and crime; 455
excessive violations of civil rights and liberties; grossly 467
inadequate provisions of health services, mass transit, edu- 479
cation and the care of the elderly. 486

As can be seen from ~~the~~ *Koenig's* description of the presidential 499

responsibilities ~~outlined by Koenig,~~ the President of the 506

United States has *a job with* many important *and varied* responsibilities. 519

REFERENCES 2

Davis, James W. *The American President: A New* 18
Perspective. New York: Harper & Row 27
Publishers, 1987. 31
Koenig, Louis W. *Chief Executive.* 5th ed. San Diego: 45
Harcourt Brace Jovanovich, Inc., 1986. 53

Document 2
Reference Page
Key a reference page using the information given at the right.

Document 3
Report from Rough Draft
Begin rekeying Document 1 as a leftbound report.

10a ▶ 8
Conditioning Practice

each line twice SS (slowly, then faster); DS between 2-line groups

all letters learned

1 a;sldkfj a;sldkfj uj cd ik rf nj ed hj tf ol gf .l
2 is cod and cut for did end off got the all oak jug
3 Hugh has just taken a lead in a race for a record.

QS

10b ▶ 20 Learn W and Right Shift Key

each line twice SS (slowly, then faster); DS between 2-line groups; if time permits, repeat each line

Reach technique for w

Reach *up* with *left third* finger.

Control of RIGHT SHIFT key

Reach *down* with *right little* finger; shift, strike, release.

Technique hint
Shift, strike key, and release both in a quick 1-2-3 count.

Follow the *Standard Plan for Learning New Keys* outlined on page 8.

Learn **W**

1 s s ws ws sow sow wow wow low low how how cow cows
2 sw sw ws ws ow ow now now row row own own tow tows
3 to sow; is how; so low; to own; too low; is to row

DS

Learn **Right Shift Key**

4 A; A; Al Al; Cal Cal; Ali or Flo; Di and Sol left.
5 Ali lost to Ron; Cal lost to Elsa; Di lost to Del.
6 Tina has left for Tucson; Dori can find her there.

DS

Combine **w** and **Right Shift**

7 Dodi will ask if Willa went to Town Center at two.
8 Wilf left the show for which he won a Gower Award.
9 Walt will go to Rio on a golf tour with Tom Spark.

QS

AIN'T LEARNED

10c ▶ 5
Review Spacing with Punctuation

each line once DS

Spacing hint
Do not space after an internal period in an abbreviation.

No space | Space once

1 Use i.e. for that is; cs. for case; ck. for check.
2 Dr. Wong said to use wt. for weight; in. for inch.
3 R. D. Roth has used ed. for editor; Rt. for Route.
4 Wes said Ed Rowan got an Ed.D. degree last winter.

QS

150c ▶ 37
Evaluate Document Processing Skill: Reports

Time Schedule
Plan and prepare .... 4'
Document processing .... 25'
Proofread; compute *n-pram* .. 8'

Document 1
Report from Rough Draft
Format the document shown at the right as an unbound report. Correct your errors as you key.

THE PRESIDENT OF THE UNITED STATES — 7

The highest elected office in the United States is that — 18
of President. The President who is elected by the Citizens — 30
of the United States represents all the people. The Presi- — 43
dent plays a major role in determining the course of direction for — 56
the United States under a democratic form of government. — 68

Term in Office — 73

Since the enactment of the twenty-second amendment to the Con- — 86
stitution, the President can serve only two terms. Prior to — 98
the this amendment the President could serve as long as the — 109
people would elected him to the office. Franklin Roosevelt was — 121
the last President to serve more than two terms. — 131

Qualifications — 136

The qualifications required for running for the execu- — 147
tive office of the United States are outlined in the Con- — 158
stitution (article II, section 1, paragraph 5). The person — 170
must be 35 years of age, a natural-born citizen of the United States, and — 185
a resident of the United States for the past 14 years. — 194

Responsibilities — 200

Also outlined in the Constitution (article II, sections — 211
2 and 3) are the responsibilities of the executive office. — 223
The outlined responsibilities are, however, quite general — 235
and are often open for interpretation. The Constitution — 246
states that the President is the Commander in Chief of the — 258

10d ▶ 17 Improve Keyboarding Technique

1. Key the lines once as shown: SS with a DS between 2-line groups.

2. Key the lines again at a faster pace.

Goal: finger-action reaches; quiet hands and arms

w and
r. shift

1 Dr. Rowe is in Tulsa now; Dr. Cowan will see Rolf.
2 Gwinn took the gown to Golda Swit on Downs Circle.
DS

➔
n/g

3 to go|go on|no go|an urn|dug in|and got|and a sign
4 He is to sign for the urn to go on the high chest.
DS

key
words

5 if ow us or go he an it of own did oak the cut jug
6 do all and for cog odd ant fig rug low cue row end
DS

key
phrases

7 we did|for a jar|she is due|cut the oak|he owns it
8 all of us|to own the|she is to go|when he has gone
DS

all keys
learned

9 Jan and Chris are gone; Di and Nick get here soon.
10 Doug will work for her at the new store in Newton.

Lesson 11   **B and Y**   *Line length (LL): 50 spaces*
Line spacing (LS): single (SS)

Fingers curved

Fingers upright

11a ▶ 8 Conditioning Practice

each line twice SS (slowly, then faster); DS between 2-line groups

reach
review

1 uj ws ik rf ol cd nj ed hj tf .l gf sw ju de lo fr

c/n

2 an can and cut end cue hen cog torn dock then sick

all letters
learned

3 A kid had a jag of fruit on his cart in New Delhi.
QS

11b ▶ 5 Improve Space-Bar/Return Technique

1. Key each line once SS; return and start each new line quickly.

2. On line 4, see how many words you can key in 30 seconds (30″).

1 Dot is to go at two.

2 He saw that it was a good law.

3 Rilla is to take the auto into the town.

4 Wilt has an old gold jug he can enter in the show.
QS

gwam 1′ | 1 | 2 | 3 | 4 | 5 | 6 | 7 | 8 | 9 | 10 |

A standard word in keyboarding is 5 characters or any combination of 5 characters and spaces, as indicated by the number scale under line 4.

gwam = gross words a minute

To find 1-minute (1′) *gwam*:

1. Note on the scale the figure beneath the last word you keyed. That is your 1′ *gwam* if you key the line partially or only once.

2. If you completed the line once and started over, add the figure determined in Step 1 to the figure 10. The resulting figure is your 1′ *gwam*.

To find 30-second (30″) *gwam*:

1. Find 1′ *gwam* (total words keyed).

2. Multiply 1′ *gwam* by 2. The resulting figure is your 30″ *gwam*.

words

Table 3

center column headings; decide on appropriate number of spaces to leave between columns

Table 4

center column headings; CS: 8
Rekey Table 1 with the names in alphabetical order.

PRESIDENTS OF THE UNITED STATES			6
1923 - 19 --			8
President	Term	Party	18
Calvin Coolidge	1923 - 1929	Republican	25
Herbert Hoover	1929 - 1933	Republican	32
Franklin Roosevelt	1933 - 1945	Democrat	40
Harry Truman	1945 - 1953	Democrat	46
Dwight Eisenhower	1953 - 1961	Republican	54
John Kennedy	1961 - 1963	Democrat	60
Lyndon Johnson	1963 - 1969	Democrat	67
Richard Nixon	1969 - 1974	Republican	74
Gerald Ford	1974 - 1977	Republican	81
Jimmy Carter	1977 - 1981	Democrat	87
Ronald Reagan	1981 - 1989	Republican	94
George Bush	1989 -	Republican	100

104

Source: Collier's Encyclopedia.

114

Lesson 150 — Evaluate Report Processing Skills

150a ▶ 5
Conditioning Practice

each line twice SS (slowly, then faster); DS between 2-line groups; if time permits, rekey selected lines

alphabet 1 Dr. Joswiak gave both of us excellent marks on the final physics quiz.

figures 2 Homes were built at 1683 Kari Road, 2705 Truax Drive, and 49 Oak Lane.

bottom row 3 A man and a woman came to exchange a dozen boxes of venison on Monday.

speed 4 When I visit the man in the wheelchair, I may go downtown to the firm.

| 1 | 2 | 3 | 4 | 5 | 6 | 7 | 8 | 9 | 10 | 11 | 12 | 13 | 14 |

150b ▶ 8 Check
Straight-Copy Skill

1. Take a 5' writing on 148b, page 262.

2. Find *gwam* and number of errors.

3. Record score.

11c ▶ 20
Learn B and Y

each line twice SS (slowly, then faster); DS between 2-line groups; if time permits, practice selected lines again

Follow the *Standard Plan for Learning New Keys* outlined on page 8.

Reach technique for b

Reach *down* with *left first* finger.

Reach technique for y

Reach *up* with *right first* finger.

Learn **b** ▼

1 f f bf bf fib fib rob rob but but big big fib fibs
2 bf bf rob rob lob lob orb orb bid bid bud bud ribs
3 a rib; to fib; rub it; an orb; or rob; but she bid
DS

Learn **y** ▼

4 j j yj yj jay jay lay lay hay hay day day say says
5 yj yj jay jay eye eye dye dye yes yes yet yet jays
6 a jay; to say; an eye; he says; dye it; has an eye
DS

Combine **b** and **y**

7 by by buy buy boy boy bye bye byte byte buoy buoys
8 by it; to buy; by you; a byte; the buoy; by and by
9 Jaye went by bus to the store to buy the big buoy.
QS

11d ▶ 17 Improve Keyboarding Technique

1. Key the lines once as shown: SS with a DS between 2-line groups.
2. Key the lines again at a faster pace.

Goals
- reach *up* without moving hands away from you
- reach *down* without moving hands toward your body
- use quick-snap keystrokes

reach review
1 a;sldkfj bf ol ed yj ws ik rf hj cd nj tf .l gf uj
2 a kit low for jut led sow fob ask sun cud jet grow
DS

3d/1st rows
3 no in bow any tub yen cut sub coy ran bin cow deck
4 Cody wants to buy this baby cub for the young boy.
DS

key words
5 by and for the got all did but cut now say jut ask
6 work just such hand this goal boys held furl eight
DS

key phrases
7 to do|can go|to bow|for all|did jet|ask her|to buy
8 if she|to work|and such|the goal|for this|held the
DS

all letters learned
9 Kitty had auburn hair with big eyes of clear jade.
10 Juan left Bobby at the dog show near our ice rink.

gwam 1' | 1 | 2 | 3 | 4 | 5 | 6 | 7 | 8 | 9 | 10 |

149a ▶ 5
Conditioning Practice

each line twice SS (slowly, then faster); DS between 2-line groups; if time permits, rekey selected lines

alphabet	1	Both campus organizations Faye would like to join are quite expensive.
figures	2	You can reach us at 632-5498 before 1 p.m. or at 632-7043 after 1 p.m.
fig/sym	3	The date on the bill (#580A473) from Baxter & Smythe was May 26, 1992.
speed	4	The city official paid the men for the handiwork they did on the dock.

| 1 | 2 | 3 | 4 | 5 | 6 | 7 | 8 | 9 | 10 | 11 | 12 | 13 | 14 |

149b ▶ 8 Check
Straight-Copy Skill

1. Take a 5' writing on 148b, page 262.

2. Find *gwam* and number of errors.

3. Record score.

149c ▶ 37
Evaluate Document Processing Skill: Tables

Time Schedule
Plan and prepare .... 4'
Document processing .... 25'
Proofread; compute *n-pram* ..... 8'

4 full sheets; format the tables given at the right; DS all lines; correct errors

Table 1
block column headings; CS: 10

words

STATE OFFICERS — 3

Name	Position	Phone	
Laura Wesphal	President	836-4978	10 / 17
Josh Rubinstein	Vice President	739-2075	25
Maria Fernandez	Membership Director	684-7825	34
Chris Chan	Secretary	836-2091	40
Mark Strasman	Treasurer	235-6511	47
Brett DeWitz (lc)	Past President	412-4010	54
Jacqueline McCain	President Elect	633-7189	63

Table 2
center column headings; CS: 8

19-- BANKING INSTITUTE ~~PROGRAM~~ SCHEDULE — 6

Seminar	Date	Location	
Game Plans for Loan Originators	January 15	Boston	17 / 27
Creative Financing	March 16	Chicago	35
Symposium for Branch Managers	April 20	Portland	44
Today's Automated Banking	June 10	Atlanta	53
Accounting Update in Banking	August 15	Tuscon	62
Customer Advertising	October 1	Houston	70
Managing Human Resources	November 13	Milwaukee	79

Before you begin each practice session:
- Position your body directly in front of the keyboard; sit erect, with feet on the floor for balance.
- Curve your fingers deeply and place them in an upright position over the home keys.
- Position the textbook or screen for easy reading (at about a 90° angle to the eyes).

Fingers properly curved

Body properly positioned

Fingers properly upright

12a ▶ 8
Conditioning Practice

each line twice SS (slowly, then faster); DS between 2-line groups; if time permits, practice each line again

all keystrokes learned

1 we ok as in be on by re no us if la do ah go C. J.
2 for us; in a jet; by the bid; cut his leg; to work
3 Fran knew it was her job to guide your gold truck.
QS

12b ▶ 12 Improve Space-Bar/Shift-Key Technique

1. Key the lines once as shown: SS with a DS between 2-line groups.

2. Key the lines again at a faster pace.

Down-and-in spacing

Out-and-down shifting

Space bar (Space *immediately* after each word)

1 an by win buy den sly won they than flay when clay
2 in a way│on a day│buy a hen│a fine day│if they win
DS

3 Jay can bid on the old clay urn he saw at the inn.
4 I know she is to be here soon to talk to the club.
DS

Shift keys (Shift; strike key; release both quickly)

5 Lt. Su; Nan and Dodi; Karl and Sol; Dr. O. C. Goya
6 Kara and Rod are in Italy; Jane and Bo go in June.
DS

7 Sig and Bodie went to the lake with Cory and Lana.
8 Aida Rios and Jana Hardy work for us in Los Gatos.
QS

148c ▶ 37
Evaluate Document Processing Skills: Letters/Memo

LP pp. 147-151

Time Schedule

Plan and prepare .... 4′
Document processing .... 25′
Proofread; compute *n-pram* .. 8′

1. Arrange materials for ease of handling.

2. Format and key Documents 1-4 for 25′. Proofread and correct errors before removing documents from machine.

3. After time is called (25′), proofread again and circle any uncorrected errors. Compute *n-pram*.

Document 1 LP p. 147
block format; open punctuation

Special features:

CERTIFIED
Subject: **19-- Banking Institute Schedule**
c Mark L. Kostner

Document 2 LP p. 149
modified block format; blocked ¶s; mixed punctuation

Insert the following information for the numbers in parentheses: (1) **May** (2) **Houston** (3) **managing human resources** (4) **November 13** (5) **Milwaukee** (6) **Marc Plaza**

Special features:

Company name in closing lines:
BANKING INSTITUTE
c Natasha J. Bartlett
Mark L. Kostner
Postscript: **Will I see you at next week's convention in Hawaii? I'm looking forward to some warmer weather.**

Document 3
Format the document at the right as a simplified memorandum. The document is from you to your teacher. Use the **current date** and **"Report on the Office of the President"** for the subject line.

Document 4 LP p. 151
block format; open punctuation

Rekey Document 2 with the following changes:

Ms. Renae A. Santiago
Suwannee National Bank
5507 Ranchero Road
Tallahassee, FL 32304-9340

(1) **June** (2) **Pittsburgh** (3) **customer advertising** (4) **October 1** (5) **Houston** (6) **Hyatt Regency**

Special features:
same as Document 2; no postscript

---

words

October 13, 19-- | Ms. Natasha J. Bartlett, President | Banking Institute Corporate Office | 628 Nicolet Avenue, N | Chicago, IL 60631-6485 | Dear Ms. Bartlett — 17 / 30 / 39

Attached is a tentative listing of the seminars we plan to offer through the Banking Institute next year. If you would like any of the titles changed before we start promoting the seminars in November, please let me know by October 23. — 54 / 69 / 84 / 86

In addition to distributing materials at this year's two remaining seminars, we will be processing a mailing to current members and advertising in two banking publications. Any other suggestions you may have for promoting next year's seminars would be appreciated. Our goal for this coming year is a 20 percent increase in attendance. — 102 / 116 / 131 / 146 / 154

Sincerely yours | Ryan S. Woodward | Institute Director | xx | Attachment — 170/195

November 15, 19-- | Mr. Lewis G. Mackenzie | Human Resources Manager | Bank of Nottingham | 1295 Kensington Avenue | Detroit, MI 48230-5286 | Dear Mr. Mackenzie: — 13 / 27 / 30

The seminar you presented last __(1)__ in __(2)__ for the Banking Institute on __(3)__ was very well received. Several Institute members have requested that the seminar be offered again this coming year. — 45 / 63 / 74

The seminar is scheduled for __(4)__ in __(5)__ at the __(6)__. Are you available on this date to present the seminar? The honorarium for conducting the seminar has been increased to $1,800. Of course, all your expenses would be paid by the Institute. — 92 / 107 / 122 / 127

Please let me know by December 1 whether you will be able to work with us on this year's seminar. — 142 / 147

Sincerely, | Ryan S. Woodward | Institute Director | xx — 160

closing lines 187/210

---

opening lines 14

Here is the report on the office of the President of the United States that you assigned last week. The report gives a brief description of the term in office, the qualifications needed to run for the office, and the responsibilities of this very important position. — 30 / 45 / 61 / 67

I have also included in the appendix a table of the individuals holding the office since 1923. The table outlines each President's term in office and his party affiliation. — 83 / 98 / 102

I have enjoyed learning more about this important position in our democratic government. Please let me know if you have additional suggestions for improvement. — 116 / 131 / 135

closing lines 140

12c ▶ 15 Improve Keyboarding Skill

1. Key the lines once as shown: SS with a DS between 2-line groups.

2. Key the lines again at a faster pace.

Goals
- curved, upright fingers
- quiet hands and arms
- quick spacing -- no pause between words
- finger-reach action to shift keys

Finger-action keystrokes

Down-and-in thumb motion

Key words and phrases (*Think, say,* and *key* words and phrases.)

```
1 by dig row off but and jet oak the cub all got rid
2 ah she own dug irk buy cog jak for yet ask led urn
                                                          DS
3 of us|if the|all of|and do|cut it|he got|to do the
4 is to be|as it is|if we do|in all the|if we own it
                                                          DS
```

All letters learned (Strike keys at a brisk, steady pace.)

```
5 Judy had gone for that big ice show at Lake Tahoe.
6 Jack said that all of you will find the right job.
                                                          DS
7 Cindy has just left for work at the big ski lodge.
8 Rudy can take a good job at the lake if he wishes.
                                                          QS
```

gwam 1′ | 1 | 2 | 3 | 4 | 5 | 6 | 7 | 8 | 9 | 10 |

12d ▶ 15 Check Keyboarding Skill

1. Key each line once DS. To DS when in SS mode, return twice at the end of the line.

2. Take a 20-second (20″) timed writing on each line. Your rate in gross words a minute (*gwam*) is shown word-for-word above the lines.

3. Take another 20″ writing on each line. Try to increase key-stroking speed.

Goal: At least 15 *gwam*.

20″ gwam

```
        3|    6|    9|   12|   15|   18|   21|   24|   27|   30|

1 Al is to do it.

2 Di has gone to work.

3 Jan is to go to the sale.

4 Rog is to row us to your dock.

5 Harl has an old kayak and two oars.

6 She told us to set a goal and go for it.

7 It is our job to see just how high we can go.

8 Jake will go to the city to work on the big signs.
                                                          QS
```

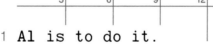

ENRICHMENT ACTIVITY: Reach Review

1. Key each line twice SS (slowly, then faster); DS between 2-line groups.

2. Rekey the drill for better control of reaches.

```
1 June had left for the club just as the news ended.
2 Bro led a task force whose goal was to lower cost.
3 Lyn knew the surf was too rough for kids to enjoy.
4 Ceil hikes each day on the side roads near school.
```

gwam 1′ | 1 | 2 | 3 | 4 | 5 | 6 | 7 | 8 | 9 | 10 |

Evaluate Keyboarding/Document Processing Skills

Measurement Goals

1. To evaluate straight-copy speed and accuracy.
2. To evaluate letter processing skills.
3. To evaluate report processing skills.
4. To evaluate table processing skills.

Format Guides

1. Paper guide at *0* (for typewriters).
2. LL: 70 spaces for drills; as required by document formats.
3. LS: SS for drills; as required by document formats.
4. PI: 5 spaces, when appropriate.

Lesson 148	*Evaluate Letter Processing Skills*

148a ▶ 5
Conditioning Practice

each line twice SS (slowly, then faster); DS between 2-line groups; if time permits, rekey selected lines

alphabet	1	Beatriz might complete five quilting projects by the end of next week.
figures	2	The May 8 test over pages 396-417 had 20 problems worth 5 points each.
space bar	3	Jan and Kay may also bid to work with the men on the map for the city.
speed	4	The girls may go to the social held at the giant chapel on the island.

| 1 | 2 | 3 | 4 | 5 | 6 | 7 | 8 | 9 | 10 | 11 | 12 | 13 | 14 |

148b ▶ 8 Check Straight-Copy Skill

1. A 5' writing on all ¶s.
2. Determine *gwam* and number of errors.
3. Record score.

all letters used | A | 1.5 si | 5.7 awl | 80% hfw

gwam 3' | *5'*

Something that you can never escape is your attitude. It will be — 4 | 3 | 45
with you forever. However, you decide whether your attitude is an asset — 9 | 6 | 48
or a liability for you. Your attitude reflects the way you feel about — 14 | 8 | 50
the world you abide in and everything that is a part of that world. It — 19 | 11 | 53
reflects the way you feel about yourself, about your environment, and — 23 | 14 | 56
about other people who are a part of your environment. Oftentimes, people — 28 | 17 | 59
ple with a positive attitude are people who are extremely successful. — 33 | 20 | 62

At times we all have experiences that cause us to be negative. The — 37 | 22 | 64
difference between a positive and a negative person is that the positive — 42 | 25 | 67
person rebounds very quickly from a bad experience; the negative person — 47 | 28 | 70
does not. The positive person is a person who usually looks to the — 52 | 31 | 73
bright side of things and recognizes the world as a place of promise, — 56 | 34 | 76
hope, joy, excitement, and purpose. A negative person generally has just — 61 | 37 | 79
the opposite view of the world. Remember, others want to be around those — 66 | 40 | 82
who are positive but tend to avoid those who are negative. — 70 | 42 | 84

gwam 3' | 1 | 2 | 3 | 4 | 5
5' | 1 | 2 | 3

13a ▶ 8
Conditioning Practice

each line twice SS (slowly, then faster); DS between 2-line groups

reach review 1 bf ol rf yj ed nj ws ik tf hj cd uj gf by us if ow
b/y 2 by bye boy buy yes fib dye bit yet but try bet you
all letters learned 3 Robby can win the gold if he just keys a new high.
QS

13b ▶ 20
Learn M and X

each line twice SS (slowly, then faster); DS between 2-line groups; if time permits, practice selected lines again

Follow the *Standard Plan for Learning New Keys* outlined on page 8.

Reach technique for m

Reach *down* with *right first* finger.

Reach technique for x

Reach *down* with *left third* finger.

Learn **m**

1 j j mj mj am am am me me ma ma jam jam ham ham yam
2 mj mj me me me may may yam yam dam dam men men jam
3 am to; if me; a man; a yam; a ham; he may; the hem
DS

Learn **X**

4 s s xs xs ox ox ax ax six six fix fix fox fox axis
5 xs xs sx sx ox ox six six nix nix fix fix lax flax
6 a fox; an ox; fix it; by six; is lax; to fix an ax
DS

Combine **m** and **X**

7 me ox am ax ma jam six ham mix fox men lax hem lox
8 to fix; am lax; mix it; may fix; six men; hex them
9 Mala can mix a ham salad for six; Max can fix tea.
QS

13c ▶ 5
Review Spacing with Punctuation

each line once DS

▽ Do not space after an internal period in an abbreviation.

1 Mrs. Dixon may take her Ed.D. exam early in March.
2 Lex may send a box c.o.d. to Ms. Fox in St. Croix.
3 J. D. and Max will go by boat to St. Louis in May.
4 Owen keyed ect. for etc. and lost the match to me.
QS

147c ▶ 35
Reinforce Document Processing Skills: Reports

plain full sheets; correct errors as you key

1. Process the copy at the right as a leftbound report with internal citations. Use **THE JOB INTERVIEW** for the title of the report.

2. Using the information given below, prepare a reference list on a separate sheet.

Reynolds, Caroline. **Dimensions in Professional Development.** 3d ed. Cincinnati: South-Western Publishing Co., 1988.

Payne, Richard A. **How to Get a Better Job Quicker.** 3d. ed. New York: NAL Penguin, Inc., 1987.

3. Prepare a title page. Use **your name, your school's name,** and the **current date.**

The result of a successful letter of application and data   15

sheet is an invitation from a potential employer for an interview.   29

Preparing Preparation for the interview is just as important in obtaining   40

employment as the planning preparation required to prepare develop an   52

effective application letter and data sheet.   61

The interviewers first impression of the applicant is   72
crucial to the success of the interview. This impression,   84
which may take as little as 60 seconds to form, determines   96
whether the interviewer is interested in learning more about   108
the potential employee. Therefore, the prospective employee   120
must make a special effort to assure a positive first im-   131
pression. Reynolds (229-233, 1988) suggests that in order   143
to make that positive first impression the applicant must be   155
prepared mentally as well as physically.   164

Preparing Mentally DS   171
Preparing mentally includes learning as much as possible about the   184
Company prior to the interview and anticipating questions   196

that the employer may ask during the interview. The inter-   208

viewee should also plan questions to learn as much as pos-   219

sible about the position and the co. op The purpose of the in-   232

terveiw is to provide the interviewer and the interviewee   243

the opportunity to exchange information and to form impres-   255

sions (Payne, 1987, 88-94). More information will be exchanged   268

and a better impression made when the interviewee comes to   280

the inter view well prepared.   286

Preparing Physically DS   294
Preparing physically also plays an important part in plan-   305

ning for a successful interview. The interviewee employee   315

should learn about appropriate company dress and grooming   327
prior to the interview
standards. The interviewer has to be able to picture the   343

job applicant as a person who would fit in well with current   356
Extreme
employees. Differences in appearance between current em-   369

ployees and the applicant make it difficult for the inter-   380

viewer to picture the aplicant as an employee of his/her their com-   392

pany.   393

13d ▶ 17 Improve Keyboarding Technique

1. Key the lines once as shown: SS with a DS between 2-line groups.

2. Key the lines again at a faster pace.

Technique goals
- reach *up* without moving hands away from you
- reach *down* without moving hands toward your body
- use quick-snap keystrokes

Goal: finger-action keystrokes; quiet hands and arms

3d/1st rows	1	by am end fix men box hem but six now cut gem ribs
	2	me ox buy den cub ran own form went oxen fine club
		DS
space bar	3	an of me do am if us or is by go ma so ah ox it ow
	4	by man buy fan jam can any tan may rob ham fun guy
		DS
key words	5	if us me do an sow the cut big jam rub oak lax boy
	6	curl work form born name flex just done many right
		DS
key phrases	7	or jam|if she|for me|is big|an end|or buy|is to be
	8	to fix|and cut|for work|and such|big firm|the call
		DS
all keys learned	9	Jacki is now at the gym; Lex is due there by four.
	10	Joni saw that she could fix my old bike for Gilda.

Lesson 14	P and V	LL: 50 LS: SS

  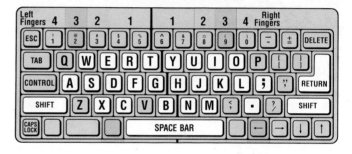

14a ▶ 8 Conditioning Practice

each line twice SS (slowly, then faster); DS between 2-line groups; if time permits, practice each line again

all letters learned

one-hand words	1	in we no ax my be on ad on re hi at ho cad him bet
phrases	2	is just|of work|to sign|of lace|to flex|got a form
all letters learned	3	Jo Buck won a gold medal for her sixth show entry.
		QS

14b ▶ 6 Improve Shift-Key/Return Technique

Key each 2-line sentence once SS as "Return" is called every 30 seconds (30"). Leave a DS between sentences.

Goal: To reach the end of each line just as the 30" guide ("Return") is called.

The 30" *gwam* scale shows your gross words a minute if you reach the end of each line as the 30" guide is called.

Eyes on copy as you shift and as you return

gwam 30" | 20"

1	Marj is to choose a high goal	12	18
2	and to do her best to make it.	12	18
	DS		
3	Gig said he had to key from a book	14	21
4	for a test he took for his new job.	14	21
	DS		
5	Alex knows it is good to hold your goal	16	24
6	in mind as you key each line of a drill.	16	24
	DS		
7	Nan can do well many of the tasks she tries;	18	27
8	she sets new goals and makes them one by one.	18	27
	QS		

146c ▶ 10
Reinforce Language Skills: Word Choice
plain full sheet; LL: 70

As you key each sentence at the right, select the word in each set of parentheses needed to complete each sentence correctly. Key the line number and period; correct errors as you key.

1. (Hear, Here) are the (to, too, two) books that are (do, due) tomorrow.
2. (Its, It's) (to, too) bad you only have (for, four) days of vacation.
3. By (then, than), the (cite, site) you may (choose, chose) could be sold.
4. (Do, Due) you (know, no) what (hour, our) the English class is taught?
5. The company's (lead, led) pipe fittings (passed, past) inspection.

6. If (your, you're) going to (buy, by) the tickets, let me (know, no).
7. (Some, Sum) prices will (vary, very) depending on the day of the week.
8. If you (raise, raze) the rent, the (poor, pour) man will have to move.
9. To learn to (sew, sow) the (right, rite) way, you should take lessons.
10. Take a (peak, peek) at the (knew, new) (stationary, stationery).

11. Do (farther, further) tests to determine the full (affects, effects).
12. You should follow the (principal's, principle's) (advice, advise).
13. The (lessen, lesson) presents the (bases, basis) for decision making.
14. The (plain, plane) (flew, flue) (through, threw) the (air, heir).
15. Dennis did not (accept, except) the results of the latest (pole, poll).

Lesson 147   Reinforce Report Processing Skills

147a ▶ 5
Conditioning Practice
each line twice SS (slowly, then faster); DS between 2-line groups; if time permits, rekey selected lines

alphabet	1	Judge Wirtz quickly thanked both of them for giving excellent reports.
figures	2	The study guides for the next exam are on pages 56, 197, 280, and 304.
shift lock	3	BASIC and COBOL as well as APL, TRAC, and LISP are computer languages.
speed	4	The man with the problems may wish to see the proficient tax official.

| 1 | 2 | 3 | 4 | 5 | 6 | 7 | 8 | 9 | 10 | 11 | 12 | 13 | 14 |

147b ▶ 10
Reinforce Language Skills: Verb Agreement
plain full sheet; LL: 70

As you key each sentence at the right, select the word in parentheses needed to complete each sentence correctly. Key the line number and period; correct errors as you key.

1. The manager (is, are) going to announce the final cuts tomorrow.
2. Almost everyone (is, are) planning to attend the New Year's dance.
3. Either the manager or his secretary (has, have) the purchase orders.
4. The band (has, have) been selected to participate in the parade.
5. The band directors (is, are) going to be meeting in Room 205.

6. The number of individuals buying computers (has, have) increased.
7. Some of the expenses for the banquet (is, are) still being received.
8. Many of the movies about the war (is, are) based on true stories.
9. Neither Alyssa nor Nicole (is, are) aware of the surprise party.
10. The entire department (is, are) going to attend the next meeting.

11. Dean and Tom (has, have) their own computer consulting business.
12. The disks (don't, doesn't) need to be formatted again before using.
13. All of the dinner guests (has, have) already left for the play.
14. A number of changes (has, have) been made in the starting lineup.
15. The manager and the trainers (is, are) meeting with team members today.

14c ▶ 20
Learn P and V

each line twice SS (slowly, then faster); DS between 2-line groups; if time permits, practice selected lines again

Follow the *Standard Plan for Learning New Keys* outlined on page 8.

Reach technique for p

Reach *up* with *right little* finger.

Learn p

1 ; ; p; p; pa pa up up apt apt pen pen lap lap kept
2 p; p; pa pa pa pan pan nap nap paw paw gap gap rap
3 a pen; a cap; apt to pay; pick it up; plan to keep
DS

Learn v

4 f f vf vf via via vie vie have have five five live
5 vf vf vie vie vie van van view view dive dive jive
6 go via; vie for; has vim; a view; to live; or have
DS

Reach technique for v

Reach *down* with *left first* finger.

Combine p and v

7 up cup vie pen van cap vim rap have keep live plan
8 to vie; give up; pave it; very apt; vie for a cup;
9 Vic has a plan to have the van pick us up at five.
QS

14d ▶ 16 Improve Keyboarding Technique

1. Key the lines once as shown: SS with a DS between 2-line groups.

2. Key the lines again at a faster pace.

Technique goals
- reach *up* without moving hands away from you
- reach *down* without moving hands toward your body
- use quick-snap keystrokes

Goal: finger-action keystrokes; quiet hands and arms

reach review
1 vf p; xs mj ed yj ws nj rf ik tf ol cd hj gf uj bf
2 if lap jag own may she for but van cub sod six oak
DS

3d/1st rows
3 by vie pen vim cup six but now man nor ton may pan
4 by six but now may cut sent me fine gems five reps
DS

key words
5 with kept turn corn duty curl just have worn plans
6 name burn form when jury glad vote exit came eight
DS

key phrases
7 if they|he kept|with us|of land|burn it|to name it
8 to plan|so sure|is glad|an exit|so much|to view it
DS

all letters learned
9 Kevin does a top job on your flax farm with Craig.
10 Dixon flew blue jets eight times over a city park.

146b ▶ 35
*Reinforce Document
Processing Skills:
Tables*

3 plain full sheets

Tables 1 and 2
**Tables with Main, Secondary,
and Column Headings**

CS: 8; center column headings

Format the tables given at the
right; DS all lines; correct errors.

COST OF A $50,000 LOAN			
15-Year Period			8
Rate	Monthly Payment	Total Repaid	21
9%	$507.50	$ 91,350	26
10%	537.50	96,750	32
11%	568.50	102,330	37
12%	600.50	108,090	43
13%	633.00	113,940	49
14%	666.00	119,880	54
15%	700.00	126,000	60

COST OF A $50,000 LOAN			5
30-year Period			8
Rate	Monthly Payment	Total Repaid	21
9%	$ 402.50	$144,900	26
10%	439.00	158,040	32
11%	476.50	171,540	37
12%	514.50	185,220	43
13%	553.50	199,260	49
14%	592.50	213,300	54
15%	632.50	227,700	60

Table 3
**Table with Main and Column
Headings with Total Line**

Decide on the appropriate number
of spaces to leave between
columns; center column headings.

SECOND QUARTER SALES, 19--				
Employee	April	May	June	14
Edwards, Martin	$ 29,365	$ 26,875	$ 30,650	23
Mahoney, Ryan	24,050	33,195	38,720	30
Merrick, Sheryl	39,540	36,095	37,550	37
North, Annette	16,215	15,385	12,380	44
Reid, Dinah	43,720	38,650	36,380	51
Richardson, Dyan	24,390	26,820	29,650	59
Sheridan, Douglas	19,815	18,790	19,500	66
Soto, Felix	32,100	27,580	30,850	73
Warren, Margo	27,950	35,600	29,380	85
Totals	$257,145	$258,990	$265,060	91

15a ▶ 8
Conditioning Practice

each line twice SS (slowly, then faster); DS between 2-line groups; if time permits, practice selected lines again

all letters learned 1 do fix all cut via own buy for the jam cop ask dig

p/v 2 a map; a van; apt to; vie for; her plan; have five

all letters learned 3 Beth will pack sixty pints of guava jam for David.

QS

15b ▶ 20 *Learn Q and , (Comma)*

each line twice SS (slowly, then faster); DS between 2-line groups; if time permits, practice each line again

Follow the *Standard Plan for Learning New Keys* outlined on page 8.

Reach technique for q

Reach *up* with *left little* finger.

Learn **q**

1 a qa qa aq aq quo quo qt. qt. quad quad quit quits

2 qa quo quo qt. qt. quay quay aqua aqua quite quite

3 a qt.; pro quo; a quad; to quit; the quay; a squad

DS

Learn **, (comma)**

4 k k ,k ,k kit, kit; Rick, Ike, or I will go, also.

5 a ski, a ski; a kit, a kit; a kite, a kite; a bike

6 Ike, I see, is here; Pam, I am told, will be late.

DS

Reach technique for , (comma)

Reach *down* with *right second* finger; space once after , used as punctuation.

Combine **q** and **,**

7 Enter the words quo, quote, quit, quite, and aqua.

8 I have quit the squad, Quen; Raquel has quit, too.

9 Marquis, Quent, and Quig were quite quick to quit.

QS

15c ▶ 5
Review Spacing with Punctuation

each line once DS

▽ Space once after comma used as punctuation.

1 Aqua means water, Quen; also, it is a unique blue.

2 Quince, enter qt. for quart; also, sq. for square.

3 Ship the desk c.o.d. to Dr. Quig at La Quinta Inn.

4 Q. J. took squid and squash; Monique, roast quail.

QS

145c ▶ 25
Reinforce Document Processing Skills: Letters/Memorandums

plain full sheets; correct errors

Document 1
Letter

Format and key the letter at the right in block format with open punctuation.

Current date | Miss Roberta J. Payson | 310 Ledgewood Road | Portland, ME 04108-6482 | Dear Miss Payson   14 / 20

Here are the two tables that show the cost of a $50,000 home loan. The first table displays various interest rates for a 15-year loan while the second one gives the rates for a 30-year loan. As you can see from the tables, you would decrease your monthly payment by approximately $100 per month by assuming a 30-year loan. The total amount repaid, however, would be considerably more.   35 / 50 / 66 / 79 / 94 / 98

The tables can also be used to determine the difference between the monthly payments for a fixed mortgage versus the adjustable rate mortgage. Currently our adjustable mortgage rate is 9 percent. As I mentioned yesterday, this type of loan is based on the index tied to the U.S. Treasury securities. The initial rate is guaranteed for two years. At the end of two years the rate can be increased or decreased by two percentage points each year up to a maximum rate of 15 percent.   113 / 127 / 142 / 158 / 174 / 189 / 195

If you have any additional questions about the loans we discussed yesterday, please give me a call. (195)   210 / 215

Sincerely | Mark R. Nelson | Loan Officer | xx | Enclosures | c Marshall S. Gagne   229

Document 2
Simplified Memorandum

Format and key the copy at the right as a simplified memorandum. The enclosure will be keyed in Lesson 146.

Document 3
Letter

Rekey 145b in modified block format with indented ¶s and mixed punctuation.

July 7, 19-- | Nichole A. Russell, Marketing Manager | SECOND QUARTER SALES REPORT   14 / 16

Here are the sales figures for the second quarter. Overall they represent a 7.3 percent increase over the previous quarter and a 3.8 percent increase over the second quarter sales of a year ago.   31 / 46 / 55

Annette North has given notice that she is resigning effective August 12 to return to school to work on an advanced degree. I believe we should discuss the feasibility of combining her territory with that of Douglas Sheridan. He has indicated a concern about the lack of growth potential in his area. I believe this would be a solution to his concern. He has done a fine job with his current territory, and I agree that there is not much potential for growth.   70 / 86 / 101 / 117 / 133 / 148

I'll bring additional information about the two territories for discussion at our July 20 meeting.   164 / 168

James R. Woodward, District Manager | xx | Enclosure   178

Lesson 146   Reinforce Table Processing Skills

146a ▶ 5
Conditioning Practice

each line twice SS (slowly, then faster); DS between 2-line groups; if time permits, rekey selected lines

alphabet 1 Marjorie quickly realized the beautiful mauve gown was very expensive.

figures 2 After a delay of 45 minutes, Flight 837 left from Gate 26 at 1:09 p.m.

fig/sym 3 My policy (#35-62A-748) with Barnes & Bennett expired on May 30, 1991.

speed 4 They may pay both of us to work for them when they dismantle the dock.

| 1 | 2 | 3 | 4 | 5 | 6 | 7 | 8 | 9 | 10 | 11 | 12 | 13 | 14 |

15d ▶ 17 Improve Keyboarding Technique

1. Key the lines once as shown: SS with a DS between 2-line groups.

2. Key the lines again at a faster pace.

Technique goals

- reach *up* without moving hands away from you
- reach *down* without moving hands toward your body
- use quick-snap keystrokes

Goal: finger-action keystrokes; quiet hands and arms

reach review

1 qa .l ws ,k ed nj rf mj tf p; xs ol cd ik vf hj bf
2 yj gf hj quo vie pay cut now buy got mix vow forms
DS

3d/1st rows

3 six may sun coy cue mud jar win via pick turn bike
4 to go│to win│for me│a peck│a quay│by then│the vote
DS

key words

5 pa rub sit man for own fix jam via cod oak the got
6 by quo sub lay apt mix irk pay when rope give just
DS

key phrases

7 an ox│of all│is to go│if he is│it is due│to pay us
8 if we pay│is of age│up to you│so we own│she saw me
DS

all letters learned

9 Jevon will fix my pool deck if the big rain quits.
10 Verna did fly quick jets to map the six big towns.

Lesson 16 — Review

LL: 50
LS: SS

Fingers properly curved

Fingers properly aligned

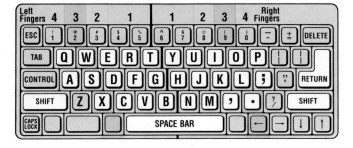

16a ▶ 8 Conditioning Practice

each line twice SS (slowly, then faster); DS between 2-line groups; if time permits, practice each line again

all letters learned

review 1 Virgil plans to find that mosque by six with Jack.
shift keys 2 Pam, Van, and Quin have to be in New Hope by five.
easy sentence 3 Vi is to aid the girl with the sign work at eight.
QS

gwam 1' │ 1 │ 2 │ 3 │ 4 │ 5 │ 6 │ 7 │ 8 │ 9 │ 10 │

16b ▶ 10 Key Block Paragraphs

each paragraph (¶) once SS as shown; DS between ¶s; then key the ¶s again at a faster pace

To find 1-minute (1') *gwam*:

1. Note the figure at the end of your last complete line.

2. Note from the scale under the ¶s the figure below where you stopped in a partial line.

3. Add the two figures; the resulting number is your *gwam*.

Paragraph 1

gwam 1'

Do not stop at the end of the line before you make   10
a return. Keep up your pace at the end of a line,   20
and return quickly after you strike the final key.   30
DS

Paragraph 2

Make the return with a quick motion, and begin the   10
next line with almost no pause. Keep your eyes on   20
the copy as you return to save time between lines.   30
QS

gwam 1' │ 1 │ 2 │ 3 │ 4 │ 5 │ 6 │ 7 │ 8 │ 9 │ 10 │

Reinforce Document Processing Skills

Learning Goals

1. To reinforce letter/memorandum processing skills.
2. To reinforce table processing skills.
3. To reinforce report processing skills.
4. To reinforce language skills.

Format Guides

1. Paper guide at 0 (for typewriters).
2. LL: 70 for drills and language skills activities; as required by document formats.
3. LS: SS for drills and language skills activities unless otherwise instructed; as required by document formats.
4. PI: 5 spaces, when appropriate.

Lesson 145 | *Reinforce Letter/Memo Processing Skills*

145a ▶ 5
Conditioning Practice

each line twice SS (slowly, then faster); DS between 2-line groups; if time permits, rekey selected lines

alphabet	1	Major Quantz will leave the five packages by the box next to the desk.
figures	2	I delivered pizzas to 3910 Lake Road, 876 B Street, and 425 Lana Lane.
double letters	3	Will Emmalou be successful when she attempts to pass the zoology exam?
speed	4	If the firm pays for the social, the eight city officials may also go.

| 1 | 2 | 3 | 4 | 5 | 6 | 7 | 8 | 9 | 10 | 11 | 12 | 13 | 14 |

145b ▶ 20
Build Speed: Letters/Memos

plain full sheets; block format; open punctuation

1. Review special letter parts on page 222.
2. A 5' writing on the letter to determine *gwam*.
3. Take two 1' writings on date through subject line of the letter. If you complete the lines before time is called, QS and start over.
4. Take two 1' writings on complimentary close through enclosures. If you complete the lines before time is called, QS and start over.
5. Take another 5' writing on the letter. Try to increase your *gwam* by 4-8 words.

gwam 5'

February 10, 19-- REGISTERED Attention Ms. Claudia W. Seymore Fenton   3
Manufacturing Company 3829 Douglas Road Fort Wayne, IN 46835-7553   5
Ladies and Gentlemen Subject: Education Classes   7

(¶ 1) Even the most user-friendly computer hardware/software will gather   10
dust unless employees have been properly trained. When you purchased   13
your system from us, we told you we provide the necessary training.   16

(¶ 2) Our next session of beginner's classes in word processing and   18
spreadsheets will be offered again in March. The word processing class   21
is scheduled for Monday nights. This class starts on March 6 and runs   24
through April 24. The spreadsheet applications class is scheduled for   27
Wednesday nights starting on March 8. April 26 will be the completion   30
date of this class. Both classes meet from 7 p.m. to 8 p.m.   32

(¶ 3) Registration materials are enclosed. Since the classes fill quite   35
rapidly, you must register as soon as possible.   37

Sincerely COMPUTER SPECIALISTS Todd W. Rush Education Specialist xx   39
Enclosures: Registration Materials Course Syllabi   43

gwam 5' | 1 | 2 | 3 |

16c ▶ 12 Build Keyboarding Skill: Space Bar/Shift Keys

each line twice SS; DS between 4-line groups

Goals
- to reduce the pause between words
- to reduce the time taken to shift/strike key/release when making capital letters

Down-and-in spacing

Out-and-down shifting

Space bar (Space *immediately* after each word.)

1 so an if us am by or ox he own jay pen yam own may
2 she is in│am to pay│if he may│by the man│in a firm
DS

3 I am to keep the pens in a cup by a tan mail tray.
4 Fran may try to fix an old toy for the little boy.
DS

Shift keys (Shift; strike key; release both quickly.)

5 J. V., Dr. or Mrs., Ph.D. or Ed.D., Fourth of July
6 Mrs. Maria Fuente; Dr. Mark V. Quin; Mr. T. C. Ott
DS

7 B. J. Marx will go to St. Croix in March with Lex.
8 Mae has a Ph.D. from Miami; Dex will get his Ed.D.
QS

16d ▶ 10 Improve Keyboarding Skill

each line twice SS (slowly, then faster); DS between 4-line groups

Technique goals
- quick-snap keystrokes
- quick joining of letters to form words
- quick joining of words to form phrases

Key words and phrases (*Think, say,* and *key* words and phrases.)

1 ox jam for oak for pay got own the lap via sob cut
2 make than with them such they when both then their
DS

3 to sit│an elf│by six│an oak│did go│for air│the jam
4 to vie│he owns│pay them│cut both│the quay│for they
DS

Key sentences (Strike keys at a brisk, steady pace.)

all letters learned
5 I may have six quick jobs to get done for low pay.
6 Vicky packed the box with quail and jam for Signe.
DS

all letters learned
7 Max can plan to bike for just five days with Quig.
8 Jim was quick to get the next top value for Debby.
QS

16e ▶ 10 Check Keyboarding Skill

1. Take a 30-second (30") timed writing on each line. Your rate in gross words a minute (*gwam*) is shown word-for-word above the lines.

2. If time permits, take another 30" writing on each line. Try to increase your keyboarding speed.

Goal: At least 18 *gwam*.

SUN
3/28/98

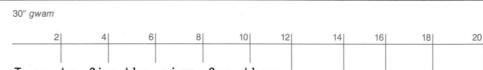

30" gwam

	2	4	6	8	10	12	14	16	18	20

1 I am to fix the sign for them.
2 Jaye held the key to the blue auto.
3 Todd is to go to the city dock for fish.
4 Vi paid the girl to make a big bowl of salad.
5 Kal may keep the urn he just won at the quay show.

	2	4	6	8	10	12	14	16	18	20

If you finish a line before time is called and start over, your *gwam* is the figure at the end of the line PLUS the figure above or below the point at which you stopped.

Job 11

LP p. 141

Processing Instructions From **Annette O'Toole**

Mr. Caswell would like the items on the attached sheet ordered. Prepare Purchase Order #387-609 to order these items. You will need to figure and enter the extensions in the total column and grand total of the order.

Job 12

LP p. 143

Processing Instructions From **Annette O'Toole**

Attached is a handwritten sales report prepared by Mr. Colfax. Prepare the report in final form.

March 4, 19--

Order from LaSalle Computer Supplies, 3418 Biscayne Street, Miami, FL 33139-5812

2	No. D83-98	Computer workstation--at $279.50 each
1	No. A23-56	Computer printer stand--at $249.50
1	No. A15-70	File cabinet--at $169.99
2	No. M26-63	Computer workstation chair--at $184.59 each

LaSalle's terms of sale are 3/10, net 30. Have order shipped by United Freight.

∎EPI

MONTHLY SALES REPORT

Month of _____February_____

Sales Representative	Territory	Sales For Month	Total Sales For Year
Adams, Becky	South Carolina	$ 18,760	$ 34,810
Brown, Janice	Tennessee	5,195	5,195
Chan, Regina	Tennessee	21,240	39,490
Rodriguez, Mario	Florida	12,560	22,380
Vanberg, Shawn	Georgia	13,500	27,980
Russell, Karin	Alabama	12,345	23,120
Jones, Lisa	North Carolina	15,895	33,125
Hernandez, Felipe	Florida	6,870	6,870
Nelson, Nancy	Virginia	18,755	34,900
Conrad, Greg	Kentucky	21,179	37,500
Vue, Cha	Mississippi	12,790	23,410
Spencer, Briget	North Carolina	16,050	36,185
McCarver, Maureen	South Carolina	7,385	7,385
Ryan, Shari	Alabama	15,380	25,790
Okenek, Jarom	Georgia	14,760	31,850
Lange, Diane	Mississippi	13,780	27,650
Cloud, Lee	Florida	10,980	21,860
Newton, Steve	Florida	15,760	29,485
Thomas, Jan	Georgia	15,675	27,390
Total Sales		$268,859	$496,375

17a ▶ 8
Conditioning Practice

each line twice SS; then a 1' writing on line 3; find *gwam*: total words keyed

all letters learned	1 Jim won the globe for six quick sky dives in Napa.
spacing	2 to own|is busy|if they|to town|by them|to the city
easy sentence	3 She is to go to the city with us to sign the form.

gwam 1' | 1 | 2 | 3 | 4 | 5 | 6 | 7 | 8 | 9 | 10 |

17b ▶ 20 Learn Z and : (Colon)

each line twice SS (slowly, then faster); DS between 2-line groups; if time permits, practice selected lines again

Follow the *Standard Plan for Learning New Keys* outlined on page 8.

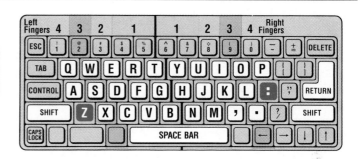

Reach technique for **z**

Reach *down* with *left little* finger.

Reach technique for : (colon)

Left shift and strike ; key; space twice after : used as punctuation.

Language skills notes
- Space twice after : used as punctuation.
- Capitalize the first word of a complete sentence following a colon.

Learn **Z**

1 a a za za zap zap zap zoo zoo zip zip zag zag zany
2 za za zap zap zed zed oz. oz. zoo zoo zip zip maze
3 zap it, zip it, an adz, to zap, the zoo, eight oz.

Learn **:** (colon)

4 ; ; :; :; Date: Time: Name: Room: From: File:
5 :; :; To: File: Reply to: Dear Al: Shift for :
6 Two spaces follow a colon, thus: Try these steps:

Combine **Z** and **:**

7 Zelda has an old micro with : where ; ought to be.
8 Zoe, use as headings: To: Zone: Date: Subject:
9 Liza, please key these words: zap, maze, and zoo.
10 Zane read: Shift to enter : and then space twice.

17c ▶ 5
Spacing Checkup

Key each line once SS. In place of the blank line at the end of each sentence, key the word "once" or "twice" to indicate the proper spacing.

1 After a . at the end of a sentence, space _____ .
2 After a ; used as punctuation, space _____ .
3 After a . following an initial, space _____ .
4 After a : used as punctuation, space _____ .
5 After a , within a sentence, space _____ .
6 After a . following an abbreviation, space _____ .

Processing
Instructions From
Annette O'Toole

Key the attached material as a formal memorandum for **Lynda V. Lopez, Committee Chair.** *Make all the changes marked on the copy as well as any un-marked errors you detect. Be sure to include an en-closure notation. Date the memo* **February 28.**

Product Development Evaluation Committee Members

MARCH 15 COMMITTEE MEETING

The next meeting of the Product development Evaluation Committee will be held wednesday, march ~~fifteenth~~ 15, at 2:30 P.M. in the con-ference room. Mark Sanderson will be demonstrating the computer math program, "Back to ~~the~~ Math Basics," which he recently developed. Because of the timeliness of the product, mr. Caswell has re-quested Susan St. Claier and Dave Master's to present information at our meeting on production costs and sales potential. Jason Hibbard will present an estimate of the cost/price structure for the software package. Mr. Caswell and I agree that we should move as quickly as possible in order to assure that this very innovative program is on the market before something similar appears from another company. A copy of Mr. Caswells letter to president Boswell which provides additional background information is enclosed ~~attached~~.

Job 10
LP p. 141

Processing
Instructions From
Annette O'Toole

Prepare an invoice from the order form prepared by Ms. Jan Thomas. Be sure to check the accu-racy of extensions and the total column before keying. Use today's date **(February 28).** *Order No.* **892-611A,** *and* **Net 30** *days. Our Order No.* **385.**

■EPI■ EDUCATIONAL PRODUCTS, INC.   PURCHASE ORDER

▲ 3929 Braddock Road, Fort Meyers, FL 33912-8357 (813) 277-6600

Purchase Order No.:

Carlton School of Business
488 Willowbrook Drive, SW
Atlanta, GA 30311-7485

Date:

Terms:

Shipped Via:

Quantity	Description/Stock Number	Price		Per	Total	
20 Sets	Creative Business Letters --E561	125	00	set	2,400	00
20 sets	Quick Key WP -- B731	75	00	set	1,500	00
5 sets	English Enhancement -- E320	219	00	set	1,095	00
2 sets	The Art Gallery -- B839	249	00	set	498	00
					5,493	00

By _____

17d ▶ 17 Improve Keyboarding Technique

1. Key the lines once as shown: SS with a DS between 2-line groups.

2. Key the lines again at a faster pace.

Technique goals
- curved, upright fingers
- quiet hands and arms
- steady keystroking pace

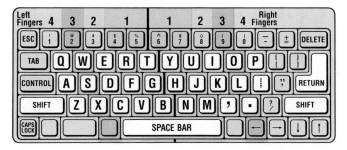

q/z
1 zoo qt. zap quo zeal quay zone quit maze quad hazy
2 Zeno amazed us all on the quiz but quit the squad.

p/x
3 apt six rip fix pens flex open flax drop next harp
4 Lex is apt to fix apple pie for the next six days.

v/m
5 vim mam van dim have move vamp more dive time five
6 Riva drove them to the mall in my vivid lemon van.

easy sentences
7 Glen is to aid me with the work at the dog kennel.
8 Dodi is to go with the men to audit the six firms.

alphabet
9 Nigel saw a quick red fox jump over the lazy cubs.
10 Jacky can now give six big tips from the old quiz.

Lesson 18	CAPS LOCK and ? (Question Mark)	LL: 50 LS: SS

18a ▶ 8 Conditioning Practice

each line twice SS; then a 1' writing on line 3; find *gwam*: total words keyed

alphabet 1 Lovak won the squad prize cup for sixty big jumps.

z/: 2 To: Ms. Mazie Pelzer; From: Dr. Eliza J. Piazzo.

easy sentence 3 He is to go with me to the dock to do work for us.

gwam 1' | 1 | 2 | 3 | 4 | 5 | 6 | 7 | 8 | 9 | 10 |

18b ▶ 7 Key Block Paragraphs

Key each paragraph (¶) once as shown; DS between ¶s; then key the ¶s again at a faster pace.

If your teacher directs, take a 1' writing on each ¶; find your rate in *gwam* (see page 30).

Paragraph 1   gwam 1'

The space bar is a vital tool, for every fifth or   10
sixth stroke is a space when you key. If you use   20
it with good form, it will aid you to build speed.   30

Paragraph 2

Just keep the thumb low over the space bar. Move   10
the thumb down and in quickly toward your palm to   20
get the prized stroke you need to build top skill.   30

gwam 1' | 1 | 2 | 3 | 4 | 5 | 6 | 7 | 8 | 9 | 10 |

---

significant decrease in Georgia can be attributed to a depleted sales force. ~~having~~

two sales representatives terminated employment ~~quit~~ during the year without

giving prior notice. This not only created a problem in there

districts, but also in the districts of the representatives

~~that tried to~~ who covered ~~two districts~~ for them while replacements were

being hired and trained.

<u>Comments and Projections</u>

Overall, the past year was a vary successful one. Our goal for this year is to increase total sales by 10 percent, with no state falling below a 7.5 percent gain.

The new products showcased at the January board meeting along with the improvements made to existing product lines should have a significant impact on sales during the next year. The addition of much needed sales representatives in Tennessee Florida and South Carolina will also create a positive impact on the total sales picture. } DS

Steps are being taken to establish a new policy for

distribution of sales commissions. This is being done to

prevent future occurrences of the problems such as those ~~we~~ experienced in

Georgia. The combination of all these factors should make

it quite easy for the Southern region to achieve and exceed the 10

percent projected increase.

Processing Instructions From Annette O'Toole

Ms. Lopez would like the attached agenda keyed as soon as possible.

AGENDA

Product Development Evaluation Committee Meeting

2:30 p.m., March 15

1. Introductory Comments . . . . Lynda Lopez

2. Presentation of "Back to Math Basics" . . . . . . Mark Sanderson

3. Special Reports

Production Cost Projections . . . . Susan St. Claire

Market Projections . . . . Dave Masters

Cost / Price Structure Projections . . . . . . Jason Hibbard

4. Discussion of Proposal . . . . Committee Members

5. Summary of Discussion: Pros and Cons . . . . . Griffin Caswell

6. Call for Vote . . . . Lynda Lopez

7. Adjournment

18c ▶ 15 Learn CAPS LOCK and ? (Question Mark)

each line twice SS (slowly, then faster); DS between 2-line groups; if time permits, practice each line again

Depress the CAPS LOCK to key a series of capital letters.

To release the LOCK to key lowercase letters, strike LEFT or RIGHT SHIFT key on most typewriters; strike the LOCK again on most computers. Learn now how this is done on the equipment you are using.

Reach technique for CAPS LOCK

Reach *left* with *left little* finger.

Reach technique for ? (question mark)

Left shift; reach *down* with *right little* finger; space twice after **?** at end of sentence.

Learn **CAPS LOCK**

1 Hal read PENTAGON and ADVISE AND CONSENT by Drury.

2 Oki joined FBLA when her sister joined PBL at OSU.

3 Zoe now belongs to AMS and DPE as well as to NBEA.

Learn **?** (question mark)   Space twice

4 ; ; ?; ?; Who? What? When? Where? Why? Is it?

5 Who is it? Is it she? Did he go? Was she there?

6 Is it up to me? When is it? Did he key the line?

18d ▶ 20 Improve Keyboarding Technique

1. Key the lines once as shown: SS with a DS between 2-line groups.

2. Key the lines again at a faster pace.

3. If time permits, take a 1' writing on line 11 and then on line 12; find *gwam*.

Technique goals
- reach *up* without moving hands away from you
- reach *down* without moving hands toward your body
- use CAPS LOCK to make ALL CAPS

Goal: finger-action keystrokes; quiet hands and arms

CAPS LOCK/?
1 Did she join OEA? Did she also join PSI and DECA?
2 Do you know the ARMA rules? Are they used by TVA?

z/v
3 Zahn, key these words: vim, zip, via, zoom, vote.
4 Veloz gave a zany party for Van and Roz in La Paz.

q/p
5 Paul put a quick quiz on top of the quaint podium.
6 Jacqi may pick a pink pique suit of a unique silk.

key words
7 they quiz pick code next just more bone wove flags
8 name jack flax plug quit zinc wore busy vine third

key phrases
9 to fix it|is to pay|to aid us|or to cut|apt to own
10 is on the|if we did|to be fit|to my pay|due at six

alphabet 11 Lock may join the squad if we have six big prizes.
easy sentence 12 I am apt to go to the lake dock to sign the forms.

gwam 1' | 1 | 2 | 3 | 4 | 5 | 6 | 7 | 8 | 9 | 10 |

To find 1' gwam: Add 10 for each line you completed to the scale figure beneath the point at which you stopped in a partial line. The total is your 1' *gwam*.

Processing
Instructions From
Annette O'Toole

Mr. Colfax would like the attached report prepared in unbound format. The last two columns of the table you prepared for Job 6 will be needed to complete the table in the report. Correct any unmarked errors.

SOUTHERN REGION SALES REPORT _DS_
Educational Products, Inc. _— QS_

The Southern Region of ~~EPI~~ *sp* increased overall sales by 5.5 percent /~~last~~ *over the previous* year /~~with~~ total sales amounting too *ed* $3,014,730; This increase was 1.5% *sp* higher then forecast for the year.

Sales by States

The figures for each state in the *e* rgion are outlined below. ~~The~~ *Sales* figures are presented for total dollar sales and for percentage of increase or decrease for the state for the year.

<u>Total dollar sales</u>. Florida replaced Georgia as the state generating the highest total dollar sales with sales of $525,650. Georgia ($406,310) was the only other state with ~~total~~ sales in excess of $400,000. The remaining seven states /*in the region* generated sales between $265,300 *and* ~~to~~ $338,250. A complete breakdown /*for each* by state in the /*Southern* region is shown below:

State	19-- Sales	% Change
Alabama		
Florida		
Georgia		
Kentucky		
Mississippi		
North Carolina		
South Carolina		
Tennesses		
Virginia		

Use information from the last two columns of Southern Region Sales Comparison table.

<u>Percentage increase/decrease</u>. ~~As can been seen from the above table,~~ *The sales information shows that* Virginia had the greatest percentage of total sales increase with 30.3 percent; Florida was second with a 22.4 percent increase. ~~Both states~~ *The* increase /*in both states* is do to the addition of a sales representative. A knew ~~rep~~ *sp* was added to Florida's sales force in March and to Virginia's in July.

Two states decreased in sales ~~this year~~--Georgia by 18.7 percent and North Carolina by 1.6 percent. The

19a ▶ 8
Conditioning Practice

each line twice SS; then a 1′ writing on line 3; find *gwam:* total words keyed

On most typewriters: **Comma** and **period** as well as **colon** and **question mark** can be keyed when the CAPS LOCK is on.

On most computers: CAPS LOCK affects only the letter keys; shifted punctuation marks require the use of one of the SHIFT keys.

alphabet 1 Zosha was quick to dive into my big pool for Jinx.

CAPS LOCK 2 Vi found ZIP Codes for OR, MD, RI, NV, AL, and PA.

easy sentence 3 Ian kept a pen and work forms handy for all of us.

gwam 1′ | 1 | 2 | 3 | 4 | 5 | 6 | 7 | 8 | 9 | 10 |

19b ▶ 12 Learn Tabulator

TYPEWRITERS

To clear electric tabs:
1. Move print element to *extreme* right using SPACE BAR or TAB key.
2. Hold CLEAR key down as you return print element to *extreme* left to remove all tab stops.

To clear electronic tabs:
1. Strike TAB key to move print element to the tab stop you want to clear.
2. Depress the TAB CLEAR key to remove the stop.
3. To remove all stops, depress TAB CLEAR key, then REPEAT key.

To set tab stops (all machines):
1. Move print element to desired tab position by striking SPACE BAR or BACKSPACE key.
2. Depress TAB SET key. Repeat procedure for each stop needed.

Tabulating procedure:
Strike the TAB key with the closest little finger; release it quickly and return the finger to home-key position.

COMPUTERS

Most computer programs have preset (default) tabs as shown in the following tab line:

----T----T----T----T----T----T
  5   10 15 20 25 30

Procedures for removing default tabs and setting tab stops vary. Use the Operator's Manual for your equipment/software to learn proper procedures.

Drill procedure:
1. Clear all tab stops, as directed above.
2. Set a tab stop 5 spaces to the right of left margin stop.
3. Set the LINE-SPACE SELECTOR on "2" for DS.
4. Key the paragraphs (¶s) once DS as shown, indenting the first line of each ¶.

Tab ⟶ The tab key is used to indent blocks of copy such as these.

Tab ⟶ It should also be used for tables to arrange data quickly and neatly into columns.

Tab ⟶ Learn now to use the tab key by touch; doing so will add to your keying skill.

Processing
Instructions From
Annette O'Toole

Process the attached letter for Mr. Colfax's signature. Date the letter **February 28** *and address the letter to*

Ms. Regina R. Chan
EPI Sales Representative
310 Rushmore Drive, NW
Knoxville, TN 37923-
7492

Correct any unmarked errors you find in the copy.

Dear Ms. Chan:

Your proposal that EPI sponsor a software institute for business education teachers prior to the Tennessee vocational conference is excellent. When teachers preview our software programs, they are much more receptive if they have received instruction during the preview from one of our specialists. This conference would be a perfect place to provide such instruction.

On March 17 I will be meeting with President Boswell to discuss the merits of your proposal. Prior to the meeting, I will need a detailed budget outlining the anticipated expenditures for the institute.

Sincerely,

Troy S. Colfax
Regional Vice President

Job 6

plain full sheet

Processing
Instructions From
Annette O'Toole

Prepare the attached table in final form for Mr. Colfax.

SOUTHERN REGION

19--/19-- Sales Comparison

State	Previous Year	Current Year	% Change
Alabama	$ 258,960	$ 275,980	+6.6
Florida	429,395	525,650	+22.4
Georgia	499,800	406,310	⁻18.7
Kentucky	265,290	275,390	+3.8
Mississippi	320,180	338,250	+5.6
North Carolina	340,395	334,970	-1.6
South Carolina	288,345	325,390	+12.8
Tennessee	250,200	265,300	+6.0
Virginia	205,320	267,490	+30.3
Totals	$ 2,857,885	$ 3,014,730	+5.5

19c ▶ 10 Improve Keyboarding Technique

each pair of lines twice
SS; DS between 4-line
groups

Lines 1-2

1. Clear tab stops; then, beginning at left margin, set a tab stop every 9 spaces until you have set 5 tab stops.

2. Key the first word in Column 1; tab to Column 2 and key the first word in that column, and so on. There will be 5 blank spaces between the columns.

		Tab		Tab		Tab		Tab		Tab	
tabulator 1 coal · turn · they · paid · worn · right
2 them · kept · fuel · corn · dual · their

shift-key 3 The best dancers are: Ana and Jose; Mag and Boyd.
sentences 4 Did Ms. Paxon send us the letter from Dr. LaRonde?

CAPS LOCK 5 Masami saw the game on ESPN; Krista saw it on NBC.
6 The AMS meeting is on Tuesday; the DPE, on Friday.

19d ▶ 14 Build Keyboarding Speed

1. Key each pair of lines once as shown: SS with a DS between pairs.

2. Take a 1' writing on each of lines 5-8; find *gwam* on each writing. (1' *gwam* = total 5-stroke words keyed.)

3. If time permits, take another 1' writing on line 7 and line 8 to improve speed.

Goal: At least 21 *gwam*.

Key words and phrases (*Think, say,* and *key* words and phrases.)

1 ad my we in be on at up as no are him was you gets
2 girl quay turn rush duty down maps rich laid spend

3 an ad|to fix|an oak|to get|the zoo|via jet|in turn
4 if they|to risk|by them|the duty|and paid|she kept

Key easy sentences (Key the words at a brisk, steady pace.)

5 He is to aid the girls with the work if they wish.
6 Jan may go to the city for the bid forms for them.

7 He may go to the lake by dusk to do the dock work.
8 I did all the work for the firm for the usual pay.

gwam 1' | 1 | 2 | 3 | 4 | 5 | 6 | 7 | 8 | 9 | 10 |

19e ▶ 6 Check Keyboarding Skill

1. Clear tab stops and set a new stop 5 spaces to the right of the left margin.

2. Set your equipment to DS the lines of the paragraphs (¶s).

3. Key each ¶ once DS as shown.

4. Take a 1' writing on each ¶; find *gwam* on each writing. (1' *gwam* = figure above the last word keyed.)

Key easy paragraphs containing all letters

¶ 1　　Good form means to move with speed and quiet control. My next step will be to size up the job and to do the work in the right way each day.

¶ 2　　To reach my goal of top speed, I have to try to build good form. I will try for the right key each time, but I must do so in the right way.

Processing Instructions From
Annette O'Toole

Mr. Griffin Caswell, Director of Product Development, would like the attached material formatted as a two-page letter to **Mr. Henry Boswell, President.** *Date the letter* **February 28** *and use* **New Software Developments** *for the subject line.*

Job 4
plain full sheet

Processing Instructions From
Annette O'Toole

Mr. Griffin Caswell, Director of Product Development, would like the same letter reformatted as a simplified memorandum to the **Product Development Staff.** *Date the memorandum* **February 28** *and use* **New Software Developments** *for the subject line.*

The information from the educational survey you had conducted has been most helpful in planning. Jay Hancock of Research Associates conduct for us — for the future. The responses from 350 elementary school teachers support our belief that teachers are eager for additional computer-aided instructional materials.

Over 40 percent of the respondents indicated that they are currently using some type of instructional materials requiring the computer. A very high percentage (93%) of the respondents felt that future curricular revisions will require the use of computers in their classrooms.

Math was the subject area the survey respondents listed as the course in which they would like to see additional software materials developed. Many of the respondents indicated that they would like to have an individualized math program for students with math difficulties.

Currently two computer programs for individualized math instruction are being pilot tested by our department. These programs appear to meet the elementary teachers' requirements. Mark Sanderson's individualized computer program, "Back to Math Basics," has great sales potential. With a few modifications the software could serve a wide market. Instructional objectives, periodic self-checks, and post-tests are all enhanced by the computer graphics which should be very appealing to elementary students. Jennifer Shields has worked with Mark to develop a more advanced math package which can be used after completing the "Back to Math Basics" program. It is our plan to have a comprehensive elementary math individualized program completed within the next two years. I will provide periodic updates will be provided periodically on the progress of these two individualized math programs.

20a ▶ 8
Conditioning Practice

each line twice SS;
then a 1' writing on
line 3; find *gwam*

alphabet	1	Quig just fixed prize vases he won at my key club.
spacing	2	Marcia works for HMS, Inc.; Juanita, for XYZ Corp.
easy sentence	3	Su did vow to rid the town of the giant male duck.

gwam 1' | 1 | 2 | 3 | 4 | 5 | 6 | 7 | 8 | 9 | 10 |

20b ▶ 20 Check/Improve Keyboarding Technique

each line once SS; if time permits, key each line again at a
faster pace

Ask your teacher to check your
keyboarding technique as you
key the following lines.

Fingers curved

Fingers upright

Finger-action keystroking

Down-and-in spacing

Reach review (Keep on home row the fingers not used for reaching.)

1 old led kit six jay oft zap cod big laws five ribs
2 pro quo|is just|my firm|was then|may grow|must try
3 Olga sews aqua and red silk to make six big kites.

Space-bar emphasis (*Think, say,* and *key* the words.)

4 en am an by ham fan buy jam pay may form span corn
5 I am|a man|an elm|by any|buy ham|can plan|try them
6 I am to form a plan to buy a firm in the old town.

Shift-key emphasis (Reach *up* and reach *down* without moving the hands.)

7 Jan and I are to see Ms. Han. May Lana come, too?
8 Bob Epps lives in Rome; Vic Copa is in Rome, also.
9 Oates and Co. has a branch office in Boise, Idaho.

Easy sentences (*Think, say,* and *key* the words at a steady pace.)

10 Eight of the girls may go to the social with them.
11 Corla is to work with us to fix the big dock sign.
12 Keith is to pay the six men for the work they did.

gwam 1' | 1 | 2 | 3 | 4 | 5 | 6 | 7 | 8 | 9 | 10 |

20c ▶ 6
Think as You Key

Key each line once SS. In place of
the blank line at the end of each
sentence, key the word that correctly completes the adage.

1 All that glitters is not _____ .
2 Do not cry over spilt _____ .
3 A friend in need is a friend _____ .
4 A new broom always sweeps _____ .
5 A penny saved is a penny _____ .

February 1, 19--   *(25)*

<Sales Representative>
<Address>
<City>, <State> <Zip>

Dear <Name>:

Subject: New Product Sales Information

~~Nine~~ *Sixteen* new/revised software programs have been released by
our Product Development Division since you received the
first quarter price list. Attached is a listing of those
products, the purchase order numbers, and the prices.
The second quarter price list will be mailed to you prior
to April 1.

Our Shipping Department has been instructed to send copies of these software packages along with the promotional
materials that have been developed. You should receive
them within the next ten days. Any questions you may
have about these programs should be directed to our support specialists at (813) 277-6601.

If there are additional materials that will assist you
in your sales efforts, please let us know.

Sincerely,

Sarah R. McLaughlin
Director of Marketing

xx

Attachment

■EPI■ EDUCATIONAL PRODUCTS, INC.

▲ 3929 Braddock Road, Fort Meyers, FL 33912-8357

Miss Janice B. Brown
Representative

(813) 277-6600

Home address:
310 Rossville Avenue
Chattanooga, TN 37408-8340

EPI■ EDUCATIONAL PRODUCTS
3929 Braddock Road, Fort Meyers, FL 3391

Mrs. Maureen C. McCarver
Representative

(813) 277-6600

Home address:
849 Rockridge Drive
Columbia, SC 29203-7401

■EPI■ EDUCATIONAL PRODUCTS, INC.

▲ 3929 Braddock Road, Fort Meyers, FL 33912-8357

Mr. Felipe R. Hernandez
Representative

(813) 277-6600

Home address:
2230 Atlantic Road
Miami, FL 33149-1745

20d ▶ 7
Check/Improve Keyboarding Speed

1. Take a 30-second (30″) timed writing on each line. Your rate in *gwam* is shown word-for-word above the lines.

2. If time permits, take another 30″ writing on each line. Try to increase your keyboarding speed.

Goal: At least 22 *gwam*.

30″ gwam

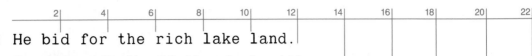

| | 2 | 4 | 6 | 8 | 10 | 12 | 14 | 16 | 18 | 20 | 22 |

1 He bid for the rich lake land.

2 Suzy may fish off the dock with us.

3 Pay the girls for all the work they did.

4 Quen is due by six and may then fix the sign.

5 Janie is to vie with six girls for the city title.

6 Duane is to go to the lake to fix the auto for the man.

| | 2| | 4| | 6| | 8| | 10| | 12| | 14| | 16| | 18| | 20| | 22| |

If you finish a line before time is called and start over, your *gwam* is the figure at the end of the line PLUS the figure above or below the point at which you stopped.

20e ▶ 9
Check/Improve Keyboarding Speed

1. Take a 1′ writing on each paragraph (¶); find *gwam* on each writing.

2. Using your better *gwam* as a base rate, select a *goal rate* and take two 1′ guided writings on each ¶ as directed at the bottom of the page.

Copy used to measure skill is triple-controlled for difficulty:

E = easy   HA = high average
LA = low average   D = difficult
A = average

Difficulty index
(shown above copy)

E	1.2 si	5.1 awl	90% hfw
1	**2**	**3**	
Syllable intensity	Average word length	High-frequency words	

Difficulty index
all letters used | E | 1.2 si | 5.1 awl | 90% hfw |

        .   2   .   4   .   6   .   8   .

Tab   How you key is just as vital as the copy you

   10   .   12   .   14   .   16   .   18   .

work from or produce. What you put on paper is a

   20   .   22   .   24   .   26   .   28   .

direct result of the way in which you do the job.

        .   2   .   4   .   6   .   8   .

Tab   If you expect to grow quickly in speed, take

   10   .   12   .   14   .   16   .   18   .

charge of your mind. It will then tell your eyes

   20   .   22   .   24   .   26   .   28   .

and hands how to work through the maze of letters.

Guided (Paced) Writing Procedure

Select a practice goal

1. Take a 1′ writing on ¶ 1 of a set of ¶s that contain superior figures for guided writings, as in 20e above.

2. Using the *gwam* as a base, add 4 *gwam* to determine your goal rate.

3. Choose from Column 1 of the table at the right the speed nearest your goal rate. At the right of that speed, note the ¼′ points in the copy you must reach to maintain your goal rate.

Quarter-minute checkpoints

gwam	¼′	½′	¾′	Time
16	4	8	12	16
20	5	10	15	20
24	6	12	18	24
28	7	14	21	28
32	8	16	24	32
36	9	18	27	36
40	10	20	30	40

4. Note from the word-count dots and figures above the lines in ¶ 1 the checkpoint for each quarter minute. (Example: Checkpoints for 24 *gwam* are 6, 12, 18, and 24.)

Practice procedure

1. Take two 1′ writings on ¶ 1 at your goal rate guided by the quarter-minute calls (¼, ½, ¾, time).

Goal: To reach each of your checkpoints just as the guide is called.

2. Take two 1′ writings on ¶ 2 of a set of ¶s in the same way.

3. If time permits, take a 2′ writing on the set of ¶s combined, without the guides.

Speed level of practice

When the purpose of practice is to reach out into new speed areas, use the *speed* level. Take the brakes off your fingers and experiment with new stroking patterns and new speeds. Do this by:

1. Reading 2 or 3 letters ahead of your keying to foresee stroking patterns.

2. Getting the fingers ready for the combinations of letters to be keyed.

3. Keeping your eyes on the copy in the book.

Warm up daily before starting job tasks by keying each line twice (slowly, then faster).

alphabet	1	Jack was extremely hopeful of having the Marquette jazz bands perform.
figures	2	You can call her at 836-4807 before 9 a.m. or at 836-2510 after 9 a.m.
fig/sym	3	Invoice #8604 totalled $371.29 after deducting the 15% sales discount.
speed	4	The girl may dismantle the bicycle and then go to the island to visit.

| 1 | 2 | 3 | 4 | 5 | 6 | 7 | 8 | 9 | 10 | 11 | 12 | 13 | 14 |

Job 1

plain full sheet

Processing Instructions From **Annette O'Toole**

Attached is a copy of the **New Product Price List.** *Rekey the document with the changes marked on the document.*

NEW PRODUCT PRICE LIST

February ~~1~~ 25, 19--

Number	Software	Price
B929	Basic Spreadsheets	$ 139
E246	Computer Geography	~~269~~ 259
E786	Computerized Reading	189
E561	Creative *Business* Letters	125
B821	Data Controller	~~329~~ 309
E320	English Enhancement	219
B689	Financial Advisor	99
E758	Keyboarding Composition Skills	155
E615	Language Arts Skills	139
B731	Quick Key WP	75
E641	Spelling Mastery	139
B658	Telephone Directory	119
B839	The Art Gallery	249
~~B658~~	~~Telephone Directory~~	~~119~~
B794	Your Time Manager	69
B952	*Tax Assistant*	*129*
B586	*Graphics Designer*	*165*

Improve Keyboarding/Language Skills

Learning Goals

1. To improve keyboarding technique.
2. To improve control of letter reaches and letter combinations.
3. To improve speed on sentence and paragraph copy.
4. To review and improve language skills: capitalization.

Format Guides

1. *Paper Guide* at *0* (for typewriters)
2. Line length (LL): 50 spaces; see *Get Ready to Keyboard: Typewriters* (p. x) or *Computers* (p. xii).
3. Line spacing (LS): Single-space (SS) drills; double-space (DS) paragraphs (¶s).
4. Paragraph indention (PI): 5 spaces when appropriate.

Lesson 21	*Keyboarding/Language Skills*	LL: 50 LS: SS

21a ▶ 6
Conditioning Practice

each line twice SS; then a 1' writing on line 3; find *gwam*

alphabet	1	Nat will vex the judge if she bucks my quiz group.
punctuation	2	Al, did you use these words: vie, zeal, and aqua?
easy sentence	3	She owns the big dock, but they own the lake land.

gwam 1' | 1 | 2 | 3 | 4 | 5 | 6 | 7 | 8 | 9 | 10 |

21b ▶ 22 *Improve Keyboarding Technique*

1. Key the lines once as shown: SS with a DS between 2-line groups.

2. If time permits, key the lines again to improve keying ease and speed.

Technique goals

- fingers deeply curved and upright
- eyes on copy
- finger-action keystrokes
- hands and arms quiet, almost motionless

Reach review

ed/de	1	ed de led ode need made used side vied slide guide
	2	Ned said the guide used a video film for her talk.
ju/ft	3	ju ft jug oft jet aft jug lift just soft jury loft
	4	Judy left fifty jugs of juice on a raft as a gift.
ol/lo	5	ol lo old lot lob lox log sold loan fold long told
	6	Lou told me that her local school loans old books.
ws/sw	7	ws sw was saw laws rows cows vows swam sways swing
	8	Swin swims at my swim club and shows no big flaws.
ik/ki	9	ik ki kit ski kin kid kip bike kick like kiwi hike
	10	The kid can hike or ride his bike to the ski lake.
za/az	11	za az zap adz haze zany lazy jazz hazy maze pizzas
	12	A zany jazz band played with pizzazz at the plaza.
alphabet	13	Olive Fenz packed my bag with six quarts of juice.
	14	Jud aims next to play a quick game with Bev Fritz.

gwam 1' | 1 | 2 | 3 | 4 | 5 | 6 | 7 | 8 | 9 | 10 |

Educational Products, Inc. (An Office Job Simulation)

Learning Goals

1. To become familiar with the keyboarding/formatting tasks in a firm that produces/markets educational software.

2. To learn selected terms frequently used in word processing.

3. To improve your ability to work from different copy sources and to detect and correct unidentified errors.

Documents Processed

1. Tables
2. Letters
3. Memorandums
4. Report/Sales Report
5. Agenda
6. Forms: Invoice and Purchase Order

EDUCATIONAL PRODUCTS, INC. AN OFFICE JOB SIMULATION

Before you begin processing the documents in this unit, read the information at the right carefully.

Make notes of any standard procedures that you think will save you time during the completion of the document production activities.

Daily work plan:

Conditioning practice .... 5′
Work on simulation ....45′

Mr. Henry Boswell
Page 2
February 28, 19--
It is our plan to have a comprehensive elementary math program completed within the next two years. Updates on the progress will

Second-Page Heading

Work Assignment

You have accepted a part-time position in the document processing center of Educational Products, Inc. (EPI) as a document processing trainee. EPI manufactures and sells educational software. The company is located at 3929 Braddock Road, Fort Meyers, FL 33912-8357. Your supervisor is Ms. Annette O'Toole, supervisor of the document processing center. In addition to training personnel, Ms. O'Toole is responsible for scheduling and coordinating the work load of the center's document processing specialists and trainees.

During your training program, you were instructed to format all company letters in block format with mixed punctuation. The originator's business title is to be keyed on the line below the originator's keyed name in the closing lines. The originators of the documents will specify the format they prefer for the memorandums you format.

Processing instructions from the supervisor of the center will be attached to each document you are given to complete. For some documents specific instructions are not given; you will be expected to make appropriate decisions on the basis of your knowledge and experience. Since EPI has based its word processing manual on your textbook, you can also use the text as a reference to assist you in making formatting decisions.

Some documents contain undetected errors that have been overlooked by the individual submitting the document. Correct those errors along with any keying errors you make before submitting your work to Ms. O'Toole.

Special guides for jobs requiring unusual specifications are provided in "Excerpts from EPI's Document Processing Procedures Manual." Review these guides before you begin your work.

Note: Students using electronic equipment should utilize the capabilities of the equipment in creating, editing, and storing documents. For example, Job 2 should be completed using the mail merge function.

Excerpts from EPI's Document Processing Procedures Manual

Leaders. Leaders are a series of periods and spaces (. . .) that are keyed between two items in tabular material to make reading easier. They "lead the reader's eye" from one columnar item to another. They are primarily used when the distance between certain items in two columns is so great that matching columnar items is difficult.

Leaders are made by alternating the period (.) and a space. The lines of leaders should be aligned in vertical rows and should end at the same point at the right.

To align leaders, key all periods on either the odd or the even numbers on the line-of-writing scale guided by their position in the first line of leaders. Begin the first line of leaders on the second space after the first item in the column and end the leaders 2 or 3 spaces to the left of the beginning of the next column.

Agenda. An agenda is one example of a business document that makes use of leaders. Educational Products, Inc. uses the nonjustified format for agendas (all items in Column 2 begin at the same horizontal point). The margins used for the agenda are: top, 1 or 1½″; side 1″; and bottom, 1″. The heading as well as the body of the agenda are double spaced. Study carefully the agenda shown below.

AGENDA

Marketing Meeting

February 12, 19--

1. Call to Order . . . . Sarah McLaughlin

2. Minutes of Last Meeting . . . . Greg White

3. Special Reports

    Southern Region Sales . . . . . . Troy Colfax

    Eastern Region Sales . . . . Sally Marshall

Second-page heading for correspondence. The heading for a two-page letter or memorandum begins on line 6. Key the heading SS in block format at the left margin. Include the name of the addressee, the page number, and the date. DS between the heading and the body.

21c ▶ 12
Check/Improve Keyboarding Speed

1. Take one 1' timed writing and two 1' *guided* writings on ¶ 1 as directed on page 38.

2. Take one 1' timed writing and two 1' *guided* writings on ¶ 2 in the same way.

3. As time permits, take one or two 2' timed writings on ¶s 1 and 2 combined *without* the call of the guide; find *gwam*.

1' *gwam* goals
▽ 17 = acceptable
⊡ 21 = average
⊙ 25 = good
◇ 29 = excellent

all letters used | E | 1.2 si | 5.1 awl | 90% hfw

gwam 2'

Keep in home position all of the fingers not   5
being used to strike a key. Do not let them move   10
out of position for the next letters in your copy.   15
Prize the control you have over the fingers.   19
See how quickly speed goes up when you learn that   24
you can make them do just what you expect of them.   29

gwam 2' | 1 | 2 | 3 | 4 | 5 |

21d ▶ 10 Improve Language Skills: Capitalization

1. Read the first rule highlighted in color at the right.

2. Key the **Learn** sentence below it, noting how the rule has been applied.

3. Key the **Apply** sentence, supplying the needed capital letters.

4. Read and practice the other rules in the same way.

5. If time permits, key the three **Apply** sentences again to increase decision-making speed.

> Capitalize the first word in a sentence.

Learn 1 Mindy left her coat here.   Can she stop by for it?
Apply 2 do you plan to go today?   the game begins at four.

> Capitalize personal titles and names of people.

Learn 3 I wrote to Mr. Katz, but Miss Dixon sent the form.
Apply 4 do you know if luci and lex bauer are with dr. tu?

> Capitalize names of clubs, schools, organizations, and companies.

Learn 5 The Beau Monde Singers will perform at Music Hall.
Apply 6 lennox corp. now owns the hyde park athletic club.

Lesson 22 — Keyboarding/Language Skills

LL: 50
LS: SS

22a ▶ 6
Conditioning Practice

each line twice SS; then a 1' writing on line 3; find *gwam*

alphabet 1 Wusov amazed them by jumping quickly from the box.
spacing 2 am to|is an|by it|of us|an oak|is to pay|it is due
easy 3 It is right for the man to aid them with the sign.

gwam 1' | 1 | 2 | 3 | 4 | 5 | 6 | 7 | 8 | 9 | 10 |

22b ▶ 12
Check/Improve Keyboarding Speed

1. Take one 1' timed writing and two 1' *guided* writings on ¶ 1 of 21c, above, as directed at the bottom of page 38.

2. Key ¶ 2 of 21c, above, in the same way.
Goal: To increase speed.

3. As time permits, take one or two 2' timed writings on ¶s 1 and 2 combined; find *gwam*.

139a ▶ 5
Conditioning Practice

each line twice SS (slowly, then faster); DS between 2-line groups; if time permits, rekey selected lines

alphabet	1	Mrs. Waxler enjoyed checking the problems on the quiz she gave Friday.
figures	2	My 1992 salary was $28,741.56; however, after taxes it was $20,683.12.
fig/sym	3	This model (#94A-683) is $1,250; the other model (#94A-783) is $1,495.
speed	4	The proficient man did the work on the bicycle for them on the island.

| 1 | 2 | 3 | 4 | 5 | 6 | 7 | 8 | 9 | 10 | 11 | 12 | 13 | 14 |

139b ▶ 15
Language Skills: Compose at Keyboard

plain full sheets; SM: 1″

1. Applicants are often asked to respond to the questions at the right during an interview. Select four of the questions and compose your response. Number your responses and DS between paragraphs.

2. Edit your copy, marking corrections and changes to improve sentence structure and organization.

1 What would you like to be doing five years from now?
2 Give me three reasons why our firm should hire you.
3 Do your grades accurately reflect your ability? Explain why or why not?
4 Are you considering further education? Explain why or why not.
5 What are your greatest weaknesses.
6 What salary do you feel you should be paid during the first year?
7 What are your major accomplishments in life?
8 What have you learned from previous employment?

139c ▶ 30 Prepare Follow-Up Letters

plain full sheets; modified block format; blocked paragraphs; mixed punctuation; proofread and correct errors

Document 1

Format and key the follow-up letter at the right. Use personal-business letter format. Refer to page 240 for Ms. Murphy's address. Use **May 27, 19--** for the date. Supply missing letter parts.

Document 2

Study the guides for follow-up letters on page 239. Assume that you interviewed for the job you applied for in 136b, Document 2. Compose your follow-up letter; edit and prepare a final copy. Submit your first draft and final copy.

words

opening lines 10

Mr. Juan R. Gutierrez Director of Human Resources Creswell Manufacturing Co. 8352 West Oxford Avenue Denver, CO 80236-7483   20 / 29 / 38

Thank you for talking with me about the secretarial opening with Creswell Manufacturing Co. From our discussion, I have a more complete understanding of the requirements for the position.   48 / 58 / 68 / 76

My meeting with Ms. Karlstad was very beneficial. Why those working with her speak so highly of her was quickly apparent. Replacing Ms. Karlstad would be a challenge. I would like the opportunity to face that challenge.   87 / 98 / 110 / 120

If there is further information that would be helpful as you consider my application, please let me know.   132 / 142

closing lines 149

22c ▶ 20 Improve Keyboarding Technique: Response Patterns

1. Key each pair of lines twice SS; DS between 4-line groups.

2. Take a 1′ writing on line 10 and then on line 12; find *gwam* (total words keyed) on each writing.

3. Take another 1′ writing on the slower line to increase your speed on more difficult copy.

PRACTICE HINTS

Balanced-hand lines:
Think, say, and *key* the words by word response at a fast pace.

One-hand lines:
Think, say, and *key* the words by letter response at a steady but unhurried pace.

> **Letter response**
> Many one-hand words (as in lines 3-4) are not easy to key. Such words may be keyed letter-by-letter and with continuity (steadily, without pauses).

> **Word response**
> Short, balanced-hand words (as in lines 1-2) are so easy to key that they can be keyed as words, not letter-by-letter. Think and key them at your top speed.

balanced-hand words	1	ah do so go he us if is of or to it an am me by ox
	2	ha for did own the for and due pay but men may box
one-hand words	3	as up we in at on be oh ax no ex my ad was you are
	4	ad ink get ilk far him few pop set pin far imp car
balanced-hand phrases	5	of it|he is|to us|or do|am to|an ox|or by|is to do
	6	do the|and for|she did|all six|the map|for the pay
one-hand phrases	7	as on|be in|at no|as my|be up|as in|at him|saw you
	8	you are|oil tax|pop art|you get|red ink|we saw him
balanced-hand sentences	9	The man is to go to the city and do the auto work.
	10	The girl is to go by bus to the lake for the fish.
one-hand sentences	11	Jimmy saw you feed a deer on a hill up at my mill.
	12	Molly sat on a junk in oily waters at a bare reef.

gwam 1′ | 1 | 2 | 3 | 4 | 5 | 6 | 7 | 8 | 9 | 10 |

22d ▶ 12 Improve Language Skills: Capitalization

1. Read each rule and key the **Learn** and **Apply** sentences beneath it.

2. If time permits, practice the **Apply** lines again to increase decision-making speed.

> Capitalize the days of the week.

Learn 1 Did you ask if the OEA contest is to be on Friday?
Apply 2 does FBLA meet on wednesday, thursday, and friday?

> Capitalize the months of the year.

Learn 3 August was very hot, but September is rather cool.
Apply 4 they are to spend july and august at myrtle beach.

> Capitalize names of holidays.

Learn 5 Kacy and Zoe may visit their parents on Labor Day.
Apply 6 gus asked if memorial day comes at the end of may.

> Capitalize the names of historic periods and events and special events.

Learn 7 The Fourth of July honors the American Revolution.
Apply 8 bastille day is in honor of the french revolution.

138c ▶ 7
Simulated Employment Test: Straight-Copy Timed Writing

1. A 5' writing on all ¶s.
2. Find *gwam* and number of errors.

all letters used | A | 1.5 si | 5.7 awl | 80% hfw

gwam 3' | 5'

Preparing employment documents is a vital part of securing a job. | 4 | 3

These documents consist of a letter of application, a data sheet, and a | 9 | 6

follow-up letter. Since these documents may be the most important docu- | 14 | 8

ments that you will ever prepare, it is crucial that extra care be taken | 19 | 11

to assure high quality. Within a few seconds a prospective employer | 24 | 14

forms an initial opinion of you based on the letter of application and | 28 | 17

the data sheet. If the opinion is a positive one, the documents will | 33 | 20

be looked at further, and you may be invited for an interview. | 37 | 22

An impressive data sheet is one that leaves the reader with a favor- | 42 | 25

able impression of you and your abilities. The data sheet provides the | 47 | 28

reader with detailed information about you. The reader learns who you | 51 | 31

are, where you live, and how to contact you from the specifics outlined | 56 | 34

by the first section of the data sheet. Other sections inform the reader | 61 | 37

of your education, school activities, and work history. The last part of | 66 | 40

the data sheet is often used to supply the reader with the names of peo- | 71 | 42

ple to contact to acquire further specifics about you and your potential. | 76 | 45

The letter of application accompanies the data sheet. It emphasizes | 80 | 48

how you are qualified and why you should be hired for the job. If the | 85 | 51

data sheet and letter impress the reader, you will be invited for an in- | 90 | 54

terview. During the interview, you will be given the time to convince | 95 | 57

the interviewer that you have the background and are the appropriate per- | 99 | 60

son for the job. A day or two after the interview, a follow-up letter to | 104 | 63

convey your appreciation to the interviewer for spending time with you | 109 | 65

and to specify again your interest in the job is appropriate. | 113 | 68

gwam 3' | 1 | 2 | 3 | 4 | 5
5' | 1 | 2 | 3

23a ▶ 6
Conditioning Practice

each line twice SS; then a 1' timed writing on line 3; find *gwam*

alphabet 1 Marjax made five quick plays to win the big prize.

CAPS LOCK 2 Did you say to send the cartons by UPS or by USPS?

easy 3 I am to pay the six men if they do the work right.

gwam 1' | 1 | 2 | 3 | 4 | 5 | 6 | 7 | 8 | 9 | 10 |

23b ▶ 20 Improve
Keyboarding Technique: Response Patterns

1. Key each set of lines twice SS (slowly, then faster); DS between 6-line groups.

2. Take a 1' writing on line 10, on line 11, and on line 12; find *gwam* on each; compare rates.

3. If time permits, rekey the slowest line.

> **Combination response**
> Normal copy (as in lines 7-9) includes both word- and letter-response sequences.   Use *top* speed for easy words, *lower* speed for words that are harder to key.

letter response
1 be in as no we kin far you few pin age him get oil
2 see him|was nil|vex you|red ink|wet mop|as you saw
3 Milo saved a dazed polo pony as we sat on a knoll.

word response
4 ox if am to is may end big did own but and yam wit
5 do it|to cut|he got|for me|jam it|an owl|go by air
6 He is to go to the city and to do the work for me.

combination response
7 am at of my if on so as to be or we go up of no by
8 am in|so as|if no|is my|is up|to be|is at|is up to
9 Di was busy at the loom as you slept in the chair.

letter 10 Jon gazed at a phony scarab we gave him in a case.
combination 11 Pam was born in a small hill town at the big lake.
word 12 Keith is off to the lake to fish off the big dock.

gwam 1' | 1 | 2 | 3 | 4 | 5 | 6 | 7 | 8 | 9 | 10 |

23c ▶ 12 Improve
Language Skills: Capitalization

1. Read each rule and key the **Learn** and **Apply** sentences beneath it.

2. If time permits, practice the **Apply** lines again to increase decision-making speed.

> Capitalize names of cities, states, and other important places.

Learn 1 When you were in Nevada, did you visit Hoover Dam?
Apply 2 did he see paris from the top of the eiffel tower?

> Capitalize geographic names, regions, and locations.

Learn 3 Val drove through the Black Hills in South Dakota.
Apply 4 we canoed down the missouri river near sioux city.

> Capitalize names of streets, roads, avenues, and buildings.

Learn 5 Jemel lives at Bay Towers near Golden Gate Bridge.
Apply 6 our store is now in midtown plaza on kenwood road.

Document 3
Unbound Report
Format and key the material given at the right as an unbound report using the internal citation method for referencing. Use **INTEGRATED SOFTWARE** for the title of the report.

Document 4
Prepare a reference page from the information given below.

References

Clark, J. F., and others. Computers and Information Processing. 2d ed. Cincinnati: South-Western Publishing Co., 1990.

VanHuss, S. H., and W. R. Daggett, Jr. Electronic Information Systems. Cincinnati: South-Western Publishing Co., 1990.

words

title 4

Software packages *for computers* are now available that combine word 18
processing, data base, and spreadsheet applications. This 29
allows the user to perform each of the applications 40
a seperately, or to merge information between *many* applications. 53
¶ Software packages that have this capability are called in- 64
tegrated software. These packages may include several dif- 76
ferent applications; however, word *#* processing, data base, and 88
spreadsheets are currently *among* the most common applications. 101

Word Processing 107

Word Processing software ~~provides the~~ program*s* to enable 115
a computer to do word processing applications. ~~This~~ *The program* allows 129
a user to create*,* *store,* edit, and print documents using a computer. 143

The editing capability is extremely valuable. Editing 154
can be done at any time by loading a *stored* document back into 166
memory and display*ing* it on the scr*e*n. Various function keys 179
are used to insert, delete, copy, replace, and move informa- 191
tion *with minimal keystrokes*. This has a great effect on the time and effort re- 207
quired to edit documents. 212

Spreadsheets 217

Spreadsheet programs allow the ~~use~~ *manipulation* of data for deci- 229
sion-making purposes. Various forms of manual spreadsheets 241
have been used for many years. Computers which utilize cur- 253
rent spreadsheet softwar*e* provide users with electronic 264
spreadsheets. *These electronic* Spreadsheets are being used by *many of today's* business firms 283
for financial analysis. *The* Information gained from spread- 295
sheets decreases the uncertainty related to the outcomes of 307
potential decisions (VanHuss *and Daggett*, 1990, 254-255). 318

Data Base 322

¶ Data base software is used for collecting and maintaining 334
information (Clark and others, 1990, 215). This application 346
allows the extraction of information in different ways. 357
Those in decision-making positions are provided with more 369
information in a timely as well as cost-effective manner, 381
allowing the various alternatives to be considered more 393
thoroughly. 394

23d ▶ 12
Check/Improve Keyboarding Speed

1. Take one 1' timed writing and two 1' *guided* writings on ¶ 1 as directed on page 38.

2. Take one 1' timed writing and two 1' *guided* writings on ¶ 2 in the same way.

3. As time permits, take one or two 2' timed writings on ¶s 1 and 2 combined *without* the call of the guide; find *gwam*.

1' gwam goals
▽ 19 = acceptable
⊡ 23 = average
⊙ 27 = good
◇ 31 = excellent

all letters used | E | 1.2 si | 5.1 awl | 90% hfw

gwam 2'

```
               .    2    .    4    .    6    .    8
        The level of your skill is a major item when        5
      10   .   12   .   14   .   16   .   18
   you try to get a job.  Just as vital, though, may        10
      20   .   22   ⊡  24   .   26   ⊙   28   .
   be how well you can express ideas in written form.       15
               .    2    .    4    .    6    .    8    .
        It might amaze you to learn what it is worth         19
      10   .   12   .   14   .   16   .   18
   to a company to find those who can write a letter         24
      20   .   22   ⊡  24   .   26   ⊙   28   .
   of quality as they key.  Learn to do so in school.        29
```

gwam 2' | 1 | 2 | 3 | 4 | 5 |

Lesson 24	Keyboarding/Language Skills	LL: 50
		LS: SS

24a ▶ 6
Conditioning Practice

each line twice SS; then a 1' writing on line 3; find *gwam*

alphabet 1 Jack viewed unique forms by the puzzled tax agent.

? 2 Where is Elena? Did she call? Is she to go, too?

easy 3 Title to all of the lake land is held by the city.

gwam 1' | 1 | 2 | 3 | 4 | 5 | 6 | 7 | 8 | 9 | 10 |

24b ▶ 12 Improve Language Skills: Capitalization

1. Read each rule and key the **Learn** and **Apply** sentences beneath it.

2. If time permits, practice the **Apply** lines again to increase decision-making speed.

> Capitalize an official title when it precedes a name and elsewhere if it is a title of high distinction.

Learn 1 In what year did Juan Carlos become King of Spain?
Learn 2 Masami Chou, our class president, made the awards.
Apply 3 will the president speak to us in the Rose Garden?
Apply 4 mr. koch, our company president, chairs the group.

> Capitalize initials; also capitalize letters in abbreviations if the letters would be capitalized when the words are spelled out.

Learn 5 Does Dr. R. J. Anderson have an Ed.D., or a Ph.D.?
Learn 6 He said that UPS stands for United Parcel Service.
Apply 7 we have a letter from ms. anna m. bucks of boston.
Apply 8 m.d. means Doctor of Medicine, not medical doctor.

24c ▶ 12
Check/Improve Keyboarding Speed

Practice again the 2 ¶s above, using the directions in 23d.

Goal: To improve your speed by at least 2 *gwam*.

138a ▶ 5
Conditioning
Practice

each line twice SS
(slowly, then faster);
DS between 2-line
groups; if time permits,
rekey selected lines

alphabet 1 Jared Buckly reviewed the next eight steps required for modernization.

figures 2 The librarian purchased 5,790 books during 1991 and 4,863 during 1992.

fig/sym 3 The order for 19 desks (invoice #8A23) came to $7,640 with the 5% tax.

speed 4 The neighbor of the tax auditor of the firm did the work on the docks.

| 1 | 2 | 3 | 4 | 5 | 6 | 7 | 8 | 9 | 10 | 11 | 12 | 13 | 14 |

138b ▶ 38 Simulated
Employment Test:
Letter, Table, Report

Time Schedule

Applicant Time to Review
Documents and Ask
Questions . . . . 8'
Employment Production
Test . . . . 30'
(includes proofreading time--
applicant will be notified when
five minutes remain)

plain full sheet; correct errors
as you key

Document 1
Letter
block format; open punctuation

words

November 15, 19--|Mr. Joshua D. Cline, President|Chadwick Insurance   14
Company|3209 Roosevelt Way, NE|Seattle, WA 98105-6385|Dear Mr. Cline| 28
Subject: Bellevue Branch Office   34

The renovation of the building we leased for the new branch office in   48
Bellevue is scheduled to be completed by December 1. This schedule should   63
give us ample time to have the branch operational by the target date of   78
December 15.   81

Erika Tudor from the Seattle home office has been promoted to branch   94
manager and will be in Bellevue by the first of December. Jason Reeves has   110
agreed to transfer from the Tacoma branch to be Erika's assistant. I am   124
confident they will do an exceptional job.   133

A complete roster of the Bellevue office personnel is enclosed. Two of   147
the agents are transferring from Seattle. The others are new and will have   163
completed our trainee program by December 10.   172

I will keep you informed on the progress of the Bellevue branch; I am sure   187
that it will be an excellent addition to our company. (163)   198

Sincerely|Parker S. Hawthorne|District Supervisor|xx|Enclosure   210/231

Document 2
Table
plain full sheet; DS;
CS: 8; center column headings

Bellevue Branch   3
November 15, 19--   7

Name and Position	Location	Phone	
Erika Tudor, Branch Manager	100b	252-1903	29
Jason Reeves, Assistant	102	252-4871	37
Dyan Silverhill, Secretary	100a	252-3010	46
Courtney Edinburg, Agent	110	252-9618	54
Phillip Guerrero, Agent	104	252-1765	62
Forrest Hewitt, Agent	108	252-6913	69
Chieh Kaneko, Agent	106	252-1655	76

(Name and Position header row: 21)

24d ▶ 20 Master Difficult Reaches

1. Key each set of lines twice SS (slowly, then faster); DS between 8-line groups.

2. Note the lines that caused you difficulty; practice them again to develop a steady pace (no pauses between letters).

Adjacent (side-by-side) keys (as in lines 1-4) can be the source of many errors unless the fingers are kept in an upright position and precise motions are used.

Long direct reaches (as in lines 5-8) reduce speed unless they are made without moving the hands forward and downward.

Reaches with the outside fingers (as in lines 9-12) are troublesome unless made without twisting the hands in and out at the wrist.

Adjacent-key letter combinations

1 Rena saw her buy a red suit at a new shop in town.
2 Opal will try to stop a fast break down the court.
3 Jeremy knew that we had to pool our points to win.
4 Her posh party on their new patio was a real bash.

Long direct reaches with same finger

5 Herb is under the gun to excel in the second race.
6 My fervor for gym events was once my unique trait.
7 Music as a unique force is no myth in any country.
8 Lynda has since found many facts we must now face.

Reaches with 3d and 4th fingers

9 The poet will opt for a top spot in our port town.
10 Sam said the cash price for gas went up last week.
11 Zane played a zany tune that amazed the jazz band.
12 My squad set a quarter quota to equal our request.

| Lesson 25 | Keyboarding/Language Skills | LL: 50 LS: SS |

25a ▶ 6 Conditioning Practice

each line twice SS; then a 1' writing on line 3; find *gwam*

alphabet 1 Kevin can fix the unique jade owl as my big prize.
capitalization 2 Rule: When : precedes a sentence, cap first word.
easy 3 Dodi is to make a visit to the eight island towns.

gwam 1' | 1 | 2 | 3 | 4 | 5 | 6 | 7 | 8 | 9 | 10 |

25b ▶ 20 Improve Keyboarding Technique: Response Patterns

1. Key each set of lines twice SS; DS between 6-line groups.

2. Take a 1' writing on line 10, on line 11, and on line 12 to increase speed; find *gwam* on each.

Goal: At least 24 *gwam* on line 12.

letter response
1 kilo beef yams were only date upon gave milk rates
2 my car|oil tax|you are|was him|raw milk|as you see
3 We ate plump plum tarts in a pink cafe on a barge.

word response
4 also form town risk fuel auto goal pens iris visit
5 apt to|go for|is also|the goal|fix them|go for the
6 Roxie is also apt to go for the goal of good form.

combination response
7 an in of at is fix pop for him ham are pen far men
8 in the|at the|and tar|for him|due you|she saw them
9 An odor of wax and tar was in the air at the mill.

letter 10 Zac gave only a few facts in a case on wage taxes.
combination 11 He set off for the sea by dusk to see a rare loon.
word 12 It is right for them to audit the work of the men.

gwam 1' | 1 | 2 | 3 | 4 | 5 | 6 | 7 | 8 | 9 | 10 |

APPLICATION FOR EMPLOYMENT

PLEASE PRINT WITH BLACK INK OR USE TYPEWRITER

AN EQUAL OPPORTUNITY EMPLOYER

NAME (LAST, FIRST, MIDDLE INITIAL)	SOCIAL SECURITY NUMBER	CURRENT DATE
Murphy, Leslie-Ann	520-38-8151	May 21, 19--

ADDRESS (NUMBER, STREET, CITY, STATE, ZIP CODE)	HOME PHONE NO.
358 Knox Court, Denver, CO 80219-6482	(303) 492-2950

REACH PHONE NO.	U.S. CITIZEN?	DATE YOU CAN START
	YES X NO	June 10, 19--

ARE YOU EMPLOYED NOW?	IF SO, MAY WE INQUIRE OF YOUR PRESENT EMPLOYER?
No	

TYPE OF WORK DESIRED	REFERRED BY	SALARY DESIRED
Secretarial	Ms. Carolyn Baxter	$ Open

IF RELATED TO ANYONE IN OUR EMPLOY, STATE AND NAME AND POSITION

DO YOU HAVE ANY PHYSICAL CONDITION THAT MAY PREVENT YOU FROM PERFORMING CERTAIN KINDS OF WORK?	YES	NO X	IF YES, EXPLAIN

HAVE YOU EVER BEEN CONVICTED OF A FELONY?	YES	NO X	IF YES, EXPLAIN

EDUCATION

	EDUCATIONAL INSTITUTION	LOCATION (CITY, STATE)	DATES ATTENDED FROM MO. YR.	DATES ATTENDED TO MO. YR.	DIPLOMA, DEGREE, OR CREDITS EARNED	CLASS STANDING (CHK QUARTER) 1	2	3	4	MAJOR SUBJECTS STUDIED
COLLEGE										
HIGH SCHOOL	Lincoln High School	Denver, Colorado	8 87	5 91	Diploma	X				Admin. Services
GRADE SCHOOL										
OTHER										

LIST BELOW THE POSITIONS THAT YOU HAVE HELD (LAST POSITION FIRST)

1. NAME AND ADDRESS OF FIRM	DESCRIBE POSITION RESPONSIBILITIES
The Exercise Place 315 Bellaire Way Denver, CO 80233-4302	Maintained customer data base, responded to customer inquiries, and
NAME OF SUPERVISOR Miss Linda Morrison	assisted with customer billing.
EMPLOYED (MO-YR) FROM: 9/90 TO: 5/91	REASON FOR LEAVING Co-op program during school year.

2. NAME AND ADDRESS OF FIRM	DESCRIBE POSITION RESPONSIBILITIES
Copper Mountain Resort P.O. Box 3001 Copper Mountain, CO 80443-7011	Processed mail and telephone reservations for resort guests.
NAME OF SUPERVISOR Mr. Jarome Nielson	
EMPLOYED (MO-YR) FROM: 5/90 TO: 8/90	REASON FOR LEAVING Summer employment.

3. NAME AND ADDRESS OF FIRM	DESCRIBE POSITION RESPONSIBILITIES
Lakeside Amusement Park 4601 Sheridan Boulevard Denver, CO 80212-1240	Ride attendant.
NAME OF SUPERVISOR Mr. Jason Anderson	
EMPLOYED (MO-YR) FROM: 5/89 TO: 8/89	REASON FOR LEAVING Summer employment.

I UNDERSTAND THAT I SHALL NOT BECOME AN EMPLOYEE UNTIL I HAVE SIGNED AN EMPLOYMENT AGREEMENT WITH THE FINAL APPROVAL OF THE EMPLOYER AND THAT SUCH EMPLOYMENT WILL BE SUBJECT TO VERIFICATION OF PREVIOUS EMPLOYMENT, DATA PROVIDED IN THIS APPLICATION, ANY RELATED DOCUMENTS, OR RESUME. I KNOW THAT A REPORT MAY BE MADE THAT WILL INCLUDE INFORMATION

CONCERNING ANY FACTOR THE EMPLOYER MIGHT FIND RELEVANT TO THE POSITION FOR WHICH I AM APPLYING, AND THAT I CAN MAKE A WRITTEN REQUEST FOR ADDITIONAL INFORMATION AS TO THE NATURE AND SCOPE OF THE REPORT IF ONE IS MADE.

Leslie-Ann Murphy
SIGNATURE OF APPLICANT

Application for Employment Form

25c ▶ 14 Check/Improve Keyboarding Speed

1. Take a 1' writing on each ¶; find *gwam* on each; record the better *gwam*.

2. Take a 2' writing on ¶s 1 and 2 combined; find *gwam*.

3. Using your better *gwam* in Step 1 as a base rate, take two 1' *guided* writings on ¶ 1 as directed on page 38.

4. Using the same goal rate, take two 1' writings on ¶ 2 in the same way.

5. Take another 2' writing on ¶s 1 and 2 combined; find *gwam*.

6. Record your best 1' *gwam* and your better 2' *gwam*.

Goals

1': At least 22 *gwam*.
2': At least 20 *gwam*.

all letters used | E | 1.2 si | 5.1 awl | 90% hfw

gwam 2'

. 2 . 4 . 6 . 8
You must realize by now that learning to key   5
10 . 12 . 14 . 16 . 18
requires work. However, you will soon be able to   10
20 . 22 . 24 . 26 . 28
key at a higher speed than you can write just now.   15

. 2 . 4 . 6 . 8
You will also learn to do neater work on the   19
10 . 12 . 14 . 16 . 18
machine than you can do by hand. Quality work at   24
20 . 22 . 24 . 26 . 28
higher speeds is a good goal for you to have next.   29

gwam 2' | 1 | 2 | 3 | 4 | 5 |

25d ▶ 10 Check Language Skills: Capitalization

1. Key each sentence once SS, capitalizing words according to the rules you have learned in this unit.

2. Check with your instructor the accuracy of your application of the rules.

3. If time permits, rekey the lines in which you made errors in capitalization.

The references refer to previous lesson parts containing capitalization rules.

lesson references		
21d	1	this stapler is defective. please send a new one.
21d	2	ask if alma and suzan took the trip with ms. diaz.
23c	3	texas and mexico share the rio grande as a border.
21d, 23c, 24b	4	miss jackson is an auditor for irs in los angeles.
21d, 22d	5	alice said thanksgiving day is always on thursday.
21d, 23c	6	marcus saw the play at lincoln center in new york.
21d, 22d	7	our school year begins in august and ends in june.
23c	8	is the dubois tower on fifth avenue or oak street?
21d, 24b	9	send the dental supplies to byron c. tubbs, d.d.s.
21d, 24b	10	when did senator metcalf ask to see the president?

ENRICHMENT ACTIVITY: Think as You Key

Key each line once SS. At the end of each line, supply the information (noted in parentheses) needed to complete the sentence. In Items 3 and 6, also choose the correct article (*a* or *an*) to precede the information you supply.

1 My full name is *(first/middle/last)*.

2 I attend *(name of school)*.

3 I am learning to key on a/an *(brand of typewriter/computer)*.

4 My main goal has been to develop *(technique/speed/accuracy)*.

5 My favorite class in school is *(name of subject)*.

6 My career goal is to be a/an *(name of job)*.

7 My main hobby is *(name of hobby)*.

8 I spend most of my free time *(name of activity)*.

Document 2

Review the application letter guidelines on p. 239. Compose at the keyboard a rough-draft letter applying for one of the positions shown at the right. Edit/revise your letter; then process it in final form.

SECRETARY

Immediate opening for school secretary. Full-time position requires good communication skills, telephone etiquette, and keyboarding skill of 45-55 wpm. Knowledge of modern office equipment is a must.

Must be able to work with students, faculty, and school visitors. Send data sheet and letter of application to

Wayne S. Jorgenson
Superintendent
North School District
7523 Mcgregor Street
Detroit, MI 48209-2431

ADMINISTRATIVE ASSISTANT

Assistant to the Marketing Vice President. Large company seeks outgoing individual with good keyboarding and shorthand skills.

Interested applicants must have a minimum keyboarding skill of 50 wpm and a minimum shorthand skill of 80 wpm. Experience preferred, but will consider applicants with no previous experience who possess excellent keyboarding and shorthand skills.

To apply, send letter of application and data sheet to

Director of Human Resources
Steele Manufacturing Company
697 Brookwood Court
Joliet, IL 60435-9203

WORD PROCESSING

Bachman Consulting Services has an opening in the Word Processing Department for a detail-oriented individual with excellent transcription skills.

Machine transcription and word processing training desirable. Must have keyboarding skill of 50 wpm.

Send letter of application and data sheet to
Miss Judith L. Painter
Personnel Director
Bachman Consulting Services
840 Belvidere Street
Boston, MA 02115-7301

KEYBOARDING OPERATOR

Small insurance company has full-time position for a keyboarding operator. Applicant must be able to key 40 wpm, perform basic math operations, and project professional telephone image.

Apply to

Ms. Mary A. Stetson
Office Manager
Crandall Insurance Company
330 University Drive
Pine Bluff, AR 71601-4011

Lesson 137 | Application Form/Composing

137a ▶ 5
Conditioning Practice

each line twice SS (slowly, then faster); DS between 2-line groups; if time permits, rekey selected lines

alphabet 1 I would be very amazed if he objects to the back exercising equipment.

figures 2 Table A on page 3 lists 2,068 births in 1991 and 3,754 births in 1992.

fig/sym 3 A 17% discount off the marked price ($26,930.00) amounts to $4,578.10.

speed 4 If all the girls go to the formal social, she may pay for their gowns.

| 1 | 2 | 3 | 4 | 5 | 6 | 7 | 8 | 9 | 10 | 11 | 12 | 13 | 14 |

137b ▶ 45 *Prepare Application Forms*
LP pp. 125-127

Document 1 LP p. 125
Format and key the application form on p. 243. Correct any errors you make as you key the copy.

Document 2 LP p. 127
Use LP p. 127 as the application for employment form to apply for the position you selected in 136b.

You should review the form and make a few notes before entering your personal data on the form.

LEARN ALPHANUMERIC KEYBOARDING TECHNIQUE AND CORRESPONDENCE FORMATTING

In the 25 lessons of this phase, you will:

1. Learn to key figures and basic symbols by touch and with good technique.

2. Improve speed/control on straight copy, handwritten (script) copy, rough-draft (corrected) copy, and statistical copy (copy containing figures and some symbols).

3. Review/improve language skills.

4. Apply your keyboarding skill in preparing simple personal and business documents.

The copy from which you have keyed up to now has been shown in pica (10-pitch) typewriter type. In Phase 2 much of the copy is shown in large, easy-to-read printer's type.

All drill lines are written to an exact 60-space line to simplify checking. Some paragraphs and problem activities, however, contain lines of variable length. Continue to key them line-for-line as shown until you are directed to do otherwise.

135a ▶ 5
Conditioning Practice

each line twice SS (slowly, then faster); DS between 2-line groups; if time permits, rekey selected lines

alphabet 1 Vicky Lopez is extremely qualified for a management job with our firm.

figures 2 Crowds of 49,872 and 51,360 saw the games between the Giants and Mets.

fig/sym 3 The invoice (96A103) which is for $2,745 should be paid before June 8.

speed 4 She is apt to yell when they cut down the iris by the giant cornfield.

| 1 | 2 | 3 | 4 | 5 | 6 | 7 | 8 | 9 | 10 | 11 | 12 | 13 | 14 |

135b ▶ 45
Prepare Data Sheets

plain full sheets; SM: 1"; PB: 1"

Document 1
Format and key the data sheet shown on page 240.

Document 2
Compose at the keyboard a rough-draft data sheet for yourself using the guidelines on p. 239 and the model on p. 240. Edit; then key a final copy.

136a ▶ 5
Conditioning Practice

each line twice SS (slowly, then faster); DS between 2-line groups; if time permits, rekey selected lines

alphabet 1 Gavin expects the banker to formalize quite a few details before July.

figures 2 Jay hit .359 with 86 singles, 20 doubles, 7 triples, and 14 home runs.

fig/sym 3 Our 1993-1994 service & supply budget was $16,780, an increase of 25%.

speed 4 The eight girls and the auditor may burn down the shanty by city hall.

| 1 | 2 | 3 | 4 | 5 | 6 | 7 | 8 | 9 | 10 | 11 | 12 | 13 | 14 |

136b ▶ 45
Prepare Application Letters

plain full sheets; modified block format; blocked ¶s; mixed punctuation; proofread and correct errors

Document 1

Format and key the application letter for Ms. Leslie-Ann Murphy. If necessary, refer to the illustration on p. 239. Use personal-business letter format and begin return address on line 10. Refer to data sheet on p. 240 for Ms. Murphy's return address.

words

May 15, 19-- | Mr. Juan R. Gutierrez | Director of Human Resources | Creswell 14
Manufacturing Co. | 8352 West Oxford Avenue | Denver, CO 80236-7483 | Dear 28
Mr. Gutierrez: 31

Ms. Carolyn Baxter, my administrative services instructor, informed me of 46
the secretarial position with your company that will be available June 10. 61
She speaks very highly of your organization. After learning more about the 77
position, I am confident that I am qualified and would like to be considered 92
for the assignment. 96

Currently I am completing my senior year at Lincoln High School. All of my 111
elective courses have been in the administrative services area. This includes 127
courses in information processing, shorthand, and business procedures. I 142
have a keyboarding skill of 60 words a minute and a shorthand skill of 80 157
words a minute. The information processing class was taught using com- 171
puters. We were instructed in word processing, spreadsheet, and data base 186
applications. As an office assistant, I have been able to utilize these skills 202
on the job. 204

My work experience and school activities have given me the opportunity to 219
work with people to achieve group goals. Participating in FBLA has given 234
me a better appreciation for the business world. 244

I would appreciate the opportunity to interview with you to discuss the pos- 259
sibility of employment. You may call me weekdays after 3:30 p.m. 272

Sincerely, | Ms. Leslie-Ann Murphy | xx | Enclosure 281

UNIT 3   LESSONS 26 – 30
Learn the Figure Keyboard

Learning Goals

1. To learn the location of each figure key.
2. To learn how to strike each figure key properly and with the correct finger.
3. To build keyboarding speed and technique on copy containing figures.
4. To improve keyboarding speed and technique on alphabetic copy.
5. To learn to center lines horizontally (side-to-side).

Format Guides

1. *Paper guide* at *0* (for typewriters).
2. Line length (LL): 60 spaces; see *Get Ready to Keyboard: Typewriters* (p. x) or *Computers* (p. xii).
3. Line spacing (LS): single-space (SS) drills; double-space (DS) paragraphs (¶s).
4. Paragraph indention (PI): 5 spaces when appropriate.

Lesson 26	8 and 1	Line length (LL): 60 spaces Line spacing (LS): single (SS)

26a ▶ 6
Conditioning Practice

each line twice SS; then a 1' writing on line 3; find *gwam*

alphabet	1	Max was quick to fly a big jet plane over the frozen desert.
spacing	2	Any of them can aim for a top goal and reach it if they try.
easy	3	Nan is to go to the city hall to sign the land forms for us.

gwam 1' | 1 | 2 | 3 | 4 | 5 | 6 | 7 | 8 | 9 | 10 | 11 | 12 |

26b ▶ 18
Learn 8 and 1

each line twice SS (slowly, then faster); DS between 2-line groups; if time permits, practice each line again

Reach technique for **8**

Reach *up* with right second finger.

Reach technique for **1**

Reach *up* with left little finger.

Follow the *Standard Plan for Learning New Keys* outlined on page 8.

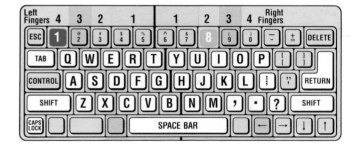

Learn **8**

1 k k 8k 8k kk 88 k8k k8k 88k 88k Reach up for 8, 88, and 888.
2 Key the figures 8, 88, and 888. Please open Room 88 or 888.

Learn **Figure 1**

3 a a 1a 1a aa 11 a1a a1a 11a 11a Reach up for 1, 11, and 111.
4 Add the figures 1, 11, and 111. Has just 1 of 111 finished?

Combine **8** and **1**

5 Key 11, 18, 81, and 88. Just 11 of the 18 skiers have left.
6 Reach with the fingers to key 18 and 188 as well as 1 and 8.
7 The stock person counted 11 coats, 18 slacks, and 88 shirts.

Leslie-Ann Murphy
358 Knox Court
Denver, CO 80219-6482
(303) 492-2950 _{QS}

EDUCATION _{DS}

    Senior at Lincoln High School
    High School Diploma, pending graduation
    Major Emphasis: Administrative Services
    Grade Average: 3.50; upper 15% of class _{DS}

SCHOOL ACTIVITIES _{DS}

    <u>Future Business Leaders of America Secretary</u>, senior year;
    member for three years. _{DS}

    <u>National Honor Society</u>, junior and senior years. _{DS}

    <u>High School Yearbook Treasurer</u>, senior year; member for two
    years. _{DS}

WORK EXPERIENCE

    <u>Office Assistant</u>, The Exercise Place, Denver, Colorado, Sep-
    tember 1990 to present. Work 15 hours a week as an office
    assistant; maintain customer data base, respond to customer
    inquiries, and assist with customer billing.

    <u>Reservations Clerk</u>, Copper Mountain Resort, Copper Mountain,
    Colorado, summer 1990. Processed mail and telephone reserva-
    tions for resort guests.

    <u>Concessionnaire</u>, Lakeside Amusement Park, Denver, Colorado,
    summer 1989.

REFERENCES (by permission)

    Ms. Carolyn M. Baxter, Administrative Services Instructor,
    Lincoln High School, 2285 South Federal Boulevard, Denver, CO
    80219-4312 (303) 329-3300.

    Miss Linda A. Morrison, Owner, The Exercise Place, 3850 Jordan
    Drive, Denver, CO 80221-9020 (303) 243-2561.

    Mr. Jarome C. Nielson, Resort Manager, Copper Mountain Resort,
    P.O. Box 3001, Copper Mountain, CO 80443-7011 (303) 458-2000.

Data Sheet

26c ▶ 14 Improve Keyboarding Technique

1. Each pair of lines (1-6) twice SS (slowly, then faster); DS between 4-line groups.

2. A 1' writing on line 7 and on line 8; find *gwam* on each writing.

Technique goals

● reach *up* without moving the hand forward

● reach *down* without twisting the wrists or moving the elbows in and out

Row emphasis

home/3d	1 she quit │ with just │ that play │ fair goal │ will help │ they did go
	2 Dru said you should try for the goal of top speed this week.
home/1st	3 hand axe│lava gas│can mask│jazz band│lack cash│a small flask
	4 Ms. Hamm can call a cab, and Max can flag a small black van.
figures	5 The quiz on the 18th will be on pages 11 to 18 and 81 to 88.
	6 Just 11 of the 118 boys got 81 of the 88 quiz answers right.
easy	7 Ty is to pay for the eight pens she laid by the audit forms.
	8 Keith is to row with us to the lake to fix six of the signs.

gwam 1' │ 1 │ 2 │ 3 │ 4 │ 5 │ 6 │ 7 │ 8 │ 9 │ 10 │ 11 │ 12 │

26d ▶ 12 Improve Keyboarding Speed: Guided Writing

1. A 1' writing on each ¶; find *gwam* on each writing.

2. Using your better *gwam* as a base rate, select a *goal rate* 2-4 *gwam* higher than your base rate.

3. Take three 1' writings on each ¶ with the call of the quarter-minute guide (see page 38 for directions).

Quarter-minute checkpoints

gwam	¼'	½'	¾'	Time
16	4	8	12	16
20	5	10	15	20
24	6	12	18	24
28	7	14	21	28
32	8	16	24	32
36	9	18	27	36
40	10	20	30	40

all letters used │ E │ 1.2 si │ 5.1 awl │ 90% hfw │   *gwam 2'*

      •   2   •   4   •   6   •   8   •   10

How much time does it take you to return at the end of   6

 12   •   14   •   16   •   18   •   20   •   22   •

the line? Do you return with a lazy or a quick reach? Try   12

 24   •   26   •   28   •   30   •   32   •   34

not to stop at the end of the line; instead, return quickly   18

 36   •   38   •   40   •   42

and move down to the next line of copy.   21

      •   2   •   4   •   6   •   8   •   10   •

How much time does it take you to strike the shift key   27

 12   •   14   •   16   •   18   •   20   •   22   •

and the letter to make a capital? Just a bit more practice   33

 24   •   26   •   28   •   30   •   32   •   34

will help you cut by half the time you are now using. When   39

 36   •   38   •   40   •   42   •

you cut the time, you increase your speed.   43

gwam 2' │ 1 │ 2 │ 3 │ 4 │ 5 │ 6 │

Lesson 27   *9 and 4*   LL: 60   LS: SS

27a ▶ 6 Conditioning Practice

each line twice SS; then a 1' writing on line 3; find *gwam*

alphabet	1 Joby quickly fixed a glass vase and amazed the proud owners.
figures	2 She told us to add the figures 11, 88, 18, 81, 118, and 881.
easy	3 Ciel may make a bid on the ivory forks they got in the city.

gwam 1' │ 1 │ 2 │ 3 │ 4 │ 5 │ 6 │ 7 │ 8 │ 9 │ 10 │ 11 │ 12 │

27b ▶ 12 Improve Keyboarding Speed: Guided Writing

Practice again the 2 ¶s above, using the directions in 26d.

Goal: To improve your speed by at least 2-4 *gwam*.

Process Office Employment Documents

Learning Goals

1. To learn/apply guides for preparing a data sheet, application letter, application form, and follow-up letter.
2. To compose and process personal employment documents.
3. To improve language skills through composing activities.
4. To process documents for a simulated employment test.

Format Guides

1. Paper guide at *0* (for typewriters).
2. LL: 70 for drills and language skills activities; as required by document formats.
3. LS: SS for drills and language skills activities; as required by document formats.
4. PI: 5 spaces, when appropriate.

FORMATTING GUIDES: DATA SHEET, APPLICATION LETTER, APPLICATION FORM, AND FOLLOW-UP LETTER

Application Letter

Employment Documents

Extreme care should be given to the preparation of all employment documents. The data sheet, application letter, and application form are generally the basis of the first impression you make on a prospective employer; they may also determine whether you are invited for an interview.

Prepare application documents on a keyboard with the possible exception of the application form. You may be asked to complete the application form at the time of the interview, in which case it may be prepared with a pen. Always use high-quality paper when preparing your data sheet and application letter. Make sure that each document you prepare is attractively arranged, neat, grammatical, and that it presents both accurate and appropriate information.

Data Sheet

In most cases, a data sheet should be limited to one page. The information presented usually covers five major areas: personal information (your name, address, and telephone number), education, school activities, work experience, and references. It may also include sections listing community activities and hobbies and/or special interests.

Top, bottom, and side margins may vary depending on the amount of information presented. The specific format may also vary with personal preference. In general, the most important information is presented first, which means that a person who has been out of school for several years and has considerable work experience may place that information before educational background information. References, however, are usually the last item on the page. (Always get permission from the individuals you plan to include as references on your data sheet before using their names.)

Application Letter

An application letter should always accompany the data sheet. The letter is formatted as a personal-business letter and should be limited to one page.

The first paragraph of the application letter should indicate the position for which you are applying and how you learned of the position. It is also appropriate to include something positive that you know about the company or someone who works for the company in the opening paragraph.

The next one or two paragraphs are used to convince the reader that you understand the requirements for the position and to explain how your background experiences qualify you for the position for which you are applying. You may do this by elaborating on some of the information on your data sheet and inviting the reader to refer to the enclosed data sheet for additional information.

The final paragraph is used to request an interview. Information is also provided to make it easy for the reader to contact you to make arrangements for the interview.

Follow-Up Letter

Appreciation for an interview is conveyed in a follow-up letter. In addition to thanking the person for the interview, the follow-up letter may also be used to let the interviewer know you are still interested in the job. The letter also may provide any additional relevant information and give positive impressions of the company and/or people you met. To be effective, the letter should be written immediately following the interview. This will increase the likelihood that the interviewer will receive the letter before a decision is made.

27c ▶ 18
Learn 9 and 4

each line twice SS (slowly, then faster); DS between 2-line groups; if time permits, practice each line again

Reach technique for **9**

Reach *up* with *right third* finger.

Reach technique for **4**

Reach *up* with *left first* finger.

Follow the *Standard Plan for Learning New Keys* outlined on page 8.

Learn 9

use the letter "l"

1 l l 9l 9l ll 99 l9l l9l 99l 99l ▼ Reach up for 9, 99, and 999.
2 Key the figures 9, 99, and 999. Have only 9 of 99 finished?

Learn 4

3 f f 4f 4f ff 44 f4f f4f 44f 44f ▼ Reach up for 4, 44, and 444.
4 Add the figures 4, 44, and 444. Please study pages 4 to 44.

Combine 9 and 4

5 Key 44, 49, 94, and 99. Only 49 of the 94 joggers are here.
6 Reach with the fingers to key 49 and 499 as well as 4 and 9.
7 My goal is to sell 44 pizzas, 99 tacos, and 9 cases of cola.

27d ▶ 5 Improve Keyboarding Skill: Figures

1. Key each of lines 1-3 twice SS (slowly, then faster); DS between 2-line groups.
2. If time permits, key each line again to improve speed.

Figure sentences

use the figure "1"

1 Keep the fingers low as you key 11, 18, 19, 48, 94, and 849.
2 On March 8, 1991, 44 people took the 4 tests for the 8 jobs.
3 He based his May 1 report on pages 449 to 488 of Chapter 19.

27e ▶ 9 Learn to Center Lines Horizontally
plain full sheet

Get ready to center

1. Set LM and paper guide at *0;* set RM at 85 (10-pitch) or 102 (12-pitch).

2a. *If machine has an automatic centering feature,* learn to use it and follow the *Drill procedure* given in Column 2.

2b. *If machine does not have an automatic centering feature:*
(1) clear all tab stops.
(2) set a tab stop at center point: 42, 10-pitch; 51, 12-pitch.
(3) Study *How to center on a typewriter* in the color block at the right.

(4) Follow the *Drill procedure* below.

Drill procedure

1. Beginning on line 10, center each line of Drill 1 horizontally (side to side), SS.
2. Space down 4 times and center each line of Drill 2 horizontally, SS.
3. Center Drill 3 in the same manner.

How to center on a typewriter

1. Tabulate to center point.
2. From center, backspace *once* for each 2 letters, spaces, figures, or punctuation marks in the line.
3. Do not backspace for an odd or leftover stroke at the end of the line.
4. Begin keying where backspacing ends.

Example:

● center point

backspace ▶ | 1 | 1 | 1 | 1 | 1 | 1 | 1 | 1 | 1 |

LE|AR|NI|NG|space T|O|space CE|NT|ER

1	2	3
to	a	I
wish	the	work
profit	their	handle
problems	foreign	quantity
amendments	committee	patient

134c ▶ 35 Measure Document Processing: Forms/Memorandums

Time Schedule
Plan and prepare .... 4'
Timed production .... 25'
Proofread, mark errors, and
    compute *n-pram* .... 6'

Document 1
Purchase Order
LP p. 119

Prepare a purchase order using the information given at the right.

LACONTE JEWELERS INC		Purchase Order No.:	**59Z48-3**	6
210 BROADWAY		Date:	**April 15, 19--**	11
NEW YORK NY 10038-7103		Terms:	**2/10, n/30**	18
		Shipped Via:	**Freight Specialists**	22

Quantity	Description/Stock No.	Price	Total	
5	14K Yellow Gold Rope Bezel (A44-98)	95.95/ea	479.75	34
5	Diamond Pendant (C28-95)	149.50/ea	747.50	43
10	Diamond and Pearl Ring (B95-17)	95.00/ea	950.00	54
2	Diamond "V" Necklace (Q39-50)	1250.00/ea	2500.00	65
10	Diamond Bee Pin (M66-29)	249.95/ea	2499.50	77
			7176.75	75

Document 2
Invoice
LP p. 121

Prepare an invoice using the information given at the right. Calculate the final total.

YOUR OFFICE FURNITURE STORE	Date:	**June 2, 19--**	13
406 MONTGOMERY STREET	Cust. Order No.:	**39V881**	20
SAN FRANCISCO CA 94104-2486	Terms:	**2/10, n/30**	22
	Shipped Via:	**Bay Shipping**	25
	Our Order No.:	**B92-8751**	26
	Date Shipped:	**June 2, 19--**	29

Quantity	Description/Stock No.	Price	Total	
1	Executive Desk (871-56B)	799.95	799.95	37
1	Executive Credenza Bookcase (296-88B)	649.50	649.50	48
1	Printer Stand (391-29C)	399.95	399.95	56
1	Computer Table (218-30C)	359.49	359.49	64
1	Executive Swivel Chair (119-20A)	314.49	314.49	75
			2523.38	77
	Sales Tax		126.17	82

Document 3
Formal Memorandum
LP p. 123

Key a formal memorandum using the information given at the right and the information given below.

To: **Martin F. Jensen, Chief Financial Officer**
From: **Karl L. Hayward, Facilities Manager**
Date: **June 12, 19--**
Subject: **Office Renovation**

Document 4
Simplified Memorandum
plain full sheet

Rekey Document 3 as a simplified memo.

All of the furniture ordered for your office has arrived except for the computer table. It is back ordered, and it should arrive within the next week.   37 / 53

Arrangements have been made for your new carpet to be installed on Saturday, June 26. Since your old furniture will be left in the hallway during the weekend, we will need to take the necessary security precautions. Mike Jackson has agreed to let you store your file cabinets in his office over the weekend. Please let me know by Friday if there are other things you would like stored along with the files, and I will make the necessary arrangements.   67 / 83 / 97 / 113 / 128 / 143

closing lines 144/**159**

28a ▶ 6
Conditioning Practice

each line twice SS; then a
1' writing on line 3; find *gwam*

alphabet	1	Roz may put a vivid sign next to the low aqua boat for Jack.
figures	2	Please review Figure 8 on page 94 and Figure 14 on page 189.
easy	3	Tien may fix the bus panel for the city if the pay is right.

gwam 1' | 1 | 2 | 3 | 4 | 5 | 6 | 7 | 8 | 9 | 10 | 11 | 12 |

28b ▶ 18
Learn 0 and 5

each line twice SS (slowly, then faster); DS between 2-line groups; if time permits, practice each line again

Follow the *Standard Plan for Learning New Keys* outlined on page 8.

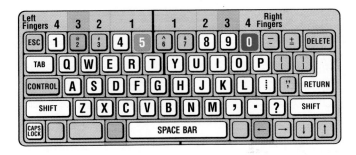

Reach technique for 0

Reach *up* with *right little* finger.

Reach technique for 5

Reach *up* with *left first* finger.

Learn **0** (zero)

1 ; ; 0; 0; ;; 00 ;0; ;0; 00; 00; Reach up for 0, 00, and 000.
2 Snap the finger off the 0. I used 0, 00, and 000 sandpaper.

Learn **5**

3 f f 5f 5f ff 55 f5f f5f 55f 55f Reach up for 5, 55, and 555.
4 Reach up to 5 and back to f. Did he say to order 55 or 555?

Combine **0** and **5**

5 Reach with the fingers to key 50 and 500 as well as 5 and 0.
6 We asked for prices on these models: 50, 55, 500, and 5500.
7 On May 5, I got 5 boxes each of 0 and 00 steel wool for her.

28c ▶ 12 Improve Keyboarding Technique: Figures

each line twice SS; DS between 2-line groups

Language skills notes
1. No space is left before or after : when used with figures to express time.
2. Most nouns before numbers are capitalized; exceptions include *page* and *line*.

No space

1 Flight 1049 is on time; it should be at Gate 48 at 5:50 p.m.
2 The club meeting on April 5 will be in Room 549 at 8:10 a.m.
3 Of our 105 workers in 1989, 14 had gone to new jobs by 1991.
4 I used Chapter 19, pages 449 to 458, for my March 10 report.
5 Can you meet us at 1954 Maple Avenue at 8:05 a.m. August 10?
6 Of the 59 students, 18 keyed at least 40 w.a.m. by April 18.

133a ▶ 5
Conditioning Practice

each line twice SS (slowly, then faster); DS between 2-line groups; if time permits, rekey selected lines

alphabet	1	Major plans for the next job will be finalized very quickly in August.
figures	2	On January 20, 1990, I moved from 2468 Bay Street to 1357 Lake Street.
space bar	3	She may see us when we go to the big city to pay and to sign the form.
speed	4	Pamela's neighbor is apt to dismantle the small cubicle in the chapel.

| 1 | 2 | 3 | 4 | 5 | 6 | 7 | 8 | 9 | 10 | 11 | 12 | 13 | 14 |

133b ▶ 10
Language Skills: Compose at Keyboard

plain full sheet
LL: 70 spaces

1. Compose at the keyboard 1 or 2 paragraphs on one of the questions at the right. DS paragraph(s).
2. Edit your copy, marking corrections and changes to improve sentence structure and organization.
3. Prepare the final copy.

Questions

If you received a check for $100,000 in the mail today, what would you do with it?

What qualities do you think an employer would be looking for in a prospective employee?

Would you buy a stereo on credit? Explain.

133c ▶ 35 Build Sustained Document Processing: Forms and Special Documents

LP pp. 115-119
company envelopes for formal memos

Time Schedule
Plan and prepare .... 4'
Timed production .... 25'
Proofread, mark errors, and
   compute *n-pram* .... 6'

1. Arrange forms, supplies, and correction materials for easy access.
2. Make a list of documents to be processed.
page 232, 130d, Document 1
page 232, 130d, Document 2
page 233, 131c, Document 1
page 234, 131c, Document 2
page 234, 131c, Document 3

3. Process as many documents as you can in 25'. Proofread and correct errors as you key.
4. After 25' timing, proofread again, mark any additional errors not found during keying, and compute *n-pram*.
5. Arrange documents in order listed in Step 2; turn in work.

n-pram = (total words keyed − penalty*) ÷ time
*Penalty is 10 words for each uncorrected error.

134a ▶ 5
Conditioning Practice

each line twice SS (slowly, then faster); DS between 2-line groups; if time permits, rekey selected lines

alphabet	1	Zachary bought two exquisite paintings of Alaska just before he moved.
figures	2	On March 29 they learned the 7, 1, and 5; on March 30 the 4, 6, and 8.
home row	3	Sally Ash has a faded glass doll. Josh Jakes was a sad lad last fall.
speed	4	The man in the wheelchair was down at the dock with my neighbor's dog.

| 1 | 2 | 3 | 4 | 5 | 6 | 7 | 8 | 9 | 10 | 11 | 12 | 13 | 14 |

134b ▶ 10 Figures and Tab-Key Drill

plain full sheet
LL: 65 spaces
CS: 6

1. Three 1' writings; find *gwam* on each.
2. Two 2' writings; find *gwam* on each.

Concentrate on figure locations; quiet hands; quick tab spacing.

words

1029	3847	5616	2738	4950	1089	4462	7
1392	5705	6783	7887	2954	1036	2198	14
2034	6905	4130	5977	6816	2543	6150	21
2831	9876	4231	9087	5641	8622	3939	28
4705	4507	9988	1055	6436	7221	3470	35

| 1 | | 2 | | 3 | | 4 | | 5 | | 6 | | 7 | |

28d ▶ 14 Improve Keyboarding Technique: Response Patterns

1. Each pair of lines twice SS (slowly, then faster); DS between 4-line groups.

2. A 1' writing on line 2 and on line 4; find *gwam* on each writing.

3. If time permits, rekey the slower line.

letter response	1	face pump ever milk area jump vast only save upon safe union
	2	As we were in a junk, we saw a rare loon feast on a crawdad.
word response	3	quay hand also body lend hang mane down envy risk corn whale
	4	Tisha is to go to the lake with us if she is to do the work.
combination response	5	with only | they join | half safe | born free | firm look | goal rates
	6	I sat on the airy lanai with my gaze on the sea to the east.

gwam 1' | 1 | 2 | 3 | 4 | 5 | 6 | 7 | 8 | 9 | 10 | 11 | 12 |

Lesson 29	7 and 3	LL: 60 LS: SS

29a ▶ 6 Conditioning Practice

each line twice SS; then a 1' writing on line 3; find *gwam*

alphabet	1	Gavin made a quick fall trip by jet to Zurich six weeks ago.
figures	2	Key 1 and 4 and 5 and 8 and 9 and 0 and 190 and 504 and 958.
easy	3	The man is to fix the big sign by the field for a city firm.

gwam 1' | 1 | 2 | 3 | 4 | 5 | 6 | 7 | 8 | 9 | 10 | 11 | 12 |

29b ▶ 18 Learn 7 and 3

each line twice SS (slowly, then faster); DS between 2-line groups; if time permits, practice each line again

Follow the *Standard Plan for Learning New Keys* outlined on page 8.

Reach technique for 7

Reach *up* with right first finger.

Reach technique for 3

Reach *up* with left second finger.

Learn 7

1 j j 7j 7j jj 77 j7j j7j 77j 77j Reach up for 7, 77, and 777.
2 Key the figures 7, 77, and 777. She checked Rooms 7 and 77.

Learn 3

3 d d 3d 3d dd 33 d3d d3d 33d 33d Reach up for 3, 33, and 333.
4 Add the figures 3, 33, and 333. Read pages 3 to 33 tonight.

Combine 7 and 3

5 Key 33, 37, 73, and 77. Just 37 of the 77 skiers have come.
6 Please order 7 Model 337 computers and 3 Model 737 printers.
7 On August 7, the 33 bikers left on a long trip of 377 miles.

Document 2
Purchase Order
LP p. 113

Prepare a purchase order using the information given at the right and listed below. Correct errors.

Order No.: **8391B**
Date: **February 12, 19--**
Terms: **2/10, n/30**
Ship Via: **McVay Transport**
(total words: 76)

Browning Office Equipment
3338 Creighton Avenue SE
Portland, OR 97267-1498

Quantity	Description/Stock Nos.	Unit Price
3	Microcassette Dictation System (39-69)	489.95
1	Microcassette Transcriber (39-85)	449.95
6	Microcassette Recorder (39-742)	89.95
25	Microcassettes (39-979)	1.95

Rebecca Granger, Purchasing Agent

Document 3
Letter Placement Guide
LP p. 113

Prepare a letter placement guide from the handwritten copy at the right. Correct errors.

LETTER PLACEMENT GUIDE

Letter Classification	5-Stroke Words in Letter Body	Side Margins	Margin Settings		Dateline Position (from Top Edge of Paper)
			Elite	Pica	
Short	Up to 100	2"	24-78*	20-65*	18
Average	101-200	1½"	18-84*	15-70*	16
Long	201-300	1"	12-90*	10-75*	14
Two-Page	Over 300	1"	12-90*	10-75*	14
6" Line	All letters	1¼"	15-87*	12-72*	As above

*Plus 3 to 7 spaces for the bell cue — *usually add 5 (see p. 76)*

132d ▶ 10
Improve Language Skills: Word Choice

Study the spelling and definition of each word. Note how it is used in the **Learn** sentence. Key the **Learn** sentence (with number and period) and the **Apply** sentences (with number and period) selecting the proper word in parentheses to complete each sentence correctly.

principal (n) a person in authority; a capital sum

principle (n) a rule

personal (adj) private; individual

personnel (n) employees

Learn 1. Our principal understood the principle of shared governance.
Apply 2. Each management (principal, principle) was presented in the speech.
Apply 3. Mrs. Gilbertson, our (principal, principle), will return on Monday.

Learn 4. The personnel committee took a personal interest in all employees.
Apply 5. The (personal, personnel) director will deal with employee problems.
Apply 6. Rinji felt the problem was too (personal, personnel) to discuss.

29c ▶ 12 Improve Keyboarding Technique: Figures

each line twice SS (slowly, then faster); DS between 2-line groups; if time permits, practice each line again

3/7	1	Flights 337 and 377 will be replaced by Flights 733 and 737.
5/0	2	You had 500 books and 505 workbooks but returned 50 of each.
4/9	3	For the answer to Problem 94, see Unit 9, page 494, line 49.
1/8	4	Irv will be 18 on Tuesday, October 18; he weighs 181 pounds.
all figures learned	5	Key these figures as units: 18, 37, 49, 50, 73, 81, and 94.
	6	We sold 18 spruce, 37 elms, 49 maples, and 50 choice shrubs.

29d ▶ 14 Practice Centering Lines

1. Review *Get ready to center* and *How to center on a typewriter* in 27e, page 49, and adjust your equipment as directed there.

2. Beginning on line 8 of a half sheet (long edge at top), center each line of Problem 1. DS the lines.

3. Beginning on line 10, center the lines of Problem 2 in the same way.

1	IMPORTANT TERMS
	income tax
	gross national product
	balance of trade
	consumer price index
	national debt
	social security

2	FBLA ANNOUNCES
	NEW OFFICERS
	Christopher Linden, President
	Mary Ann Stokes, Vice President
	ElVon Gibbs, Secretary
	Carla Johnson, Treasurer

Lesson 30 **6 and 2** LL: 60 / LS: SS

30a ▶ 6 Conditioning Practice

each line twice SS; then a 1' writing on line 3; find *gwam*

alphabet	1	Jared helped Mazy quickly fix the big wood stove in the den.
figures	2	Bella lives at 1847 Oak Street; Jessi, at 5039 Duard Circle.
easy	3	They may make their goals if they work with the usual vigor.

gwam 1' | 1 | 2 | 3 | 4 | 5 | 6 | 7 | 8 | 9 | 10 | 11 | 12 |

30b ▶ 14 Check Keyboarding Technique

1. Key each of lines 1-10 twice SS as your teacher checks your keyboarding technique; DS between 4-line groups.

2. If time permits, take a 1' writing on line 11 and on line 12; find *gwam* on each writing.

finger reaches to top row	1	if 85| am 17| or 94| me 73;| dot 395| lap 910| kept 8305| corn 3947
	2	In 1987, we had 305 workers; in 1991, we had a total of 403.
quiet hands and arms	3	Celia doubts if she can exceed her past record by very much.
	4	Brian excels at softball, but many say he is best at soccer.
quick-snap keystrokes	5	Ella may go to the soap firm for title to all the lake land.
	6	Did the bugle corps toot with the usual vigor for the queen?
down-and-in spacing	7	Coy is in the city to buy an oak chair he wants for his den.
	8	Jan may go to town by bus to sign a work form for a new job.
out-and-down shifting	9	Robb and Ty are in Madrid to spend a week with Jae and Aldo.
	10	Are you going in May, or in June? Elena is leaving in July.
easy sentences	11	Rick paid for both the visual aid and the sign for the firm.
	12	Glena kept all the work forms on the shelf by the big chair.

gwam 1' | 1 | 2 | 3 | 4 | 5 | 6 | 7 | 8 | 9 | 10 | 11 | 12 |

132a ▶ 5
Conditioning Practice

each line twice SS (slowly, then faster); DS between 2-line groups; if time permits, rekey selected lines

alphabet 1 Evelyn was just shocked by the extremely crazy sequence of happenings.

figures 2 James drove 487 miles on May 19 and the remaining 356 miles on May 20.

double letters 3 Their committee allocated three million dollars to the school project.

speed 4 My buddy may go with me when I visit the firms with the antique autos.

| 1 | 2 | 3 | 4 | 5 | 6 | 7 | 8 | 9 | 10 | 11 | 12 | 13 | 14 |

132b ▶ 10
Preapplication Drill: Using a Typewriter to Key on Ruled Lines

plain full sheet

1. Strike the underline key to make a line 3 inches long (30 pica spaces; 36 elite spaces).

2. Center and key **your school name** on the line.

3. Study the relationship of the letters to the underline. Only a slight space separates the letters from the underline.

4. Remove the paper from the machine.

5. With a pencil and ruler (or other straight edge), draw 3 hori-zontal lines 3″ long and approximately ½″ apart.

6. Reinsert and align the paper using the variable line spacer (if your machine has one) and/or the paper release so that only a slight space separates the letters from the underline. Key the information shown at the right on the 3″ lines.

7. Repeat Steps 4-6 but key your name and address on the lines.

```
Roberto Santiago
_____

894 Guinevere Drive
_____

Spokane, WA   99218-1307
_____
```

132c ▶ 25
Key on Ruled and Unruled Forms

Document 1
Index Cards
LP p. 111

1. Key an index card using the information and format illustrated in the model.

2. Using the same format, key index cards for the following information.

Dr. Troy Sheridan
396 Columbia View Drive
Vancouver, WA 98661-2139
(206) 831-2949

Miss Claudia Cepeda
2821 Four Winds Drive N
Salem, OR 97303-4110
(503) 839-4829

```
JORDAN, KELLEE (MS.)


Ms. Kellee Jordan
Liberty Art Gallery
2057 Beacon Street
San Francisco, CA   94131-4130


(414) 326-5610
```

30c ▶ 12 Check Keyboarding Speed

1. A 1' writing on ¶ 1 and then on ¶ 2; find *gwam* on each ¶.

2. Two 2' writings on ¶s 1 and 2 combined; find *gwam* on each writing.

3. A 3' writing on ¶s 1 and 2 combined (or if your teacher prefers, an additional 1' writing on each ¶).

1' *gwam* goals
▽ 21 = acceptable
⊡ 25 = average
⊙ 29 = good
◇ 33 = excellent

all letters used | E | 1.2 si | 5.1 awl | 90% hfw

	gwam 2'	3'
Time and motion are major items in building our keying	6	4
power. As we make each move through space to a letter or a	12	8
figure, we use time. So we want to be sure that every move	18	12
is quick and direct. We cut time and aid speed in this way.	24	16
A good way to reduce motion and thus save time is just	29	19
to keep the hands in home position as you make the reach to	35	23
a letter or figure. Fix your gaze on the copy; then, reach	41	27
to each key with a direct, low move at your very best speed.	47	31

gwam 2' | 1 | 2 | 3 | 4 | 5 | 6
3' | 1 | 2 | 3 | 4

30d ▶ 18
Learn 6 and 2

each line twice SS (slowly, then faster); DS between 2-line groups; if time permits, practice each line again

Follow the *Standard Plan for Learning New Keys* outlined on page 8.

Reach technique for 6

Reach *up* with *right first* finger.

Reach technique for 2

Reach *up* with *left third* finger.

Learn **6**

1 j j 6j 6j jj 66 j6j j6j 66j 66j Reach up for 6, 66, and 666.
2 Key the figures 6, 66, and 666. Have only 6 of 66 finished?

Learn **2**

3 s s 2s 2s ss 22 s2s s2s 22s 22s Reach up for 2, 22, and 222.
4 Add the figures 2, 22, and 222. Review pages 2 to 22 today.

Combine **6, 2,** and other figures

5 Key 22, 26, 62, and 66. Just 22 of the 66 scouts were here.
6 Reach with the fingers to key 26 and 262 as well as 2 and 6.

7 Key figures as units: 18, 26, 37, 49, 50, 62, 162, and 268.
8 The proxy dated April 26, 1990, was vital in Case No. 37584.

131c (continued)

Document 2
Purchase Order
LP p. 107

Key purchase order
as shown at right.

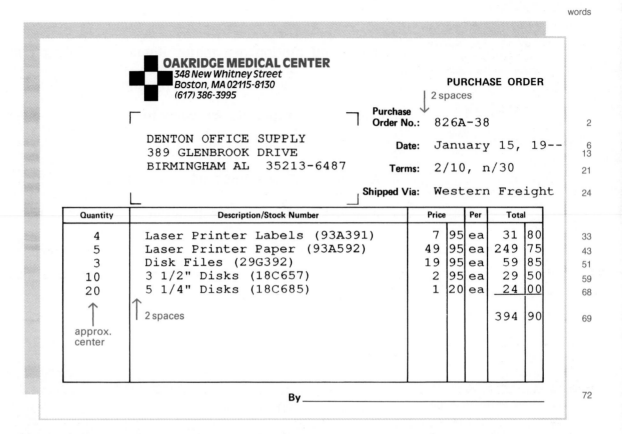

Quantity	Description/Stock Number	Price		Per	Total		
4	Laser Printer Labels (93A391)	7	95	ea	31	80	33
5	Laser Printer Paper (93A592)	49	95	ea	249	75	43
3	Disk Files (29G392)	19	95	ea	59	85	51
10	3 1/2" Disks (18C657)	2	95	ea	29	50	59
20	5 1/4" Disks (18C685)	1	20	ea	24	00	68
					394	90	69

OAKRIDGE MEDICAL CENTER
348 New Whitney Street
Boston, MA 02115-8130
(617) 386-3995

PURCHASE ORDER

↓ 2 spaces

Purchase Order No.: 826A-38 — 2

DENTON OFFICE SUPPLY
389 GLENBROOK DRIVE
BIRMINGHAM AL 35213-6487

Date: January 15, 19-- — 6 / 13

Terms: 2/10, n/30 — 21

Shipped Via: Western Freight — 24

By _____ — 72

Document 3
Invoice
LP p. 109

Key invoice as
shown at right.

Document 4
LP p. 109

Repeat Document 3
changing the quantities to 3, 5, 7, 4, 2,
and 6. Calculate
the total and add
5% sales tax.

The Photo Gallery
5817 Wild Flower Drive Carson City, NV 89701-1901 (702) 325-6715

INVOICE

↓ 2 spaces

NATIONAL PHOTOGRAPHY INC
9399 MOUNTAIN VIEW DRIVE
THOUSAND OAKS CA 91320-4311

Date: January 30, 19-- — 8

Customer Order No.: AJ-8937 — 13 / 21

Terms	Shipped Via	Our Order No.	Date Shipped	
3/10, n/30	Reed Transit, Inc.	B 388-99	1/30/--	30

Quantity	Description/Stock No.	Unit Price		Amount		
5	Mini Camera Bag	27	95	139	75	36
3	Shutter Tester	39	95	119	85	42
2	Table Top Viewer	79	50	159	00	50
3	Flash Attachment	93	49	280	47	56
5	Electronic Camera	259	95	1299	75	64
5	Tripod	28	75	143	75	68
				2142	57	73
	Sales Tax			107	13	76
				2249	70	77

Improve Keyboarding/Language Skills

Learning Goals

1. To improve alphabetic keyboarding technique and speed.

2. To improve numeric keyboarding technique and control (accuracy).

3. To review/improve language skills in number expression.

4. To acquire skill in keying longer paragraph writings.

Format Guides

1. *Paper guide* at *0* (for typewriters).

2. LL: 60 spaces; see *Get Ready to Keyboard: Typewriters* (p. x) or *Computers* (p. xii).

3. LS: SS drills; DS ¶s.

4. PI: 5 spaces when appropriate.

Lesson 31	*Keyboarding/Language Skills*	LL: 60 LS: SS

31a ▶ 6
Conditioning Practice

each line twice SS; then a 1' writing on line 3; find *gwam*

alphabet 1 Linda may have Jack rekey parts two and six of the big quiz.

6/2 2 Our house at 622 Gold Circle will be paid for June 26, 2006.

easy 3 Jena is to go to the lake towns to do the map work for them.

| 1 | 2 | 3 | 4 | 5 | 6 | 7 | 8 | 9 | 10 | 11 | 12 |

31b ▶ 10 Improve
Language Skills: Number Expression

1. Read the first rule highlighted in color at the right.

2. Key the **Learn** sentence below it, noting how the rule has been applied. Use the 60-space line for which your machine is set.

3. Key the **Apply** sentence, supplying the appropriate number expression.

4. Practice the other rules in the same way.

5. If time permits, key the three **Apply** sentences again to improve number control.

> Spell a number that begins a sentence even when other numbers in the sentence are shown in figures.

Learn 1 Twelve of the new shrubs have died; 38 are doing quite well.

Apply 2 40 members have paid their dues, but 15 have not done so.

> Use figures for numbers above ten, and for numbers one to ten when they are used with numbers above ten.

Learn 3 She ordered 2 word processors, 15 computers, and 3 printers.

Apply 4 Did he say they need ten or 12 sets of Z11 and Z13 diskettes?

> Use figures to express dates and times.

Learn 5 He will arrive on Paygo Flight 62 at 10:28 a.m. on March 21.

Apply 6 Candidates must be in Ivy Hall at eight ten a.m. on May one.

31c ▶ 18 Improve
Keyboarding Technique: Service Keys

1. Each pair of lines twice SS (slowly, then faster); DS between 4-line groups.

Note: For lines 5-6, clear all tabs and set 7 new ones 8 spaces apart, beginning at the left margin.

2. Two 1' writings on line 7 and on line 8; find *gwam* on each writing.

space 1 to my│is in│of the│to buy│for the│may sign│the form│pay them
bar 2 Kenton may sign the form at my farm for the corn and barley.

shift keys 3 Aida or Coyt; Hafner and Co.; Have you read OF MICE AND MEN?
& CAPS LOCK 4 Frankie read LINCOLN by Vidal; Kate read ALASKA by Michener.

tabulator 5 ape   tab 103   tab six   tab 282   tab she   tab 263   tab cut   tab 375
6 for   tab 495   tab nap   610   tab own   926   tab and   163

alphabet 7 Roz fixed the crisp okra while Jan made a unique beef gravy.
easy 8 Alfie is to go to work for the city to fix bus sign emblems.

gwam 1' | 1 | 2 | 3 | 4 | 5 | 6 | 7 | 8 | 9 | 10 | 11 | 12 |

**131a ▶ 5
Conditioning
Practice**

each line twice SS
(slowly, then faster);
DS between 2-line
groups; if time permits,
rekey selected lines

alphabet 1 The fabulous zoology complex will be located quite near Bjerke Avenue.

figures 2 Of the 830 surveyed, only 256 knew the importance of December 7, 1941.

long
reaches 3 The umpire received a number of unusual gifts at the special ceremony.

speed 4 The heir to the endowment may work on the problems with the six firms.

| 1 | 2 | 3 | 4 | 5 | 6 | 7 | 8 | 9 | 10 | 11 | 12 | 13 | 14 |

**131b ▶ 10 Improve
Language Skills:
Word Choice**

Study the spelling and
definition of each word.
Note how it is used in
the **Learn** sentence. Key
the **Learn** sentence (with
number and period) and
the **Apply** sentences (with
number and period) se-
lecting the proper word in
parentheses to complete
each sentence correctly.

stationary (adj) fixed; unchanging in condition

stationery (n) paper for writing

weather (n) state of the atmosphere

whether (conj) used to indicate alternatives; if

Learn 1. The stationery is on the stationary cabinet at the front of the room.

Apply 2. Richard will need tools to remove the (stationary, stationery) desks.

Apply 3. The (stationary, stationery) will go on sale this Friday.

Learn 4. The weather will determine whether the meeting has been cancelled.

Apply 5. The (weather, whether) forecast predicts snow before Friday evening.

Apply 6. I am not sure (weather, whether) I will be able to finish the project on time.

**131c ▶ 35 Process
Special Forms**

Review the Format-
ting Guides for pro-
cessing purchase
requisitions, pur-
chase orders, and
invoices on page
230. Proofread
carefully and cor-
rect errors.

**Document 1
Purchase
Requisition**
LP p. 107

Key purchase req-
uisition as shown
at right.

words

OAKRIDGE MEDICAL CENTER
348 New Whitney Street
Boston, MA 02115-8130
(617) 386-3995

PURCHASE REQUISITION

↓ 2 spaces

Deliver to: Anne Jackson   Requisition No. B7983   4

Location: Information Processing Center Date January 13, 19--   13

Job No. 8729   Date Required January 30, 19--   18

Quantity	Description	
4	Laser Printer Labels	22
5	Laser Printer Paper	27
3	Disk Files	29
10	3 1/2" Disks	33
20	5 1/4" Disks	36

↑ approx. center   ↑ 2 spaces

Requisitioned by: Martha Landon   39

1. Take one 1' timed writing and two 1' *guided* writings on ¶ 1 as directed on page 38.

2. Take one 1' timed writing and two 1' *guided* writings on ¶ 2 in the same way.

3. Take two 2' timed writings on ¶s 1 and 2 combined; find *gwam* on each.

4. Take one 3' timed writing on ¶s 1 and 2 combined; find *gwam*.

1' gwam goals

▽ 23 = acceptable
⊡ 27 = average
⊙ 31 = good
◇ 35 = excellent

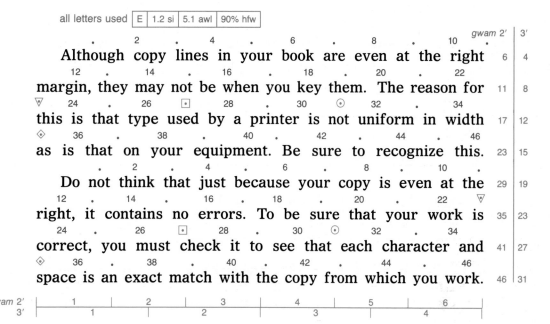

all letters used | E | 1.2 si | 5.1 awl | 90% hfw

| | | | | | gwam 2' | 3' |

Although copy lines in your book are even at the right — 6 | 4

margin, they may not be when you key them. The reason for — 11 | 8

this is that type used by a printer is not uniform in width — 17 | 12

as is that on your equipment. Be sure to recognize this. — 23 | 15

Do not think that just because your copy is even at the — 29 | 19

right, it contains no errors. To be sure that your work is — 35 | 23

correct, you must check it to see that each character and — 41 | 27

space is an exact match with the copy from which you work. — 46 | 31

Lesson 32 — Keyboarding/Language Skills

LL: 60
LS: SS

32a ▶ 6
Conditioning Practice

each line twice SS; then a 1' writing on line 3; find *gwam*

alphabet 1 Jung quickly baked extra pizzas for the film festival crowd.

figures 2 I moved from 3748 Oak Street to 1059 Jaymar Drive on May 26.

easy 3 She paid the big man for the field work he did for the city.

gwam 1' | 1 | 2 | 3 | 4 | 5 | 6 | 7 | 8 | 9 | 10 | 11 | 12 |

32b ▶ 10 *Improve Language Skills: Number Expression*

1. Read the first rule highlighted in color at the right.

2. Key the **Learn** sentence below it, noting how the rule has been applied. Use the 60-space line for which your machine is set.

3. Key the **Apply** sentence, supplying the appropriate number expression.

4. Practice the other rules in the same way.

5. If time permits, key the three **Apply** sentences again to improve number control.

Use figures for house numbers except house number *One*.

Learn 1 My home is at 9 Vernon Drive; my office, at One Weber Plaza.
Apply 2 The Nelsons moved from 4037 Pyle Avenue to 1 Maple Circle.

Use figures to express measures and weights.

Learn 3 Gladys Randoph is 5 ft. 6 in. tall and weighs 119 lbs. 6 oz.
Apply 4 This carton measures one ft. by six in. and weighs five lbs.

Use figures for numbers following nouns.

Learn 5 Review Rules 1 to 22 in Chapter 6, pages 126 and 127, today.
Apply 6 Case 2659 is reviewed in Volume five, pages eight and nine.

Stratford Manufacturing Company
5410 Redwood Drive, NW, Albuquerque, NM 87120-4130

INTEROFFICE MEMORANDUM

	words
2 spaces	

TO: Mark R. Goodwin, Assistant Manager — 7

FROM: Stacey P. McKinney, Marketing Manager — 15

DATE: January 20, 19-- — 18

SUBJECT: Western Region Sales Data — 23

Mark, the sales reports that I received yesterday for the fourth — 36
quarter indicate that there is a potential problem with the West- — 49
ern Region. The overall sales for that region have been down ap- — 62
preciably during the last two quarters. For the year they are — 75
down by almost 15 percent compared to last year. — 85

The reports I receive break down sales only by region. I would — 98
like to see sales for each individual state in the region to de- — 110
termine if this is a problem for the entire region or only for — 123
one or two states. — 127

Since I am meeting with regional representatives next Monday, I — 140
would like to have the information to review this week. — 151

xx — 151/163

1" (left margin)   1" (right margin)

Formal Memorandum

---

words

words in heading 18

130d ▶ 20
Format Documents: Interoffice Memorandums

Document 1
Formal Memorandum
LP p. 103

Review the Formatting Guides for interoffice memorandums and company envelopes on page 230. Format and key the memorandum from the model copy above. Proofread and correct errors. Prepare a company envelope to

Mr. Mark R. Goodwin
Assistant Manager
Marketing Department

Note: If you do not have Lab Pac (LP) pages to use for the formal memos, use plain sheets of paper. Begin on line 10 and set 1" side margins. Key the heading information flush left with the margin. Space twice after the colon and key the information following each heading.

Last week at the convention I picked up the attached brochure on a comput- — 33
erized mileage logging device from the exhibit area. This instrument looks — 48
like it (might, mite) be the answer to the problems we have been having with — 62
company vehicles being used excessively for personal use. — 73

In order to determine the (affect, effect) of the device, we are planning to — 87
pilot test it in two states from June (threw, through) August. Doing so will — 101
provide us with (farther, further) information to make a recommendation to — 113
Vice President Dewitz. I believe he will (accept, except) our (advice, ad- — 124
vise) regarding its purchase. — 130

Please suggest two states in which to pilot test the device--one where the ex- — 146
penses appear to be excessive and one where the expenses are below the — 160
company average. — 164

closing lines 177/191

Document 2
Simplified Memorandum
plain full sheet

Format and key the simplified memo above to **Steven M. Blythe, Assistant Fleet Manager,** from **Ramona S. Gonzalez, Fleet Manager.** Date the memo **June 21.**

Supply an appropriate subject line. Select the proper word in parentheses to complete the sentences correctly. Include your reference initials and indicate a copy to **Blake L. Dewitz.** Proofread/correct errors.

Document 3
Formal Memorandum
LP p. 105

Rekey Document 2 as a formal memorandum.

Prepare a company envelope to **Mr. Steven M. Blythe, Assistant Fleet Manager, Transportation.**

32c ▶ 12
Check/Improve Keyboarding Speed

1. Two 1' writings on each ¶; find *gwam* on each writing.

2. A 2' writing on ¶s 1 and 2 combined; find *gwam*.

3. A 3' writing on ¶s 1 and 2 combined; find *gwam*.

Goals

1': At least 24 *gwam*.
2': At least 23 *gwam*.
3': At least 22 *gwam*.

all letters used | E | 1.2 si | 5.1 awl | 90% hfw

	gwam 2'	3'
Success does not mean the same thing to everyone. For	6	4
some, it means to get to the top at all costs: in power, in	12	8
fame, and in income. For others, it means just to fulfill	18	12
their basic needs or wants with as little effort as required.	24	16
Most people fall within the two extremes. They work quite	30	20
hard to better their lives at home, at work, and in the social	36	24
world. They realize that success for them is not in being at	42	28
the top but rather in trying to improve their quality of life.	48	32

gwam 2' | 1 | 2 | 3 | 4 | 5 | 6
3' | 1 | 2 | 3 | 4

32d ▶ 12
Learn to Proofread Your Copy

1. Note the kinds of errors marked in the ¶ at right.

2. Note how the proofreader's marks above the copy are used to make corrections in the ¶.

3. Proofread the copy you keyed in the 3' writing above and mark for correction each error you made.

Goal: To learn the first step in finding and correcting your errors.

\# = space   ∧ = insert   ⊂ = close up   ℓ = delete   ∩ = transpose (tr)

Sucess does not mean thesame thing to every one. For
some, it means to get the top att all costs: in power, in
fame, and in income. For others it means juts to fulfill
thier basic needs or or wants with as little effort required.

Line 1	Line 2	Line 3	Line 4
1 Omitted letter	1 Omitted word	1 Misstroke	1 Transposition
2 Failure to space	2 Added letter	2 Omitted comma	2 Added word
3 Faulty spacing	3 Faulty spacing	3 Transposition	3 Omitted word

32e ▶ 10
Think as You Key

Key each line once SS. In place of the blank line at the end of each sentence, key the word or word group that correctly completes the sentence.

1 A small mass of land surrounded by water is a/an _____.

2 A large mass of land surrounded by water is a/an _____.

3 The earth rotates on what is called its _____.

4 When the sun comes up over the horizon, we say it _____.

5 When the sun goes down over the horizon, we say it _____.

6 A device used to display temperature is a/an _____.

7 A device used to display atmospheric pressure is a/an _____.

8 A device used to display time is a/an _____.

130a ▶ 5
Conditioning Practice

each line twice SS
(slowly, then faster);
DS between 2-line
groups; if time permits,
rekey selected lines

alphabet	1	Kay may quit publicizing the major events before the end of next week.
figures	2	Of the 12,874 votes cast, Kern received 6,305 and Bahr received 6,569.
adjacent keys	3	Officers stopped the reception before conditions deteriorated further.
speed	4	The visit by the six sorority girls may be a problem for their mentor.

| 1 | 2 | 3 | 4 | 5 | 6 | 7 | 8 | 9 | 10 | 11 | 12 | 13 | 14 |

130b ▶ 15
Check/Improve Keyboarding Skill

1. A 1' writing on ¶ 1; find *gwam*.

2. Add 4-8 *gwam* to the rate attained in Step 1, and note quarter-minute checkpoints from table below.

3. Take two 1' guided writings on ¶ 1 to increase speed.

4. Practice ¶ 2 in the same way.

5. Two 3' writings on ¶s 1-2 combined; find *gwam* and circle errors.

Quarter-Minute Checkpoints

gwam	¼'	½'	¾'	Time
24	6	12	18	24
28	7	14	21	28
32	8	16	24	32
36	9	18	27	36
40	10	20	30	40
44	11	22	33	44
48	12	24	36	48
52	13	26	39	52
56	14	28	42	56
60	15	30	45	60

all letters used | A | 1.5 si | 5.7 awl | 80% hfw

	gwam 3'	5'
Records are extremely vital for a business enterprise to maintain.	5	3 39
They give executives insight into the day-to-day dealings of a firm.	9	6 42
They also are often the sole basis for executives to make major decisions	14	8 44
on the future direction of a firm. Many different types of documents are	19	11 47
used to record data about a firm. Three such documents that are vital to	24	14 50
the operation of a firm are the purchase requisition, the purchase order,	29	17 53
and the invoice.	30	18 54
A purchase requisition is a document utilized by a firm to request	34	21 57
the purchasing agent to order goods or services. A purchase order is a	39	24 60
document used by the purchasing department of one firm to order goods or	44	26 62
services from another firm. An invoice is a document used by one firm	49	29 65
to bill another firm for goods or services purchased from the firm that	54	32 68
sends the invoice. All three documents will become a record of the	58	35 71
firm's purchasing transactions.	60	36 72

gwam 3' | 1 | 2 | 3 | 4 | 5 |
5' | 1 | 2 | 3 |

130c ▶ 10
Language Skills: Compose at Keyboard

plain full sheet
LL: 70 spaces

1. Compose at the keyboard 1 or 2 paragraphs on one of the questions at the right. DS paragraph(s).

2. Edit your copy, marking corrections and changes to improve sentence structure and organization.

3. Prepare the final copy.

Questions

Who is your favorite singing star? Explain why.

Is an education important? Explain why you believe it is or why you believe it is not.

What qualities do you feel are necessary for a good leader to possess? Why?

Practice Procedure

1. Key each line of a group (words, phrases, and sentences) 3 times: first, to improve keyboarding technique; next, to improve keyboarding speed; then, to build precise control of finger motions.

2. Take several 1' writings on the 2 sentences at the end of each set of lines to measure your skill on each kind of copy.

3. As time permits, repeat the drills, keeping a record of your speed scores to see how your skill grows.

Each of the 120 *different* words used in the drills is among the 600 most-used words in the English language. In a study of over 2 million words in personal and business communications, these 120 words accounted for over 40 percent of all word occurrences. Thus, they are important to you in perfecting your keyboarding skill. Practice them frequently for both speed and accuracy.

Balanced-hand words of 2-5 letters (Use word response.)

words
1 of is it he to by or us an so if do am go me the six and but
2 a box may did pay end man air own due big for they with when
3 make them also then such than form work both city down their
4 end they when wish hand paid name held down sign field world

phrases
5 to me | of us | and may | pay for | big box | the six | but due | own them
6 am to work | is to make | a big city | by the name | to do such work

sentences
7 He may wish to go to the city to hand the work form to them.
8 The city is to pay for the field work both men did for them.

gwam 1' | 1 | 2 | 3 | 4 | 5 | 6 | 7 | 8 | 9 | 10 | 11 | 12 |

One-hand words of 2-5 letters (Use letter response.)

words
9 a in be on we up as my at no was you are him get few see set
10 far act war tax only were best date case fact area rate free
11 you act few ever only fact card upon after state great water

phrases
12 at no | as my | on you | we are | at best | get set | you were | only date
13 get you in | act on my case | you set a date | get a rate on water

sentences
14 Get him my extra tax card only after you set up a case date.
15 As you see, you are free only after you get a case date set.

gwam 1' | 1 | 2 | 3 | 4 | 5 | 6 | 7 | 8 | 9 | 10 | 11 | 12 |

Double-letter words of 2-5 letters (Speed up double letters.)

words
16 all see too off will been well good miss feel look less call
17 too free soon week room fill keep book bill tell still small
18 off call been less free look need week soon will offer needs

phrases
19 a room | all week | too soon | see less | call off | need all | will see
20 see a need | fill a book | miss a bill | all will see | a good offer

sentences
21 It is too soon to tell if we will need that small book room.
22 They still feel a need to offer a good book to all who call.

gwam 1' | 1 | 2 | 3 | 4 | 5 | 6 | 7 | 8 | 9 | 10 | 11 | 12 |

Balanced-hand, one-hand, and double-letter words of 2-5 letters

words
23 of we to in or on is be it as by no if at us up an my he was
24 and all war six see you men too are may get off pay him well
25 such will work best then keep were good been only city needs
26 make soon ever wish tell area name bill upon paid tell great

phrases
27 is too great | they will be | box was small | their offer was good
28 if at all | may get all | off the case | to tell him | to keep after

sentences
29 If you wish to get to the rate you set, keep the hand still.
30 All of us do the work well, for only good form will pay off.

gwam 1' | 1 | 2 | 3 | 4 | 5 | 6 | 7 | 8 | 9 | 10 | 11 | 12 |

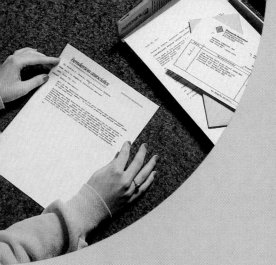

Learning Goals

1. To learn to format and process formal and simplified interoffice memorandums.

2. To learn to format and process special business forms.

3. To learn to format and process information on ruled forms.

4. To improve language skills.

Format Guides

1. Paper guide at *0* (for typewriters).

2. LL: 70-space lines for drills, ¶s, and language skills; as required for documents.

3. LS: SS drills; DS ¶s; as required by document formats.

4. PI: 5 spaces, when appropriate.

FORMATTING GUIDES: FORMS AND SPECIAL DOCUMENTS

Formal Memo and Company Envelope

Simplified Memo

Interoffice Memorandum

Communications within an organization are often formatted as memorandums rather than as letters. Two styles of the interoffice memorandum are commonly used. The *formal memorandum* is processed on a form having special printed headings. The *simplified memorandum* is prepared on plain paper or letterhead without internal headings.

Formatting guides for the interoffice memo are listed below.

1. Use either a full or half sheet.

2. Use block format.

3. Use side margins of approximately 1″.

4. Omit personal titles (Miss, Mr., Ms., Dr., etc.) on memo, but include them on the company envelope.

5. Omit salutation and complimentary close.

6. Use a subject line.

7. SS the body, but DS between ¶s.

8. Use plain envelope with COMPANY MAIL typed in the usual stamp position. Include on the envelope the receiver's personal title, name, and business title; also, include receiver's department (see illustration at left).

Formal memorandum. Begin heading information 2 spaces to the right of printed headings (as shown on page 232). Note that headings are printed in the 1″ left margin so that the lines of the heading data and the message can begin at the 1″ left margin setting. A memo may be sent to more than one individual; if so, each name is included on the same line as the "To:" heading. DS between all parts of the formal memorandum.

Simplified memorandum. Begin the date on line 6 for a half sheet and line 10 for a full sheet. DS between all parts of the simplified memo, *except* below date and the last paragraph of the body. Quadruple-space (QS) below the dateline and below the last paragraph of the body.

Special Forms (See models on pp. 233–234).

Purchase requisitions, purchase orders, invoices, and other similar documents are prepared on printed forms. Although forms vary from company to company, well-designed forms allow the keyboard operator to follow the general guidelines listed below.

1. Set left margin stop so that items are approximately centered in the Quantity column of purchase requisitions, purchase orders, and invoices. (This stop is also used to begin the *Deliver to* block of Purchase Requisitions.)

2. Set a tab stop to begin the Description items of Purchase Requisitions, Purchase Orders, and Invoices 1 or 2 spaces to the right of the vertical rule. Place the address (ALL CAPS) so that it will show through the window of a window envelope.

3. Set a tab stop for keying information in the upper right-hand area of the form (1 or 2 spaces to the right of printed items). This stop may also be used to key items in the Price column, or an additional stop may be set for that purpose.

4. Set additional tab stops for aligning and keying items in remaining column(s).

5. SS column entries, beginning on the first or second space below the horizontal rule under the column headings.

6. If the form has a vertical line to separate dollars and cents in monetary columns, key the cents so they are to the right of the vertical rule. Use of commas to indicate thousands in figure columns is optional.

7. Underline the last figure in the Total column; then, DS before keying the total amount.

8. Tabulate and key across the form rather than keying all items in one column before moving to the next column.

Learn Symbol-Key Operation

Learning Goals
1. To learn locations of basic symbol keys.
2. To learn how to strike symbol keys properly, with the correct fingers.
3. To improve keyboarding speed/technique on alphabetic and statistical copy.
4. To review/improve language skills.
5. To improve horizontal centering skill.

Format Guides
1. **Paper guide** at *0* (for typewriters).
2. LL: 60 spaces; see *Get Ready to Keyboard: Typewriters* (p. x) or *Computers* (p. xii).
3. LS: SS drills; DS ¶s.
4. PI: 5 spaces when appropriate.

Lesson 33	/ and $	LL: 60 LS: SS

33a ▶ 6
Conditioning Practice

each line twice SS; then a 1' writing on line 3; find *gwam*

alphabet 1 Di will buy from me as prizes the six unique diving jackets.

figures 2 The January 17 quiz of 25 points will test pages 389 to 460.

easy 3 Both of us may do the audit of the work of a big title firm.

| 1 | 2 | 3 | 4 | 5 | 6 | 7 | 8 | 9 | 10 | 11 | 12 |

33b ▶ 18
Learn / and $

each line twice SS (slowly, then faster); DS between 4-line groups; if time permits, practice the lines again

/ = diagonal
$ = dollar sign

Do not space between a figure and the **/** or the **$** sign.

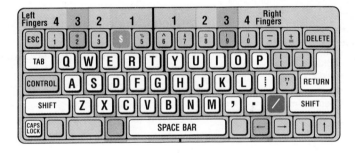

Reach technique for **/**

Reach *down* to **/** with *right little* finger.

Reach technique for **$**

Shift; then reach *up* to **$** with *left first* finger.

Learn **/** (diagonal)

1 ; ; /; /; ;; // ;/; ;/; 2/3 4/5 and/or We keyed 1/2 and 3/4.

2 Space between a whole number and a fraction: 7 2/3, 18 3/4.

Learn **$** (dollar sign)

3 f f $f $f ff $$ f$f f$f $4 $4 for $4 Shift for $ and key $4.

4 A period separates dollars and cents: $4.50, $6.25, $19.50.

Combine **/** and **$**

5 I must shift for $ but not for /: Order 10 gal. at $16/gal.

6 Do not space on either side of /: 1/6, 3/10, 9 5/8, 4 7/12.

7 We sent 5 boxes of No. 6 3/4 envelopes at $11/box on June 2.

8 They can get 2 sets of disks at $49.85/set; 10 sets, $39.85.

The two sets of paragraphs on this page are counted internally for 1' guided and unguided writings. The paragraphs at the bottom of the page are counted for 3' and 5' timed writings. They may be used at any time additional drills and/or timed writings are desired.

Straight-Copy Drill

1. A 1' writing on the ¶ at the top to establish a base rate.

2. Add 4-8 words to base rate to set goal rate. Note quarter-minute checkpoints.

3. Three 1' writings on the same paragraph, trying to achieve goal rate each quarter minute as guides are called. Set goal rate higher each time the goal is achieved.

4. Three 1' writings at reduced speed for control (not more than one error a minute).

Note: The same procedure may be used for ¶s 2 and 3 for additional guided writing copy.

Quarter-Minute Checkpoints

gwam	¼'	½'	¾'	1'
28	7	14	21	28
32	8	16	24	32
36	9	18	27	36
40	10	20	30	40
44	11	22	33	44
48	12	24	36	48
52	13	26	39	52
56	14	28	42	56
60	15	30	45	60
64	16	32	48	64
68	17	34	51	68
72	18	36	54	72
76	19	38	57	76
80	20	40	60	80

Timed Writings

Two 3' or 5' writings on the ¶s at the right. Find *gwam* and errors. Record the better of the 3' and 5' writings.

---

all letters used | A | 1.5 si | 5.7 awl | 80% hfw

A basic knowledge of parliamentary procedure is an excellent skill to acquire. Those who possess this skill will be able to put it to use in any organization they belong to that conducts meetings based on parliamentary law. A meeting which is run by this procedure will be conducted in a proper and very orderly fashion. Just as important, the rights of each member of the group are protected at all times.

---

all letters used | A | 1.5 si | 5.7 awl | 80% hfw

	gwam 3'	5'

More time is devoted to business meetings than ever before. Today a group rather than an individual is deciding the direction of many organizations. Meetings provide the forum for decisions to be made by a group. These meetings do not succeed or fail by accident. A successful business meeting is more likely to occur when advance notice of the time, date, site, and agenda are provided. The agenda quickly informs the group members of the items of business to be conducted at the next meeting. It allows them to plan and to prepare prior to the time of the meeting.

Even though the decisions are made by a group, the leader of the group is the key to the success of a meeting. The leader determines when the meeting starts and when it will conclude, the facilities, the agenda items to be discussed, and the people to be invited to the meeting. Effective group leaders strive to start and conclude meetings on time. They provide members with information on major agenda items prior to the meeting. They make sure that the meeting site and facilities contribute to the success of the meeting rather than detract from it.

gwam 3'	5'
5	3	48
9	6	51
14	9	54
19	12	57
24	14	60
29	17	63
34	20	66
38	23	68
43	26	71
48	29	74
53	32	77
57	34	80
62	37	82
67	40	85
72	43	88
76	45	91

gwam 3' | 1 | 2 | 3 | 4 | 5 |
5' | 1 | 2 | 3 |

33c ▶ 10 Check Language Skills: Number Expression

page references

1. Read each handwritten (script) line, noting mentally where changes are needed in spacing and number expression.

2. Key each line once SS, making needed changes; then check accuracy of work against rules on pages listed at left of sentences.

3. If time permits, key each line again at a faster speed.

54	1	*15 voted for the amendment, but 12 voted against it.*
54	2	*Of the twenty divers, only three advanced to the state finals.*
54	3	*The curtain rises at eight thirty p.m. on Saturday, October ten.*
55	4	*My office is at ten Park Place; my home, at 1 Key Largo.*
55	5	*Buy one doz. eggs, two lbs. of butter, and 8 oz. of cream.*
55	6	*Check your answers on pages ten and eleven of Chapter One.*

33d ▶ 16 Improve Keyboarding Skill

plain full sheet; begin on line 10

1. Clear tabs; set a tab at the center point.

2. Center each of lines 1-5; DS.

3. QS and key each of lines 6-11 once SS; DS between 2-line groups.

4. If time permits, rekey the drill.

Quick-snap keystroke

	1	WORD PROCESSING TERMS
center lines	2	automatic centering
	3	delete and insert
	4	store and retrieve
	5	global search and replace
space bar	6	by us of an am to go by an urn of elm to pay she may and jam
	7	Karen is to pay the man for any of the elm you buy from him.
CAPS LOCK	8	They are to see the musical play INTO THE WOODS on Saturday.
	9	HBO will show THE KING AND I on Monday, May 13, at 8:30 a.m.
alphabet	10	Sprague is amazed at just how quickly he fixed the blue van.
figures	11	Invoice No. 2749 totals $163.85 plus $4.20 shipping charges.

| 1 | 2 | 3 | 4 | 5 | 6 | 7 | 8 | 9 | 10 | 11 | 12 |

Lesson 34 % and - LL: 60 LS: SS

34a ▶ 6 Conditioning Practice

each line twice SS; then a 1' writing on line 3; find *gwam*

alphabet	1	Lopez knew our squad could just slip by the next five games.
figures	2	Check Numbers 267, 298, 304, and 315 were still outstanding.
easy	3	Dixie works with vigor to make the theory work for a profit.

| 1 | 2 | 3 | 4 | 5 | 6 | 7 | 8 | 9 | 10 | 11 | 12 |

34b ▶ 16 Improve Keyboarding Technique

1. Key lines 1-11 of 33d, above, once each as shown.

2. Take a 1' writing on line 7 and on line 10 of 33d.

Goals: ● to refine technique
● to increase speed

129d ▶ 30 Evaluate Document Processing: Letters with Special Features

LP pp. 97-101 or plain full sheets, supply current date, salutation, complimentary close, and special features as directed

Time Schedule
Plan and prepare .... 4′
Timed production .... 20′
Proofread/compute *n-pram* ... 6′

Document 1
modified block format; indented ¶s; mixed punctuation

Special features:
CERTIFIED
Subject: Research on Employee Morale

Company name in closing lines:
THE RESEARCH SPECIALISTS
Enclosure

Document 2
block format; open punctuation

Special features:
SPECIAL DELIVERY
Company name in closing lines:
WESTRIDGE PUBLISHING, INC.
**Enclosures: Scripts
Brochure**

---

	words
Mr. Chad A. Landis | Martin Insurance Company | 726 Lakeshore Drive | Athens,	19
GA 30606-7496	33

Enclosed is our proposal for the research project you would like completed (48) on employee morale. Your decision to hire someone from outside the orga- (63) nization to do the research was a wise one. Our experience has shown em- (77) ployees to be more willing to express their opinions and attitudes to a person (93) from the outside. (97)

This research project is designed to address four work-related areas which (112) most frequently influence employee morale. These include economic reward, (127) job satisfaction, co-workers, and management. (136)

We are confident that the findings from these four areas will provide your (151) company with the information that you will need to make future decisions on (166) issues related to employee morale. (140) (174)

Ms. Erica J. Collins \| Research Consultant \| xx — 191/211

Mr. Gordon S. Jennings \| Summer Productions, Inc. \| 3120 Mount Meeker (20) Road \| Boulder, CO 80301-2001 (29)

Here are copies of the two scripts I discussed with you at the National (43) Theaters Guild Convention in Dallas. Either play would be a good addition (58) to the plays you already have planned for your summer productions. (72)

If your goal is to appeal to a younger audience, I would recommend <u>Studio</u> (88) <u>'93</u>. It is a light comedy that we have had excellent feedback on from those (104) who have seen it performed. The other script, <u>36 Bradford Street</u>, is one of (123) our newest publications. Since it just appeared in print this month, I am not (139) sure what type of audience appeal it will have. From reading it, however, I (154) feel it has great possibilities. (161)

The enclosed brochure lists and describes the plays which were most popu- (175) lar last year. If any of these interest you, please let me know. (160) (189)

Ms. Melissa M. Masters \| Manager \| xx \| postscript I look forward to attending (215) one of your productions this summer when I am in Boulder. — 226/248

Document 3
modified block format; blocked ¶s; mixed punctuation

Special features:
Attention Human Resources Director
Subject: Lakeland MBA Program
**Enclosures:
MBA Announcement
Information Cards**

Document 4
Rekey Document 1 in block format with open punctuation. Do not include the company name in the closing lines.

Griffin Computer Systems, Inc. \| 1434 John Hancock Drive \| Tallahassee, FL (24) 32304-1617 (37)

The enclosed announcement provides information on the Master of Business (52) Administration degree at Lakeland University. Please share this informa- (66) tion with employees you feel would benefit from completing this program. (81)

Lakeland offers a quality MBA program designed to provide advanced and spe- (96) cialized training in management, research, and decision making. Individuals (111) completing the program become more valued employees who generally ad- (125) vance more rapidly in their organizations. (134)

Those interested in more details about the program should complete and (148) return one of the cards enclosed with the announcement. (122) (159)

Carlos J. Santos \| Admissions Director \| xx — 179/202

34c ▶ 18
Learn % and -

each line twice SS (slowly, then faster); DS between 4-line groups; if time permits, practice the lines again

% = percent sign
- = hyphen

Do not space between a figure and the %, nor before or after - or -- (dash) used as punctuation.

Reach technique for %

Shift; then reach *up* to % with *left first* finger.

Reach technique for -

Reach *up* to – with *right little* finger.

Learn % (percent sign)

1 f f %f %f ff %% f%f f%f 5% 5% Shift for the % in 5% and 15%.
2 Do not space between a number and %: 5%, 75%, 85%, and 95%.

Learn - (hyphen)

3 ; ; -; -; ;; -- ;-; ;-; 4-ply I use a 2-ply tire on my bike.
4 I gave each film a 1-star, 2-star, 3-star, or 4-star rating.

Combine % and -

5 He can send the parcel by fourth-class mail at a 50% saving.
6 A dash is two unspaced hyphens--no space before or after it.
7 The new prime rate is 12%--but you have no interest in that.
8 You need 60 signatures--51% of the members--on the petition.

34d ▶ 10 Build Keyboarding Skill Transfer

1. Take a 1' writing on ¶ 1; find *gwam.*

2. Take a 1' writing on ¶ 2 and on ¶3; find *gwam* on each writing.

3. Compare rates. On which ¶ did you have the highest *gwam?*

4. Take two 1' writings on each of the slower ¶s, trying to equal your highest *gwam* of the first 3 writings.

Note: Most students key straight copy at the highest *gwam;* handwritten (script) copy at the next highest; and statistical copy at the lowest *gwam.*

To find *gwam,* use the 1' *gwam* for partial lines in ¶s 1 and 2, but *count* the words in a partial line in ¶ 3.

all letters/figures used | LA | 1.4 si | 5.4 awl | 85% hfw |

gwam 1'

You should try now to transfer to other types of copy   11
as much of your straight-copy speed as you can. Handwritten   23
copy and copy in which figures appear tend to slow you down.   35
You can increase speed on these, however, with extra effort.   48

An immediate goal for handwritten copy is at least 90%   11
of the straight-copy rate; for copy with figures, at least   23
75%. Try to speed up balanced-hand figures such as 26, 84,   35
and 163. Key harder ones such as 452 and 890 more slowly.   47

Copy that is written by hand is often not legible, and   11
the spelling of words may be puzzling. So give major atten-   23
tion to unclear words. Question and correct the spacing used   35
with a comma or period. You can do this even as you key.   47

gwam 1' | 1 | 2 | 3 | 4 | 5 | 6 | 7 | 8 | 9 | 10 | 11 | 12 |

128c ▶ 30 Build Sustained Document Processing: Letters with Special Features

LP pp. 89-95 or plain full sheets proofread; correct errors

Time Schedule

Plan and prepare .... 4′
Timed production ....20′
Proofread/compute *n-pram* ...... 6′

1. Arrange paper and correction materials for easy access.
2. Make a list of letters to be processed:

page 224, 126b, Letter 2
page 225, 127c, Letter 1
page 225, 127c, Letter 2
page 226, 128b

3. Process as many letters as you can in 20′. Proofread and correct errors as you key.

4. After 20′ timing, proofread again, mark any additional errors not found during keying, and compute *n-pram*.
5. Arrange letters in order listed in Step 2 and turn in work.

n-pram = (total words keyed − penalty*) ÷ time
(*Penalty is 10 words for each uncorrected error.)

129a ▶ 5 Conditioning Practice

each line twice SS (slowly, then faster); DS between 2-line groups; if time permits, rekey selected lines

alphabet 1 Three dozen packages of equipment were expected to arrive before July.
figures 2 Chapter 20, pages 253-264, of the 1987 edition contains grammar rules.
fig/sym 3 The deductible was changed to $250 on your policy (Q194-837) on May 6.
speed 4 The six haughty men did the work on the bus for the neurotic neighbor.

| 1 | 2 | 3 | 4 | 5 | 6 | 7 | 8 | 9 | 10 | 11 | 12 | 13 | 14 |

129b ▶ 7 Check Language Skills: Number Expression

SS sentences; DS between groups of sentences

Key line number (with period); space twice, then key the sentences, supplying the correct form of number expression.

If time permits, key the sentences again to increase decision-making speed.

1. 10 members of our delegation will not arrive until Friday, June first.
2. Only two of the twelve computers were damaged during shipment.
3. The final exam is scheduled for May 23 at nine a.m. in Room Twelve.
4. 1 office is located at 1 Oak Drive; the other, at 33 Lake Road.

5. The American boxer is five ft 7 in tall and weighs 126 lbs one oz.
6. Please reserve Rooms six and seven for the keyboarding event.
7. The 2 desks were returned to the store located at Six Nyman Drive.
8. Problems six and seven from Chapter twelve are due on Monday, April 5.

9. The bus stops each hour at 5th Avenue and at 75th Street.
10. Exactly 1/2 of the students taking the CPS exam passed.
11. About 50 members voted for Joshua; that is nearly 2/3.
12. Flight eighty-four, the last flight of the day, leaves at nine p.m.

129c ▶ 8 Improve Language Skills: Word Choice

Study the definition and spelling of each word. Read the **Learn** sentence. Key the **Learn** sentence (with number and period) and the **Apply** sentences (with number and period), selecting the proper word in parentheses to complete each sentence correctly.

farther (adv) greater distance	**threw** (vb) past tense of throw
further (adv) additional	**through** (prep) passage from one end to another; indicates a period of time

Learn 1. To discuss the matter further, we walked farther down the hall.
Apply 2. The item will be placed on the next agenda for (farther, further) discussion.
Apply 3. Our home is (farther, further) out of town than Jensen's home.

Learn 4. Steve threw the ball through the broken window into the classroom.
Apply 5. Karl drove (through, threw) the tunnel.
Apply 6. When he (threw, through) the bat after striking out, he was ejected.

35a ▶ 6
Conditioning Practice

each line twice SS; then a 1′ writing on line 3; find *gwam*

alphabet 1 Racquel just put back five azure gems next to my gold watch.

figures 2 Joel used a comma in 1,203 and 2,946 but not in 583 and 750.

easy 3 The auto firm owns the big signs by the downtown civic hall.

| 1 | 2 | 3 | 4 | 5 | 6 | 7 | 8 | 9 | 10 | 11 | 12 |

35b ▶ 10 Check
Language Skills: Capitalization

1. Read and key each line once SS, making needed changes in capitalization.

2. Check accuracy of work against rules on pages listed; rekey any line that contains errors in capitalization.

page references

40, 41 1 did mr. reid assign Unit 8 for monday? beth read it sunday.

40 2 did miss perez excuse john and anita xica from history class?

40 3 gloria said that juan will attend midway college next year.

40, 42 4 the golden gate bridge connects san francisco and sausalito.

40, 41 5 our labor day holiday is the first monday in september.

40, 42 6 concordia bank is located at mason street and laurel avenue.

40, 43 7 muriel getz, the club secretary, wrote to president marquis.

40, 43 8 dr. p. c. vickers has an m.d. and a ph.d. from johns hopkins.

35c ▶ 18
Learn # and &

each set of lines twice SS (slowly, then faster); DS between groups; if time permits, practice the lines again

= number/pounds
& = ampersand (and)

Do not space between # and a figure; space once before and after & used to join names.

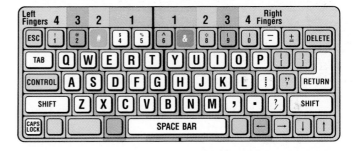

Reach technique for #

Shift; then reach *up* to # with *left second* finger.

Reach technique for &

Shift; then reach *up* to & with *right first* finger.

Learn **#** (number/pounds)

1 d d #d #d dd ## d#d d#d 3# 3# Shift for # as you enter #33d.

2 Do not space between a number and #: 3# of #633 at $9.35/#.

Learn **&** (ampersand)

3 j j &j &j jj && j&j j&j 7& 7& Have you written to Poe & Son?

4 Do not space before or after & in initials; i.e., CG&E, B&O.

Combine **#** and **&**

5 Shift for # and &. Recall: # stands for number and pounds.

6 Names joined by & require spaces; a # sign alone does, also.

7 Letters joined by & are keyed solid: List Stock #3 as C&NW.

8 I bought 20# of #830 grass seed from Locke & Uhl on March 4.

127d ▶ 10 Improve Language Skills: Word Choice

Study the definition and spelling of each word. Read the **Learn** sentence. Key the **Learn** sentence (with number and period) and the **Apply** sentences (with number and period), selecting the proper word in parentheses to complete each sentence correctly.

affect (vb) to influence	**advice** (n) opinion; recommendation
effect (n) result; consequence (vb) to cause; to accomplish	**advise** (vb) to give advice, to recommend

Learn 1. The effect of the recent change will affect our previous decision.
Apply 2. Cutting our staff 25 percent will (affect, effect) employee morale.
Apply 3. What (affect, effect) did the new equipment have on productivity?

Learn 4. If you want my advice, I would advise that you accept the offer.
Apply 5. The only (advice, advise) she offered was to consider all my options.
Apply 6. Mr. Martin will (advice, advise) students on Wednesday mornings.

Lesson 128   Letters with Special Features

128a ▶ 5 Conditioning Practice

each line twice SS (slowly, then faster); DS between 2-line groups; if time permits, rekey selected lines

alphabet 1 Umezaki, the exchange student from Japan, plays racquetball very well.

figures 2 He was born on May 25, 1987, at 4:30 a.m. and weighed just over 6 lbs.

fig/sym 3 The shipping expenses ($29.76) were not included on Invoice #A184-350.

speed 4 The widow of the tax auditor of the firm did handiwork for the chapel.

| 1 | 2 | 3 | 4 | 5 | 6 | 7 | 8 | 9 | 10 | 11 | 12 | 13 | 14 |

128b ▶ 15 Formatting Drill: Letters

plain full sheets; modified block format; open punctuation

1. A 3' writing on the letter to determine *gwam*.

2. Take three 1' writings on date through subject line of the letter. If you complete the lines, QS and start over.

3. Take three 1' writings on the complimentary close through the postscript. If you complete the lines, QS and start over.

4. Take another 3' writing on the letter. Try to increase your *gwam* by 4-8 words.

gwam 3'

July 5, 19-- SPECIAL DELIVERY Attention Ms. Mary A. Fields Carlson Elec-   5

tronics 897 Rust Street Fairfax, VA 22030-7341 Ladies and Gentlemen   9

Subject: Office Layout Designs   11

(¶ 1) Attached is the information you requested on office layout designs.   16

This plan combines both conventional and open design layouts. The con-   21

ventional layout will isolate some work areas with walls which will pro-   26

vide for the privacy you require. The open portion of the plan allows   30

for flexibility, reduces communication barriers, and better utilizes the   35

available space.   36

(¶ 2) A rough estimate of the cost of the project is also included. I   41

look forward to hearing your branch manager's reaction to your proposal.   45

Sincerely OFFICE CONSULTANTS, INC. Todd P. Harmon Design Consultant xx   50

Attachments: Layout Design Price Estimate c Janice Eastman *postscript*   54

The price estimate reflects the 15 percent business discount.   58

35d ▶ 16 Improve Keyboarding Skill Transfer

1. Take a 1' writing on ¶ 1; find *gwam*.

2. Take a 1' writing on ¶ 2; find *gwam*.

3. Take two more 1' writings on the slower ¶.

4. Take a 2' writing on ¶ 1 and on ¶ 2; find *gwam* on each writing (2' *gwam* = 1' *gwam* ÷ 2).

5. Take 2 more 2' writings on the slower ¶.

Goal: To transfer at least 75% of your straight-copy speed to statistical copy.

To determine % of transfer:
¶ 2 *gwam* ÷ ¶ 1 *gwam*

all letters/figures used | LA | 1.4 si | 5.4 awl | 85% hfw

Figures appear often in personal and business documents. It is vital, therefore, that you learn to key them rapidly. If you will just keep your hands in position and reach with your fingers, you will soon be amazed at your ability to key all figures with ease.

Learn to read and key figures in distinct groups. For example, read 165 as one sixty-five and key it that way. Tackle the longer sequences in like manner. Read 1078 as ten seventy-eight and handle it as 2 units. Try this trick for 2493, also.

Lesson 36   (and)

LL: 60
LS: SS

36a ▶ 6 Conditioning Practice

each line twice SS; then a 1' writing on line 3; find *gwam*

alphabet 1 Jacques could win a prize for eight more dives by next week.

figures 2 In 1987, we had only 135 computers; as of 1990 we owned 264.

easy 3 The girls paid for the eight antique urns with their profit.

| 1 | 2 | 3 | 4 | 5 | 6 | 7 | 8 | 9 | 10 | 11 | 12 |

36b ▶ 12 Recall/Improve Language Skills: Capitalization and Number Expression

1. Read the first rule highlighted in color.

2. Key the **Learn** sentence below it, noting how the rule has been applied.

3. Key the **Apply** sentence, supplying the appropriate capitalization and/or number expression.

4. Practice the other rules in the same way.

5. If time permits, key the four **Apply** lines again to improve decision-making speed.

Capitalize nouns preceding numbers (except *page* and *line*).

Learn 1 Please see Rule 10 in Unit 3, page 45, lines 27 and 28.
Apply 2 See volume 12, section 38, page 564, lines 78-90.

Spell (capitalized) names of small-numbered streets and avenues (ten and under).

Learn 3 I walked several blocks along Third Avenue to 65th Street.
Apply 4 At 6th Street she took a taxi to his home on 43d Avenue.

Use figures for a series of fractions, but spell isolated fractions and indefinite numbers.

Learn 5 Carl has a 1/4 interest in Parcel A, 1/2 in B, and 2/3 in C.
Learn 6 Nearly forty-five members voted; that is almost two thirds.
Apply 7 Guide calls: one fourth, 1/2, 3/4, and 1--each 15 seconds.
Apply 8 Over 50 students passed the test; that is about 1/2.

127a ▶ 5
Conditioning Practice

each line twice SS (slowly, then faster); DS between 2-line groups; if time permits, rekey selected lines

alphabet	1	Everyone except Jake was amazed by how quickly the fight was finished.
figures	2	The editor made changes on pages 40, 63, 71, 82, and 95 of the script.
fig/sym	3	Their assets ($153,450) were greater than their liabilities ($96,782).
speed	4	The maid paid the men for the work they did on the shanty by the lake.

| 1 | 2 | 3 | 4 | 5 | 6 | 7 | 8 | 9 | 10 | 11 | 12 | 13 | 14 |

127b ▶ 10
Formatting Drill: Letters with Special Features

plain full sheets

1. Two 1' writings on date through subject line of letter on page 223. Concentrate on correct placement of letter parts.

2. Two 1' writings on complimentary close through postscript of letter on page 223. Concentrate on correct placement of letter parts.

3. A 3' writing on correct letter format on the complete letter. Stress correct placement of letter parts.

127c ▶ 25 Improve
Formatting Skill: Letters with Special Features

plain full sheets; supply special features as directed; proofread and circle errors

Letter 1
block format; open punctuation

Special Features:

Attention Purchasing Department

Subject: Architecture Designs
Company name in closing lines:
CARLTON PUBLISHING
Enclosures: Reeves Pamphlet
Blueprint Listing

words

October 13, 19-- | Marshall Construction Company | 7695 Industrial Way | Vancouver, WA 98660-3120 | Ladies and Gentlemen — 20 / 35

The 1988 edition of Innovative Home Floor Plans by Bart Reeves and Chan Inoue is no longer in print. Architectural Home Designs for the 1990s is the only publication by Reeves and Inoue we currently have in stock. — 55 / 79 / 92

A pamphlet describing the publication is enclosed. If you decide that you want a copy of the book, return the card which is attached to the pamphlet and the book will be shipped the same day we receive your order. — 107 / 122 / 135

A listing of our current publications that include blueprints of home designs is also enclosed. If you want to review any of the publications on the list, we will be happy to send them to you. (words in body: 140) — 151 / 167 / 174

Sincerely | Ms. Marjorie A. Reynolds | Manager — 196/218

Letter 2
modified block format; blocked ¶s; mixed punctuation

Special Features:

SPECIAL DELIVERY
Attention Connie L. Parkinson
Enclosures: Blueprints
Proposal
Postscript: In order to guarantee completion by April 1, 19--, construction should begin by November 1, 19--.

Letter 3
reformat letter 2 in block format; open punctuation

Special Features:

Company name in closing lines:
MARSHALL CONSTRUCTION COMPANY
c Barry B. Horn

October 13, 19-- | Bayfield Insurance Agency | 415 North Fifth Street | Kelso, WA 98626-4210 | Ladies and Gentlemen — 24 / 31

Here is the revised proposal for remodeling your information processing center. All the changes you requested during our last meeting are included in the revised blueprints. — 46 / 61 / 67

The changes did not increase the total cost significantly. The largest expense will be the addition of a small conference room. The increase in cost can be held to a minimum by decreasing the size of the storage area to accommodate a small conference room adjacent to the manager's office. — 81 / 97 / 111 / 125

The plans are flexible enough to allow for further expansion of the center as your company continues to grow. (116) — 141 / 147

Sincerely | Parker A. Dixon | Contractor — 182/205

36c ▶ 18
Learn (and)
each set of lines twice SS (slowly, then faster); DS between groups; if time permits, practice the lines again

(= left parenthesis
) = right parenthesis

Do not space between ( ) and the copy they enclose.

Reach technique for (

Shift; then reach *up* to (with *right third* finger.

Reach technique for)

Shift; then reach *up* to) with *right little* finger.

Learn **(** (left parenthesis)

use the letter "l"

1 l l (l (l ll ((l(l l(l 9(9(Shift for the (as you key (9.
2 As (is the shift of 9, use the l finger to key 9, (, or (9.

Learn **)** (right parenthesis)

3 ; ;);); ;;)) ;); ;); 0) 0) Shift for the) as you key 0).
4 As) is the shift of 0, use the ; finger to key 0,), or 0).

Combine **(** and **)**

5 Hints: (1) depress shift; (2) strike key; (3) release both.
6 Tab steps: (1) clear tabs, (2) set stops, and (3) tabulate.
7 Her new account (#495-3078) draws annual interest at 6 1/2%.

36d ▶ 14 Improve Keyboarding Skill
full sheet; line 10

1. Clear tabs; set a tab at center point.

2. Center each of lines 1-5; DS.

3. QS and key each of lines 6-13 once SS; DS between 2-line groups.

4. If time permits, rekey the drill.

center lines

1   DENTAL SERVICES, INC.

2   Announces New Dental Center

3   in

4   Eastwood Circle Mall

5   Opening the First of March

letter response

6 upon ever join save only best ploy gave pink edge pump facts
7 You acted on a phony tax case only after a union gave facts.

word response

8 visit risks their world field chair proxy throw right eighty
9 Lana may sign the form to pay for the giant map of the city.

combination response

10 also fast sign card maps only hand were pair link paid plump
11 To get to be a pro, react with zest and care as the pros do.

alphabet
12 Shep quickly coaxed eight avid fans away from the jazz band.
fig/sym
13 Of 370 students, only 35 (9.46%) failed to type 18-20 w.a.m.

126a ▶ 5
Conditioning Practice

each line twice SS (slowly, then faster); DS between 2-line groups; if time permits, rekey selected lines

alphabet 1 Just before moving back to Venezuela, they acquired a few exotic pets.

figures 2 The main office was located at 4623 Oxford Drive from 1970 until 1985.

fig/sym 3 You can save 25% ($376.98) by purchasing the 20 desks before March 15.

speed 4 Their neighbors on the island did the handiwork for them at the shanty.

| 1 | 2 | 3 | 4 | 5 | 6 | 7 | 8 | 9 | 10 | 11 | 12 | 13 | 14 |

126b ▶ 25 *Format Documents: Letters with Special Features*

2 plain full sheets

Review the formatting guides for correspondence with special features on p. 222.

Letter 1 (LL: 1½" SM; line 12)
Format and key the letter on p. 223 in modified block format, giving careful attention to the placement of the special features. Proofread and circle errors. Keep the copy to use as a model in the next lesson.

Letter 2
Rekey the letter on p. 223 in block format with open punctuation. Make the changes listed at the right. Proofread and circle errors.

Addressee:
Ms. Robin A. McIntyre
Mahoney Medical Center
2457 Baltimore Street
Mesa, AZ 85203-6493
Salutation: **Dear Ms. McIntyre**

126c ▶ 10 *Check Language Skills: Capitalization*

SS sentences; DS between groups of sentences

Key line number (with period); space twice, then key the sentence, supplying the needed capital letters.

If time permits, key the sentences again to increase decision-making speed.

1. dr. dixon indicated he would spend three days in washington, d.c.
2. she will be in orlando on wednesday and in jacksonville on thursday.
3. their convention will be held in april, the week before passover.
4. christmas day is on sunday and new year's eve is on saturday.
5. was the boston tea party part of the american revolution?
6. during june the carne art gallery will display work by botticelli.
7. the art gallery is in king towers, located on hollywood boulevard.
8. ms. j. b. keynes will speak at the next delta kappa gamma meeting.
9. the company president will meet with division managers on friday.
10. mrs. jay told me that president ruiz will be at the board meeting.
11. they will see the grand canyon during their trip to arizona.
12. they hired dr. kellee harper who has a ph.d. in chemistry.
13. greenwich village is located in new york city in manhattan.
14. the two major sponsors were anderson printing and carling realty.
15. one of the world war I treaty signings was held in versailles.

126d ▶ 10 *Improve Language Skills: Word Choice*

Study the definition and spelling of each word. Read the **Learn** sentence. Key the **Learn** sentence (with number and period) and the **Apply** sentences (with number and period), selecting the proper word in parentheses to complete each sentence correctly.

might (vb) used to express permission, probability, and possibility

mite (n) tiny insects, a very little; bit

accept (vb) to receive, to give approval, to take

except (vb) to exclude

Learn 1. He might be able to exchange the flour containing mites.
Apply 2. It (might, mite) cost more to fix the machine than to replace it.
Apply 3. It was not the first (might, mite) she had found in her food.

Learn 4. I believe they will accept all of the revisions except for Unit 5.
Apply 5. Mary is available every day (accept, except) Friday.
Apply 6. Tom will attend the banquet to (accept, except) the award.

37a ▶ 6
Conditioning Practice

each line twice SS; then a
1' writing on line 3; find *gwam*

alphabet   1   Bowman fixed prized clocks that seven judges say are unique.

figures   2   Only 1,473 of the 6,285 members were at the 1990 convention.

easy   3   She lent the field auditor a hand with the work of the firm.

| 1 | 2 | 3 | 4 | 5 | 6 | 7 | 8 | 9 | 10 | 11 | 12 |

37b ▶ 20 Learn ' (Apostrophe) and " (Quotation Mark)

Apostrophe: The ' is to the right of ; and is controlled by the *right little finger.*

Quotation mark: Key " (the shift of ') with the *right little finger.* Remember to depress the left shift before striking ".

Learning procedure

1. Locate new symbol on appropriate chart above. Read the reach technique given below the chart.

2. Key twice SS the appropriate pair of lines given at right; DS between pairs.

3. Repeat Steps 1 and 2 for the other new symbol.

4. Key twice SS lines 5-8.

5. If time permits, rekey the lines with which you had difficulty.

Language skills note
Capitalize the first and all important words in titles of publications.

Learn ' (apostrophe)

1   ; ; '; '; ;; '' ;'; ;'; it's he's I'm I've It's hers, I see.
2   I'm not sure if it's Hal's; but if it's his, I'll return it.

Learn " (quotation mark)

3   ; ; "; "; ;; "" ;"; ;"; "Keep on," she said, but I had quit.
4   I read "Ode on a Grecian Urn," "The Last Leaf," and "Trees."

Combine ' and "

5   "If it's Jan's or Al's," she said, "I'll bring it to class."
6   "Its" is an adjective; "it's" is the contraction of "it is."
7   Miss Uhl said, "To make numbers plural, add 's: 8's, 10's."
8   O'Shea said, "Use ' (apostrophe) to shorten phrases: I'll."

Alternative practice

On some keyboards, ' is the shift of **8** and " is the shift of **2**. If these are the locations of ' and " on your keyboard, key each set of lines at right twice SS; then key each of lines 5-8 in 37b, above, twice SS.

apostrophe   1   k k 'k 'k kk '' k'k k'k Is this tie Ike's? No, it's Dick's.
  2   On Vic's keyboard the ' is on 8; on Lei's, it's in home row.

quotation mark   3   s s "s "s ss "" s"s s"s 2" 2" "Go for a high goal," he said.
  4   Did Mrs. Negron use "there" for "their" and "two" for "too"?

SOFTWARE SPECIALISTS
4501 MONARCH STREET • DALLAS, TX 75204-3011
(214) 683-4012

Line 12 September 16, 19-- DS   4   4

Mailing notation   SPECIAL DELIVERY DS   7   7

Attention line   Attention Ms. Dyane E. Ellsworth   14   14
Remington Associates   18   18
784 Winterhaven Drive   22   22
Mesa, AZ 85203-8563 DS   27   27

Ladies and Gentlemen: DS   31   31

Subject line   Subject: Desktop Publishing Software DS   8   39

I enjoyed demonstrating the desktop publishing software   19   50
to you and members of your department yesterday. You   30   61
are fortunate to work with such progressive and enthusi-   41   72
astic individuals.   45   76

Based on our discussion, I am convinced that your de-   55   86
partment is ready to move into the area of desktop pub-   66   97
lishing. The professional image that your company is   77   108
trying to project will be greatly enhanced through the   88   119
use of such software.   93   124

After you have had an opportunity to review the material   104   135
you received, I would like to discuss further with you   115   146
and members of your staff the advantages/disadvantages   126   157
of each package. Before the end of the month, I will   137   168
call you to arrange a time.   142   173

Sincerely, DS   4   178

Company name   SOFTWARE SPECIALISTS QS   10   184

Richard R. Mathews

Richard R. Mathews   16   190
Software Consultant DS   22   196

xx DS   23   196

Enclosure notation   Enclosures: Price List   28   201
Brochure DS   29   203

Copy notation   c Gregory P. Schultz DS   34   207

Postscript   Should you have any questions that you would like an-   44   218
swered prior to our meeting, call me at (813) 839-4899.   55   229

Letter with Special Features

64

37c ▶ 10 Improve Language Skills: Capitalization

1. Read the first rule highlighted in color.

2. Key the **Learn** sentences below it, noting how the rule has been applied.

3. Key the **Apply** sentences, supplying the appropriate capitalization.

4. Practice the other rule in the same way.

5. If time permits, key the **Apply** lines again at a faster speed.

> Capitalize the first word of a direct quotation unless the quote is built into the structure of the sentence.

Learn 1 Yu-lan quoted the rule: "Spell the hour used with o'clock."
Learn 2 I didn't say that "making more errors makes us more human."

Apply 3 Kathleen quoted Pope: "to err is human, to forgive divine."
Apply 4 Ms. Ohms said to "Keep your eyes on the copy as you key."

> Capitalize the first word of the first part of an interrupted quotation, but not the first word of the second part.

Learn 5 "To reduce errors," he said, "drop back slightly in speed."
Apply 6 "curve your fingers," she urged, "and keep them upright."

37d ▶ 14 Improve Keyboarding Technique

1. Key each pair of lines once as shown: SS with a DS between pairs.

2. Take two 1' writings on line 11 and on line 12; find *gwam* on each writing.

3. If time permits, rekey the slower line.

Technique goals
- curved, upright fingers
- quick-snap keystrokes
- quiet hands and arms

shift-key sentences
1 He and Vi crossed the English Channel from Hove to Le Havre.
2 J. W. Posner has left Madrid for Turin for some Alps skiing.

fig/sym sentences
3 I signed a 20-year note--$67,495 (at 13.8%)--with Coe & Han.
4 Order #29105 reads: "16 sets of Cat. #4718A at $36.25/set."

adjacent-key sentences
5 We spent a quiet week at the shore prior to the open season.
6 If we buy her coffee shop, should we buy the gift shop, too?

long-reach sentences
7 My niece has a chance to bring the bronze trophy back to us.
8 We once had many mussels, but not since the recent harvests.

alphabetic sentences
9 Pam was quickly given the bronze trophy by six fussy judges.
10 Quent got six big jigsaw puzzles from the very dapper clerk.

easy sentences
11 Did he rush the rotor of the giant robot to the island firm?
12 The busy girl works with a fury to fix the signals by eight.

| 1 | 2 | 3 | 4 | 5 | 6 | 7 | 8 | 9 | 10 | 11 | 12 |

Lesson 38	___ and *	LL: 60 LS: SS

38a ▶ 6 Conditioning Practice

each line twice SS; then a 1' writing on line 3; find *gwam*

alphabet 1 Quig was just amazed by the next five blocks of his players.
figures 2 On October 30, 1991, the 287 members met from 5 to 6:45 p.m.
easy 3 Keith may hang the sign by the antique door of the big hall.

| 1 | 2 | 3 | 4 | 5 | 6 | 7 | 8 | 9 | 10 | 11 | 12 |

38b ▶ 14 Improve Keyboarding Technique

1. Key lines 1-12 of 37d, above, once SS as shown; DS between pairs.

2. Take two 1' writings on line 11 and one on line 12; find *gwam* on each writing.

Goals: • to refine technique
• to increase speed.

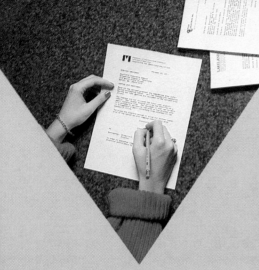

Process Correspondence with Special Features

Learning Goals

1. To learn to format and process letters with special features such as mailing notation, attention line, subject line, company name in closing lines, multiple enclosures, copy notation, and postscript.

2. To learn to format letter addresses with long lines.

3. To check/improve language skills.

Format Guides

1. Paper guide at *0* (for typewriters).

2. LL: 70 spaces for drills and ¶s; as specified in placement table for letters, p. 76.

3. LS: SS for drill lines and letters, unless otherwise directed.

4. PI: 5 spaces, when appropriate.

FORMATTING GUIDES: CORRESPONDENCE WITH SPECIAL FEATURES

On occasion you will find several special features used in business letters. These features are illustrated in the model letter on page 223. In some cases, alternative formats for special parts are chosen (for example, the subject line may be placed in various positions). The simplest and most efficient formats, however, are illustrated in this unit.

Mailing notations. Mailing notations (REGISTERED, CERTIFIED, SPECIAL DELIVERY or AIRMAIL) begin at the left margin in ALL CAPS a double space below the dateline and a double space above the first line of the letter address. (Note: AIRMAIL is used only on foreign mail.)

Attention line. When an attention line is used in a letter addressed to a company, key it as the first line of the letter and envelope address:

Attention Personnel Officer
InfoMaster Office Equipment, Inc.
3200 Erie Avenue
Cincinnati, OH 45208-2837

When a letter is addressed to a company, the correct salutation is "Ladies and Gentlemen," even though an attention line may name an individual.

Subject line. Place the subject line a double space below the salutation. If the body paragraphs are blocked, block the subject line at the left margin. If the body paragraphs are indented, indent the subject line the same number of spaces or center it. The word "Subject" may be used. If used, follow the word "Subject" by a colon and two spaces before completing the subject line.

Company name. When used, place the company name a double space below the complimentary close in ALL CAPS. QS (quadruple-space) to signature line.

Enclosure notation. Place enclosure (or attachment) notation a double space

below reference initials. If multiple enclosures are referred to in the letter, follow the word "Enclosures" with a colon and two spaces and list each enclosure.

Enclosures: Quarterly Report
             Travel Expenses

Copy notation. A copy notation indicates that a copy of a letter is being sent to someone other than the addressee. Use "c" followed by the name of the person(s) to receive a copy. Place copy notation a double space below the last line of the enclosure notation or the reference line if there is no enclosure.

c Claudia Gullikson
  Dale Ogden
  Roberto Griffin

Postscript. A postscript is an additional paragraph that may be added after a letter has been completed. It is the last item in the letter. Begin a postscript a double space below the preceding item. Use the same paragraph format (indented or blocked) as the body paragraphs.

Notes. Long lines in the letter address may be carried to the next line even with the left margin.

In both the letter address and closing lines, professional titles may be placed on the same line as the name separated by a comma or placed on the following line without a comma.

Ms. Karen M. Ming, Executive Director
                  or
Ms. Karen M. Ming
Executive Director

Use the form which gives the best balance and attractiveness.

When several special features are used in a letter, the dateline may be raised to present a more attractive appearance on the page. Generally, raise the dateline one line for each two special-feature lines used.

38c ▶ 18 Learn __ (Underline) and * (Asterisk)

Underline: Key __ (the shift of -) with the *right little finger*. Remember to depress the left shift before striking __ .

Asterisk: Key * (the shift of **8**) with the *right second finger*. Remember to depress the left shift before striking *.

Learning procedure

1. Locate new key on appropriate chart above. Read the reach technique given below the chart.

2. Key twice SS the appropriate pair of lines given at right; DS between pairs.

3. Repeat Steps 1 and 2 for the other new key.

4. Key twice SS lines 5-6.

5. If time permits, rekey the lines with which you had difficulty.

Note: If you are using a computer, insert the proper codes for underlining.

Learn __ (underline)

> Key the word; backspace to beginning to underline it.

1 ; ; _; _; ;; _ _ ;_; ;_; We are to underline <u>ready</u> and <u>begin</u>.
2 To <u>succeed</u>, you should <u>plan</u> the work and then <u>work</u> the plan.

Learn * (asterisk)

3 k k *k *k kk ** k*k k*k She used * for a single source note.
4 All discounted items show an *, thus: 48K*, 588*, and 618*.

Combine __ and *

5 Use an * to mark often-confused words such as <u>then</u> and <u>than</u>.
6 *Note: Book titles (like <u>Lorna Doone</u>) are often <u>underlined</u>.

38d ▶ 12
Check/Improve Keyboarding Skill

1. A 1′ writing on each ¶; find *gwam* on each.

2. A 2′ writing on ¶s 1-2 combined; find *gwam*.

3. An additional 1′ writing on each ¶; find *gwam*.

4. An additional 2′ writing on ¶s 1-2 combined; find *gwam*.

5. If time permits, take a 3′ writing on ¶s 1-2 combined; find *gwam*.

1′ gwam goals
▽ 25 = acceptable
▫ 29 = average
⊙ 33 = good
◇ 37 = excellent

all letters used | LA | 1.4 si | 5.4 awl | 85% hfw

	gwam 2′	3′
One reason we learn to key is to be able to apply that	6	4
skill as we format personal and business documents--letters,	12	8
reports, and tables, for example. Your next major goal will	18	12
be to learn the rules that govern how we arrange, place, and	24	16
space the most commonly used documents.	28	18
In one way or another, we must memorize the features	33	22
that distinguish one style of letter or report from another.	39	26
Our ability to retain in our minds the vital details will	45	30
help us place and space documents quickly and avoid having	51	34
to look up such facts as we key letters or reports.	56	37

gwam 2′ | 1 | 2 | 3 | 4 | 5 | 6 |
3′ | 1 | 2 | 3 | 4 |

PHASE 6 PROCESS SPECIAL DOCUMENTS

In the 25 lessons of Phase 6, you will:

1. Improve basic keyboarding and language skills.

2. Learn to format letters with special features, formal memorandums, forms, and employment documents.

3. Compose at the keyboard.

4. Enhance decision-making skills.

5. Apply formatting skills to process information for a firm that markets computer-aided educational products.

6. Measure and evaluate document processing skills.

The ¶s are counted internally for 1' guided and unguided writings and at the side and bottom for 2' and 3' measurement writings. The ¶s may be used whenever additional timed writing practice is desired.

1. Take a 1' writing on ¶ 1; determine *gwam*.

2. Add 4 *gwam* to set a new goal rate.

3. Take two 1' writings on ¶ 1, trying to maintain your goal rate each 1/4 minute.

4. Key ¶ 2 in the same way.

5. Take a 2' unguided writing on each ¶. If you complete a ¶ before time is called, begin that ¶ again.

6. Take a 3' writing on ¶s 1-2 combined; determine *gwam*.

gwam	¼'	½'	¾'	Time
16	4	8	12	16
20	5	10	15	20
24	6	12	18	24
28	7	14	21	28
32	8	16	24	32
36	9	18	27	36
40	10	20	30	40
44	11	22	33	44
48	12	24	36	48

all letters used | LA | 1.4 si | 5.4 awl | 85% hfw

	gwam 2'	3'
When you need to adjust to a new situation in which new	6	4
people are involved, be quick to recognize that at first it	12	8
is you who must adapt. This is especially true in an office	18	12
where the roles of workers have already been established. It	24	16
is your job to fit into the team structure with harmony.	30	20
Learn the rules of the game and who the key players are;	6	23
then play according to those rules at first. Do not expect	12	27
to have the rules modified to fit your concept of what the	18	31
team structure and your role in it should be. Only after you	24	36
become a valuable member should you suggest major changes.	30	39

gwam 2' | 1 | 2 | 3 | 4 | 5 | 6
gwam 3' | 1 | 2 | 3 | 4

plain full sheets; begin on line 24

1. Clear tabs; set a tab at center point.

2. Set line spacing to DS.

3. Center each line of the first announcement.

4. Center each line of the second announcement, correcting errors as marked.

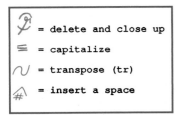

= delete and close up
= capitalize
= transpose (tr)
= insert a space

Announcement 1

SUPER SAVER SALE

Up to 35% Off

Rings, Necklaces, Bracelets

at

THE GEM SHOP

December 1 through 15

10 a.m.-6 p.m.

Towne Shopping Center

Announcement 2

SCHOOL OF PERFORMMING ARTS

presents

"The Mouse that Roared"

on

January 21 and 22

2:30 and 8:00 p.m.

Marx Theatre

Matinee: $4.50; Evening: $5.50

125c ▶ 37
Evaluate Table Processing Skills

Time Schedule
Plan and prepare .... 4'
Document processing ....25'
Proofread/compute n-pram....... 8'

correct all errors

Table 1
plain full sheet; short edge at top; CS: 8; DS data; center all headings

FILE RETENTION SCHEDULE 5

Adopted January 19-- 9

File	Years Retained	
Accounts payable	5	24
Accounts receivable	5	29
Annual reports	permanent	34
Articles of incorporation	permanent	41
Bank statements	7	45
Bids	3	48
Contracts (employee)	permanent	54
General correspondence	3	60
		63

Source: Administrative Information Systems, 1987. 80

Table 2
plain full sheet; short edge at top; CS: 6; SS data; center all headings

SALES DEPARTMENT BUDGET PERFORMANCE 7

Month Ended July 31, 19-- 12

Expense Item	Budget Allocation	Amount Spent	
Salaries	$18,600	$18,450	34
Benefits	4,985	4,857	38
Supplies	1,125	1,250	43
Telephone	650	595	48
Postage	475	515	52
Travel	3,275	3,075	59
Totals	$29,110	$28,742	65

Table 3
plain full sheet; short edge at top; CS: 8; DS data; center all headings

Table 4
If time permits, reformat Table 1 on a half sheet with short edge at top; CS: 6; DS data; center all headings.

Accounting Department 4

Proposed Salary Increases for 19-- 11

Employee	Cost of Living Increase	Merit Increase	New Salary	
				18
Sandra Morris	$1,500	$ 900	$ 32,400	34 / 42
Jane Raleigh	1,140	1,140	25,080	48
William Bossey	990	792	21,582	55
Rita Perez	945	850	20,695	61
Hiro Hito	930	1,116	20,646	67
Harry Kaskie	500	450	12,950	78
Totals	$6,005	$5,248	$133,353	85

Learn to Format Personal-Business Correspondence

Learning Goals

1. To learn how to format personal-business letters in block style.

2. To learn how to format simplified memos in block style.

3. To learn how to divide words correctly at line endings.

4. To improve basic keyboarding skills.

Format Guides

1. *Paper guide* at *0* (for typewriters).

2. LL: 60 spaces or as directed for documents; see *Get Ready to Keyboard: Typewriters* (p. x) or *Computers* (p. xii).

3. LS: SS except when formatting special parts of letters and memos which require DS and QS.

FORMATTING GUIDES: LETTERS AND MEMORANDUMS IN BLOCK STYLE

Personal-Business Letter

Simplified Memorandum

Block Format

When *all* lines of a letter or memorandum begin at the left margin (LM) as shown in the illustrated models, the document is arranged in *block format* (style). Block format is easy to learn and easy to arrange. It is widely used for both personal and business correspondence.

Parts of a Personal-Business Letter

The basic parts of personal-business letters (those written by individuals to conduct business) are described below in order of their occurrence. (See model letter on p. 70.)

Return address. The return address consists of a line for the street address and one for the city, state, and ZIP Code. Key the street address (or post office box or route number) on line 14 from the top edge of the sheet; key the city, state name abbreviation, and ZIP Code on line 15.

Date. Key the date (month, day, and year) a single space (SS) below the last line of the return address.

Letter address. Begin the letter address on the fourth line space (QS) below the date. If the letter is addressed to a company, the address *may* include an attention line (the first line of the address) to call the letter to the attention of a specific person, department, or job title.

Salutation. Key the salutation (greeting) a double space (DS) below the letter address.

Body. Begin the letter body (message) a DS below the salutation. Block the paragraphs (¶s) of the body and SS them with a DS between ¶s.

Complimentary close. Key the complimentary close (farewell) a DS below the last line of the body.

Name of writer. Key the name of the writer (the originator of the message) a QS below the complimentary close. The name may be preceded by a personal title such as *Miss, Mrs.,* or *Ms.* to indicate how a female prefers to be addressed in a response.

Enclosure notation. An enclosure notation indicates that something other than the letter is included in the envelope. When appropriate, key the word *Enclosure* or *Enclosures* a DS below the name of the writer.

Parts of a Simplified Memorandum

Simplified memorandums are often used as a quick and easy means of written communication between members of clubs, by schools for making announcements and summarizing information, and by people who frequently exchange information. (See model memorandum on p. 74.)

The parts of simplified memorandums are described below in order of their occurrence. By eliminating the address of the addressee, the salutation, and the complimentary close, the simplified memo format saves time and reduces opportunity for error.

Date. Key the date (month, day, and year) on line 10 from the top edge of a full sheet or on line 6 of a half sheet.

Name of addressee. Key the name(s) of the person(s) to receive the memo a QS below the date. No personal title(s) should be used before the name(s), but an official title (such as *Principal* or *President*) may follow a name, preceded by a comma.

Subject. The subject line specifies the topic discussed in the memo. Key the subject line in ALL CAPS a DS below the name of the addressee.

Body. Block the ¶s in the body (message) a DS below the subject line. SS the ¶s with a DS between them.

Name of writer. Key the name of the writer a QS below the last line of the body. A personal title does not precede the name, but an official title may follow it, preceded by a comma.

Reference initials. If the keyboard operator is not the writer of the message, key the operator's initials (lowercased) a DS below the name of the writer.

Attachment/enclosure notation. If a supporting document is attached to the memo, key an attachment notation a DS below the name of the writer (or below the reference initials, if any). If the enclosure is not attached to the memo, use the word *Enclosure* rather than *Attachment.*

[1]Joyce Kupsch and Sandra Whitcomb, **The Electronic Office** (Mission Hills, CA: Glencoe Publishing Company, 1987), p. 131.

[2]Arnold Rosen, **Telecommunications** (San Diego: Harcourt Brace Jovanovich, Publishers, 1987), p. 4.

[3]Thomas Keller and Ernest N. Savage, **Administrative Information Systems** (Boston: Kent Publishing Company, 1987), p. 68.

[4]Susie H. VanHuss and Willard R. Daggett, Jr., **Electronic Information Systems** (Cincinnati: South-Western Publishing Co., 1990), pp. 307-308.

Document 2
Bibliography

Keller, Thomas and Ernest N. Savage. **Administrative Information Systems.** Boston: Kent Publishing Company, 1987.

Kupsch, Joyce and Sandra Whitcomb. **The Electronic Office.** Mission Hills, CA: Glencoe Publishing Company, 1987.

Rosen, Arnold. **Telecommunications.** San Diego: Harcourt Brace Jovanovich, Publishers, 1987.

VanHuss, Susie H. and Willard R. Daggett, Jr. **Electronic Information Systems.** Cincinnati: South-Western Publishing Co., 1990.

words

Networking. Networking is a relatively new technology that is rapidly 207
changing the way information can be transmitted from one place to an- 221
other. Networking can link telecommunication equipment (telephones, com- 235
puters, teletypewriters, facsimile units, copiers, etc.) to each other so that 251
information can be transmitted between people in the same office or build- 265
ing or another building in the same or different country. 277

Electronic mail. Electronic mail includes Telex and TWX services, elec- 294
tronic messaging on communicating computer systems, facsimile units, and 309
intelligent copiers and printers. 316

Teleconferencing. VanHuss and Daggett[4] describe teleconferencing as 333
follows: 335

Teleconferencing is an electronic meeting of individuals in different lo- 349
cations.... Teleconferencing is not used very extensively. Perhaps the 365
major reason is that teleconferencing requires a significant change in the 380
behavior of those participating. 386

Listed below are three basic forms of telecommunicating which can be 400
used separately or in combination with each other. 411

1. Audio teleconferencing--transmission of voices. 421

2. Written teleconferencing--transmission of keyboarded messages by 435
way of connected computer terminals. 443

3. Video teleconferencing--transmission of still or full motion pictures. 458

Telecommunication Carriers 467

Various carriers are used to telecommunicate information from place to 483
place. Common carriers include telephone wires, coaxial cables, fiber op- 497
tics, microwaves, and satellites. 504

124c ▶ 8
Evaluate Straight-Copy Skill

1. Take a 5' writing on 123b, p. 216.

2. Determine *gwam* and number of errors.

3. Record *gwam* and errors; compare to scores on 123b.

| Lesson 125 | Evaluate Table Processing/Straight-Copy Skills |

125a ▶ 5
Conditioning Practice

each line twice SS (slowly, then faster); DS between 2-line groups; if time permits, rekey lines 1 and 4

alphabet 1 Becky poured the liquid wax from the old jug into a dozen glass vials.

figures 2 I had 489 points, 160 rebounds, 57 assists, and 36 steals in 24 games.

fig/sym 3 The computers will cost $34,679 (less discounts of 20%, 15%, and 18%).

speed 4 The rich widow and the maid may make the usual visit to the city dock.

| 1 | 2 | 3 | 4 | 5 | 6 | 7 | 8 | 9 | 10 | 11 | 12 | 13 | 14 |

125b ▶ 8
Evaluate Straight-Copy Skill

1. Take a 5' writing on 123b, p. 216.

2. Determine *gwam* and number of errors.

3. Record *gwam* and errors; compare to scores on 123b and 124c.

39a ▶ 6
Conditioning Practice

each line twice SS; then a
1' writing on line 3; find *gwam*

alphabet 1 Jake led a big blitz which saved the next play for my squad.

fig/sym 2 Beth has ordered 26 5/8 yards of #304 linen at $7.19 a yard.

speed 3 Good form is the key if all of us wish to make the big goal.

| 1 | 2 | 3 | 4 | 5 | 6 | 7 | 8 | 9 | 10 | 11 | 12 |

39b ▶ 9 Improve Language Skills: Word Division

1. Read each rule and key the **Learn** and **Apply** lines beneath it.

Note: As you key the **Apply** lines, insert a hyphen in each word at the point (if any) where the word can best be divided.

2. Check with your teacher the accuracy of your **Apply** lines; if time permits, rekey the **Apply** lines in which you made word-division errors.

Divide a word only between syllables; words of one syllable, therefore, should not be divided.

Learn 1 per-sons, through, in-come, straight, pur-pose, con-tracts
Apply 2 expects, brought, control, methods, thoughts, practice

Do not separate a one-letter syllable at the beginning of a word or a one- or two-letter syllable at the end of a word.

Learn 3 ideal, prior, ready, ahead, around, event, lengthy, ef-fort
Apply 4 again, early, party, ideal, quickly, about, adhere, enough

Divide a word between double consonants except when adding a syllable to a word that ends in double letters.

Learn 5 mat-ters, writ-ten, sud-denly, add-ing, will-ing, run-ning
Apply 6 summer, college, carried, current, telling, stopping

39c-40c ▶ 35 (daily)
Format Personal-Business Letters in Block Style

plain full sheets
LL: 60 spaces
LS: single
PB: line 14

1. Study the formatting guides for personal-business letters on p. 68 and the model letter illustrating block format on p. 70. Note the vertical and horizontal placement of letter parts and the spacing between them.

2. On a plain full sheet, format and key line-for-line a copy of the letter on p. 70. Do not correct your errors as you key.

3. Proofread your copy of the letter and mark it for correction. (See list of proofreader's marks on Reference Guide p. RG10 at back of book.)

4. Format and key the letter again from your own copy, errors corrected.

5. If time permits, begin processing the letters on p. 71. Save any partially completed letter to finish during the next class period. Correct your errors as you key.

40a ▶ 6
Conditioning Practice

each line twice SS; then a
1' writing on line 3; find *gwam*

alphabet 1 Jacki had won first place by solving my tax quiz in an hour.

fig/sym 2 Our 1990 profit was $58,764 (up 23% from the previous year).

speed 3 Roddy may sign the six forms and work with the city auditor.

| 1 | 2 | 3 | 4 | 5 | 6 | 7 | 8 | 9 | 10 | 11 | 12 |

123c (continued)

Document 3
Long Letter

modified block format; PI: 5; mixed punctuation; use **current date;** use following address in ALL CAP, unpunctuated format

DR FERNANDO L RUIZ
DEAN SCHOOL OF BUSINESS
ELLIS UNIVERSITY
8975 EDEN AVENUE
ST LOUIS MO 63123-3244

Use **OFFICE OF THE FUTURE** as a subject line.

Document 4
Average Letter

If you finish Documents 1-3 before time is called, rekey Document 2 on p. 217 in block format, open punctuation; use plain full sheet.

opening lines 27

Our school district is planning to implement an "Office of the Future" program in the business education department. The main purpose of this project is to develop an exemplary business education curriculum and facility which will enable our faculty to prepare students who will work in high-tech environments. — 41 / 56 / 70 / 85 / 89

To meet this purpose, we need to secure the expertise of various agencies outside the public school sector. Since extensive curriculum revision is likely to be a major part of this project, we request that you appoint three faculty members to serve on a steering committee. They will be joined by five representatives from business and three of our business education teachers. — 104 / 120 / 136 / 151 / 166

The first meeting of the steering committee will be scheduled early next month. The meeting will be held in our senior high school and will provide an opportunity for the committee members to meet each other, review our curriculum, and tour the business education facilities. — 180 / 195 / 210 / 221

We are looking forward to hearing from you at your earliest convenience and having your college become a partner in this exciting project. — 236 / 249

Sincerely | Dr. Yolanda K. Degini | Superintendent | xx — 259/279

Lesson 124   *Evaluate Report Processing/Straight-Copy Skills*

124a ▶ 5
Conditioning Practice

each line twice SS (slowly, then faster); DS between 2-line groups; if time permits, rekey lines 1 and 4

alphabet	1	Mary's parents will quickly join Geoff to criticize both taxi drivers.
figures	2	Bad weather canceled 35 flights with 2,460 passengers on June 7, 1989.
fig/sym	3	Parsit & Brown received Model #239-089/A with Serial #465-17-40 today.
speed	4	Dirk may hand the girls eight shamrocks when they are at their formal.

| 1 | 2 | 3 | 4 | 5 | 6 | 7 | 8 | 9 | 10 | 11 | 12 | 13 | 14 |

124b ▶ 37
Evaluate Report Processing Skills:

Time Schedule
Plan and prepare .... 4'
Document processing .... 25'
Proofread/compute *n-pram* ... 8'

Document 1
Leftbound Report with Footnotes

Format the document shown at the right and on the next page as a leftbound report with footnotes. Correct errors as you key. Footnotes are listed in the left margin on p. 219.

words

TELECOMMUNICATIONS

4

Every time you speak on the telephone, watch television, or listen to the radio you benefit from telecommunications technology. Similarly, those who use a telephone, microcomputer network, teletypewriter, or facsimile unit to conduct business also benefit from telecommunications.[1] — 19 / 33 / 48 / 61

Telecommunications Defined

71

Telecommunications is "a technology that provides for the movement of information between two locations by electronic means."[2] The information that is transmitted can be sounds, pictures, or data in the form of words and/or numbers.[3] — 85 / 99 / 115 / 118

Common Methods of Telecommunicating

133

Telegraph services were the principal means of sending messages quickly between distant points until the 1850's. After the invention of the telephone, it became the chief way to transmit voice messages. Recent developments in computer communications provide new methods of communicating. — 147 / 163 / 178 / 191

2 SPACES

			words in parts	total words
Return address	2274 Cogswell Road ▼ Line 14		4	4
	El Monte, CA 91732-3846		9	9
Date	October 15, 19--		12	12

Quadruple-space (QS):
strike return key 4 times

Letter address	Mrs. Alice M. Wiggins		17	17
	11300 Lower Azusa Road		21	21
	El Monte, CA 91732-4725		26	26

Double-space (DS):
strike return key twice

| Salutation | Dear Mrs. Wiggins DS | | 30 | 30 |

Body	The El Monte PTA is devoting its next meeting to the important	13	42
	topic "Computer Literacy." The meeting is on November 18 and	25	55
	begins at 7 p.m. DS	29	59

Our speaker will be Dr. Mark C. Gibson. For the past several — 41 | 71
years, he has written the "Personal Computer" column in the — 53 | 83
Los Angeles Post. His talk will combine wisdom and wit. DS — 68 | 98

To assure Dr. Gibson a large audience, we are asking selected — 80 | 110
members to bring as guests two parents who are not active mem- — 93 | 123
bers of our group. Please use the enclosed return card to — 105 | 134
give me the names of your guests by November 1. DS — 114 | 144

I shall appreciate your assistance. DS — 121 | 152

Complimentary close	Cordially yours QS	3	155

Laura J. Marsh

Writer	Ms. Laura J. Marsh DS	7	159
Enclosure notation	Enclosure	9	160

Shown in pica (10-pitch)
type on a 60-space line,
photo-reduced

Personal-Business Letter in Block Format

123c ▶ 37
Evaluate Letter Processing Skills

Time Schedule

Plan and prepare	4'
Document processing	25'
Proofread/compute *n-pram*	8'

1. Arrange materials for ease of handling. (LP pp. 75-79 and one plain full sheet)

2. Format and key Documents 1-4 for 25'. Proofread and correct errors before removing paper from machine.

3. After time is called, proofread again and circle any uncorrected errors. Compute *n-pram.*

Document 1
Short Letter

block format; open punctuation; address envelope

Document 2
Average Letter

modified block format; block ¶s; mixed punctuation; address envelope

Date the letter **May 27, 19--.**
Address the letter to

Attention Customer Relations
Haynes and Jones, Inc.
1697 Wilson Avenue
Ames, IA 50010-5365

Close the letter

Henrietta J. Hadley, M.D.

xx

Enclosure

Add the following postscript:

I have bought many other electronic appliances from your store; this is the first time I have been dissatisfied.

Document 3 is on p. 218.

May 15, 19-- | Mr. Gene M. Sakely | Highlands High School | 700 Elm Street | 14
Muncie, IN   47302-2346 | Dear Mr. Sakely   22

Thank you for inviting me to the "Career Planning" conference that was held   37
at your school last week. The session topics were relevant and all the pre-   52
senters were excellent.   57

The panel of recent graduates was the highlight of the day for me. Their   72
remarks on college studies and the first few months of employment were   86
very enlightening.   90

The conference will benefit my students, too, because it provided me with   105
information about careers I can share with them.   115

Sincerely | Ms. Anita B. Redacki | Business Educator | xx | c Dr. Geraldine W.   129
Greene, Principal   132/148

---

words

opening lines 21

25

Ladies and Gentlemen:

Enclosed is a copy of my receipt for the stereo sys-   36
tem I purchased at your East Mall store. The system   46
includes an AM/FM radio, cassette player/recorder,   56
compact disc player, and two speakers.   64

I am very satisfied with the system except for   74
one of the speakers. It seems that a bass speaker   84
in one of them has developed a small tear which   94
distorts the sound. The salesperson who sold me   103
the system indicated that tears are not covered   113
by the one-year limited warranty.   120

While I suspect the tear was caused by de-   128
fective speaker material, I cannot prove it. I can   139
assure you, however, that it was not a result   148
of unreasonable use or improper care by me.   157

Will you please authorize a new speaker so   165
my patients can enjoy the excellent sound the   175
system produced when it was installed.   182

Sincerely yours,   186

closing lines 216/**234**

40b ▶ 9 Improve Language Skills: Word Division

1. Read each rule and key the **Learn** and **Apply** lines beneath it.

Note: As you key the **Apply** lines, insert a hyphen in each word at the point (if any) where the word can best be divided.

2. Check with your teacher the accuracy of your **Apply** lines; if time permits, rekey the **Apply** lines in which you made word-division errors.

> Divide a word after a single-letter vowel syllable that is not a part of a word ending.

Learn 1 ori-ent, usu-ally, vari-ous, sepa-rate, genu-ine, situ-ated
Apply 2 editor, educate, holiday, evaluate, celebrate, maximum

> Divide a word before the word endings -able, -ible, -acle, -ical, and -ily when the vowel **a** or **i** is a separate syllable.

Learn 3 mir-acle, heart-ily, prob-able, convert-ible, opti-cal
Apply 4 edible, handily, lyrical, tropical, variable, musical

> Do not divide a word that contains a contraction (a word in which one or more omitted letters have been replaced by an apostrophe).

Learn 5 we've, didn't, hadn't, you're, haven't, they'll, couldn't
Apply 6 we'll, hasn't, you'll, you've, aren't, doesn't, shouldn't

---

39c-40c ▶ 35 (continued)

4-27-98

1. Continue processing the series of personal-business letters given below and on p. 72. See 39c-40c, p. 69, for formatting guides. Color verticals indicate line endings.

2. Before removing a letter from the machine, proofread it and correct any errors.

Letter 1 · words

5802 Lehman Drive	4
Colorado Springs, CO 80918-1123	10
October 20, 19--	14

QS

Ms. Lorna K. Ryan, Director	19
Placement Services, Inc.	24
350 E. Colfax Avenue	28
Denver, CO 80203-6285	33

DS

Dear Ms. Ryan · 36

DS

Today's <u>Times Star</u> quotes you as saying in a · 47
recent talk that | "more workers fail as a result · 56
of personal traits than because | of weak techni- · 66
cal skills." · 67

DS

I want to quote this statement in a paper I am · 78
writing titled | "Why Beginning Workers Fail," · 87
and I would like to know the | research studies · 96
to which you referred so that I can include | them · 106
in my reference list. · 111

DS

If you will send me the research references you · 120
used to sup- | port your statement, I shall be most · 130
grateful. I am sure the | references will be of · 139
great help to me in preparing my paper. · 147

DS

Sincerely yours · 151

QS

Edward R. Shields · 154

Letter 2 · words

2405 Siesta Avenue	4
Las Vegas, NV 89121-2683	9
October 22, 19--	12

Learning Tutor, Inc.	17
752 S. Bascom Avenue	21
San Jose, CA 95128-3605	26

Ladies and Gentlemen · 30

On October 8 I ordered from your fall catalog a · 40
copy of MATH | TUTOR IX (Catalog #A2937) de- · 48
signed for use on the Eureka GS. | I have had the · 57
diskette a week. · 61

I follow the booting instructions step-by-step · 70
but am unable | to boot the program on my · 78
Eureka GS. I took the diskette to | the store · 87
where I bought my computer, but the manager · 96
could | not boot the program on the same model · 105
computer. · 107

Will you please check the booting instructions · 117
in the User's | Guide to see if they are correct. · 127
If they are, please send a | replacement diskette · 136
and I will return the faulty one to you. · 145

Sincerely yours · 148

Miss Ellen M. Marcos · 152

Letters 3, 4, and 5 are on p. 72.

UNIT 28 LESSONS 123 – 125

Evaluate Letter, Report, and Table Processing Skills

Measurement Goals

1. To evaluate your ability to process tables, letters, and reports in correct format.

2. To measure your ability to key straight-copy material.

Format Guides

1. Paper guide at *0* (for typewriters).

2. LL: 70 spaces for drills and ¶s; as required for documents.

3. LS: SS drills; DS ¶s; as required for tables, letters, and reports.

4. PI: 5 spaces for ¶s and documents.

Lesson 123	Evaluate Straight-Copy/Letter Processing Skills

123a ▶ 5
Conditioning Practice

each line twice SS (slowly, then faster); DS between 2-line groups; if time permits, rekey lines 2 and 3

alphabet 1 Jim wants both freshmen guards to execute the zone press very quickly.

figures 2 They won the last three games by scores of 135-117; 102-94; and 80-76.

fig/sym 3 Ed called (505) 257-5980 before 1:15 p.m. and 413-6766 after 4:15 p.m.

speed 4 Pamela may name an official tutor to work for the widow and eight men.

| 1 | 2 | 3 | 4 | 5 | 6 | 7 | 8 | 9 | 10 | 11 | 12 | 13 | 14 |

123b ▶ 8
Evaluate Straight-Copy Skill

1. A 5' writing on all ¶s.

2. Determine *gwam* and number of errors.

3. Record *gwam* and errors to compare with 124c and 125b.

all letters used | A | 1.5 si | 5.7 awl | 80% hfw

gwam 3' | 5'

		gwam 3'	5'

A business is an entity that uses investment money, raw materials, `4` `3` `41`
and/or labor to make a profit or offer a service to consumers. The `9` `5` `43`
success of the business depends to a large extent on the management `14` `8` `46`
skills of the people who start, organize, and operate the business. `17` `10` `48`
The owners are certain to earn profits if the business is successful. `22` `13` `51`

All businesses should try to improve society. They can do this `26` `16` `54`
by selling quality products and services that are valued and demanded. `31` `19` `57`
A thriving business can be a way for a worker to earn an income, gain `36` `22` `60`
security, and grow as a person and as a professional. Also, a dutiful `41` `24` `62`
business can help by aiding civic affairs. `44` `26` `64`

In our country's economic system, the public plays a major part in `48` `29` `67`
determining which businesses will be successful and which ones will not. `53` `32` `70`
The public gets this critical part because it has the freedom to choose `58` `35` `73`
to buy or not to buy the goods and services that businesses bring to the `63` `38` `76`
marketplace. `63` `38` `76`

gwam 3' | 1 | 2 | 3 | 4 | 5 |
5' | 1 | 2 | 3 |

39c-40c (continued)

Letter 3 words

5209 W. Grand Avenue   4
Chicago, IL 60639-3372   9
October 23, 19--   12

Dr. Dallas T. Johnson   17
Drug Rehabilitation Center   22
4056 W. Melrose Street   27
Chicago, IL 60641-2940   32

Dear Dr. Johnson   35

With the approval of the principal of Columbus   44
High School, the Student Leadership Club is   53
sponsoring a series of assembly programs this   62
year dealing with student problems in learn-   71
ing and life. One of these student assemblies   81
will address the serious problem of teenage drug   90
abuse.   92

As chair of the program committee, I would es-   101
pecially like you, or a member of your staff, to   111
talk to us on this timely topic. A presentation   121
similar to the one you made last year on local   130
TV would be ideal.   134

Can you give us 45 minutes of your time on   143
Friday, March 10, at 10:15 a.m. We need your   152
help, and we will appreciate it. If you prefer   162
to call, my telephone number (after 4 p.m.) is   171
277-2048.   173

Sincerely yours   176

Juan F. Ramirez   179

Letter 4 words

11300 Lower Azusa Road   5
El Monte, CA 91732-4725   10
October 24, 19--   13

Ms. Laura J. Marsh   17
2274 Cogswell Road   21
El Monte, CA 91732-3846   26

Dear Ms. Marsh   29

How fortunate you are to have Dr. Mark C.   37
Gibson as a speaker for the November 18 meet-   46
ing of the El Monte PTA. If he speaks as well   55
as he writes, your meeting will be a success.   65

Because I strongly support the effort El Monte   74
schools are mak- ing to assure computer liter-   83
acy for all students, I would like to bring three   93
guests, not two, to the meeting. All three names   103
are listed on the enclosed card. If the limit is   113
two guests per member, please let me know.   122

We need parental support for the computer lit-   131
eracy program to be the success it should be.   140
You are to be commended for ar- ranging this   149
informative program for us.   155

Cordially yours   158

Mrs. Alice M. Wiggins   162

Enclosure   164

Letter 5

1. Format and key the handwritten copy as a personal-business letter in block style. Key it on a plain full sheet, line-for-line as shown.

2. Use your own **return address**; date the letter **October 25** of the **current year.**

3. Address the letter to:

Shutterbug Shops, Inc.
812 Olive Street
St. Louis, MO 63101-4460

4. Use your **full name** (first name, middle initial, and surname) in the closing lines. Females should include a personal title (Miss, Ms., or Mrs.).

words
opening lines 25

Ladies and Gentlemen   29

The enclosed copy of my credit card statement shows that you   42
have not yet issued a credit for the Lycon Camera (Catalog   53
#C288) that I returned to you more than three weeks ago.   65

Will you please check to see whether a credit of $137.95 has   77
now been issued; and, if not, see that it is issued promptly.   90
I wish to pay the invoice less the appropriate credit.   101

Sincerely yours/Enclosure   106

121b-122b (continued)

computing resources in Room 101 be upgraded 778
and used and that the room be named the Busi- 787
ness Technologies Computer Laboratory. When 796
completed, this room will be able to support in- 805
struction which utilizes word processing, data 815
base, graphics, spreadsheet, and communica- 823
tions computer software packages. 830

Evaluation and Grading 839

Students will be evaluated according to their 848
performance on written examinations, the qual- 857
ity and quantity of documents produced, and 866
classroom participation. Written examinations 876
will be given near the end of each grading 884
period, unannounced quizzes will be given pe- 893
riodically during each grading period, and re- 902
quired documents will be due throughout the 911
course. Grades will be computed based on the 920
following weighting: 924

1. Desktop publishing documents--50%. 932
2. Unannounced quizzes--10%. 939
3. Written examinations--30%. 945
4. Classroom participation--10%. 952

Conclusion 956

The business education faculty believes that 965
the desktop publishing course must be added to 975
the curriculum so the department can continue 984

to equip graduates with up-to-date skills and 993
knowledge they need to enter and perform well 1002
in the business world. 1007

Truly, desktop publishing is a technology 1015
whose time has come. It will have a signifi- 1024
cant impact on the way information is handled 1033
and presented and will become a productivity 1042
tool in most businesses. And, like all present 1052
computer applications in business education, 1061
the teaching of desktop publishing is being de- 1070
fined by those business teachers who are will- 1079
ing to experiment, test, fail periodically, and 1089
try again.[5] 1091

ENDNOTES 1093

1. Michael Antonoff, "Setting Up for Desk- 1102
top Publishing," Personal Computing, July 1987, 1115
p. 76. 1116

2. Janice Schoen, Henry and Heide R. 1124
Perrault, "Guidelines for Choosing and Using 1133
Desktop Publishing Software," Instructional 1144
Strategies, Winter 1989, p. 1. 1153

3. Rose Mary Wentling, "Desktop Publish- 1161
ing: A New Approach," Business Education 1173
Forum, March 1989, p. 29. 1179

4. Wentling, pp. 27-28. 1184

5. Wentling, p. 28. 1188

ENRICHMENT ACTIVITY: Timed Writing

1. Take two 5' writings; find *gwam* on each.
2. Proofread and circle errors on each.
3. Record better *gwam* rate.

all letters used | A | 1.5 si | 5.7 awl | 80% hfw

gwam 3' | 5'

	3'	5'
There are few job skills more important than being able to present	4	3	43
your ideas clearly. This skill is needed when you are speaking to your	9	6	46
boss, co-workers, or customers. If you cannot present your ideas in a	14	8	48
skillful manner, you will not be able to establish the trust, credi-	19	11	51
bility, or rapport needed to be a valued worker.	22	13	53
Fortunately, there are techniques and strategies that you can use	26	16	56
to improve your skills in this area. Many of them are easy to under-	31	19	59
stand and can be controlled by you when you are speaking. First, you	36	21	61
should make eye contact with the person who is listening because the	40	24	64
contact suggests that you express a sincere interest in the listener.	45	27	67
The volume of your voice is also critical. You should always speak	50	30	70
loud enough to be heard but not so loud as to make the listener uncom-	54	33	73
fortable. Also, the volume of your voice should be varied. You should	59	35	75
talk louder than required to emphasize major points and talk softer than	64	38	78
usual at some points to encourage listening.	67	40	80

gwam 3' | 1 | 2 | 3 | 4 | 5
5' | 1 | 2 | 3

41a ▶ 6
Conditioning Practice

each line twice SS; then a
1′ writing on line 3; find *gwam*

alphabet	1	Five kids quickly mixed the prizes, baffling one wise judge.
fig/sym	2	Joe asked, "Is the ZIP Code 45209-2748 or is it 45208-3614?"
speed	3	The firms may make a profit if they handle their work right.

| 1 | 2 | 3 | 4 | 5 | 6 | 7 | 8 | 9 | 10 | 11 | 12 |

41b ▶ 9 Improve Language Skills: Word Division

1. Read each rule and key the **Learn** and **Apply** lines beneath it.

Note: As you key the **Apply** lines, insert a hyphen in each word at the point (if any) where the word can best be divided.

2. Check with your teacher the accuracy of your **Apply** lines; if time permits, rekey the **Apply** lines in which you made word-division errors.

> When two words are hyphenated to make up a compound word, divide only after the designated hyphen.

Learn 1 ill-advised, self-satisfied, well-groomed, self-concerned
Apply 2 illmannered, self con-tained, well-mean-ing, self centered

> When two single-letter syllables occur together in a word, divide between them.

Learn 3 gradu-ate, gradu-ation, evalu-ate, evalu-ation, initi-ation
Apply 4 devaluation, insinuation, variation, anxiety, attenuation

> Avoid dividing proper names, dates, and figures.

Learn 5 Edna J. Jackson; May 15, 1997; $300,000; Atlanta or Savannah
Apply 6 Sep-tember 28, 1996; Portland, Cali-fornia; Edward S. Ebe-ling

41c-42c ▶ 35 (daily) Format Memorandums in Simplified Style

plain full sheets
LL: 1-inch side margins
    Pica (10-pitch) = 10-75
    Elite (12-pitch) = 12-90
LS: single
PB: line 10

1. Study the formatting guides for simplified memos on p. 68 and the model memo illustrating the simplified format on p. 74. Note the vertical and horizontal placement of memo parts and the spacing between them.

2. On a plain full sheet, format and key a copy of the memo on p. 74; do not correct your errors as you key. Center the assembly topic as shown.

3. Proofread your copy of the memo, marking any errors that need to be corrected.

4. Format and key the memo again from your own copy, errors corrected.

5. If time permits, begin processing the memos on p. 75. Save any partially completed memo to finish during the next class period. Correct your errors as you key.

MANAGING LINE ENDINGS

The format for memos requires 1-inch side margins (10 pica spaces; 12 elite). Thus, the line length for pica or 10-pitch machines is 65 spaces; for elite or 12-pitch machines, 78 spaces. As a result, line endings for pica and elite equipment will differ.

Users of standard typewriters should add about 5 spaces to the right margin stop setting and be guided by the warning bell to return, add a short word, or divide a word at the end of the line. Doing so will cause the right margin to be more nearly 1 inch and will result in a less-ragged right margin.

Users of computers or word processors should study their software to learn how to manage line endings. Procedures vary from program to program and depend upon whether hard returns or the word wrap feature is used.

words

A COURSE PROPOSAL

The business education faculty has voted unanimously to propose that a one-semester desktop publishing (DTP) course be added to the curriculum next fall. The course could be an elective course for all students who have completed the existing word processing or business computer applications courses.

Rationale for the Course

Desktop publishing is one of the fastest-growing computer applications because its use saves businesses money and reduces the time required to create professional-looking documents and presentation graphics.[1] Because of this increased use and the resulting demand for employees who can use DTP software, the business education faculty has a responsibility to teach students about this technology.[2]

In addition to learning DTP applications, students will apply their writing, problem-solving, decision-making, and creativity skills as they prepare text, plan graphics, and lay out the various documents they have to process in the course.[3]

Course Description

Desktop publishing provides students with an opportunity to learn about desktop publishing and how to use DTP software. Students write text, plan graphics, and design document layout for various business documents. Experience with laser printers and scanners is also acquired. Being a competent user of word processing and graphics software is a prerequisite for the course.

Course Objectives

Students who complete the desktop publishing course will:

1. Understand what desktop publishing is, the benefits of desktop publishing, and how desktop publishing works.[4]

2. Have gained "hands on" experience using a microcomputer, desktop publishing software, a laser printer, and a scanner.

3. Have designed and created newsletters, certificates, business cards, letterheads, report covers, fliers, and directories which are used extensively in business.

words

4. Understand the desktop publishing field and know of the employment opportunities in the field.

Teaching/Learning Strategies

Readings, lectures, demonstrations, and class discussions will be used for about 25 percent of the class time to accomplish the course objectives relating to acquisition of knowledge and understanding. Students will spend the remaining class time applying what they have learned. During this time, they will use DTP and other software which supports DTP to produce the required documents.

Teaching/Learning Resources

Recommendation. It is recommended that this course be taught in a classroom with microcomputers, printers, and at least one scanner on a network. Furthermore, it is recommended that section enrollment not exceed 25 students and that each student have a microcomputer workstation.

If this recommendation is accepted, the following equipment will be needed:

1. Twenty-seven 80286 microcomputers (25 for students, 1 for the teacher, and 1 to be used as the file server on the network). Each with two floppy disk drives, one fixed disk, graphics board, one serial port, one parallel port, LAN board, and enhanced keyboard.

2. Twenty-four black and white monochrome monitors with video adapters.

3. Three VGA color monitors with VGA video adapters.

4. Twenty-six mouse units. (A mouse unit is a handheld pointer used to manipulate the cursor on the microcomputer monitor.)

5. One desktop, flatbed design scanner with interface kit and scanner software.

6. Three laser printers with 8½" × 11" paper tray.

Cost and location. It is estimated that it will cost no more than $15,000 to upgrade the hardware and software in one of the existing microcomputer classrooms to meet the specifications needed to offer this desktop publishing course. The faculty recommends that the

		words in parts	total words
Date	October 29, 19-- ⟶ Line 10 (line 6 of a half sheet)	3	3
	QS		
Addressee	**Student Leadership Program Committee**	11	11
	DS		
Subject	**DALLAS JOHNSON TO ADDRESS ASSEMBLY**	18	18
	DS		
Body	Dr. Dallas T. Johnson telephoned to say that he will be pleased	13	31
	to address the special student assembly on March 10 on the topic	26	44
	DS		
	TEENAGE DRUG ABUSE	30	47
	DS		
	Dr. Johnson will use slides to present data on the incidence of	42	60
	drug use among teenagers. He will use a short film to highlight	55	73
	differences in attitudes and behavior before and after drug use.	69	86
	Finally, a young adult who has undergone treatment at the Drug Re-	82	100
	habilitation Center will tell us about her experiences with drugs.	95	113
	DS		
	This assembly should be very interesting, but sobering.	106	125
	QS		
Writer	*Juan F. Ramirez*	3	128
	Juan F. Ramirez		

Shown in pica (10-pitch) type
with 1-inch side margins,
photo-reduced

Simplified Memorandum in Block Format

42a ▶ 6
Conditioning Practice
each line twice SS; then a
1' writing on line 3; find *gwam*

alphabet 1 Quincy worked six jigsaw puzzles given him for his birthday.

fig/sym 2 I deposited Hahn & Ober's $937.48 check (#1956) on March 20.

speed 3 Vivian may lend them a hand with the audit of the soap firm.

| 1 | 2 | 3 | 4 | 5 | 6 | 7 | 8 | 9 | 10 | 11 | 12 |

NETWORKING--A STATUS REPORT   6

The purpose of this report is to inform you 14
of the status of the project to network the micro- 24
computers assigned to the Public Relations and 34
Advertising departments. 39

Decisions Made 45

Based on the recommendations made in Mr. 53
John Boyer's report,[1] it has been decided to in- 63
stall a star network: 67

One of the most popular ways of creating 75
local area networks is with physical coaxial 84
and a host computer. The cables physically 93
connect to the central host computer and 101
thus "hardwire" the network. This is often 110
called a star network because workstation 119
connections (nodes) radiate from the host 127
computer like the many points of a star.[2] 136

The decision has been made to network 25 144
computers, 5 printers, and a scanner; to pur- 153
chase a higher level graphics package; and to 162
delay adding an electronic mail system. 170

Current Activities 178

The director of computing is seeking prices 186
on the following items which are needed to in- 196
stall the network. 200

1. Network software, network cards, active 208
and passive hubs, cabling, etc. 215

2. Network versions of existing word pro- 223
cessing, desktop publishing, data base, and 232
spreadsheet applications software packages. 241

words

3. Graphics software which will run on the 250
network. 252

4. A microcomputer capable of serving as 260
the host computer on the network. 267

5. Furniture to accommodate the equipment 276
which will be purchased. 281

Advantages and Disadvantages 293

Advantages. The chief advantage of net- 303
working is that the department's 25 micro 311
users will share computer files, software pack- 320
ages, a scanner, and computer printers.[3] 329
Sharing will improve the quantity and quality 338
of the documents and presentations. 346

Disadvantages. One drawback to network- 356
ing is the large initial investment in hardware 366
and software that must be made. Another 374
relates to security in that a "greater effort to 384
protect the system and its sensitive file infor- 393
mation"[4] will need to be taken. 400

ENDNOTES   402

[1]John A. Boyer, "Networking--A Preliminary 410
Report," (Pittsburgh: Office Network Consul- 419
tants, Inc., 1990), p. 5, photocopied. 427

[2]Mark G. Simkin, Computer Information 439
Systems for Business (Dubuque, Iowa: Wm. C. 452
Brown Publishers, 1987), p. 161. 459

[3]"The Future, According to Wang," The 467
Office, June 1988, p. 40. 474

[4]Simkin, Computer Information Systems for 488
Business, p. 163. 493

Lessons 121-122   *Leftbound Report with Endnotes/Title Page*

121a-122a ▶ 5 *(daily)*
Conditioning Practice
each line twice SS
(slowly, then faster);
DS between 2-line
groups; if time permits,
rekey selected lines

alphabet 1 Viki will begin to expedite the zone office's major quarterly reports.

fig/sym 2 Catalog item #9087 will cost Anessi & Co. $432.65 (less 10% for cash).

figures 3 The team averages 28,915 fans per game in a stadium that seats 34,760.

speed 4 The toxic gas odor in the air did make the girls sick when they slept.

| 1 | 2 | 3 | 4 | 5 | 6 | 7 | 8 | 9 | 10 | 11 | 12 | 13 | 14 |

121b-122b ▶ 45 *(daily)*
Format Leftbound Report with Endnotes/Title Page
plain full sheets; correct errors

1. Format and key the report with endnotes presented on the next two pages in leftbound format.

2. Use the report title, your name, your school's name, and current date to prepare a title page in leftbound format.

Note: If your equipment permits you to raise the reference numbers, raise them; otherwise, place the reference numbers on the line preceded and followed by diagonals: /1/.

42b ▶ 9
Language Skills: Composing Sentences
Compose a 1- or 2-sentence answer to each question.

1 Why are you learning to operate a typewriter or computer?

2 By the end of the course, in what ways do you want to be able to use your skill?

3 In what ways could this course be made more helpful to you?

4 In what ways do you think you could improve your performance?

41c-42c ▶ 35 (continued) See 41c-42c, p. 73, for formatting guides. Correct your errors as you key.

Memo 1   words

October 24, 19--	3
QS	
All Seniors	6
DS	
CHOOSING A COLLEGE OR UNIVERSITY	12
DS	
A voluntary assembly for seniors is planned for	22
3 p.m. next Friday, November 5, in the cafete-	31
ria. The purpose is to give you information and	41
answer your questions about choosing and get-	50
ting into the college or university of your choice	60
upon graduation.	64
DS	
Each guest speaker will summarize entrance	72
requirements and opportunities at his or her	81
college or university. A question/answer period	91
will follow. You may direct your questions to	101
the person of your choice: Miss Micaela Stokes	110
of Central Community College, Dr. Louise	118
Bolan of Midland State University, or Mr. John	128
Hawkes of Metropolitan College of Business.	137
DS	
If you plan to attend, sign your name below.	146
QS	
Melissa Briggs, Senior Class President	154

Memo 2   words

October 28, 19--	3
Leon Deitz	6
FOREIGN EXCHANGE STUDY	10
On Thursday, November 15, Mr. Earl Bosma	18
of Rotary, International will be here to discuss	28
the foreign study program with prospective	37
exchange students.	41
The meeting will be at 11:15 a.m. in Conference	50
Room A of Tredwell Library. After the general	60
session, Mr. Bosma will visit with each applicant	70
separately. Your appointment is at 2:30 p.m.	79
Please be prompt for these meetings and bring	88
all your application materials with you.	97
Eileen P. Roth, Assistant Principal	104
xx (Use your own initials for reference)	104

Memo 3
Format and key Memo 2 again but address it to **Cora Jordan**.
Change the appointment time to **1:15 p.m.**

Memo 4

1. Read the rough-draft memo, noting the changes to be made. (See key to proofreader's marks below.)

2. Format and key the copy as a simplified memo. Use the **current date** and use **Keyboarding Students** as the addressee. Correct marked errors and any errors you make as you key. **Note:** Try to maintain an acceptable right margin of 1 inch, fairly even.

∧	=	insert
#	=	add space
∿	=	transpose
✗	=	delete
⌒	=	close up
≡	=	capitalize

words

opening lines 7

AUTOMATICLY CONTROLLED RIGHT MARGINS   15

Some machines have built-in software that control the right mar-   28

gin; others, such as computers, depend upon a separate software   41

disk too control how the lines end.   48

However the rihgt margin is controlled though, you can override   61

the defaults to change a line ending, adding or dividing a   74

wrod may make the right margin less ragged. You must follow the   87

procedure in your user's guide to make line ending changes.   99

Liang Chih, *Keyboarding Teacher*   106

xx   106

BIBLIOGRAPHY line 10 pica
line 12 elite

QS

Cunningham, William H., Ramon J. Aldag, and Christopher M.
 Swift. <u>Introduction to Business</u>. 2d ed. Cincinnati:
 South-Western Publishing Co., 1989. DS

Kalinski, Burton S., and Peter F. Meggison. <u>Management of
 Administrative Office Systems</u>. 2d ed. San Diego:
 Harcourt Brace Jovanovich, Publishers, 1988. DS

Simkin, Mark G. <u>Computer Information Systems for Business</u>.
 Dubuque, Iowa: Wm. C. Brown Publishers, 1987. DS

Smith, Harold T., William H. Baker, and Marvin P. Evans. <u>The
 Administrative Manager</u>. 2d ed. Chicago: Science Research Associates, Inc., 1987.

1½"
left margin

1"
right margin

119b (continued)

Document 2 — Bibliography
plain full sheet; SS entries with a DS between; correct errors
Key model bibliography above.

Top margin: line 10 pica;
line 12 elite
Side margins: left, 1½";
right, 1"
Bottom margin: at least 1"

Learning Cues
1. Key page number on line 6 at the right margin.
2. ALL CAP heading.
3. Begin first line of each entry at left margin; indent remaining lines 5 spaces.
4. SS each entry; DS between entries.

Lesson 120 — Leftbound Report with Endnotes

120a ▶ 5 Conditioning Practice

each line twice SS (slowly, then faster); DS between 2-line groups; if time permits, rekey selected lines

alphabet 1 Jo quickly sighted seven African whydahs by the bear complex at the zoo.

fig/sym 2 Here are my latest costs: #621-3A, $54; #908/5, $76; and #56-89, $38.

figures 3 Janice ordered 27 pants, 36 skirts, 50 belts, 48 socks, and 19 shirts.

speed 4 A problem for the ill ensign was to focus on the rigor of the rituals.

| 1 | 2 | 3 | 4 | 5 | 6 | 7 | 8 | 9 | 10 | 11 | 12 | 13 | 14 |

120b ▶ 45 Learn to Format a Leftbound Report with Endnotes

plain full sheets; leftbound report format; correct errors

1. Format the leftbound report given on p. 213. DS the body of the report.
2. Raise the endnote reference numbers or use /1/ if your equipment cannot raise the reference numbers.

Learning Cues: Endnotes
Endnotes are keyed on a separate sheet of paper which follows the last page of the report. They are arranged in the same order as footnotes.

In endnotes, the reference number is either *elevated* or is placed *on the line and followed by a period.* Vertical spacing is the same as for a reference page.

Learn to Format Business Correspondence

Learning Guides

1. To learn how to format business letters in block style.

2. To improve skill in formatting/keying simplified memos and personal-business letters.

3. To improve basic keyboarding skills.

4. To review/improve language skills.

Format Guides

1. *Paper guide* at *0* (for typewriters).

2. LL: 60 spaces for drills, ¶s, and personal-business letters; see *Get Ready to Keyboard: Typewriters* (p. x) or *Computers* (p. xii); 1" SM for memos; as directed by *Letter Placement Guide* for business letters.

3. LS: SS (except for letter/memo parts).

4. PI: 5 spaces when appropriate.

FORMATTING GUIDES: BUSINESS LETTERS IN BLOCK STYLE

Block Style, Pica

Block Style, Elite

2" = 20 pica spaces
24 elite spaces

1½" = 15 pica spaces
18 elite spaces

1" = 10 pica spaces
12 elite spaces

Block Letter Style

In block letter style (format), all lines begin at the left margin (LM). Open punctuation is used, which means that no punctuation follows the salutation or complimentary close.

Letter Stationery

Most business letters are processed on standard-size letterheads (8½" × 11") with the company name, address, and telephone number printed at the top.

Simplified memorandums may be processed on letterheads, too. If the letterhead is too deep to key the date on line 10, place it a DS below the letterhead.

Letter Placement/Spacing

A placement guide such as the one shown below will help you place letters.

Dateline placement. Vertical placement of the dateline varies according to letter length (the longer the letter, the higher the date placement). If a deep letterhead prevents placing the date on the line suggested in the *Letter Placement Guide*, place it a DS below the letterhead.

Letter address. The letter address is always started a QS below the dateline. If the letter is addressed to a company, the address may include an attention line (the first line of the address) to call the letter to the attention of a specific person, department, or job title.

Salutation. The salutation is placed a DS below the letter address. If the first line of the address is a company name, the salutation *Ladies and Gentlemen* is used. If the first line of the letter address is a person's name, the salutation includes the name: *Dear Mr. Wells; Dear Ms. Sanchez.*

Subject line. A subject line identifies the topic of the letter. It is placed a DS below the salutation in ALL CAPS.

Body. The body or letter message begins a DS below the salutation (or below the subject line, if any). Body paragraphs (¶s) are SS with a DS between ¶s.

Complimentary close. The complimentary close is placed a DS below the last line of the body.

Writer's name and title. The writer's name is placed a QS below the complimentary close. The writer's business title may follow the name on the same line, preceded by a comma, or may be placed on the next line.

Reference initials. If the keyboard operator is not the writer of the message, the operator's initials (lowercased) are keyed a DS below the writer's name or title.

Enclosure notation. If anything other than the letter is to be included in the envelope, the word *Enclosure* (or *Enclosures*) is keyed a DS below the initials.

Copy notation. If a copy of the letter is to be sent to someone other than the addressee, the letter *c*, followed by a space and the recipient's name, is placed a DS below the enclosure notation. If two people are to receive copies, both names are placed on the same line with a comma and space between them.

Note: Not all letters require subject lines, reference initials, enclosure notations, and copy notations. Regardless of which special elements are needed, key them in the order given with a DS between them.

LETTER PLACEMENT GUIDE

Letter Classification	5-Stroke Words in Letter Body	Side Margins	Margin Settings		Dateline Position (from Top Edge of Paper)
			Elite	Pica	
Short	Up to 100	2"	24-78*	20-65*	18
Average	101-200	1½"	18-84*	15-70*	16
Long	201-300	1"	12-90*	10-75*	14
Two-Page	More than 300	1"	12-90*	10-75*	14
6" Line	All letters	1¼"	15-87*	12-72*	As above

*Plus 3-7 spaces for the typewriter bell cue — usually add 5.

119a ▶ 5
Conditioning Practice

each line twice SS (slowly, then faster); DS between 2-line groups; if time permits, rekey selected lines

alphabet 1 Max will authorize me to get quality products from major bike vendors.

fig/sym 2 Each computer desk (42″ wide × 36″ long × 27″ high) will cost $158.90.

figures 3 Mary served 138 donuts, 279 danish, 60 cupcakes, and 45 elephant ears.

speed 4 They are proficient for the quantity and rigor of work they are to do.

| 1 | 2 | 3 | 4 | 5 | 6 | 7 | 8 | 9 | 10 | 11 | 12 | 13 | 14 |

119b ▶ 35 Process a Leftbound Report with Footnotes/Bibliography

words

Document 1—Leftbound Report with Footnotes
leftbound; DS; correct errors; review format features on p. 206 if necessary

words

COMPUTERS AND DECISION MAKING 6

Computers have widespread use in today's 14 world. Computers are used by workers who pro- 23 duce goods and services and by consumers who 32 use goods and services. 37

Computers in Business 46

People who pursue a career in business will 55 learn that computers have helped reduce the 64 cost of and time devoted to managing and pro- 73 cessing information. Computers have had no 81 equal for computing, classifying, sorting, mov- 91 ing, editing, or storing information. 99

New Uses 102

Computers have been used to provide "the 110 right information to the right manager at the 119 right time in a cost-effective manner."[1] This 129 use is taking on a new dimension as other in- 138 novative computer applications are introduced. 147 The new use is to provide top-level managers 156 with resources to improve decision making. 165 Three such resources are decision support sys- 174 tems, expert systems, and decision modeling. 184

Decision support systems. Decision support 197 systems are computer applications which sup- 206 port the decision-making process in a business. 216

Decision support systems allow managers 224 to ask a series of "what if" questions about 233 business problems. With a decision support 242 system, a manager and computer essen- 249 tially engage in a dialogue. That is, the 258 manager sits at the microcomputer and asks 266 a series of questions to which the computer 275 responds. The computer does not make a 283 decision; instead, it provides information 292 which the manager can use for decision 299 making.[2] 301

Expert systems. Expert systems are com- 312 puter applications which "store knowledge about 322 a given subject in a data base."[3] The knowledge 332 stored is the data and decision rules pertain- 341 ing to a specialized knowledge area a nonex- 350 pert needs to be able to perform at the level 359 comparable to that of an expert in that knowl- 368 edge area. 370

Decision modeling. The term decision mod- 382 eling refers to computer applications designed 392 to free managers from having to make routine 401 decisions. A computer model "is designed to 410 behave as the decision maker behaves."[4] Once 419 the model meets accuracy standards of the 427 decision maker, it then becomes the decision 436 maker's replacement. 441

These computer applications are significant 450 enhancements to the functions of the computer, 459 and they are likely to become more prevalent 468 as a means to improve decision making.[5] 478

_____ 482

[1]Mark G. Simkin, Computer Information 494 Systems for Business (Dubuque, Iowa: Wm. C. 507 Brown Publishers, 1987), p. 305. 513

[2]William H. Cunningham, Ramon J. Aldag, 521 and Christopher M. Swift, Introduction to 533 Business, 2d ed. (Cincinnati: South-Western 544 Publishing Co., 1989), pp. 69-70. 551

[3]Burton S. Kalinski and Peter F. Meggison, 559 Management of Administrative Office Systems, 577 2d ed. (San Diego: Harcourt Brace Jovanovich, 586 Publishers, 1988), p. 507. 592

[4]Cunningham, Introduction to Business, p. 70. 606

[5]Harold T. Smith, William H. Baker, and 614 Marvin P. Evans, The Administrative Manager, 628 2d ed. (Chicago: Science Research Associates, 638 Inc., 1987), p. 67. 642

43a ▶ 6
Conditioning Practice

each line twice SS; then a
1' writing on line 3; find *gwam*

alphabet 1 Rex just left my quiz show and gave back a prize he had won.

fig/sym 2 Review reaches: $40, $84, 95%, #30, 5-point, 1/6, B&O 27's.

speed 3 Di may profit by good form and a firm wish to make the goal.

| 1 | 2 | 3 | 4 | 5 | 6 | 7 | 8 | 9 | 10 | 11 | 12 |

43b ▶ 14
Learn to Format Letter Parts

2 plain full sheets

Drill 1

1. Begin return address on line 14 so that the date is placed on line 16.

2. After keying the salutation, space down 14 lines to begin closing lines.

SM: 1½"
  pica: 15-70 + 5
  elite: 18-84 + 5
PB: line 16

Drill 2

1. Study the business letter formatting guides on p. 76; check each placement point with the model letter on p. 78 and with the copy in Drill 2 at right.

2. Key the drill according to the spacing annotations in color within the drill.

Drill 1: Personal-Business Letter

3204 Mount Holly Road
Charlotte, NC 28216-3746
November 10, 19--   ←——Line 16——→
  QS
  (Return 4 times)

Mrs. Juanita L. Ruiz
1859 Boston Road
Springfield, MA 01129-3467
  DS

Dear Mrs. Ruiz
  DS

Space down 14 times (using *index* or *return/enter* key) to allow for body of letter.

Cordially yours
  QS
  (Return 4 times)

Ms. Gloria C. Ainsley
  DS

Enclosure

Drill 2: Business Letter

November 10, 19--
  QS
  (Return 4 times)

Attention Mr. Kevin J. Marx
Kendall Computers, Inc.
733 Marquette Avenue
Minneapolis, MN 55402-1736
  DS

Ladies and Gentlemen
  DS

Space down 14 times (using *index* or *return/enter* key) to allow for body of letter.

Sincerely yours
  QS
  (Return 4 times)

Evan L. Ritchey, Director
Word Processing Center
  DS

tbh
  DS

Enclosure
  DS

c Miss Mary E. Durbin

43c ▶ 30
Learn to Format Business Letters

3 plain full sheets;
SM: 1½"; PB: line 16

1. Study the model letter on p. 78 which illustrates *block style* with *open punctuation*. Note the vertical and horizontal placement of letter parts.

2. On a plain full sheet, key the letter shown on p. 78. Use the typewriter bell cue or word wrap feature to return at line endings.

3. Proofread/correct your copy.

4. If time permits, take a 2' writing on the opening lines (date through subject line); then a 2' writing on the closing lines (complimentary close to the end). Use plain full sheets.

words

Self-Check Questions

1. Do you know where you will end the first page? If not, plan ahead at this time and then check your page-ending mark or line indicator as you near the bottom of the page.

2. Do you know where the page number is keyed on the second page? If not, refer to p. 206.

3. Are you maintaining a correct right margin? If not, you should divide words according to the word division rules you have learned.

4. Do you recall that when an enumeration exceeds one line, the second and all succeeding lines begin under the number. If several lines are needed to key the enumeration(s), the left margin should be reset until the enumeration(s) is keyed.

<u>Skills</u>. An analyses of your skills is likely to reveal | 179

that your have many different kinds of skills. | 186

    1. Functional skills that determine how well you | 196
manage time, communicate, motivate people, write, etc. | 208

    2. Adaptive skills that determine how well you will | 218
fit into a specific work environment. These skills include | 230
personal traits such as flexibility, realiability, ef- | 241
ficeincy, thoroughness, and enthusiasm for the job. | 251

    3. Technical skills or work content skills that are | 260
required to perform a specific job. These skills may | 271
include such things as keyboarding, accounting, computer operation, | 285
and language arts usage skills. [3] | 291

    <u>Interests</u>. "Interests refer to the things that you | 303
like or dislike." [4] By listing and analyzing them you should | 315
be able to identify a desirable work environment. For exam- | 327
ple, your list is likely to reveal if you like to work | 338
with things or people, work alone or with others, lead or | 349
follow others, or being indoors or outdoors. | 358

    <u>Values</u>. Values are your priorities in life, and you | 370
should identify them early stet so you can pursue a career which | 382
will improve your chances to acquire them. Some of the more | 394
obvious considerations values include the importance you place on | 404
family, security, wealth, prestige, creativity, power, inde- | 416
pendence, and glamour. [5] | 421

| 425

─────────────

  [1]Susan Bernard, <u>Getting the Right Job</u>, AT&T's Col- | 439
lege Series (Elizabeth, NJ: AT&T College Market, 1988), p. | 451
2.6 | 452

  [2]William H. Cunningham, Ramon J. Aldag, and Christopher | 463
M. Swift, <u>Introduction to Business</u>, 2d ed. (Cincinnati: | 479
South-Western Publishing Co., 1989), 620. | 488

  [3]Adele Scheele, "Deciding What You Want To Do", <u>Busi-</u> | 500
<u>ness Week Careers</u>, 1988 ed., 7. | 511

  [4]Bernard, <u>Getting the Right Job</u>, 1-2. | 523

  [5]Cunningham, <u>Introduction to Business</u>, p. 617. | 537

M E R K E L - E V A N S, Inc.

1321 Commerce Street • Dallas, TX 75202-1648 • Tel. (214) 871-4400

		words in parts	total words

Date **November 10, 19--** Line 16 — 4 — 4

Quadruple-space (QS):
strike return key 4 times

Letter address **Mrs. Evelyn M. McNeil** — 8 — 8
4582 Campus Drive — 12 — 12
Fort Worth, TX 76119-1835 — 17 — 17

Double-space (DS):
strike return key twice

Salutation **Dear Mrs. McNeil** DS — 20 — 20

Body **The new holiday season is just around the corner, and** — 11 — 31
we invite you to beat the rush and visit our exciting — 22 — 42
Gallery of Gifts. Gift-giving can be a snap this year — 33 — 53
because of our vast array of gifts "for kids from one — 43 — 64
to ninety-two." DS — 47 — 67

What's more, many of our gifts are prewrapped for pre- — 57 — 78
sentation. All can be packaged and shipped right here — 68 — 89
at the store. DS — 71 — 92

A catalog of our hottest gift items and a schedule of — 82 — 103
holiday hours for special charge-card customers are en- — 93 — 113
closed. Please stop in and let us help you select that — 104 — 125
special gift, or call us if you wish to shop by phone. DS — 115 — 136

We wish you happy holidays and hope to see you soon. DS — 126 — 147

Complimentary close **Cordially yours** QS — 3 — 150

Carol J. Suess

Writer's name and title **Ms. Carol J. Suess, Manager** DS — 9 — 155

Reference initials **rj** DS — 9 — 156

Enclosure notation **Enclosures** — 11 — 158

Shown in pica (10-pitch) type
with 1½-inch side margins,
photo-reduced

Business Letter in Block Format, Open Punctuation

118a ▶ 5
Conditioning Practice

each line twice SS (slowly, then faster); DS between 2-line groups; if time permits, rekey selected lines

alphabet 1 Jeb, Dom, and I favor analyzing the weekly exchange prices frequently.

fig/sym 2 The agreement (#19-723) must state that Payment #48 is $506; not $312.

figures 3 I hope to bus 67 players, 140 band members, 23 teachers, and 598 fans.

speed 4 Diane and she may visit the ancient city chapel when they are with us.

| 1 | 2 | 3 | 4 | 5 | 6 | 7 | 8 | 9 | 10 | 11 | 12 | 13 | 14 |

118b ▶ 10 Check Language Skills

plain full sheet; LL: 70

As you read and key the ¶, correct any errors in capitalization, spelling, word choice, punctuation, etc., that you find. If you make any errors as you key, correct those also. Check work with your teacher.

The result's of Glenn Adam's pole of members of the teenagers' Club served as the bases for the dezision to reserve space on john jones' Best of the '90s tour. The usual fair fore this tur is $395.95, however the Clubs' fair will be at leased 20% lower. The club's fair is lower becuase john jones has an idol dual-engine plain which can fly Club member's to Buffalo, New York, Erie, Pennsylvania, and Dayton, Ohio tomorrow. Plan to be at the air port at 7:45 am, the plain leafs at 8;15 am.

118c ▶ 35 Process a Leftbound Report with Footnotes

plain full sheets; PI: 5; DS the body; correct unmarked as well as marked errors and errors you make as you key

Recall Hints

1. Refer to proofreader's marks on RG 10 as needed.

2. Review formatting features for leftbound reports, p. 206.

3. The left margin for long quotations is at the paragraph indention point. Long quotations are single-spaced.

4. Footnotes go on the same page as the footnote reference number is keyed.

5. Plan to end the page so there is at least 1″ of white space for the bottom margin.

6. The dividing line is 1½″ in length.

words

Career Planning — 3

Career planning is an important, onging process. It is — 15

important because the career you follow will affect your — 26

quality of your life and will help determine the respect and — 38

recognition you will recieve. Throughout your lifetime you — 49

are likely to make career changes three or four times.[1] — 59

Establish a Career Objective — 71

One important and early aspect of career planning is to — 83

define a career objective. — 89

The career objective may indicate your area of interest — 101
(such as finance or sales), the sort of organization — 111
you would like to work for (such as banking or manufac- — 122
turing), and the level of the position you want.[2] — 132

Complete a Personal Inventory — 144

Another useful step in the career planning is to devel- — 154

op a personal profile of your skills, values and interests. — 166

(continued, p. 210)

44a ▶ 6
Conditioning Practice

each line twice SS; then a 1' writing on line 3; find *gwam*

alphabet 1 Zoe just may have to plan a big, unique dance for next week.

fig/sym 2 Tami asked, "Can't you touch-key 65, 73, $840, and 19 1/2%?"

speed 3 Six of the big firms may bid for the right to the lake land.

| 1 | 2 | 3 | 4 | 5 | 6 | 7 | 8 | 9 | 10 | 11 | 12 |

44b ▶ 8
Language Skills: Simple Sentences

1. Study the guides in the color blocks at right and the sentences that illustrate the guides.

2. Key the **Learn** sentences as shown, noting the words that comprise the subject and predicate of each sentence.

3. On a separate sheet of paper, key vertically the numbers 1 through 8, DS.

4. Key the subject and predicate of each **Learn** sentence opposite the appropriate number.

5. Check work with teacher.

> A *simple* sentence consists of a single independent clause which contains a subject (noun or pronoun) and a predicate (verb).

Learn 1 Pam is president of her class. *(single subject/single predicate)*
Learn 2 Kevin walks to and from school. *(single subject/single predicate)*
Learn 3 Reading mystery novels is my favorite pastime.
Learn 4 The captain of the team is out with a badly sprained ankle.

> A simple sentence may have as its subject more than one noun or pronoun and as its predicate more than one verb.

Learn 5 She bought a new bicycle. *(single subject/single predicate)*
Learn 6 Marv and I received new bicycles. *(compound subject/single predicate)*
Learn 7 Alice washed and waxed her car. *(single subject/compound predicate)*
Learn 8 He and I cleaned and cooked the fish. *(compound subject and predicate)*

44c ▶ 6 Improve Keyboarding Skill: Rough-Draft Copy

1. Using a 60-space line, key a 2' writing on the ¶, making the marked changes as you key.

2. Proofread your copy and find *gwam*.

3. Key another 2' writing; try to increase your speed.

| ∧ = insert |
| ⨍ = delete |
| # = add space |
| ∩ = transpose |
| ⌣ = close up |

all letters used | LA | 1.4 si | 5.4 awl | 85% hfw

gwam 2'

When you key from marked copy, read just a little ahead   6
of where your keying.) Doing this will keep you from missing   12
changes that must be made. Learn to recognize quickly thee   18
correction simbols so that you don't have to reduce speed   24
or stop to read. Expect to copy rough draft at about eighty   30
five per cent of your straight copy speed.   35

44d-45d ▶ 30 (daily) Improve Formatting Skill: Letters and Memos

5 letterheads (LP pp. 29-38) or plain full sheets

Note: Correct your errors as you key unless otherwise directed.

1. Begin formatting/processing the average-length letters and the memo on pp. 81-82 (use the *Letter Placement Guide* on p.76). Try to finish the documents in two class periods.

2. Proofread/correct each document before removing it from your typewriter or the screen of your computer.

3. If a document cannot be completed within a class period, complete the line on which you are working and save the document for later completion.

Money is a resource you must learn to manage wisely so you can buy the goods and services you need and have some money left to do things you find enjoyable and worth doing. DS

A Budget DS

One way to help balance your income and expenses is to prepare a budget. A budget is an itemized spending plan that enables you to set priorities for the money that remains after you have accounted for your fixed expenses.[1] Also, a budget helps you develop effective money management habits. DS

Prepare a Budget DS

1½"
left
margin

1"
right
margin

To prepare a budget for a month, list in one column the sources of your money and note when you expect it. Include gifts you will receive, interest from your savings account, allowances, and wages and tips you earn. In another column, identify what you want to save and list the amounts for fixed expenses--the cost of the "must buys." DS

Indent quotations 5 spaces from left margin.

After you include all your fixed expenses, total each column and subtract the monthly amounts from your monthly income in the first listing you made. That will give you what you have left for comforts, self-improvements, and luxuries.[2] DS

—————————————————— DS

[1]Robert K. Gerver and Richard J. Sgroi, Dollars and Sense (Cincinnati: South-Western Publishing Co., 1989), p. 500. DS

[2]Caroline Reynolds, Dimensions in Professional Development, 3d ed. (Cincinnati: South-Western Publishing Co., 1988) p. 301.

1 line 62

(at least 1" bottom margin)

Leftbound Report with Footnotes

45a ▶ 6
Conditioning Practice

each line twice SS; then a 1' writing on line 3; find *gwam*

alphabet 1 Wayne froze the ball, having just made the six quick points.

fig/sym 2 Flo moved from 583 Iris Lane to 836 - 42d Avenue on 10/7/91.

speed 3 Suella may row to the small island to dig for the big clams.

| 1 | 2 | 3 | 4 | 5 | 6 | 7 | 8 | 9 | 10 | 11 | 12 |

45b ▶ 8 Improve Language Skills: Compound Sentences

1. Study the guides in the color blocks at right and the sentences that illustrate the guides.

2. Key the **Learn** sentences as shown, noting the words that comprise the subjects and predicates of each sentence.

3. On a separate sheet of paper, key vertically the numbers 1 through 8, DS.

4. Key the subject-predicate of both clauses in each **Learn** sentence opposite the appropriate number. Use a diagonal (/) to separate the subject-predicate of one clause from that of the other.

5. Check work with teacher.

> A *compound* sentence contains two or more independent clauses connected by a coordinating conjunction (*and, but, for, or, nor, yet, so*).

Learn 1 Jay Sparks likes to hike, and Roy Tubbs likes to swim.
Learn 2 The computer is operative, but the printer does not work.
Learn 3 You may eat in the hotel, or you may choose a cafe nearby.
Learn 4 The sky is clear, the moon is out, and the sea is very calm.

> Each clause of a compound sentence may have as its subject more than one noun/pronoun and as its predicate more than one verb.

Learn 5 Ben and I saw the game, and Bob and Marla went to a movie.
Learn 6 Nick dived and swam, but the others fished off the boat.
Learn 7 You may play solitaire, or you and Joe may play checkers.
Learn 8 Jan huffed and puffed up the hill, but Eloise scampered up.

45c ▶ 6 Improve Keyboarding Skill: Script Copy

1. Using a 60-space line, key a 2' writing on the ¶.

2. Proofread your copy and find *gwam*.

3. Key another 2' writing; try to increase speed.

all letters used | LA | 1.4 si | 5.4 awl | 85% hfw

gwam 2'

Whether you key documents for personal or for business 5
use, much of the copy will be in handwritten or rough-draft 11
form. So adjust your speed in order to do work of quality. 18
Seize the next opportunity to prove that you can handle both 24
kinds of copy without too great a loss in speed and control. 30
With practice, you can process such copy with speed and ease. 36

44d-45d ▶ 30 (continued)

letterheads and plain full sheets as listed in 44d-45d, p. 79

Use *Letter Placement Guide* on p. 76 for business letters.

1. Continue formatting/processing the average-length documents given on pp. 81-82.

2. Proofread/correct each document before removing it from the typewriter or the screen of your computer.

3. If you finish all documents before time is called, start over with Document 1; OR rekey one of the documents that contains errors. Use plain paper.

4. Assemble your work in document number order and turn it in.

Your teacher may evaluate your work in terms of number of lines or documents satisfactorily processed.

117a ▶ 5
Conditioning Practice

each line twice SS (slowly, then faster); DS between 2-line groups; if time permits, rekey selected lines

alphabet 1 Maxim just now realized his favorite racquet broke from rough playing.

fig/sym 2 My Policy #49-3816 for $75,000 will mature 20 (twenty) years from now.

figures 3 Flight 1089 leaves at 8:45 p.m. while Flight 2496 leaves at 10:37 p.m.

speed 4 They are to fix the problem with the right signal so it works at dusk.

| 1 | 2 | 3 | 4 | 5 | 6 | 7 | 8 | 9 | 10 | 11 | 12 | 13 | 14 |

117b ▶ 5 Improve Language Skills: Word Choice

1. Study the spelling and definition of each word.

2. Key the line number (with period), space twice, then key the **Learn** sentence; key the **Apply** sentences in the same format, selecting the correct word in parentheses to complete each sentence.

loan (n) a sum of money lent at interest

lone (adj) companionless; solitary

lessen (vb) to cause to decrease; to make less

lesson (n) something to be learned; a period of instruction; a class

Learn 1. The lone transaction in our department today was the loan he made.

Apply 2. I gave him a (loan, lone) so he could buy the (lone, loan) car on the lot.

Apply 3. The (loan, lone) person in the lobby wanted to make a (loan, lone).

Learn 4. This lesson will lessen the time it takes you to do the job.

Apply 5. My failure to listen will (lessen, lesson) what I can learn from this (lessen, lesson).

117c ▶ 10
Preapplication Drill: Formatting Footnotes

1. Review Formatting Guides for leftbound reports with footnotes on p. 206.

2. Set margins for a leftbound report (1½" left and 1" right margin).

3. Leaving a bottom margin of about 1", determine the line on which to begin keying the material at the right.

4. Key the last two lines of text and the footnotes in correct format.

margin 1½"   key to financial control.[1]   A budget is often created on the ₍DS₎

basis of past experience.[2] ₍DS₎   1"

dividing line 1½"   —————————— ₍DS₎

[1]Burton S. Kaliski and Peter F. Meggison, <u>Management of Administrative Office Systems</u>, 2d ed. (San Diego: Harcourt Brace Jovanovich, Publishers, 1988), p. 447. ₍DS₎

[2]Richard M. Hodgetts and Donald F. Kurato, <u>Effective Small Business Management</u>, 3d ed. (San Diego: Harcourt Brace Jovanovich, Publishers, 1989), p. 265.

117d ▶ 30 Format
Leftbound Report with Footnotes

plain full sheet; correct errors

1. Study again, if necessary, the Formatting Guides on p. 206. Note in the model report on p. 208 how the formatting and spacing guides are applied.

Note. The model report is shown in pica (10-pitch) type, camera reduced. If you are keying in elite (12-pitch) type, your line endings will be different from those in the model but the vertical spacing will be the same.

2. Key the model report, following the formatting and spacing annotations shown on it.

Footnote Placement Hints: Typewriter

1. Make a light pencil mark at the right edge of the paper 1" from the bottom.

2. As you key each footnote reference number in the body of the report, make another pencil mark ½" above the previous one. This will help you reserve about 3 line spaces for each footnote. (If you have a page line gauge, such as the one on LP p. 5, use it.)

Document 1: Business Letter in Block Format, Open Punctuation

	words
November 12, 19--	4

Miss Carmen J. Blanco, Chair	9
Business Education Department	15
Dolphin Vocational High School	22
104 N. Andrews Avenue	26
Fort Lauderdale, FL 33301-2859	32

Dear Miss Blanco	36

Your order for six Genesis GS computers and | 45
two printers is being processed. We are pleased | 54
to include you in the growing number of users | 64
of this quality equipment. | 69

We plan to deliver and install these machines at | 79
three o'clock on November 18 to avoid disrupt- | 88
ing classroom activities. Please let me know if | 98
this date and time are convenient for you. | 107

Only a few minutes are required to install the | 116
equipment, but we want to test two or three | 125
programs to be certain that everything is work- | 134
ing properly. | 137

Please telephone me at the number shown above | 147
to confirm or change the appointment. | 154

(words in body: 121)

Sincerely yours | 158

Kermit L. Dahms, Sales Manager | 164

xx (Use your own initials for reference) | 164

c DeRon S. Jackson | 168

Document 2: Business Letter in Block Format, Open Punctuation

	words
November 12, 19--	4

Mr. Duane R. Burk, Office Manager	10
Huesman & Schmidt, Inc.	15
662 Woodward Avenue	19
Detroit, MI 48226-1947	24

Dear Mr. Burk | 27

Thank you for letting our representative, Miss | 36
Tina Chun, discuss with you and your staff our | 46
new line of landscaped office modules. | 54

Using in-scale templates, Miss Chun has rede- | 63
signed the general work area of your word | 71
processing center. Her mock-up offers you | 80
important features: ideal use of space in indi- | 89
vidual workstations, stationary panels to create | 99
private work areas without a feeling of cloister, | 109
and traffic patterns that are least disruptive | 118
to others. | 121

May we show you this portable display and dis- | 130
cuss the low cost of improving the productivity | 140
and harmony of your office staff. A color photo- | 149
graph of the mock-up is enclosed. Please call | 159
me to set a convenient date and time for us to | 168
spend about an hour with you. | 174

(words in body: 149)

Sincerely yours | 178

Virgil P. Thompson | 181
Assistant Sales Manager | 186

xx (Use your initials) | 187

Enclosure | 189

Document 3
Simplified Memo in Block Format

letterhead (LP p. 33) or plain full sheet; SM: 1"; PB: line 10

Date: **November 13, 19--**
Addressees: **Ana Wells**
   DeRon Jackson
Subject: **APPOINTMENT FOR GENESIS INSTALLATION**
Writer's name: **Kermit L. Dahms**
Reference: **your initials**

Documents 4, 5, and 6 are on p. 82.

Two-Addressee Memo

October 28, 19--

Leon Deitz, Cora Jordan

FOREIGN EXCHANGE STUDY

On Thursday, November 15, Mr. Earl will be here to discuss the foreign

	words
	opening lines 16

Miss Blanco of Dolphin Vocational High School called to con- | 28
firm the appointment for DeRon Jackson to install the six | 39
Genesis GS computers and two printers in her word processing | 52
lab. The appointment is at 3 p.m. on Friday, November 18. | 64

Be sure to take the three *User's Manuals* for the basic soft- | 78
ware programs we are providing. Miss Blanco wants three | 90
of her teachers to have a brief hands-on demonstration of | 101
the basic operating procedures | 108

closing lines 111

Extend Report Formatting Skills: Leftbound Reports

Learning Goals

1. To learn to format and process leftbound reports with footnotes and endnotes.

2. To learn to format and process leftbound reference lists (bibliographies) and title pages.

3. To improve language-skill competency.

Format Guides

1. Paper guide at *0* (for typewriters).

2. LL: 70 spaces for drills; as required for documents.

3. LS: SS drills; as required for documents.

4. PI: 5 spaces for ¶s and documents.

FORMATTING GUIDES: LEFTBOUND REPORTS WITH FOOTNOTES AND ENDNOTES

Leftbound Report

Leftbound Bibliography

Many business reports, as well as personal/professional ones, are bound at the left margin. When reports are leftbound, an additional half inch is left at the left side for binding; thus, the left margin is 1½ inches wide (15 pica or 10-pitch spaces; 18 elite or 12-pitch spaces). The right margin is 1 inch wide as in unbound reports.

Vertical placement and spacing is the same as for unbound reports.

Margins Leftbound and Unbound Reports

Top	Place main heading on line 10 (pica) line 12 (elite)
Side	1½″ left and 1″ right margins for leftbound 1″ left and right margins for unbound
Bottom	At least 1″ on all pages

Headings and Subheadings

Main heading. Center the main heading in ALL CAPS over the *line of writing;* leave a quadruple space (QS) below it.

To find the center of the line of writing, add the readings at the left and right margins on the line-of-writing or format scale and divide the total by 2.

pica (10-pitch): (15 + 75) ÷ 2 = 45
elite (12-pitch): (18 + 90) ÷ 2 = 54

Backspace from these points to center titles and headings in leftbound reports.

Side headings. Begin side headings at left margin, underline, and capitalize the first letter of all main words. DS above and below side headings.

Paragraph headings. Begin paragraph headings at paragraph indention point, underline and follow by a period. Capitalize the first letter of only the first word.

Documentation (Footnotes)

When material is quoted or closely paraphrased, the source is indicated by keying a footnote reference number a half space *above* the line of writing immediately after the quoted material and a correspondingly numbered footnote at the foot of the page (separated from last line of text by a 1½″ underline).

```
. . . electronic mail."1   Special forms

may be used for formatting such mail.
```

```
    1S. H. VanHuss and W. R. Daggett, Jr.,
Electronic Information Systems (Cincinnati:
South-Western Publishing, Co., 1990), p. 308.
```

For equipment that does not permit half spacing, keying the reference figure *on the* line of writing immediately preceded and followed by a diagonal is acceptable.

```
. . . electronic mail."/1/  Special forms
```

Separate the footnote divider rule from the report body by a DS; DS below the divider rule to begin the footnote.

Indent each footnote 5 spaces and SS it; DS between footnotes. If your equipment can raise figures, key the figure in the footnote a half space *above the line of writing.* If your equipment cannot raise figures, key the figure in the footnote *on the line of writing* followed by a period and two spaces.

In planning footnote placement, allow at least a 1″ bottom margin below footnotes on all pages except the last. On the last page, the dividing line and footnotes may begin a DS below the last line of text *or* be placed at the bottom of the page with at least 1″ of white space in the bottom margin.

Number footnotes consecutively throughout a report, and place each footnote on the same page as its in-text reference figure.

Page Numbers

The first page need not be numbered, but it may be. When numbered, center the number on line 62. For the second page and subsequent pages, place numbers on line 6 approximately even with the right margin.

Document 4
Business Letter
with Attention and
Subject Lines
Use *Letter Placement Guide,*
page 76.

words

November 14, 19-- | Attention Sales Manager | Business Management   12
Systems | 748 S. Market Street | Tacoma, WA 98402-1365 | Ladies and   25
Gentlemen | IMPROVE SALES BY 10 PERCENT   33

If you could close 10 percent more sales a year, would you spend a day of   48
your time to learn how? If so, we want to welcome you to   59

SUCCESS BY VISUAL PERSUASION   65

This special seminar is designed for high-level managers like you who want   80
quick, easy ways to prepare visual presentations that are a cut above the   95
chalkboard and flipchart. Using a lecture/electronic technique, a seminar   110
leader will show you how to use built-in outlining, drawing, and charting tools.   127
You will even learn how to get full-color effects in overheads and slides.   142

To improve your sales by 10 percent a year, read the enclosed brochure   156
about the seminar; then complete and return the registration card. You will   171
be glad you did. (143)   175

Sincerely yours | Robert L. Marsh, Director | xx | Enclosure   186

Document 5
Personal-Business Letter
from Rough Draft
Recall
LL: 60 spaces; PB: line 14

words

22149 West chester Road   5
Cleveland, OH 44122-3756   10
November 15, 19--   13
         QS

Mr. Trevor L. DeLong   18
5202 Regency Drive   21
Cleveland, OH 44129-2756   27

Dear Trevor   29

never
A news item in the Shaker Hieghts <u>Gazette</u> says that you are   42
to be graduated from Case Western Reserve at midyear.   53
With honors no less. Congratulations.   61
When you were a student at Woodmere, I worried that you   73
might not put your potential to work in a serious way. But   86
evidently you have been able to continue your athletic   97
goals and at the same time pursue an academic major suc-   108
cessfully. I am glad you have done credit to us at Wood-   119
mere. We are quiet proud of you.   126

What are your plans after graduation? Whatever they are,   138
your former teachers at Woodmere wish you well. I would   149
enjoy a note from you which I would share with the others.   161

Cordiallly yours   165
         QS

Willis R. Lowenstein   169

Document 6
Business Letter with Changes

1. Rekey Document 4 with
changes; use **November 18, 19--**
as the date.

2. Address the letter to:
Mrs. Lou Ann Rich, Manager
Management Services Corp.
10778 Main Street
Bellevue, WA 98004-1946

3. Supply an appropriate
salutation.

4. Use the same closing lines.

116e ▶ 5 Improve Language Skills: Apostrophe

1. Read and key the **Learn** sentence (with number and period), noting how the rule has been applied.

2. Key the **Apply** sentences (with numbers and periods), using the correct punctuation.

3. If time permits, rekey the **Apply** lines at a faster speed.

> To *show possession,* use an apostrophe *plus s* after a proper name of one syllable that ends in *s.*

Learn 1. I will buy Tom Ross's watch if it is for sale soon.
Apply 2. Did you see Susan Chris' shoes or Tom Bess' hat near the table?
Apply 3. I just learned Tom Sams' and Rita Tess' books were found.

> To *show possession,* use *only* an apostrophe after (1) plural nouns ending in *s* and (2) a proper name of more than one syllable which ends in *s* and *z.*

Learn 4. The boys' teacher will help with Thomas' science project.
Apply 5. The ladies watches were found in Douglas Variety Store.
Apply 6. Leon Contos's agenda for the officer's meeting was clear.

ENRICHMENT ACTIVITY: Improve Keyboarding and Composing Skills

Improve Keyboarding Skill: Speed-Forcing Drill

1. Each line twice at top speed; then:

2. In each set, try to complete each sentence on the call of 15", 12", or 10" timing as directed. Force speed to higher levels as you move from line to line.

3. Move from Set 1 to Set 2 to Set 3 as you are able to complete the lines in the time allowed.

4. Two 1' speed-forcing timings on lines 1d, 2d, and 3d. Compare rates.

5. Take additional 1' timings on the sentence or sentences on which you made your lowest rate(s).

		gwam		
	Set 1: High-frequency balanced-hand words emphasized.	15"	12"	10"
1a	The girl will hand the sorority emblem to the visitors.	44	55	66
1b	The handyman is to go to the field to cut ivy for the bowls.	48	60	72
1c	Their goal is to surprise the four city officials during a visit.	52	65	78
1d	Eight girls in the dorm lend a hand to the maid to keep the dorm cozy.	56	70	84
	Set 2: High-frequency combination-response patterns emphasized.			
2a	Nancy was at the dorm cafe by six p.m. to eat with him.	44	55	66
2b	The abstract is to be added to the formal report we drafted.	48	60	72
2c	The extra pupil is to join me by the pool to work on fast starts.	52	65	78
2d	My dad attested that the barber paid the wage tax to the city auditor.	56	70	84
	Set 3: High-frequency one-hand words emphasized.			
3a	Bret saw fast deer retreat after Johnny started uphill.	44	55	66
3b	My pupil asserts that great debates are based only on facts.	48	60	72
3c	Lilli Mull addressed my pupils on minimum state tax rates on gas.	52	65	78
3d	In my opinion, only a few eager pupils read texts on careers in trade.	56	70	84

| 1 | 2 | 3 | 4 | 5 | 6 | 7 | 8 | 9 | 10 | 11 | 12 | 13 | 14 |

Compose at the Keyboard

1. Compose a paragraph describing an accomplishment of yours of which you are proud.

2. Jot down the thoughts you want to relate, arrange them in a logical order, and then compose your paragraph from your notes.

3. Review your composition, use proofreader's marks to indicate the changes you want to make.

4. Process a final copy.

46a ▶ 6
Conditioning
Practice

each line twice SS; then a
1' writing on line 3; find *gwam*

alphabet 1 Vicky landed quite a major star for her next big plaza show.

fig/sym 2 Items marked * are out of stock: #139*, #476A*, and #2058*.

speed 3 Dodi is to handle all the pay forms for the small lake town.

| 1 | 2 | 3 | 4 | 5 | 6 | 7 | 8 | 9 | 10 | 11 | 12 |

46b ▶ 14 *Learn to Address Envelopes*

1. Study the guides at right and the illustrations below.

2. Format a small (No. 6¾) and a large (No. 10) envelope for each of the addresses given below the illustration (LP pp. 39-46). Use your own return address on the small envelopes.

3. If time permits, practice folding standard-sized sheets of paper for both large and small envelopes. (See Reference Guide page RG7.)

Envelope address

Set a tab stop 10 spaces left of center of a small envelope, and 5 spaces left of center for a large envelope.

Space down 12 lines from top edge of a small envelope, and 14 spaces for a large envelope. Begin the address at the tab stop position.

Style

Use *block style*, SS. Use ALL CAPS; omit punctuation. Place city name, 2-letter state name abbreviation, and ZIP Code on last address line. Two spaces precede the ZIP Code.

Return address

Use *block style*, SS, and caps and lowercase or ALL CAPS. Begin on line 2 from top of envelope, 3 spaces from left edge.

Special notations

Place *mailing notations* such as REGISTERED and SPECIAL DELIVERY below the stamp position on line 8 or 9.

Place *addressee notations* such as PERSONAL and HOLD FOR ARRIVAL a DS below the return address and 3 spaces from left edge of envelope.

Formatting Personal and Business Envelopes as Recommended by the U.S. Postal Service

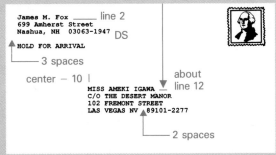

Note: The ALL CAPS unpunctuated address format may also be used for the letter address when window envelopes or automated addressing equipment (computers) is used.

MRS SONIA J CARDONA ASST VP
GENESIS ELECTRONICS INC
700 E DURANGO BLVD
SAN ANTONIO TX 78205-2649

DR NIGEL P OATMAN
407 UNIVERSITY AVENUE
SYRACUSE NY 13210-1246

MS HAN CHING YU
GOLDEN GATE REALTY CO
785 MARKET STREET
SAN FRANCISCO CA 94103-2277

MR GEORGE V WHITNEY
ROUTE 1 BOX 457
DALTON GA 30720-1457

116c ▶ 10 Improve Keyboarding Technique: Letter Emphasis

each line 3 times (slowly, faster, then in-between rate for control)

Goal: To keep hands quiet with keystroking action limited to the fingers.

Emphasize: Continuity and rhythm with curved, upright fingers.

s Susanne sat still as soon as Suno served his sushi and sashimi dishes.

t Ted took title to two tiny cottages the last time he went to the city.

u Uri usually rushes uptown to help us unload the sugar from the trucks.

v Vera voted to review the vivid videos during her visit to the village.

w Walter was waving wildly when the swimmers were wading into the water.

x Tax experts explain that we are exempt from the existing excise taxes.

y Your young boys yearn to go yachting each year on my big yellow yacht.

z Zeno puzzled over a zany zealot who seized a bronze kazoo at a bazaar.

116d ▶ 20 Measure Keyboarding Skill: Straight Copy

1. Two 3' writings; find *gwam*, circle errors on each.

2. Two 5' writings; find *gwam*, circle errors on each.

Goal: to maintain 3' rate for 5'.

3. Record better 3' and better 5' *gwam*.

4. Compare these rates with those achieved in 114d.

Skill Building (as time permits)

1. Set a goal of speed or control: If you made 6 or more errors on the 3' writings, work for control; otherwise, work for speed.

2. Take two 1' writings on each ¶ trying to increase speed or reduce errors according to your goal.

3. Take a 5' writing on ¶s 1-3 combined; find *gwam*, circle errors.

4. Record your 5' *gwam* if it exceeded the 5' rate attained earlier in the lesson.

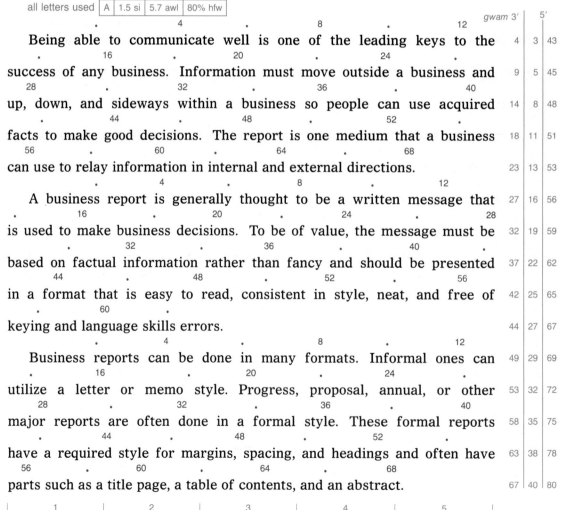

all letters used | A | 1.5 si | 5.7 awl | 80% hfw

gwam 3' | 5'

Being able to communicate well is one of the leading keys to the | 4 | 3 | 43

success of any business. Information must move outside a business and | 9 | 5 | 45

up, down, and sideways within a business so people can use acquired | 14 | 8 | 48

facts to make good decisions. The report is one medium that a business | 18 | 11 | 51

can use to relay information in internal and external directions. | 23 | 13 | 53

A business report is generally thought to be a written message that | 27 | 16 | 56

is used to make business decisions. To be of value, the message must be | 32 | 19 | 59

based on factual information rather than fancy and should be presented | 37 | 22 | 62

in a format that is easy to read, consistent in style, neat, and free of | 42 | 25 | 65

keying and language skills errors. | 44 | 27 | 67

Business reports can be done in many formats. Informal ones can | 49 | 29 | 69

utilize a letter or memo style. Progress, proposal, annual, or other | 53 | 32 | 72

major reports are often done in a formal style. These formal reports | 58 | 35 | 75

have a required style for margins, spacing, and headings and often have | 63 | 38 | 78

parts such as a title page, a table of contents, and an abstract. | 67 | 40 | 80

gwam 3' | 1 | 2 | 3 | 4 | 5
5' | 1 | 2 | 3

46c ▶ 22 Check Business Letter Formatting Skill

2 letterheads (LP pp. 47-50) or plain full sheets

Document 1
Business Letter with USPS Address

1. Format and key the average-length letter.

2. Use the USPS address format as shown; assume a window envelope will be used.

3. Proofread and correct your copy before removing it from your typewriter or computer.

Document 2
Business Letter with Variations

Format the letter again from your corrected copy, making these changes:
Date: **November 17, 19--**
Address, traditional format:
Mr. Edwin C. Phipps
Elmwood Vocational School
1262 Asylum Avenue
Hartford, CT 06105-2828
Salutation: supply one
Subject: **WORLD CHAMPIONS**
Copy notation: **c Ms. Eloise M. Rozic**

	words
November 16, 19--	4
MISS JANELLE A QUIN — *Use USPS format.*	8
CENTRAL HIGH SCHOOL	12
1000 LINCOLN AVENUE	16
EVANSVILLE IN 47714-2330	21
Dear Miss Quinn	24

Thanks/for conveying the intrest of your students inthe 36
keying speeds acheived by those who have won international 48
typewriting contests. 52
Margaret/Hama won hte last inter national contest, held 64
in 1941. She keyed for an hour on an electric typewriter 75
at a speed of 149 net words a minute (errors penalized). 87
The next highest speed was attained by Albert Tangore who 99
won the 1923 contest on a manual typewriter atthe rate of 110
147 words a minute 115
Even though later claims have been made to the title World 126
Champion Typist," the international contests were discon- 137
tinued during World War II and to our knowledge have not 149
been started again resumed. 152

Good luck to you and you students as you seek champion 163
ship speed. (141) 166
Sincerely Yours 169

Mrs. Allison K. Boyles 173
Educational director *cap* 178

xx (Use your initials) 178/195

46d ▶ 8 Language Skills: Complex Sentences

1. Study the guides in the color blocks at right and the sentences that illustrate the guides.

2. Key the **Learn** sentences as shown, noting the clauses that are independent (can stand alone as a sentence) and dependent (cannot stand alone as a sentence).

3. On a separate sheet of paper, key vertically the numbers 1 through 8, DS.

4. Key the subject and predicate of the independent clause and then of the dependent clause of each sentence opposite the appropriate number. Use a diagonal (/) to separate the subject-predicate of one clause from that of the other clause.

5. Check work with teacher.

> A complex sentence contains only one independent clause but one or more dependent clauses.

Learn 1 The book that you gave Juan for his birthday is lost.
Learn 2 If I were you, I would speak to Paula before I left.
Learn 3 Miss Gomez, who chairs the department, is currently on leave.
Learn 4 Students who use their time wisely usually succeed.

> The subject of a complex sentence may consist of more than one noun or pronoun; the predicate may consist of more than one verb.

Learn 5 All who were invited to the party also attended the game.
Learn 6 If you are to join, you should sign up and pay your dues.
Learn 7 After she and I left, Cliff and Pam sang and danced.
Learn 8 Although they don't know it yet, Fran and Bret were elected.

115c ▶ 5 Improve Language Skills: Apostrophe

1. Read and key the **Learn** sentence (with number and period), noting how the rule has been applied.

2. Key the **Apply** sentences (with numbers and periods), using the correct punctuation.

3. If time permits, rekey the **Apply** lines at a faster speed.

> Use an apostrophe *plus s* to form the plural of most figures, letters, and words (6's, A's, five's). In market quotations, form the plural of figures by the addition of *s* only.

Learn   1.   Your d's look like 4's. Chicago Growth Fund 89s are due in 2007.

Apply   2.   Reprint all ts, fs, and gs. Buy Prospect 7s this coming month.

Apply   3.   He consistently keyed %s as 5s, $s as 4s, and *s as 8s.

> To show *possession*, use an apostrophe *plus s* after (1) a singular noun and (2) a plural noun which does not end in *s*.

Learn   4.   The children's toys were expensive, but the boy's clothes were not.

Apply   5.   We went to the mens store on the left to buy a mans suit.

Apply   6.   Marys new coat was found in the womens locker room.

115d ▶ 10 Improve Keyboarding Technique: Letter Emphasis

each line 3 times (slowly, faster, then in-between rate for control)

Goal: To keep hands quiet with keystroking action limited to fingers.

Emphasize: Continuity and rhythm with curved, upright fingers.

j   Jed just objected to taking Jim's jeans and jogging jersey on the jet.

k   Karl kept Kay's knicknack in a knapsack in the keel of the knockabout.

l   All small holes in the lane to the left of my dwelling will be filled.

m   Myra meets my mama most mornings at the mall during the summer months.

n   Nora's niece and nephew can be tended by only one new nanny on Monday.

o   One of four officers opposed opening more offshore moorings for boats.

p   Pam's playful puppy pulled the paper wrapping off the apple and pears.

q   Quinten quit questioning the requirements for bouquets at the banquet.

r   Rory and Larry arrived from a rough carriage ride over the rural road.

115e ▶ 10 Compose at the Keyboard

1. Compose a paragraph describing the most memorable thing that happened to you last year.

2. Jot down the thoughts you want to relate, arrange them in a logical sequence, and then compose your paragraph from your notes.

3. Review your composition; use proofreader's marks to indicate the changes you want to make.

4. Save the copy for Lesson 116.

Lesson 116   Keyboarding/Language/Composing Skills

116a ▶ 5 Conditioning Practice

each line twice SS (slowly, then faster); DS between 2-line groups; if time permits, rekey selected lines

alphabet   1   Fay Bok's new zoo job requires her to do seven or eight complex tasks.

fig/sym   2   The cost of Model #40-79 is $352 plus 6% sales tax and 18% excise tax.

shift key   3   Dana, Jerry, and Fred plan to see the movie, <u>Let Janis Lead the Games</u>.

speed   4   The official goal of the spa downtown is to get my body in good shape.

| 1 | 2 | 3 | 4 | 5 | 6 | 7 | 8 | 9 | 10 | 11 | 12 | 13 | 14 |

116b ▶ 10 Compose at the Keyboard

1. Retrieve the revised copy you prepared in 115e, above.

2. Review the copy once more, marking any additional changes you want to make.

3. Key a final draft of your paragraph with 1½" side margins and "A Most Memorable Thing" as a title; DS the ¶.

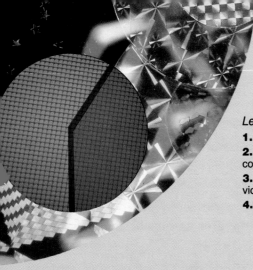

Improve Keyboarding/Language Skills

Learning Goals

1. To improve keyboarding technique.
2. To check/improve keyboarding speed and control (accuracy).
3. To check application of language skills previously learned.
4. To extend compose-as-you-key skills.

Format Guides

1. **Paper guide** at 0 (for typewriters).
2. LL: 60 spaces; see *Get Ready to Keyboard: Typewriters* (p. x) or *Computers* (p. xii).
3. LS: SS drills; DS ¶s, language skills, and composing activities.
4. PI: 5 spaces when appropriate.

Lesson 47	Keyboarding/Language Skills	LL: 60 LS: SS

47a ▶ 6
Conditioning Practice

each line twice SS; then a 1′ writing on line 3; find *gwam*

alphabet 1   Jarvis will take the next big prize for my old racquet club.

fig/sym 2   My income tax for 1990 was $5,274.62--up 3% over 1989's tax.

speed 3   A neighbor paid the girl to fix the turn signal of the auto.

| 1 | 2 | 3 | 4 | 5 | 6 | 7 | 8 | 9 | 10 | 11 | 12 |

47b ▶ 9
Check/Improve Language Skills

LL: 60 spaces; LS: DS

1. Key each line, supplying capitalization as needed.
2. Check accuracy of work with teacher.
3. If time permits, rekey each line in which you made capitalization errors.

1   elana cruz agreed to serve as president of delta pi epsilon.

2   was it pope who said, "to err is human, to forgive divine"?

3   the address by dr. morales will be given in assembly hall.

4   fujio kimura began work for miramir, inc., on september 15.

5   the giant christmas tree in rockefeller plaza was stunning.

6   "be very quiet," she said, "and listen to the stillness."

7   she said to check the data in volume 4, section 2, page 29.

8   a labor day buffet dinner will be held at 201 fifth street.

47c ▶ 15 Improve Keyboarding Technique

LL: 60 spaces; LS: SS
Tabs: Set 2, 24 spaces apart, starting at LM

1. Each line twice SS; DS between 4-line groups.
2. A 1′ writing on each of lines 8, 10, and 12; find *gwam* on each.
3. If time permits, rekey the two lines on which you had the lowest *gwam*.

tabulator 1   if they work   tab   as they fear   tab   he may serve
           2   he paid them   my land case   she may save

shift keys 3   Jane and Robb go to a New Year's party with Donna and Spiro.
           4   R. J. Appel was paid by the Apollo Insurance Co. of Jackson.

space bar 5   It is up to me to do my best in each try to make a new goal.
           6   Andy may use his pen to sign the form for a job in the city.

letter response 7   A tax rate was set in my area only after we set a case date.
           8   We are free only after we get him set up on a tax rate case.

combination response 9   I shall bid on the antique vase only if I regard it as rare.
           10   You are to sign all of the artwork you turn in to be graded.

word response 11   He is to do the work for both of us, and she is to pay half.
           12   The girl with the titian hair owns the title to the autobus.

| 1 | 2 | 3 | 4 | 5 | 6 | 7 | 8 | 9 | 10 | 11 | 12 |

114d ▶ 30 Assess/ Improve Keyboarding Speed and Control

1. A 1' writing on each ¶ for speed; find *gwam*.

2. A 1' writing on each ¶ for control; circle errors.

3. A 3' writing on ¶s 1-3 combined; find *gwam*; circle errors.

4. Record your 3' *gwam* to compare with your 3' *gwam* in 116d.

Skill Building (as time permits)

1. Set a goal of speed or control. If you made 6 or more errors on the 3' writing, work for control; otherwise, work for speed.

2. Take two 1' writings on each ¶ trying to increase speed or reduce errors according to your goal.

3. Take a 5' writing on ¶s 1-3 combined; find *gwam*; circle errors.

4. Record your 5' *gwam* to compare with your *gwam* in 116d.

all letters used | A | 1.5 si | 5.7 awl | 80% hfw

	gwam 3'		5'
The computer is an amazing machine. It is amazing because of the	4	2	38
many things it does, the speed at which it does its operations, and the	9	6	42
degree of accuracy it maintains. In short, the computer is one of man-	14	8	44
kind's most important inventions and a resource that seems to be every-	19	11	47
where and do everything.	20	12	48
Computers are used by students in many classes. They are used by	25	15	51
people who work in health, law, farming, and athletics to record, keep,	30	18	54
and process data. Rock stars use them to run concerts and to write music.	35	21	57
Computers run and work on assembly lines and are used to design many con-	40	24	60
sumer goods.	40	24	60
Computers have changed extensively in the short period they have	45	27	63
existed. Early ones had to be kept in special areas and run by trained	50	30	66
personnel. Today, young children use them to learn or for play. The	54	33	69
jumbo, slow computers of yesteryear have given way to the small, quick	59	35	71
computers in use today.	61	36	72

gwam 3' | 1 | 2 | 3 | 4 | 5 |
5' | 1 | 2 | 3 |

Lesson 115   *Keyboarding/Language/Composing Skills*

115a ▶ 5 Conditioning Practice

each line twice SS (slowly, then faster); DS between 2-line groups; if time permits, rekey selected lines

alphabet 1 The Arizona firm will quote a very good price for the jet's black box.

figures 2 Of the 13,748 people who entered this year's 10k race, 9,652 finished.

shift key 3 The North-Side Vikings beat the Ipseyville Knights on Tuesday evening.

speed 4 Profit is no problem for the sorority social when it is held downtown.

| 1 | 2 | 3 | 4 | 5 | 6 | 7 | 8 | 9 | 10 | 11 | 12 | 13 | 14 |

115b ▶ 20 Improve Keyboarding Skill: Timed Writing

1. Take two 1' writings on each ¶ of 114d, above; find *gwam* on each writing.

2. Take a 3' writing on ¶s 1-3 combined; try to equal your best 1' *gwam* in Step 1.

3. Take a 5' writing on ¶s 1-3 combined; find *gwam*; circle errors.

47d ▶ 20
Check/Improve Keyboarding Skill

1. A 1' writing on ¶ 1; find *gwam*. Add 2-4 words to set a new goal.

2. Two 1' writings on ¶ 1 at your new goal rate, guided by ¼' guide call.

3. Key ¶ 2 in the same way.

4. A 2' writing on ¶ 1 and then on ¶ 2. If you finish a ¶ before time is called, start over.

5. A 3' writing on ¶s 1-2 combined; find *gwam*.

gwam	¼'	½'	¾'	1'
20	5	10	15	20
24	6	12	18	24
28	7	14	21	28
32	8	16	24	32
36	9	18	27	36
40	10	20	30	40
44	11	22	33	44
48	12	24	36	48
52	13	26	39	52
56	14	28	42	56

all letters used | LA | 1.4 si | 5.4 awl | 85% hfw

	gwam 2'	3'
What is it that makes one person succeed and another	5	4
fail when the two seem to have about equal ability? Some	11	7
have said that the difference is in the degree of motivation	17	11
and effort each brings to the job. Others have said that an	23	16
intent to become excellent is the main difference.	28	19
At least four items are likely to have a major effect	5	22
on our success: basic ability, a desire to excel, an aim	11	26
to succeed, and zestful effort. If any one of these is ab-	17	30
sent or at a low point, our chances for success are lessened.	23	34
These features, however, can be developed if we wish.	29	38

| Lesson 48 | Keyboarding/Language Skills | LL: 60 LS: SS |

48a ▶ 6
Conditioning Practice

each line twice SS; then a 1' writing on line 3; find *gwam*

alphabet 1 Bevis had quickly won top seed for the next games in Juarez.

fig/sym 2 The Diamond Caper (Parker & Sons, #274638) sells for $19.50.

speed 3 Shana may make a bid for the antique bottle for the auditor.

| 1 | 2 | 3 | 4 | 5 | 6 | 7 | 8 | 9 | 10 | 11 | 12 |

48b ▶ 9
Check/Improve Language Skills

LL: 60 spaces; LS: SS groups, DS between groups

1. Lines 1-2: Insert hyphens where words can be divided.

2. Lines 3-5: Correct the errors in capitalization.

3. Lines 6-8: Key numbers as words/figures when appropriate.

4. Check work with teacher; rekey incorrect sentences.

Word division

1 into yearly ideals annual indeed little smaller sessions
2 suggest sizable service taxicab variation self-analysis

Capitalization

3 the junior achievement meeting will be at 3 p.m. in room 44.
4 rick reviewed the article "ethics in business" on wednesday.
5 mrs. thomas assigned lines 10-20 of beowulf for november 16.

Number expression

6 The package measures thirty-two by twenty-four by eight cm.
7 When you get to 5th Street, turn west toward 10th Avenue.
8 We are to study Units one and two of Chapter 10 this week.

Extend Keyboarding, Language, and Composing Skills

Learning Goals

1. To improve and assess keyboarding techniques.
2. To improve and assess keyboarding speed and control.
3. To improve language and composing skills.

Format Guides

1. Paper guide at *0* (for typewriters).
2. LL: 70-space line.
3. LS: SS word and sentence drills; DS ¶s; or space as directed within an activity.
4. PI: 5 spaces, when appropriate.

Lesson 114   *Keyboarding/Language Skills*

114a ▶ 5
Conditioning Practice

each line twice SS (slowly, then faster); DS between 2-line groups; if time permits, rekey selected lines

alphabet	1	Buzz expects to take his good vehicle for quick journeys on warm days.
fig/sym	2	I made Check #948 payable to O'Hare & O'Brien for $156.07 on April 23.
shift key	3	Flo Pritts told Mary White and Glenn Nance to meet her at Hall & Sons.
speed	4	Their men are in good shape to box with vigor to the end of the fight.

| 1 | 2 | 3 | 4 | 5 | 6 | 7 | 8 | 9 | 10 | 11 | 12 | 13 | 14 |

114b ▶ 5 *Improve Language Skills: Apostrophe*

1. Read and key the **Learn** sentence (with number and period), noting how the rule has been applied.

2. Key the **Apply** sentences (with numbers and periods), using the correct punctuation.

3. If time permits, rekey the **Apply** lines at a faster speed.

> Use an apostrophe as a *symbol* for *feet* in billings or tabulations, or as a symbol for minutes. (Quotation marks may be used to signify inches or seconds.)

Learn 1. I was able to install five 2″ × 4″ × 8′ studs in 10′ 30″.
Apply 2. The 6 ft. 2 in. man scored a basket every 2 min. and 30 sec.
Apply 3. I ordered 2 in. × 4 in. × 12 ft. boards 30 min. ago.

> Use an apostrophe as a symbol to indicate the omission of letters or figures (as in contractions).

Learn 4. Mary better not register for more than five classes in winter '94.
Apply 5. It's a car that is very similar to the 55 Chevy.
Apply 6. We plan to study the 72 flood at two oclock this afternoon.

114c ▶ 10 *Improve Keyboarding Technique: Letter Emphasis*

each line 3 times (slowly, then faster, then in-between rate for control)

Goal: To keep hands quiet with keystroking action limited to the fingers.

Emphasize: Continuity and rhythm with curved, upright fingers.

a After Alana and Anna ate the pancakes, each had an apple and a banana.
b Barb became the best batter by being best at batting big rubber balls.
c Cris can use pictures of a raccoon, cactus, and cacao in the calendar.
d Did Red declare he was a decoy doing deep runs to defeat the defenses?
e Ed, Eve, and Keene were elected to chaperone every late evening event.
f Fred figures fifty fast rafts floated from Fairfax to Fordstaff Falls.
g Gregg and George glanced at the gaggle of geese going over the garage.
h His healthy habits and high hopes help him through hot hockey matches.
i I think he will insist on sliding down the icy path five or six times.

Extend Keyboarding, Language, and Composing Skills

48c ▶ 15 Improve Keyboarding Speed: Skill Comparison

1. A 1' writing on each line; find *gwam* on each writing.
2. Compare rates and identify the 4 slowest lines.
3. A 1' writing on each of the 4 slowest lines.
4. As time permits in later lessons, do this drill again to improve speed and control.

fig/sym	1	Ed asked, "How much is due by May 28 on Account #4039-1657?"
figures	2	By May 25 in 1990 we had planted 375 trees and 1,648 shrubs.
one-hand	3	My war on waste at a union mill was based upon minimum data.
long-reach	4	Myra said I must curb at once my urge to glance at my hands.
adjacent-key	5	Coila hoped for a new opal ring to wear to her next concert.
double-letter	6	Bobby will sell the cookbook for a little less than it cost.
combination	7	He may join us for tea at the pool if he wishes to see them.
balanced-hand	8	Did they make the right title forms for the eight big firms?

| 1 | 2 | 3 | 4 | 5 | 6 | 7 | 8 | 9 | 10 | 11 | 12 |

48d ▶ 20 Check/Improve Keyboarding Skill

1. A 3' writing on ¶s 1-2 combined; find *gwam*, circle errors.
2. A 2' writing on ¶s 1-2 combined; find *gwam*, circle errors.
3. A 1' writing on each ¶; find *gwam* on each writing.
4. Another 3' writing on ¶s 1-2 combined; find *gwam*, circle errors.
5. As time permits, take 1' guided writings on each ¶ to improve:
- **speed** (increase goal rate).
- **accuracy** (reduce goal rate).

all letters used | LA | 1.4 si | 5.4 awl | 85% hfw

	gwam 2'	3'
Planning is the first step in composing a message. The	6	4
plan should include a goal, what you want to accomplish. It	12	8
also should include a list of the points you will use to con-	18	12
vince the reader of your point of view or of the action you	24	16
want taken. The list should be arranged in logical sequence.	30	20
Your goal is the major idea behind the topic sentence.	36	24
The topic sentence is often stated first, followed next by	41	28
facts and ideas that support it. You may instead decide to	47	32
work up to the main idea at the end. In either case, you	53	35
itemize the information and tie it to the main thought.	59	39

gwam 2' | 1 | 2 | 3 | 4 | 5 | 6 |
3' | 1 | 2 | 3 | 4 |

ENRICHMENT ACTIVITY: Composing

LL: 60 spaces; LS: DS; PB: line 12

1. Select a topic from those given at right.
2. Compose two or three ¶s giving your plans (or point of view) regarding the topic.
3. Edit and proofread your copy; then process a final draft with errors corrected.

1 My future education plans
2 The harmful effects of steroid use
3 The job I want and why
4 Why I want to excel
5 Why I do not care to be No. 1
6 How to reduce teenage drinking
7 My plans for a future career
8 Is winning the most important goal
9 Why cheating is wrong
10 How to reduce teenage drug abuse
11 My plans for next summer
12 How I do my homework

112c-113c (continued)

Document 8

LP p. 69 or
plain full sheet

1. Use block format; open punctuation.

2. Supply **current date.**

3. Address letter to
Ms. Leona X. Wilhite
High Point High School
335 Tryon Road
Raleigh, NC 27603-3595

4. Address an envelope.

Learning Cue: Center the table within the margins of the letter. DS above and below the table and below the column headings; SS the column entries. Leave an even number of spaces between columns. The table may be indented an equal number of spaces from the left and right margin settings.

opening lines 20

```
Dear Ms. Wilhite                                              23

You should be proud that your business English classes at     35
High Point have decided to participate in the Learning Cen-   46
ter's competitive spelling competition. event                53

As you know, the purpose of this year's competition is to     65
improve every student's ability to spell correctly those      76
words which are commonly misspelled in business communica-    88
tions.  A secondary purpose is to give recognition to stu-    99
dents who can spell with 100% accuracy the words which will   111
be included on a 100-item list at the end of the program.     123

Since a complete listing of each week's words will not be     134
available until early next month, I am sending you the words  147
for the first three weeks.                                    152
```

Week 1	**Week 2**	**Week 3**	162
function	interest	analysis	167
manufacturing	presently	attention	174
provisions	production	capacity	180
administrative	registration	closing	187
distribution	technical	division	194
paragraph	together	entitled	199

```
Good luck to you and your students.  We are proud that we can  212
sponsor such a valuable program and pleased that you are able  224
to participate in it. (205)                                    228

Sincerely                                                      230

Harry L. Connors                                               234
Education Liaison                                              237

xx                                                       238/254
```

ENRICHMENT ACTIVITY: *Improve Basic Skill: Statistical Copy*

1. Select a goal: Accuracy--Reduce errors by one on each writing; Speed--Increase *gwam* by 3 on each writing.

2. Take three 3' writings; determine errors and *gwam.*

all letters used | A | 1.5 si | 5.7 awl | 80% hfw

	gwam 1'	3'
The sales report for the quarter ending September 31 indicated that	14	4
sales for Easy-Korec Blue Correctable Film ribbon (Stock #B193) were	27	9
down by 40% while sales of all other ribbons were up by an average of	41	14
15%. To boost sales of B193 ribbons, the selling price will be reduced	56	19
during the next quarter from $7.50 to $4.49 per ribbon (a 40% discount).	71	24
Also, a four-color display board emphasizing that the B193 ribbon can be	85	28
used as a replacement ribbon for TJK-133 and XRT-159 will be available	100	33
to all salespersons in the region.	106	35

gwam 1' | 1 | 2 | 3 | 4 | 5 | 6 | 7 | 8 | 9 | 10 | 11 | 12 | 13 | 14 |
3' | 1 | | 2 | | 3 | | 4 | | 5 |

Measure Keyboarding/Formatting Skills

Measurement Goals
1. To demonstrate that you can key straight-copy ¶s for 3 minutes at the speed and control level specified by your teacher.
2. To demonstrate that you can format and key personal-business and business letters in block style.
3. To demonstrate that you can format and key simplified memos in block style.
4. To demonstrate that you can center lines horizontally.

Format Guides
1. *Paper guide* at *0* (for typewriters).
2. LL: 60 spaces for drills, ¶s, and personal-business letters; as format requires on business letters and memos. See *Get Ready to Keyboard: Typewriters* (p. x) or *Computers* (p. xii).
3. LS: SS drills and documents; DS ¶s.
4. PI: 5 spaces when appropriate.

Lesson 49	*Keyboarding/Formatting Skills*

49a ▶ 6
Conditioning Practice

each line twice SS; then a
1′ writing on line 3; find *gwam*

alphabet 1   Jocko will place a high bid for my next prized antique vase.

fig/sym 2   Ora asked, "Wasn't R&N's check #285367 deposited on 1/4/90?"

speed 3   When did the field auditor sign the audit form for the city?

| 1 | 2 | 3 | 4 | 5 | 6 | 7 | 8 | 9 | 10 | 11 | 12 |

49b ▶ 14 Check Keyboarding Skill

1. A 1′ writing on ¶ 1; find *gwam*; circle errors.
2. A 1′ writing on ¶ 2; find *gwam*; circle errors.
3. A 2′ writing on ¶s 1 and 2 combined; find *gwam*; circle errors.
4. A 3′ writing on ¶s 1 and 2 combined; find *gwam*; circle errors.

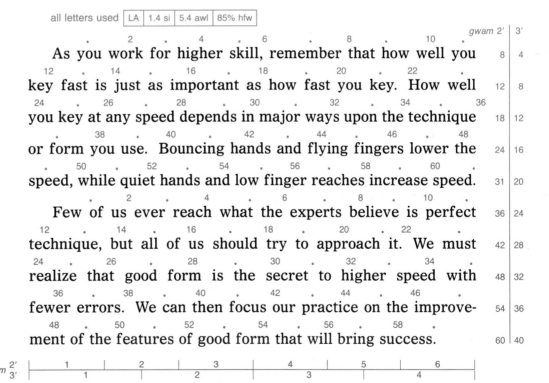

all letters used | LA | 1.4 si | 5.4 awl | 85% hfw

gwam 2′ | 3′

As you work for higher skill, remember that how well you   8 | 4

key fast is just as important as how fast you key. How well   12 | 8

you key at any speed depends in major ways upon the technique   18 | 12

or form you use. Bouncing hands and flying fingers lower the   24 | 16

speed, while quiet hands and low finger reaches increase speed.   31 | 20

Few of us ever reach what the experts believe is perfect   36 | 24

technique, but all of us should try to approach it. We must   42 | 28

realize that good form is the secret to higher speed with   48 | 32

fewer errors. We can then focus our practice on the improve-   54 | 36

ment of the features of good form that will bring success.   60 | 40

gwam 2′ | 1 | 2 | 3 | 4 | 5 | 6 |
    3′ | 1 | 2 | 3 | 4 |

49c-50c ▶ 30 (daily)
Measure Formatting Skills

3 letterheads (LP pp. 61-66)
3 plain full sheets
error correction supplies

1. Begin processing the documents on pp. 89-90 (use the *Letter Placement Guide* on p. 76). You have two class periods to complete the documents.

Note: Complete the line on which you are working when the class ends so that if necessary you can reinsert the paper and continue the document in the next class period.

2. Correct any errors you make as you key.

3. Before you remove a document from the machine or screen, proofread and correct your copy.

4. If you complete all documents before time is called, start over.

112c-113c (continued)

Document 3

plain full sheet, short edge at top; DS data; CS: 8 between longest items in columns

Document 4

Reformat Document 3 on a half sheet, long edge at top; SS data; CS: 6 between longest items in columns.

EMPLOYEE TUITION REIMBURSEMENT REPORT				8
As of Second Quarter Ended May 31, 19--				16
Name	First Quarter	Second Quarter	All Previous Quarters	23 / 38
Elaine Wilson	$ 430	$ 860	$ 5,655	47
Jean Baker	325	——	1,870	52
Surin Bajwa	890	445	4,286	57
Frances Danoff	1,115	575	8,760	64
Dolores Foseco	145	290	870	70
Cory Gentile	——	450	450	75
Cynthia Kernohan	925	470	10,270	82
Dennis Massoni	——	1,010	1,010	88
Carl Schweiger	840	——	15,780	95
Sun Yoko	750	750	2,250	99
Carla Stevens	1,400	1,400	8,400	110
Totals	$6,820	$6,250	$59,601	118

Document 5

plain full sheet, long edge at top; DS data, CS: 8 between longest items in columns

Document 6

Reformat Document 5 on a half sheet, short edge at top; DS data; CS: 4 between longest items in columns.

OFFICE SUPPLIES				4
Proposed Spring Sale Prices				9
Item	Regular Price	Sale Price	Discount Rate	14 / 26
Correction Fluid	$ 1.59	$ .89	44%	34
Tape Dispenser	4.87	1.79	63%	40
Copyholder	16.95	10.99	35%	45
List Finder	16.95	12.69	25%	51
Desk Tray	4.00	1.89	53%	56
Letter Opener	.80	.59	26%	62
Desk Stapler	21.95	5.99	73%	68

Document 7

plain full sheet, long edge at top; DS data; CS: 10 between longest items in columns

NORTH BEDFORD HIGH LADY PANTHERS					6
Section 7-AAAA Basketball Results					13
Opponent*	W-L	Score	Top Scorer	Top Rebounder	31
BLACKLICK	W	65-54	Stellar	Swalga	38
Forest Hills	L	70-61	Stellar	Swalga	45
Central	W	74-49	Montgomery	Birch	52
BELLWOOD	W	64-56	Swalga	Swalga	58
PANTHER VALLEY	W	69-64	Stellar	Birch	65
McKinley	L	65-59	Birch	Domack	71
FOREST HILLS	W	66-64	Domack	Lewis	78
CENTRAL	W	85-71	Montgomery	Birch	84
Bellwood	W	62-58	Lewis	Swalga	90
Panther Valley	L	65-60	Swalga	Domack	98
McKINLEY	W	73-68	Stellar	Lewis	104
					108

*Home games in ALL CAPS. 112

Document 8 is on p. 200.

50a ▶ 6
Conditioning Practice

each line twice SS; then a
1' writing on line 3; find *gwam*

alphabet 1 Fitz may have a jinx on our squad, but we kept the gold cup.

fig/sym 2 Pay invoice #6382 for $4,279 (less discounts of 10% and 5%).

speed 3 Sign the work form for the six men to do the city dock work.

| 1 | 2 | 3 | 4 | 5 | 6 | 7 | 8 | 9 | 10 | 11 | 12 |

50b ▶ 14 Check Keyboarding Skill

1. Repeat the timed writings called for in the directions for 49b, p. 88.

Goals: To improve your 1-, 2-, and 3-minute *gwam* or to reduce excessive errors.

2. As time permits, do additional writings to improve speed or reduce errors.

49c-50c ▶ 30 (continued)

1. Continue formatting the documents below and on p. 90 which you began in Lesson 49c.

2. Proofread and correct your work before removing it from the machine or screen.

3. If you complete all documents before time is called, start over.

Document 1: Personal-Business Letter

plain full sheet; LL: 60 spaces; PB: line 14

	words
899 Farmers Loop Road	4
Fairbanks, AK 99712-3647	9
November 18, 19--	12
Attention Customer Service	18
Outergear, Inc.	21
1354 Market Street	25
San Francisco, CA 94103-2746	31
Ladies and Gentlemen	35

On October 30 I ordered from your winter cata- 44
log a Heavyweight Fleece Tee Shirt (#M628). 53
Although the packing slip and the printed plastic 63
bag label clearly state that the shirt is a Large, 73
the shirt label shows that the size is Medium. 83
Large was the size I ordered. 89

Because I have had a similar experience twice 98
in the past, my confidence in your ability to fill 108
my orders accurately is reduced. To avoid the 118
nuisance and expense of packaging and return- 126
ing the shirt, I will keep it to use as a gift. 136

Will you please caution your packers or the 145
appropriate manufacturers to check sizes and 154
colors more carefully before placing garments 163
in prelabeled bags. I'm certain that the extra 173
care will make your other customers happier, 182
too. 183

Sincerely yours 186

Roland C. Marshall 190

Documents 3, 4, and 5 are on p. 90.

Document 2: Business Letter

LP p. 61

	words
November 18, 19--	4
Mr. Leslie D. Banks	8
George Washington High School	14
2165 E. 2700 South Street	19
Salt Lake City, UT 84109-3720	25
Dear Mr. Banks	28

Your question about the effect of word process- 37
ing equipment on the need for keying accuracy 46
is a good one. 50

Accuracy of documents processed is just as 58
vital now as ever before. The ease with which 68
keying errors can now be corrected, however, 77
has shifted the emphasis from number of input 86
errors made to skill in finding and correcting 95
these errors. 98

A major weakness of those who take employ- 106
ment tests is their inability to detect and correct 117
the errors they make. Therefore, we suggest 126
that employee training should emphasize proof- 135
reading and error correction rather than error- 144
free initial input. 148

A grading system rewarding efficient proofread- 158
ing and correction skills instead of penalizing 167
errors of initial input is worthy of your serious 177
consideration. (words in body: 152) 180

Sincerely yours 184

Ms. Audrey M. Lindsay 188
Employment Office Manager 193

xx

194/214

112a-113a ▶ 5 (daily)
Conditioning Practice

each line twice SS (slowly, then faster); DS between 2-line groups; if time permits, rekey selected lines

alphabet 1 Maxine and Peggy requested that a dozen wives join the breakfast club.

figures 2 I answered 4,978; Sidney answered 5,102; the correct answer was 5,360.

fig/sym 3 Both courses (#23-981 & #45-760) meet every Tuesday night at 6:30 p.m.

speed 4 The ensign is to make a turn to the right when the signal is in sight.

| 1 | 2 | 3 | 4 | 5 | 6 | 7 | 8 | 9 | 10 | 11 | 12 | 13 | 14 |

112b ▶ 5
Improve Language Skills: Word Choice

1. Study the spelling and definition of each word.

2. Key the line number (with period), space twice, then key the **Learn** sentence; key the **Apply** sentence in the same format, selecting the correct word in parentheses to complete each sentence.

idle (adj) inactive

idol (n) one that is adored

leased (vb) to grant use or occupation of under contract in exchange for rent

least (adj) lowest in importance or rank

Learn 1. Tom Smith's newest singing idol was idle last week due to illness.

Apply 2. During my (idle, idol) time, I read the biography of my (idle, idol).

Learn 3. The fact that he leased his new automobile is least important.

Apply 4. The (leased, least) apartment is the (leased, least) of his concerns.

112c-113c ▶ 40/45 (daily)
Process Tables

Use the time remaining in this period and in the next period to complete as many documents on pp. 198-200 as you can; center headings; correct errors.

Document 1

plain full sheet, short edge at top; DS data; CS: 6 between longest items in columns

words

RICHMOND SALES OFFICE DIRECTORY			
Name	Position	Extension	
Bill Adair	Marketing Manager	8341	26
Patricia Aley	Marketing Representative	8378	35
Walter Barnett	Service Representative	8278	44
Russell Fosia	Office Manager	8279	51
Louis Glumac	Marketing Representative	8342	60
Joy Hovanik	Administrative Specialist	8377	69
Denise Summerville	Service Representative	8276	79
Susan Vold	Marketing Representative	8228	87
Lena Wahl	Customer Service	8328	94
Janice Williamson	Administrative Specialist	8376	104

(RICHMOND SALES OFFICE DIRECTORY — 6; Name / Position / Extension — 18)

Document 2

plain full sheet, short edge at top; DS data; CS: 8 between longest items in columns

THINGS TO KNOW		
Alaska and Western Canada		
Location	Capital	Area in Square Kilometers
Alaska	Juneau	1,518,778
Alberta	Edmonton	644,392
British Columbia	Victoria	930,533
Manitoba	Winnipeg	548,497
Northwest Territories	Yellowknife	3,246,404
Saskatchewan	Regina	570,271
Yukon Territory	Whitehorse	478,036

THINGS TO KNOW — 3
Alaska and Western Canada — 8
Area in — 11
Location / Capital / Square Kilometers — 26
Alaska ... Juneau ... 1,518,778 — 31
Alberta ... Edmonton ... 644,392 — 38
British Columbia ... Victoria ... 930,533 — 46
Manitoba ... Winnipeg ... 548,497 — 52
Northwest Territories ... Yellowknife ... 3,246,404 — 62
Saskatchewan ... Regina ... 570,271 — 68
Yukon Territory ... Whitehorse ... 478,036 — 77
— 80

Source: American Automobile Association Tourbook. — 106

Document 3 is on p. 199.

49c-50c (continued)

Document 3
Simplified Memo

LP p. 63 or plain full sheet;
SM: 1"; PB: line 10

DATE: **November 19, 19--**
Addressee: **Maya Lee Aguiar**
Subject: **MAKE-UP FLU**
VACCINATIONS
Writer's name: **William D. Jent**
Reference: **your initials**
Enclosure notation: supply

opening lines 12

Maya, please prepare in final form and post on all bulletin 24
boards the enclosed rough-draft announcement of the 34
make-up flu vaccinations on November 23. 43

Dr. Preston and his assistant will be available only from 54
8:30 a.m. to 10:30 a.m. Will you please set up a schedule in- 66
dicating at what time the members of each department are 78
to arrive at the Special Events Dining Room. A copy of the 90
schedule should be sent to each affected employee a day 101
or two before November 23. 107

closing lines 112

Document 4
Announcement

plain full sheet

Beginning on line 26, center
each line of the announcement,
DS.

```
              Health Service Center              5

                   announces                     7
           MAKE-UP FLU VACINATIONS               12
                 November 24                     14
                8:30-10:30 a.m.                  18
            Specail Events Room                  24
```

Document 5
Business Letter

LP p. 65

Date: **November 20, 19--**
Address the letter to:
Mrs. Kaye E. Ott, Manager
Office Research Associates
1140 Union Street
San Diego, CA 92101-4488
Salutation: supply
Subject: **THE PROFESSIONAL**
IMAGE
Complimentary close: supply
Writer's name and title:
Miss Alexis L. Morse
Professor of Business
Reference: **your initials**
Copy notation: **J. Ellen Hicks**

opening lines 30

In the many research projects you and your associates have completed done, you 45
must have discovered soem patterns among in major companies in 57
terms of dress codes or guides to apprpriate attire dress and groom- 70
ing for the office. 74

During seminars I have conducted completed this past year on the topic of 87
grooming and dressing for succes, I have encountered found quiet a few 100
working students people who take issue with what they call my conser- 112
vative attitude. They maintain that where they work, "any- 124
thing goes. 2 sp 127

If you have surveyed business practice in this facet of 138
employe conduct, i shall appreciate your sharing your findings 151
with me. Perhaps with your help, I can ~~tell~~ convince students that any- 165
thing goes is not a viable option in most offices. (144) 175

closing lines 190/**208**

words

OFFICE SPACE RENTALS line 12   4

DS

Availability & Cost as of May 21, 19--   12

DS

Building	Square Footage	Rent per Square Foot	
			15
			27
USP Tower	332,000	$23.50	33
One Court Centre	132,000	18.00	40
PTN Building	41,673	19.50	46
Detroit Plaza	None	20.25	52
Lee Plaza	300,000	22.50	57
Riverfront Center	109,000	21.75	64
Four Steel Plaza	40,000	24.25	71
State Bank Building	7,756	17.50	78
Fifth Avenue Place	14,000	19.00	86
Corporate Tower	51,666	20.50	92

DS

Table on Special-Size Paper

PHASE 3   LEARN TO FORMAT REPORTS AND TABLES

In the 25 lessons of Phase 3, you will:

1. Learn to format and process reports, reference lists, title or cover pages, and topic outlines.

2. Learn to format and process data in columnar or table form.

3. Improve basic keyboarding and language skills.

4. Apply your formatting skills to process a series of documents typical of those prepared in the office of a recreation center.

5. Measure and evaluate your basic document processing skills.

Drills and timed writings in this phase are to be keyed on a 70-space line. Line length for problems varies according to the format required.

You will work at various times from model typescript, from print, and from handwritten (script) and rough-draft (corrected) copy. Keyboarding for personal and business purposes is often done from script and rough draft.

111d ▶ 30 Process Complex Tables on Special-Size Paper

Table 1
Study the information at the right and the model table on p. 197. Then, key the model table as illustrated using a half sheet, short edge at top; DS data; CS: 4 between longest items in columns; correct errors.

Centering on Special-Size Paper

To find horizontal center of special-size paper:

1. Note on line-of-writing or format scale the scale reading at the left edge and at the right edge of the sheet.

2. Add the two figures.
3. Divide the total by 2.
4. The resulting figure is the horizontal center point of the paper--the point from which to backspace to center copy.

On a half sheet of paper, short edge at the top:

1. There are 51 vertical line spaces available for keying.
2. The horizontal center is:
28 for pica (10-pitch)
33 for elite (12-pitch)

Table 2
half sheet, short edge at top; DS data; CS: 6 between longest items in columns; correct errors

		words
NEUROPSYCHIATRIC CLINIC INCOME REPORT		8
For Quarter Ending March 30, 19--		14
Area	Sales	21
Psychiatric Services	$ 14,320.40	28
Sleep Disorder Medicine	1,610.85	35
Anxiety Disorders	2,753.25	40
Drug and Alcohol Addiction	20,248.35	48
Stress Management Classes	11,795.00	55
Psychological Testing	17,455.90	61
Neuroelectrodiagnostics	3,944.00	68
Eating Disorders	14,987.00	73
Weight Loss Groups	25,210.50	79
Weight Gain Groups	11,100.90	87
Total Income	$123,426.15	93

Table 3
half sheet, short edge at top; DS data; CS: 6 between longest items in columns; correct errors

	Current	Next	words
EAST COAST AIRLINE TICKET INCOME			7
(In Millions of Dollars)			11
Airport	Year	Year	14 / 22
Atlanta, GA	$ 3	$ 3.3	27
Baltimore, MD	2.5	3	32
Boston, MA	2.75	3.1	36
Charleston, SC	1.12	1.41	42
Charleston, WV	.6	.85	48
Hartford, CT	1.78	1.9	53
Miami, FL	3.25	3.3	57
Newark, NJ	3.01	3.21	62
Philadelphia, PA	2.87	2.98	69
Savannah, GA	.98	1.05	76
Total Income	$21.86	$24.1	82

Table 4
plain full sheet, long edge at top; DS data; CS: 10 between longest items in columns

	This	Last	%	words
TUITION INCOME				3
For Fiscal Year Ending June 30, 19--				10
Department	Year	Year	Change	15 / 28
Accounting	$ 96,948	$ 89,052	8.9	36
Administrative Management	25,548	22,939	11.4	45
Business Teacher Education	14,750	14,180	4	54
Communications & English	124,654	126,958	−1.8	64
Computer Information Systems	44,563	48,675	−8.4	74
Economics & Finance	35,980	34,540	4.2	82
Management & Marketing	112,274	108,541	3.4	91
Quantitative & Natural Sciences	95,613	94,590	1.1	101
Social Sciences	113,542	115,652	−1.8	113
Totals	$663,872	$655,127	1.3	120

UNIT 10   LESSONS 51 – 57
Learn to Format Reports and Outlines

Learning Goals

1. To learn to format and key unbound reports, reference lists, and title pages.

2. To learn to format and key topic outlines.

3. To learn to align copy vertically and horizontally.

4. To improve basic keyboarding skills.

Format Guides

1. *Paper guide* at *0* (for typewriters).

2. LL: 70 spaces for drills and ¶s; as required for document formats.

3. LS: SS drills; DS ¶s; as required for document formats.

4. PI: 5 spaces for ¶s and reports.

FORMATTING GUIDES: UNBOUND REPORTS

Page 1

Page 2

Automatic centering of report headings

Some machines can automatically center lines horizontally. If you are using such a typewriter or computer, refer to the Operator's Manual or User's Guide to learn how to center automatically. You may then center report headings and title page lines without using the manual backspace-from-center method.

UNBOUND REPORT FORMAT

Many short reports are prepared without covers or binders. Such reports are called *unbound reports*. If they consist of more than one page, the pages are fastened together in the upper left corner by a staple or paper clip.

Standard Margins

Unbound reports are formatted with standard 1-inch (1″) *side margins* (SM): 10 pica (10-pitch) spaces; 12 elite (12-pitch) spaces. With the *paper guide* set at *0* on the *line-of-writing* or *format scale*, this means that the left margin (LM) is set at 10 on 10-pitch machines or at 12 on 12-pitch machines. If computer margins are preset, the margins may have to be reset to leave the right number of spaces in each SM.

A *top margin* of about 2″ is customarily used on the first page of unbound reports, so the title is placed on line 12. In school settings where the same report is done by users of both 10- and 12-pitch machines, a 1½″ top margin (PB: line 10) may be used for 10-pitch machines so that all students have similar end-of-page decisions to make.

A 1″ *bottom margin* is recommended. Because the internal spacing of report parts varies, a bottom margin of exactly 1″ is often not possible. For that reason, a bottom margin of *at least* 1″ is acceptable. An exact 1″ bottom margin would place the last line of copy on line 60 from the top edge of the paper.

Report Margin Summary

	10-pitch	12-pitch
Line Length (LL)	10-75	12-90
Page Beginning (PB) Page 1	line 10/12	line 12
Page 2 (page #)	line 6	line 6
Page Ending (PE)	line 60 or less	line 60 or less

Page Numbering

The first page of an unbound report is usually not numbered. On the second and subsequent pages, the page number is placed on line 6 at the right margin (RM). A DS is left below the page number so that the first line of the report body appears on line 8.

Internal Spacing of Reports

A QS is left between the report title and the first line of the body. Multiple-line titles are DS. A DS is left above and below side headings and between paragraphs, which are usually DS but may be SS when specified.

Internal (textual) Citations

References used to give credit for quoted or paraphrased material are cited in parentheses in the report body. This internal (textual) citation method of documentation is rapidly replacing the footnote method because it is easier and quicker. Internal citations should include the name(s) of the author(s), the year of publication, and the page number(s) of the material cited.

Quotation marks are used for direct quotes, but not for paraphrased material. An ellipsis (. . .) is used to indicate any material omitted from a quotation.

> "Many changes are occurring today in office organization . . . and technology" (VanHuss and Daggett, 1990, 1).

Reference Lists

All references cited in a report are listed alphabetically by author surnames at the end of a report (usually on a separate page) under the heading REFERENCES. A QS appears between the heading and the first reference. The reference page uses the same top margin and side margins as the first page of the report except that a page number appears on line 6 at the RM.

Each reference is SS with a DS between references. The first line of each reference begins at the LM; other lines are indented 5 spaces. If the reference list appears on the last page of the report body, a QS is left between the last line of copy and the heading REFERENCES.

111a ▶ 5 (daily)
Conditioning Practice

each line twice SS (slowly, then faster); DS between 2-line groups; if time permits, rekey selected lines

alphabet	1	Eight quick joggers wanted very badly many prizes and expensive gifts.
figures	2	Nearly 250 pupils and 146 adults attended the game which we won 97-83.
long words	3	The administrative manager will purchase seven bidirectional printers.
speed	4	Nancy is to make an official bid for title to the authentic dirigible.

| 1 | 2 | 3 | 4 | 5 | 6 | 7 | 8 | 9 | 10 | 11 | 12 | 13 | 14 |

111b ▶ 7 Improve Language Skills: Word Choice

1. Study the spelling and definition of each word.
2. Key the line number (with period), space twice, then key the **Learn** sentence; key the **Apply** sentence in the same format, selecting the correct word in parentheses to complete each sentence.

plain (adj) with little ornamentation or decoration
plane (n) an airplane or hydroplane

pole (n) a long, slender rounded piece of wood or other material
poll (n) a canvassing of persons to analyze public opinion

Learn	1.	The seat in the plane was covered with plain beige cloth material.
Apply	2.	I will wear my (plain, plane) suit on the (plain, plane) next week.
Learn	3.	The young person taking the poll was near the corner light pole.
Apply	4.	A recent (pole, poll) showed a need for a new basketball (pole, poll).

111c ▶ 8 Measure Basic Skill: Straight Copy

1. One 5' writing; find *gwam*.
2. Proofread; circle errors.
3. Record *gwam* rate.

all letters used | A | 1.5 si | 5.7 awl | 80% hfw

	gwam 3'	5'
Character is often described as a person's combined moral or ethical	5	3	44
strength. Most people think it is like integrity which is thought to	9	6	47
be a person's ability to adhere to a code or a set standard of values.	14	8	49
If a person's values are accepted by society, others are likely to view	19	11	52
her or him as having a somewhat high degree of integrity.	23	14	55
You need to know that character is a trait that everyone possesses	27	16	57
and that it is formed over time. A person's character reflects his or	32	19	60
her definition of what is good or just. Most children and teenagers mold	37	22	63
their character through the words and deeds of parents, teachers, and	42	25	66
other adults with whom they have regular contact.	45	27	68
Existing character helps mold future character. It is important to	50	30	71
realize that today's actions can have a lasting effect. For that reason,	54	33	74
there is no better time than now to make all your words and deeds speak	59	36	77
favorably. You want them to portray the things others require of people	64	38	79
who are thought to possess a high degree of character.	68	41	82

gwam 3' | 1 | 2 | 3 | 4 | 5 |
5' | 1 | 2 | 3 |

195

51a ▶ 6
Conditioning Practice

each line twice SS (slowly, then faster); DS between 2-line groups; if time permits, rekey selected lines

alphabet	1	The six boys quickly removed juicy chunks from a sizzling pot of stew.
figures	2	They washed 59 cars, 28 vans, 47 campers, and 30 bikes on November 16.
fig/sym	3	The 164 copies (priced at $8.75 each) may be shipped on June 29 or 30.
speed	4	Dodi may make a fuchsia gown for the civic social to be held downtown.

| 1 | 2 | 3 | 4 | 5 | 6 | 7 | 8 | 9 | 10 | 11 | 12 | 13 | 14 |

51b ▶ 6 Improve Language Skills: Word Choice

1. Study the spelling/definitions of the words in the color block at right.

2. Key line 1 (the **Learn** line), noting the proper choice of words.

3. Key lines 2-3 (the **Apply** lines), choosing the right words to complete the lines correctly.

4. Key the remaining lines in the same way.

5. Check your accuracy; rekey lines containing word-choice errors.

its (adj) of or relating to itself as the possessor

it's (contr) it is; it has

than (conj/prep) used in comparisons to show difference between items

then (n/adv) that time; at that time

Learn	1	It's time for the dog to have its food.
Apply	2	Before (its, it's) time to bid, check (its, it's) number.
Apply	3	If (its, it's) not yours, return it to (its, it's) shelf.
Learn	4	If she is older than you, then I am older than you.
Apply	5	We (than, then) decided that two hours were more (than, then) enough.
Apply	6	Fewer (than, then) half the workers were (than, then) put on overtime.

51c ▶ 8 Review How to Center Lines Horizontally

Begin on line 28 of a plain full sheet. Center each line horizontally, DS.

Automatic procedure
If your equipment has automatic centering, see your User's Guide to review centering procedure.

Manual procedure

1. Move *cursor* or *printing point indicator* to center of paper.

2. From this point, backspace once for each 2 characters and spaces in the line to be centered. (Disregard any leftover letter.)

HORIZONTAL CENTERING

Equal Left and Right Margins

Half of Copy to Left of Center

Half of Copy to Right of Center

Variance of One or Two Spaces Acceptable

51d ▶ 30 Learn to Format an Unbound Report and Reference List

1. Study the report formatting information on p. 92.

2. On 2 plain full sheets, format the model report shown on pp. 94-95. Do not correct your errors as you key.

3. When you have finished, proofread your copy, mark it for correction, and prepare a final copy with all errors corrected.

Note: Line endings of elite/pica solutions differ.

Elite (12-pitch) Layout

110c ▶ 10
Preapplication: Formatting Multiple-Line Column Headings

1. If needed, review 108b, p. 191 and 109d, p. 193 (centering column headings).

2. Center each of the lines in the multiple-line headings in Drill 1 over the longest entry in its column. Key the headings and entries on a drill sheet; DS between last line of heading and first entry; DS the entries; CS: 8; do not correct errors.

3. Complete Drill 2 in the same manner.

Drill 1

Fruit Sold	Vegetables Sold	Meat Bought
Bananas	Peas	Beef
Apples	Corn	Pork
Pears	Beans	Lamb

Drill 2

Date of Purchase	Number	Sale Price
5/1/91	95	$11,650
7/9/91	101	11,425
9/5/91	77	11,875

110d ▶ 25
Process Tables with Multiple-Line Column Headings

center all headings; correct errors

Table 1
plain full sheet; short edge at top; DS data; CS: 8 between longest items in columns

			words
	CELLULAR TELEPHONES		4
	End-of-Month Clearance Sale		10
Cellular Telephone	Regular Selling Price	Clearance Price	16 / 29
TEC P-9100	$1,699.99	$888.88	35
TEC P-9110	1,999.99	999.99	42
Rawlins CP-1000	1,549.99	825.88	49
Rawlins CP-2000	1,749.99	925.88	57
Cellatel 380	1,224.99	749.99	63
Cellatel 480	1,924.99	974.99	70
Carfone XT	1,399.99	649.99	77
Carfone ST	1,599.99	848.88	83
Carfone ZT	1,799.99	949.88	89

Table 2
plain full sheet; short edge at top; DS data; CS: 8 between longest items in columns

Table 3
Reformat Table 2 on a half sheet; long edge at top; SS data; CS: 8 between longest items in columns.

			words
	MONEY MARKET FUNDS		4
	Percents for Week Ending May 30, 19--		11
Fund	Average Annual Yield	Change from Last Week	16 / 27
AAPMny	8.35	−.02	32
ActAsMny	7.64	.01	37
AlexGrn	7.52	—	42
CDAMny	8.44	.01	47
Lndpt	8.23	.06	52
MPS Life	7.90	−.03	57
NassCash	8.31	.16	62
VenPe	6.86	−.12	67
WllngHS	7.89	.06	72
XtrMny	6.98	−.04	76

Line 10, pica (10-pitch)
Line 12, elite (12-pitch)

Title   ELECTRONIC KEYBOARD APPLICATIONS   7

QS (space down 2 DS)

Report   Learning to key is of little value unless one applies it in   19
body
        preparing something useful--a record or document of some kind.   31

        Three basic kinds of software have been developed to assist those   45

        with keyboarding skill in applying their skill electronically.   57

DS

Side   **Word Processing Software**   67
heading
DS

        Word processing software is "software specially designed to   79

        assist in the document preparation needs of an individual or busi-   92

Internal   ness" (Clark et al., 1990, 193). Word processing software permits   106
citation
        the user to enter text, format it, manipulate or revise it, and   118

        print a copy. The software can be used to process a wide variety   132

        of documents such as letters, memos, reports, and tables.   143

DS

        This software has special features such as automatic center-   155

ing and word wrap that reduce time and effort. In addition, it   168

1"   1"

        permits error corrections, format and sequence changes, and inser-   181

        tion of variables "on screen" before a copy is printed. These   193

        features increase efficiency by eliminating document rekeying.   206

DS

Side   **Database Software**   213
heading
DS

        A database is "any collection of related items stored in com-   225

Internal   puter memory" (Oliverio and Pasework, 1989, 573). The data in a   238
citation
        database may be about club members, employee payroll, company sales,   252

        and so on. Database software allows the user to enter data, re-   265

        trieve and change it, or select certain data (such as an address) to   278

        be used in documents. Software users can manipulate and print data   292

        in report form for decision-making purposes.   301

Shown in pica (10-pitch) type,
photo-reduced

At least 1"

Unbound Report

(continued, p. 95)

109d ▶ 7 Preapplication Drill: Center Column Headings Over Columns

Use the procedure in the color block at the right to center each column heading over the longest entry in the column. Key the headings and entries on a drill sheet; DS between heading and first entry; SS the entries; CS: 8 between longest items in columns.

Center Column Headings (When Column Heading is Longest Line)

1. Set the left margin and tab stops for columns.
2. Key the column headings; DS.
3. Find center point of first column heading by spacing forward once for every two characters and spaces. If a stroke is left over at the end of the heading, do not space forward for it.
4. Identify the longest line in the column entries.
5. From the center point of the heading, backspace once for every two characters and spaces in the longest entry (drop leftover or extra stroke). Set new tab where backspace stops.
6. Repeat Steps 3 through 5 for each remaining column.

Atlantic Division	Central Division	Pacific Division
Boston	Detroit	Phoenix
Philadelphia	Chicago	San Diego
Washington	St. Louis	Portland

109e ▶ 13 Format Tables with Long Column Headings

plain full sheets; short edge at top; center all headings; correct errors

Table 1
DS data; CS: 10 between longest items in columns

Table 2
Reformat Table 1; SS data; CS: 8 between longest items in columns.

			words
LOCAL FM RADIO STATIONS			5
Call Letters	Dial Location	Telephone No.	21
WYTP	88.3	918-3637	26
WLTK	91.5	321-5422	32
WBZS	100.7	879-7090	37
KLPM	102.5	273-6401	43
WMEZ	104.3	521-4343	49
WLQP	106.7	988-9889	54
WQRS	106.9	343-7899	60
WEAS	107.9	314-5454	65

Lesson 110 — Processing Tables

110a ▶ 5 Conditioning Practice

each line twice SS (slowly, then faster); DS between 2-line groups; if time permits, rekey selected lines

alphabet 1 This weekly journal gives exact sizes of old boat and plane equipment.

figures 2 I know the ZIP Code plus 4 for 49-13th Street is listed as 92057-1683.

fig/sym 3 The 72″ × 96″ tablecloth will cost $84.63 less discounts of 10% & 15%.

speed 4 The soggy field by the city dog kennels was good for a big tug of war.

| 1 | 2 | 3 | 4 | 5 | 6 | 7 | 8 | 9 | 10 | 11 | 12 | 13 | 14 |

110b ▶ 10 Format Tables with Centered Column Headings

plain full sheet; short edge at top; DS data; CS: 6 between longest items in columns; centered headings; correct errors

				words
RETURNING VARSITY LETTERMEN ROSTER				7
Name	Sophomore	Junior	Senior	19
Jim Alvarez			X	22
Tom Beatty		X		25
David Dow		X		28
Fred Litteri	X			32
Sam Selkski			X	36
Pietro Thoeni		X		39
Tim Wemblack			X	43
Raul Waurez			X	46
Earl Zetz	X			52
Totals	2	3	4	57

Side heading **Spreadsheet Software**   310
DS

"A spreadsheet is an electronic worksheet made up of columns 322

Internal citation and rows of data" (Oliverio and Pasewark, 1989, 489). Spreadsheet 335

1″   software may direct a program to apply mathematical operations to 349

the data and to print reports that are useful in summarizing and   1″ 362

analyzing business operations and in planning for the future. 374
DS

Employment personnel look favorably upon job applicants who 386

are familiar with these kinds of software and how they are used. 399
QS (space down 2 DS)

REFERENCES 402
QS, then change to SS

List of references **Clark, James F., et al.** Computers and Information Processing. 422
    2d ed. Cincinnati: South-Western Publishing Co., 1990. 433
DS

Oliverio, Mary Ellen, and William R. Pasewark. The Office. Cin- 448
    cinnati: South-Western Publishing Co., 1989. 457

Unbound Report, Page 2

Lesson 52   **Unbound Reports**   *LL: 70*
                                                          LS: SS

52a ▶ 6
Conditioning Practice

each line twice SS (slowly, then faster); DS between 2-line groups; if time permits, rekey selected lines

alphabet 1 Four giddy children were amazed by the quick, lively jumps of the fox.

figures 2 This new edition boasts 1,380 photographs, 926 charts, and 475 graphs.

fig/sym 3 Check #1657 for $48.90, dated May 23, is made out to McNeil & O'Leary.

speed 4 He may hand me the clay and then go to the shelf for the die and form.

| 1 | 2 | 3 | 4 | 5 | 6 | 7 | 8 | 9 | 10 | 11 | 12 | 13 | 14 |

52b ▶ 6 Improve Language Skills: Word Choice

1. Study the spelling/definitions of the words in the color block at right.

2. Key line 1 (the **Learn** line), noting the proper choice of words.

3. Key lines 2-3 (the **Apply** lines), choosing the right words to complete the lines correctly.

4. Key the remaining lines in the same way.

5. Check your accuracy; rekey lines containing word-choice errors.

do (vb) to bring about; to carry out

due (adj) owed or owing as a debt; having reached the date for payment

hear (vb) to gain knowledge of by the ear

here (adv) in or at this place; at this point; in this case; on this point

Learn 1 If you pay when it is due, the cost will be less.

Apply 2 (Do, Due) you expect the plane to arrive when it is (do, due)?

Apply 3 (Do, Due) you want me to indicate the (do, due) date of the invoice?

Learn 4 Did you hear the sirens while you were here in the cellar?

Apply 5 (Hear, Here) is the new CD you said you want to (hear, here).

Apply 6 To (hear, here) well, we should see if we can get seats (hear, here).

109a ▶ 5
Conditioning Practice

each line twice SS (slowly, then faster); DS between 2-line groups; if time permits, rekey selected lines

alphabet	1	Quen said subzero weather may crack six big joints in the paved floor.
figures	2	They delivered 9,821 subcompact; 6,704 mid-size; and 395 luxury autos.
fig/sym	3	At 2:45 p.m., Teams #9 & #7 (Court 3-5) and #6 & #10 (Court 1-8) play.
speed	4	The neighbor burns wood and a small bit of coal to make a giant flame.

| 1 | 2 | 3 | 4 | 5 | 6 | 7 | 8 | 9 | 10 | 11 | 12 | 13 | 14 |

109b ▶ 7
Assessing Table Formatting Skills

Follow directions at the right.

1. Move margin stops to ends of line-of-writing scale.
2. Clear all tab stops.
3. At signal to begin, format and key as much of the model table on p. 190 as you can in 5′ (plain full sheet, short edge at top; DS data; CS: 10).
4. When time is called, determine errors and verify accuracy of settings for the left margin and tab stops.

109c ▶ 18
Format Tables

plain full sheets, short edge at top; center all headings; correct errors

Table 1
DS data; CS: 8 between longest items in columns

Learning cue: Align numbers at the right or at the decimal point if one is used.

		words
SNOWIEST PLACES IN U.S.		5
Annual Average Snowfall		10
City and State	**Amount**	20
Stampede Pass, Washington	36.04 feet	27
Valdez, Alaska	24.59 feet	32
Mt. Washington, New Hampshire	20.74 feet	41
Blue Canyon, California	20.27 feet	48
Yakutat, Alaska	17.37 feet	53
Marquette, Michigan	10.14 feet	59
Sault St. Marie, Michigan	9.6 feet	67
		70
Source: National Climatic Data Center.		78

Table 2
DS data; CS: 8 between longest items in columns

Learning cue: To indicate a total, underline the last entry the full length of the total figure; DS; key the total figure.

			words
TRI-VALLEY RECREATION CLUB			5
Comparison of Estimated and Actual Incomes			14
Income Source	Est.	Actual	25
Membership Dues	$11,050	$12,370.50	32
Court Fees	15,300	14,210.75	38
Weight Room Fees	3,750	4,010.25	45
Swimming Pool Fees	2,500	2,650.00	52
Instruction & Other	3,750	3,981.45	62
Indent 5 spaces Totals	$36,350	$37,222.95	68

52c ▶ 8 *Learn to Format a Report Title Page*

A title or cover page is prepared for many reports. Using the following guides, format a title page for the report you prepared in Lesson 51.

1. Center the title in ALL CAPS on line 16 of a plain full sheet (from top edge down 8 DS).

2. Center your name in capital and lowercase letters on the 16th line below the title.

3. Center the school name a DS below your name.

4. Center the current date on the 16th line below the school name.

ELECTRONIC KEYBOARD APPLICATIONS

Your name
Your school's name

Current date

52d ▶ 30 *Format a Book Report in Unbound Report Style*

1. Review the formatting guides on p. 92.

2. Format the following material as a 2-page unbound report on 2 plain full sheets.

3. Place the reference below the last line of copy on the second page of the report.

4. Correct any errors you make as you key.

5. Staple the pages together across the upper left corner or fasten them with a paper clip.

	words
BOOK REPORT	2
by	3
George Timberwolf	6

Ordinary People is a heartrending, and at times heartwarming, family novel in which "ordinary people" under pressure become special after all. — 17, 26, 35, 38

Calvin Jarrett is a determined, successful provider. Beth is his organized and efficient, but proud and self-centered, wife. They had two sons, Buck and Conrad. Now they have just one. Buck, the older and the leader, was drowned in a storm while sailing with Conrad, the younger and the follower. Conrad held on; Buck let go. — 47, 56, 65, 74, 83, 92, 102, 105

Devastated by the death of his brother, Conrad comes to blame himself and attempts suicide. After months in a hospital for physical and psychological care, he returns, still guilt-ridden, to a home environment that is less than warm and understanding. His mother does nothing to help relieve his feelings of guilt; — 113, 121, 130, 140, 149, 159, 168

rather, she is concerned with what her friends and neighbors will think of his behavior. Empathy and affection appear alien to her nature, and Buck was her favorite son. Thus it is left to the father, who is well-intentioned but often ineffective, to maintain parental ties to the boy. — 177, 186, 194, 203, 213, 223, 226

Conrad withdraws further into himself and away from his parents and friends. Only as a result of psychiatric care with Dr. Berger and his father's growing understanding and acceptance is he able to rebuild his self-image and self-esteem and to absolve himself of guilt. Conrad manages to reaccept his former friends and even to forgive his mother for her inability to show him affection and understanding--to say nothing of forgiveness. — 234, 243, 253, 262, 271, 280, 289, 299, 308, 314

The characters are so finely drawn they seem real. The story is so carefully woven that the reader is pulled along by an unwinding string from beginning to end, as in a mystery thriller. Principles of human strength born of suffering are laced throughout the story. One is left with the conviction that even for "ordinary people" under stress, there is a way out of the darkness. — 322, 331, 339, 348, 357, 366, 375, 384, 391

	words
REFERENCE	393

Guest, Judith. Ordinary People. New York: Ballantine Books, 1979. — 405, 409

108a ▶ 5
Conditioning Practice

each line twice SS (slowly, then faster); DS between 2-line groups; if time permits, rekey selected lines

alphabet   1   Jackie Wadman's next goal is to qualify for the event's bronze trophy.

figures   2   There were 12,087; 9,365; and 8,401 fans at the last three home games.

symbols   3   Jane practiced keying *, /, and — on Monday; %, $, and # on Wednesday.

speed   4   Lay the clamshell at the end of the rug on the big shelf at the right.

| 1 | 2 | 3 | 4 | 5 | 6 | 7 | 8 | 9 | 10 | 11 | 12 | 13 | 14 |

108b ▶ 7
Preapplication Drill: Center Column Headings Over Columns

Use the procedure in the color block at the right to center each of the column headings over the longest entry in its column. Key the headings and entries on a drill sheet; DS between heading and entry; SS the entries; CS: 8 between longest items in the columns; do not correct errors.

Center Column Headings (When Column Heading is not Longest Line)

1. Identify the longest entry in each column.

2. Find center point of entry by spacing forward once for every two characters and spaces. If a stroke is left over at the end of the item, do not space forward for it.

3. From the center point of the longest column entry backspace once for every two characters and spaces in the column heading. Begin the heading where the backspacing ends.

Name	Class	Position
Harry Aine	Junior	Tackle
Tom Burrell	Sophomore	Flanker
Bill Casey	Senior	Linebacker

108c ▶ 38 Format Tables with Centered Headings

center all headings

Table 1
plain full sheet, short edge at top; DS data; CS: 8 between longest items in columns; do not correct errors

Table 2
plain full sheet, short edge at top; DS data; CS: 8 between longest items in columns; correct errors

Table 3
Reformat Table 1 on a half sheet, long edge at top; arrange deductions in alphabetical order; SS data; CS: 12 between longest items in columns; correct errors.

		words
SUE TOTH'S 19-- PAYROLL DEDUCTIONS		7
Deduction	Amount	15
Federal Income Tax	$11,070.68	21
State Income Tax	1,305.43	26
City Income Tax	652.72	31
Social Security Tax	3,131.70	37
Disability Insurance	37.68	43
Pension Plan	2,916.60	48
Medical & Dental Insurance	441.95	55

POPULATION PROJECTIONS FOR SELECTED COUNTRIES			9
Reported in Millions for Years 2000 and 2025			18
Country	2000	2025	26
Canada	29.4	34.4	30
China: Mainland	1,255.7	1,460.1	37
France	57.1	58.5	41
Japan	127.7	127.6	45
Mexico	109.2	154.1	49
Soviet Union	314.8	367.1	55
United Kingdom	56.2	56.4	61
United States	268.1	312.7	66
			70
Source: Population Division of United Nations.			79

53a ▶ 6
Conditioning Practice

each line twice SS (slowly, then faster); DS between 2-line groups; if time permits, rekey selected lines

alphabet 1 Joey paid the exotic woman a quarter each for three black gauze veils.

figures 2 Jan sold 14 rings, 293 clips, 50 watches, 168 clocks, and 70 tie pins.

fig/sym 3 After May 5, Al's new address will be 478 Pax Avenue (ZIP 92106-1593).

speed 4 Ivor may make the goal if he works with vigor and with the right form.

| 1 | 2 | 3 | 4 | 5 | 6 | 7 | 8 | 9 | 10 | 11 | 12 | 13 | 14 |

53b ▶ 6 Improve
Language Skills: Word Choice

1. Study the spelling/definitions of the words in the color block at right.

2. Key line 1 (the **Learn** line), noting the proper choice of words.

3. Key lines 2-3 (the **Apply** lines), choosing the right words to complete the lines correctly.

4. Key the remaining lines in the same way.

5. Check your accuracy; rekey lines containing word-choice errors.

hour (n) the 24th part of a day; a particular time
our (adj) of or relating to ourselves as possessors

know (vb) to be aware of the truth of; to have understanding of
no (adv/adj/n) in no respect or degree; not so; indicates denial or refusal

Learn 1 It is our intention to complete the work in an hour or two.

Apply 2 If I drive steadily, we should reach (hour, our) house in an (hour, our).

Apply 3 We should earn one credit (hour, our) for (hour, our) computer class.

Learn 4 Did you know that there are to be no quizzes this week?

Apply 5 If you (know, no) the chapter, you should have (know, no) fear of a quiz.

Apply 6 Did you (know, no) that they scored (know, no) touchdowns in the game?

53c ▶ 38 Format
an Unbound Report with Long Quotation

Document 1
Report

On two plain full sheets, format the report given at right and on the next page as a 2-page unbound report, DS. Correct any errors you make as you key.

Long quotations
When keying quotations of more than 3 typed lines, SS and indent them 5 spaces from the LM. Leave a DS above and below them.

words

TYPEWRITERS: AN ENDANGERED SPECIES? 7

    For well over a decade, experts in office automation 18
have predicted the demise of the typewriter. In their view 30
the computer is destined to take over the word processing 42
role enjoyed by the typewriter for over a century. Yet, a 53
recent report (Fernberg, 1989, 49-50) indicates that elec- 65
tronic typewriter shipments over the last three years aver- 76
aged about a billion dollars a year. Further, the Computer 88
and Business Equipment Manufacturers' Association projects 100
that the annual growth rate will remain constant at 1.5 per- 112
cent over the next five years. With sales holding steady at 124
over a million units a year, the electronic typewriter does 136
not appear endangered. It is likely here to stay--and for 148
good reasons. 151

Typewriter Familiarity 160

    Virtually anyone who has learned to key can sit down at 171
the electronic typewriter and within a few minutes operate it 184
with amazing ease and speed. According to Paez (1985, 55): 196

SS {
    A familiar keyboard, which requires fewer keystrokes and 207
has a simpler, less code-intensive user interface, makes 219
the transition to a high-end typewriter much easier than 230
the transition to a personal computer with the same func- 241
tions. 243

(continued, p. 98)

Center

words

TALL BUILDINGS IN CHICAGO line 22			5
DS			
Listed by Height in Feet and Meters			12
DS			
Building	**Feet**	**Meters**	20
		DS	
Sears Tower	1,454	443.470	25
Amoco	1,136	346.480	29
John Hancock Center	1,127	343.735	36
Water Tower Place	859	261.995	42
First National Bank	852	259.860	48
Three First National Plaza	775	236.375	56
DS			60
——————————— 1½"			
DS			
Source: **The World Almanac.**			68

Table on a Full Sheet

107e ▶ 23
Format Three-Column Tables

plain full sheets, short edge at top; correct errors

Table 1
Format model table above; DS data; CS: 6 between longest items in columns; block column headings.

Table 2
Format table at the right; DS data; CS: 8 between longest items in the columns; block column headings.

words

Tall Buildings in New York City			6
Listed by Height in Feet and Meters			14
Building	Feet	Meters	21
World Trade Center	1,350	411.750	28
Empire State (without TV tower)	1,250	381.250	37
Chrysler	1,046	319.030	41
American International	950	289.750	48
40 Wall Tower	927	282.735	53
Citicorp Center	914	278.770	59
————————			63
Source: The World Almanac.			72

53c (continued)

Typewriter Flexibility

An electronic typewriter can preform some function com- 263
puters cannot, but a personal computer (PC) cannot be used as 275
a mere typewriter (nor should it be). Perhaps that is why 287
one large survey found that 85 percent of secretaries who use 299
PCs also use typewriters. Using microchip technology, sophis- 312
ticated electronic typewriters can perform many of the auto- 324
matic functions and editing functions of which computers are 336
capable. 338
Automatic Functions. Among the features of electronic 353
typewriters are automatic centering, returning, right margin 365
justifying and hang-indenting. These features are avail-able on 378
computers as well, but some users of both kinds of equipment 390
say that the typewriter is more "user freindly." 400

Editing Functions. Some Many electronic typewriters permit 415
operators to backspace/delete, insert copy, move copy from 426
one place to another, and search and replace specific words or 439
terms in a document. Some are equiped with templates that 451
make form fill-in easy; others permits the merging of in- 462
formation from diferent sources. All these functions are 474
performed without needing to rekeying documents. 482

Typewriter Sophistication

Electronic typewriters range from low-end machines with 503
limited features and without editing windows to high-end 514
machines with full-page displays, diskette storage, and com- 526
plete text-editing capabilities. The price range varies with 539
the number amount of advanced features included. Some machines are 551
upgradable so that the appropriate level of sophistication 563
can be obtained without replacing machines. 572

Document 2
Reference Page
Format the references on a separate plain full sheet.

REFERENCES 574
Audiph, Mark. "Using Electronic Typewriters: The Basics, 584
     Plus. . . ." _Today's Office_, July 1986, 55-64. 597
Fernberg, Patricia M. "Electronic Typewriters: Understanding 610
     the Product." _Modern Office Technology_, March 1989, 625
     48-50. 627
Page, Patricia. "Typewriters: Technology with an Easy 638
     Touch." _Today's Office_, September 1985, 55-72. 650

Document 3
Title Page
Format a title page for the report on a plain full sheet. Use your own name and school name and the current date.

107a ▶ 5
Conditioning Practice

each line twice SS (slowly, then faster); DS between 2-line groups; if time permits, rekey selected lines

alphabet 1 Seven new boys qualified through expert knowledge of jazz dance music.

figures 2 Ms. Tedd excluded Chapters 19 and 20, pages 378 to 465, from the exam.

shift lock 3 SWOPWO will buy one LM-PC at AABSCO rather than a PC-WEX from WEYSCOT.

speed 4 She bid on the field by the lake as the right land for the big chapel.

| 1 | 2 | 3 | 4 | 5 | 6 | 7 | 8 | 9 | 10 | 11 | 12 | 13 | 14 |

107b ▶ 6 Improve Language Skills: Word Choice

1. Study the spelling and definition of each word.

2. Key the line number (with period), space twice, then key the **Learn** sentence; key the **Apply** sentence in the same format, selecting the correct word in parentheses to complete each sentence.

beat (vb) to strike repeatedly; to defeat

beet (n) the name of a plant with a dark-red root

basis (n) the fundamental ingredient of anything

bases (n) plural for base or basis

Learn 1. I beat the drum loudly when my canned beets won first prize.
Apply 2. Carter High (beat, beet) Dennison High for the championship.
Apply 3. Mary wanted Jim to plant at least four rows of (beats, beets).

Learn 4. The basis of good base stealing is fast speed and accurate timing.
Apply 5. The (basis, bases) of his argument is not supported by facts.
Apply 6. The runner missed first and second (basis, bases) while running.

107c ▶ 6
Preapplication Drill: Backspace and Tab Keys

1. Center each of lines 1-4 horizontally.

2. Key lines 5-6, tabbing from one column to the next. For pica machines, set left margin stop at 15 and tab stops at 31, 48, and 64. For elite machines, set left margin stop at 23 and tab stops at 39, 56, and 72.

3. Do not correct errors.

Backspace Key Drill:

1 Angela L. Robinson
2 Rogelio M. Rodriquez
3 James P. Feltenberg
4 Margaret H. Breedlove

Tab Key Drill:

5	10,432	in case	lay by	blazon
6	57,986	it will	my box	amazed
7	24,103	on base	do cut	benzol
8	97,856	no case	an elf	cozily

107d ▶ 10 Review
Horizontal Placement of Tables

1. Study horizontal placement procedures on p. 188.

2. Center horizontally on a full sheet the table at the right; DS data; CS: 6 between longest items in columns; PB: line 26; correct errors.

words

COMMONLY MISSPELLED WORDS 5

activities	necessary	professional	12
address	offered	reason	17
decision	participation	representative	24
entry	position	schedule	29
experience	premium	supervisor	35
important	procedure	transportation	42

54a ▶ 6
Conditioning Practice

each line twice SS (slowly, then faster); DS between 2-line groups; if time permits, rekey selected lines

alphabet 1   After a wild jump ball, the guards very quickly executed a zone press.

figures 2   The invoice covered 115 sofas, 270 desks, 476 chairs, and 1,398 lamps.

fig/sym 3   Order the #284, #365, and #1790 cartons (untaped) from O'Brien & Sons.

speed 4   A big firm kept half of the men busy with their work down by the lake.

| 1 | 2 | 3 | 4 | 5 | 6 | 7 | 8 | 9 | 10 | 11 | 12 | 13 | 14 |

54b ▶ 6 Improve Language Skills: Word Choice

1. Study the spelling/definitions of the words in the color block at right.

2. Key line 1 (the **Learn** line), noting the proper choice of words.

3. Key lines 2-3 (the **Apply** lines), choosing the right words to complete the lines correctly.

4. Key the remaining lines in the same way.

5. Check your accuracy; rekey lines containing word-choice errors.

> **lead** (vb) to guide or direct; to be first   **choose** (vb) to select; to decide on
>
> **led** (vb) the past tense of lead   **chose** (vb) the past tense of choose

Learn 1   Max is to lead the parade; Pam led it last year.

Apply 2   The Falcons (lead, led) now; the Friars (lead, led) at the half.

Apply 3   Marj (lead, led) at the ninth hole, but she does not (lead, led) now.

Learn 4   Jose chose a Eureka computer; I may choose a Futura.

Apply 5   After he (choose, chose) a red cap, I told him to (choose, chose) blue.

Apply 6   Mae (choose, chose) me as a partner; Janice may (choose, chose) me.

54c ▶ 38 Format an Unbound Report with Enumerated Items

Document 1
Report
On 2 plain full sheets, format and key the copy given at right and on page 100 as an unbound report. Place the reference list below the last line of copy on page 2 of the report. Correct any errors you make as you key.

words

BASIC STRATEGIES FOR EFFECTIVE STUDY   7

Effective learning depends upon good study habits. Efficient study skills   22
do not simply occur; they must first be learned and then applied consis-   37
tently. Good study strategies include a preset time for study, a desirable   52
place to study, and a well-designed study plan.   62

A Time for Study   68

All of us think we have more things to do than we have time to do, and   82
studying gets shortchanged. It is important to prepare a schedule of daily ac-   98
tivities that includes time slots for doing the studying we have to do. Within   114
each study slot, write in the specific study activity; for example, "Read Unit 6   130
of accounting; do Problems 1-5." Keep the schedule flexible so that it can be   146
modified after you assess your success in meeting your study goals within   161
each time slot.   164

A Place to Study   171

Choose the best place to study and use the same one every day. Doing so   185
will help to put you in a study mood when you enter that place. According to   201
Usova (1989, 37), "The library is not always a desirable place to study." Choose   217
a place that has the fewest distractions such as people traffic, conversation,   233
telephone, TV, and outside noises. Study is usually best done alone and in the   249
absence of sights and sounds that distract the eye and ear. In your chosen   264
quiet place, force the mind to concentrate on the task at hand.   277

A Plan for Study   284

Research on the effects of specific study skills on student performance   298
(Dansereau, 1985, 39) suggests that the following study tactics help to im-   313
prove academic performance.   319

(continued, p. 100)

Extend Table Processing Skills

Learning Goals

1. To improve skill in centering material horizontally and vertically on paper of different sizes.

2. To improve skill in formatting tables with single- and multiple-line headings, source notes, and totals.

3. To improve language-skill ability.

Format Guides

1. Paper guide at *0* (for typewriters).

2. LL: 70-space line, or as directed.

3. LS: SS word and drill lines; space tables as directed.

4. PI: 5 spaces, when appropriate.

FORMATTING GUIDES: TABLES

Table Spacing Summary

Double-Space (DS):

1. Below all heading lines.

2. Above and below column headings.

3. Column entries when so directed.

4. Above and below source note ruling separating column entries from source notes.

5. Above column TOTALS, when used.

Single-Space (SS):

1. Column entries when so directed.

2. Multiple-line column headings.

Vertical Placement

Step 1: Count all lines to be used in table (including all blank line spaces).

Step 2: Subtract this figure from total lines available on sheet. **Note.** Most machines have six line spaces to the vertical inch; therefore, paper 8½″ × 11″ has 66 vertical line spaces (11 × 6).

Step 3: Divide remainder by 2 to determine the number of the line on which to key the main heading. If a fraction results, disregard it. If the number that results is

   EVEN, space down that number from the top;

   ODD, use next lower even number.

Note. This means that the main heading of a table will always begin on an even number.

Horizontal Placement of Columns Using Backspace-from-Center Method

Step 1: Move margin stops to ends of scale and clear all tab stops.

Step 2: From the horizontal center of sheet, backspace once for each 2 strokes in the longest line in each column (carry over to the next column any extra stroke at the end of a column but ignore any extra stroke at the end of the last column); then backspace once for each 2 spaces to be left between columns. **Note.** As center point of paper 8½″ wide, use 42 for pica; 51 for elite.

Step 3: Set left margin stop at point where backspacing ends.

Step 4: From the left margin stop, space forward once for each stroke in the longest line in the first column, and once for each space to be left between the first and second columns. Set a tab stop at this point for the start of the second column. Continue procedure for any additional columns.

Spacing Between Columns

As a general rule, leave an even number of spaces between columns (4, 6, 8, 10 or more).

Column Headings

When used, column headings are often centered over the longest line in the column. When the column heading is the longest

```
lines
used
  1              REGISTERED  STUDENTS
  2
  3                             Course
  4              Name           Number        Code
  5
  6     Mary Jones              E101            3T
  7
  8     Charles Harris          E106            7P
  9
 10     Mark Stevens            G205            4C
 11
 12     Sue Booth               A443            1W
 13
 14     _____
 15
 16     Source:  Registrar, July 15, 19--.
```

line in the column, other lines are centered under it.

If a table has single- and multiple-line headings (see model above), the bottom line of each multiple-line heading is placed on the same line as the single-line headings. The lines of multiple-line headings are single-spaced.

Horizontal/Vertical Placement with a Word Processor/Computer

Horizontal. Word processors/computers usually have a function which can be used to simplify horizontal centering. You should refer to the *User's Manual* to see how this function works on your equipment. On most, a trial line (consisting of the longest line in each column plus the spaces between the columns) is keyed on the screen before or after a center function is used. After the trial line is keyed and centered, set left margin or tab stop at the beginning of each column. Delete the trial line; then key the table using the margin and tab stops.

Vertical. If your equipment has a vertical centering function key, refer to your *User's Manual* to see how it works. If not, determine the vertical line on which the last line of the table ends after it is keyed. Subtract this line number from the lines on the paper and divide the answer by 2. If necessary, round this answer to the next lower even number and then insert this number of blank lines above the first line of the table.

words

Enumerated items

1. Block a series of numbered items 5 spaces from the LM (at ¶ indent point).

2. SS each item, but DS between items and above and below the series.

3. For a long series, reset the LM (or use automatic indent if your equipment has this feature).

1. Skim a unit or a chapter, noting headings, topic sentences, key words, and definitions. This overview will clue you to what you are about to study. 334 348 350

2. As you read a unit or chapter, convert the headings into questions; then seek answers to those questions as you read. 365 374

3. If you own the book, use color marking pens to highlight important ideas: headings, topic sentences, special terms, definitions, and supporting facts. If you don't own the book, make notes of these important ideas and facts. 389 403 418 421

4. After you have completed a unit or chapter, review the highlighted items (or your notes which contain them). 435 444

5. Using the headings stated as questions, see if you can answer those questions based on your reading. 458 465

6. Test yourself to see if you can recall definitions of important terms and lists of supporting facts or ideas. 480 488

A high correlation exists between good study habits and good grades for the courses taken in school. 502 508

Document 2
Title Page
Format a suitable title page for the report, using your name and school name and the current date.

REFERENCES 510

Dansereau, D. F. "Learning Strategy Research." Thinking and Learning Skills. Vol. 1. Hillsdale, NJ: Lawrence Erlbaum, 1985, 21-40. 529 543

Usova, George M. Efficient Study Strategies. Pacific Grove, CA: Brooks/ Cole Publishing Company, 1989. 563 569

| *Lesson 55* | *Unbound Reports* | *LL: 70* *LS: SS* |

55a ▶ 6
Conditioning Practice

each line twice SS (slowly, then faster); DS between 2-line groups; if time permits, rekey selected lines

alphabet	1	Liquid oxygen fuel was used to give this big jet rocket amazing speed.
figures	2	We proofread 275 letters, 18 reports, 369 invoices, and 40 statements.
fig/sym	3	This rug (12′ × 13′6″) was $814.95, but it is now on sale for $710.50.
speed	4	Pay them for their work and then go with us to the city for the forms.

| 1 | 2 | 3 | 4 | 5 | 6 | 7 | 8 | 9 | 10 | 11 | 12 | 13 | 14 |

55b ▶ 6 Improve Language Skills: Word Choice

1. Study the spelling/definitions of the words in the color block at right.

2. Key line 1 (the **Learn** line), noting the proper choice of words.

3. Key lines 2-3 (the **Apply** lines), choosing the right words to complete the lines correctly.

4. Key the remaining lines in the same way.

5. Check your accuracy; rekey lines containing word-choice errors.

your (adj) of or relating to you or yourself as possessor

you're (contr) you are

for (prep/conj) used to indicate purpose; on behalf of; because; because of

four (n) the fourth in a set or series

Learn	1	As soon as you receive your blue book, you're to write your name on it.
Apply	2	(Your, You're) to write the letter using (your, you're) best English.
Apply	3	When (your, you're) computer is warmed up, (your, you're) to begin work.
Learn	4	All four workers asked for an appointment with the manager.
Apply	5	At (for, four) o'clock the lights went off (for, four) an hour.
Apply	6	The (for, four) boys turned back, (for, four) they feared the lightning.

Reinforce Letter Processing Skills

LP pp. 61-67
or plain full sheets
correct errors; address
envelopes

Letter 1

block format; open punctuation

Use ALL CAP, unpunctuated format for letter address. If necessary, refer to formatting guide on p. 83.

Letter 2

Reformat Letter 1 using modified block format, open punctuation. Do not use ALL CAP, unpunctuated format for the letter address.

words

April 10, 19--| Attention Mrs. Luze L. Sanchez| Compuworks| 7110 Claasen Avenue| Cleveland, OH 44105-5023| Ladies and Gentlemen| SUBJECT: GRADUATE FOLLOW UP QUESTIONNAIRE 15 26 33

It hardly seems possible that six months have passed since Maria Deucsh began working for your company as a word processor. 47 58

As you may recall, our department tries to find out how graduates of Central High School perform in the business world. We gain valuable information from these studies which enables us to evaluate the success of our program and helps us keep the content of our courses current and relevant. In addition, it provides us with employment information we can pass on to our students. 73 88 103 118 132 134

Would you have Maria's supervisor complete the enclosed questionnaire so we can learn about Maria's progress and other items pertaining to Central High. Please return the questionnaire in the enclosed envelope. 149 164 177

Thank you; we look forward to placing some of our other graduates with Compuworks. (160) 191 194

Sincerely yours| Ronald W. Thomas, Jr.| Business Department Chair| xx| Enclosures| c Guidance Office| If you could use a student on a co-op assignment, please call me. 207 222 226/**243**

Letter 3

Modified block format with indented ¶s, mixed punctuation.

Use ALL CAP, unpunctuated format for letter address. Address letter to

**Attention Office Ed. Dept.
Woodward High School
101 Ash Street
San Diego, CA 92101-3096**

Supply appropriate salutation.

Letter 4

Reformat Letter 3 using block format, open punctuation.

Use ALL CAP, unpunctuated format for letter address. Address letter to

**Attention Office Ed. Dept.
Central High School
1707 Wood Street
Oakland, CA 94607-2514**

Supply appropriate salutation; change copy notation to "c Principal."

address 18

April 10, 19--|SUBJECT: KEYBOARDING COMMITTEE MEETING 31

¶ The Keyboarding Task Force will meet at the San Diego Airport Hotel at 10:00 a.m. on Wednesday, April 15, 19--. 42 53

¶ Please plan to join us so we can review the survey results relating to the need for touch keyboarding skills in various occupational fields. A copy of the results are enclosed. 63 74 84 89

¶ A quick review of the data reveals that respondents from many different occupational areas indicate a need for employees to have touch keyboarding skills to operate computer keyboards efficiently and effectively. Once confirmed, this finding can be the basis for the conclusion that each student, regardless of expected career, should learn touch keyboarding in school. (132) 99 109 120 132 143 155 163

Yours truly/Ms. Elisa T. Witt/Task Force Chair/xx/ Enclosure/c Dr. Geoff W. Hurd, Principal/We'll have a "Dutch Treat" lunch at the hotel. 173 184 191/**209**

55c ▶ 38 Format an Unbound Report

Process report with references on page 2; prepare title page; correct errors.

words

READING FOR KEYBOARDING AND FORMATTING   8

When learning to key, format, and process 16
documents, a major portion of one's time is 25
spent reading. Two different reading processes 35
are used in learning: reading for meaning and 44
reading for "copy getting." 50

Reading for Meaning 58

When one reads an explanation and descrip- 66
tion of a document format or directions for com- 75
pleting a keying task, the purpose of reading is 85
to process information and to acquire meaning 94
or understanding (de Fossard, 1990, 1). Such 103
reading requires focusing on the content: its 113
organization, sequence, ideas, terms, and facts. 123
The objective is to assimilate them, store them, 133
and recall them in proper order for later use. 142
Reading for meaning is very important when 151
learning terms, concepts, and procedures. Such 160
reading is preferably done with speed followed 170
by review. 172

Reading for Copy Getting 182

When one reads a drill or document for the 191
purpose of copying it by means of a keyboard, 200
one reads to "get the copy" to feed through the 210
brain at the speed the fingers are able to re- 219

words

cord it by striking the keys (West, 1983, 227
130). The purpose is not to understand the 236
message or to get meaning from it; rather, the 245
purpose is to reproduce the message character 254
for character. In initial learning, this process 264
is done on a letter-by-letter basis. As skill 274
grows, however, the process begins to include 283
"chains" of letters and short words that are 292
perceived and responded to as units. Rarely, 301
though, can a keyboard operator feed the fin- 310
gers more than one or two words at a time un- 319
less the words are short. 324

Reading for copy getting requires that the 333
speed of reading be synchronized with the fin- 342
gers' ability to make the keystrokes required to 352
reproduce the words. In this process, the mind 361
is concerned with the form and sequence of the 371
letters and words, not with the meaning of the 380
message the letters and words convey. This 389
kind of reading must be done at a slower pace 398
that is deliberate but harmonious. 405

REFERENCES 407

de Fossard, Esta. Reading in Focus. 3d ed. 420
     Cincinnati: South-Western Publishing Co., 428
     1990. 430

West, L. J. Acquisition of Typewriting Skills. 446
     2d ed. Indianapolis: Bobbs-Merrill Educa- 455
     tional Publishing, 1983. 459

Lesson 56	Outlines	LL: 70
		LS: SS

56a ▶ 6
Conditioning Practice

each line twice SS (slowly, then faster); DS between 2-line groups; if time permits, rekey selected lines

alphabet	1	Suzi can equal a track record by jumping twelve feet at the next meet.
figures	2	The data are given in Figures 26 and 27 of Part 14, Unit 39, page 508.
fig/sym	3	Rizzo & Lewis wrote Check #728 for $301.95 and Check #745 for $648.50.
speed	4	Eighty of the men may work for the island firms if they make a profit.

| 1 | 2 | 3 | 4 | 5 | 6 | 7 | 8 | 9 | 10 | 11 | 12 | 13 | 14 |

56b ▶ 9 Learn to Align Roman Numerals

Use drill sheet from 56a; center heading a QS below your warm-up lines; LL: 40 spaces; LS: DS.

Automatic procedure
If your equipment has an automatic aligning feature, see the User's Guide for information on how to set tabs and align numerals.

Manual procedure
1. Clear all tab stops; from LM, space forward to set new tab stops as indicated by the KEY below and the guides above the columns at right.

2. Center the heading.

3. As you key Roman numerals, tabbing from column to column, align them at the right. To do this, space forward or backward from the tab stop as needed.

> **Margin release**
> To begin the numeral III in Column 1, depress the *margin release key* with the nearer little finger and backspace once into the LM.

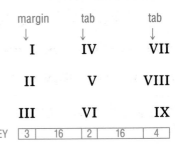

ROMAN NUMERALS

margin	tab	tab
↓	↓	↓
I	IV	VII
II	V	VIII
III	VI	IX

KEY   3   16   2   16   4

105c ▶ 30
Reinforce Letter Processing Skills
LP pp. 55-59

correct errors; address envelopes

Letter 1
modified block format; mixed punctuation

March 3, 19--	Attention Miss Terry L. Ely	Valley Area High School	375	14

March 3, 19--|Attention Miss Terry L. Ely|Valley Area High School|375 14
Baker Street|Jamestown, NY 14701-7598|Ladies and Gentlemen:|SUBJECT: 26
ADVANCED STANDING CREDIT FOR CYNTHIA BAXTER 35

Ms. Cynthia Baxter, a Valley Area High School senior, completed an ad- 49
vanced standing examination at Jamestown Business Institute (JBI) last 63
week at the freshman orientation session. 72

As a result of Cynthia's high school data processing studies, she is able to be- 88
gin her JBI computer studies at the intermediate level. In addition, she will 103
receive three credits toward a degree. 111

I want to congratulate Cynthia and her data processing teacher for their out- 127
standing accomplishments in the data processing area. (102) 138

Sincerely,|Robert L. Carr|Admission Counselor|xx|c Dr. Ray M. Ness 151/170

Letter 2
block format; open punctuation

Letter 3
Reformat Letter 1 using block format and open punctuation.

Letter 4
Use plain full sheet and reformat Letter 2 using modified block format with indented ¶s and open punctuation.

March 5, 19--|Attention Nursing Director|Computer Institute|960 Pembroke 15
Street|New Rochelle, NY 10801-3127|Ladies and Gentlemen 26

Enclosed is a signed copy of the Memorandum of Understanding agreement 40
between Computer Institute and New Rochelle Health Systems. As requested, 55
I have retained a copy for my files and am forwarding one copy to you. 70

If you have any questions regarding this agreement, please call me. (57) 83

Sincerely|NEW ROCHELLE HEALTH SYSTEMS|Fred F. Valdez|President|xx| 97
Enclosure|I will mark my calendar to remind me to contact you in 90 days to 112
discuss extending the agreement for another six months. 123/142

Lesson 106 | Processing Letters

106a ▶ 5
Conditioning Practice

each line twice SS (slowly, then faster); DS between 2-line groups; if time permits, rekey selected lines

alphabet 1 A new expert may organize both journal displays quickly for the event.

fig/sym 2 D & L Shops cashed in Policy #2847-08 for $15,986 on October 30, 1991.

shift key 3 T. J. Wurtz expects S & L Co. to merge with ROBO, a subsidiary of TMW.

speed 4 Make the panel suspend the pay of their city officials as the penalty.

| 1 | 2 | 3 | 4 | 5 | 6 | 7 | 8 | 9 | 10 | 11 | 12 | 13 | 14 |

106b ▶ 5
Improve Language Skills: Word Choice

1. Study the spelling and definition of each word.

2. Key the line number (with period), space twice, then key the **Learn** sentence; key the **Apply** sentences in the same format, selecting the correct word in parentheses to complete each sentence.

dual (adj) composed of two parts; double

duel (n) a struggle between two contending persons, groups, or ideas

fair (adj) just, equitable, visually beautiful or admirable

fare (n) a transportation charge

Learn 1. The duel between Jim and Harry served a dual purpose.

Apply 2. The unions' (dual, duel) may affect taxes for trucks with (dual, duel) axles.

Learn 3. Mary Ann thought the taxi fare was not fair for such a short trip.

Apply 4. I paid the (fare, fair) and then sat back to enjoy the (fare, fair) sky.

56c ▶ 35 Learn to Format Topic Outlines

Outline 1
Format the outline on a plain full sheet.

SM: 1″ (pica, 10 spaces; elite, 12 spaces)
PB: line 10 (pica) or line 12 (elite)

Automatic procedure
If your equipment has the land-indent feature, see the User's Guide for the appropriate tab procedure.

Manual procedure
Set margins and tabs as indicated by the color notes on the outlines.

Note: Major headings are preceded by I., II., etc.; first-order headings by A., B., etc.; and second-order headings by 1., 2., etc.

Language skills notes
1. Outline title is in ALL CAPS and may be underlined.
2. Major headings are in ALL CAPS and are not underlined.
3. Important words of first-order sub-headings are capitalized.
4. First word only of second-order subheadings is capitalized.

SPACING TOPIC OUTLINES

Leave 3 blank line spaces—
QS (quadruple space)

Space forward once from margin → 2 spaces

I. VERTICAL SPACING

Leave 1 blank line space—
DS (double space)

Reset margin → A. Title of Outline
1st tab → 1. Line 12, elite (12-pitch); line 10, pica (10-pitch)
2. Followed by 3 blank line spaces (QS)
(Set 2 tab stops 4 spaces apart)
B. Major Headings
1. First major heading preceded by a QS; all others
2d tab → preceded by 1 blank line space (DS)
2. All followed by a DS
3. All subheadings single-spaced (SS)

DS

Use margin release; backspace 5 times

II. HORIZONTAL SPACING
DS
A. Title of Outline Centered over the Line of Writing
B. Major Headings and Subheadings
1. Identifying Roman numerals at left margin (periods aligned) followed by 2 spaces
2. Identifying letters and numbers for each subsequent level of subheading aligned below the first word of the preceding heading, followed by 2 spaces

---

Outline 2
Format the outline on a plain full sheet.

SM: 1″; PB: line 10 (pica) or line 12 (elite); correct errors

EMPLOYMENT COMMUNICATIONS
QS

I. PERSONAL DATA SHEET

A. Personal Information   *lc*
1. Name, address, and Telephone number   *if needed*
2. Social Security number (work permit number)
3. Personal interests: hobbies/recreational interests
B. Educational Information
1. Schools attended *and dates of attendance*
2. Special areas of study; activities; awards *received*
C. Work Experience
1. Jobs held; what you experienced; commendations
2. Volunteer work
DS D. References (Teachers, Work Supervisors)
II. LETTER OF APPLICATION

A. Source of Information about Job *Opening*
B. Expression of Interest in Being Interviewed for the Job
C. Brief Summary of Work Skills and How They Fit the Job
1. Special courses that are applicable to the job
2. Work experiences *that* make you qualified for the job
D. Request for Interview

III. THANK-YOU LETTER FOLLOWING INTERVIEW
DS A. Appreciation for Courtesies Shown During Company Visit
B. Positive Impressions of Company and Employees
C. Expression of Continued Interest in the Job

104d ▶ 15 *Process Average-Length Letters*

plain full sheets

supply appropriate salutations; correct all errors

Letter 1--modified block format with indented ¶s; mixed punctuation

Letter 2--Reformat Letter 1 using block format; open punctuation. Address letter to

**Dr. Martin K. Jobbs
Superintendent
Highland School District
1727 Hurd Drive
Irving, TX 75038-4309**

May 10, 19-- | Mrs. Donna W. Wells | School Board President | Highland School 14
District | 1727 Hurd Drive | Irving, TX 75038-4309 | Dear Mrs. Wells 27

Computer literacy is an important concern that I believe should be addressed 43
by the Highland School District. It is important to our students while in 58
school and will be even more important to them upon graduation. 71

The level of computer literacy varies with the grade level of the student. At 86
the elementary level it may involve the use of tutorial software to improve 102
learning. For high school students it may mean the use of word processing, 117
spreadsheet, database, and other software. For all students it should include 133
the ability to operate the keyboard by touch. 142

I hope the recently appointed curriculum committee will put improving com- 157
puter literacy at the top of its priority list. 167

Sincerely | Robert L. Harris, President | Instantcare Health Services | xx 180

Lesson 105 — *Processing Letters*

105a ▶ 5 *Conditioning Practice*

each line twice SS (slowly, then faster); DS between 2-line groups; if time permits, rekey selected lines

alphabet 1 Gwen just froze the bread, chickens, pork, veal, quiche, and six yams.

figures 2 Sheila was told to call Ruth around 5:30 p.m. at 264-8498 or 264-7130.

shift key 3 Fred O'Barsky plans to advertise on WPCI-TV and KWPA-AM/FM this month.

speed 4 An auditor on the panel did not sign a key element of the small audit.

| 1 | 2 | 3 | 4 | 5 | 6 | 7 | 8 | 9 | 10 | 11 | 12 | 13 | 14 |

105b ▶ 15 *Preapplication Drill: Formatting Letter Parts*

2 plain full sheets
LL: 1½" SM
PB: line 16

1. Review the block format model letter on p. 78.

2. On a full sheet and at the signal to begin, space to line 16 and key the opening lines of Drill 1.

3. After keying the subject line, return 12 times and key the closing lines.

4. Complete Drill 2 in the same way after reviewing the modified block format model letter on p. 137.

5. Do not correct errors.

Drill 1: **Block format; open punctuation**

March 10, 19--
QS

Attention Mr. John P. Steffan
Stocker & Juarez, Inc.
430 Branner Street, SE
Topeka, KS 66607-1899
DS
Ladies and Gentlemen
DS
AGREEMENT #97-1253-46-AA

Space down 12 times (using INDEX or RETURN) to allow for body of letter.

Sincerely yours
DS
K & N SALES AND SERVICE
QS

Mrs. Marianne A. Perez, Director
DS
pjc
DS
c Betty M. Gleaner

Drill 2: **Modified block format; mixed punctuation**

April 30, 19--
DS
REGISTERED MAIL
DS
Mr. Edwin H. Whitman
Greene Trucking Co.
3200 Grand Street
Wichita, KS 67218-2923
DS
Dear Mr. Whitman:

Space down 12 times (using INDEX or RETURN) to allow for body of letter.

Sincerely,
QS

Ms. Sue P. Mori, Manager
DS
upj
DS
Enclosure
DS
Will you need a hotel room for three evenings?

57a ▶ 6
Conditioning Practice

each line twice SS (slowly, then faster); DS between 2-line groups; if time permits, rekey selected lines

alphabet 1 Marvin, the tax clerk, was puzzled by the quaint antics of the judges.

figures 2 The shop is 278.4 meters long, 90.6 meters wide, and 13.5 meters high.

fig/sym 3 Guy Moss's order (#30-967) is for 42 almanacs, 15 atlases, and 8 maps.

speed 4 Vivian may go to the ancient island city by the lake to work for them.

| 1 | 2 | 3 | 4 | 5 | 6 | 7 | 8 | 9 | 10 | 11 | 12 | 13 | 14 |

57b ▶ 35 Check
Formatting Skill: Unbound Reports

4 plain full sheets; correction supplies

1. Format and key the report in unbound style.

2. Format the reference list on a separate sheet.

REFERENCES

Hamel, Ruth. "Making Summer Earnings Work for You." USA Weekend, 2-4 June 1989, 10-11.

Kushner, John. How to Find and Apply for a Job. Cincinnati: South-Western Publishing Co., 1989.

3. If time permits, prepare a title page using your name and school name and the current date.

words

THE IMPORTANCE OF WORK EXPERIENCE   7

A part-time or summer job pays more than money. Although the money   20
earned is important, the work experience gained has a greater long-term   35
value when one applies for a full-time job after graduation from school. Job   50
application forms (the application blank and the personal data sheet) ask you   66
to list jobs you have held and to list as references the names of individuals   82
who supervised your work. As one young person was heard to remark, "You   96
can't get a job without experience and you can't get experience without a   111
job." That dilemma can be overcome, however, by starting to work early in   126
life and by accepting simpler jobs that have no minimum age limit and do not   141
require experience.   146

Jobs Teens Can Do   153

Start early at jobs that may not pay especially well but help to establish a   168
working track record: baby-sitting, delivering newspapers, mowing lawns,   183
assisting with gardening, and the like. Use these work experiences as spring-   198
boards for such later jobs as sales clerk, gas station attendant, fast food   213
worker, lifeguard, playground supervisor assistant, and office staff assistant   229
(after you have developed basic office skills). As you progress through these   245
work exploration experiences, try increasingly to get jobs that have some re-   260
lationship to your career plans. If, for example, you want a career involving   276
frequent contact with people--as in sales--seek part-time and summer work   291
that gives you experience in dealing with people (Hamel, 1989, 10).   305

How to Handle Yourself on the Job   318

Whatever the job you are able to get, the following pointers will help you   333
succeed in getting a good recommendation for the next job you seek.   347

1. Be punctual. Get to work on time and return from lunch and other   361
breaks promptly.   364

2. Get along well with others. Do your job well and offer to assist others   380
who may need help. Take direction with a smile instead of a frown.   394

3. Speak proper English. Teenage jargon is often lost on the adults who   408
are likely to be your supervisors.   416

4. Dress the part. Observe the unwritten dress code; dress as others on   430
the job do. Always be neat and clean.   438

references   487

Extend Letter Processing Skills

Learning Goals

1. To improve skill in processing block and modified block format letters using open or mixed punctuation.
2. To improve skill in processing letters with special features.
3. To use the ALL CAP, unpunctuated format for formatting letter and envelope addresses.

Format Guides

1. Paper guide at *0* (for typewriters).
2. LL: 70 spaces, or as directed.
3. LS: SS word and drill lines; space letters as directed.
4. PI: 5 spaces, when appropriate.

Lesson 104 *Processing Letters*

104a ▶ 5
Conditioning Practice

each line twice SS (slowly, then faster); DS between 2-line groups; as time permits, rekey selected lines

alphabet 1 Gwen's six jumpers quickly seize every chance to practice before dawn.

fig/sym 2 Sam will pay $1,954 for the 16-MHz EP/37 PC which is 80286-compatible.

shift key 3 Tom and Jim wanted LT/PCs; Sue wanted the WO/PC with a Q-Tron printer.

speed 4 They may do the handiwork for the panel with the usual vigor and rush.

| 1 | 2 | 3 | 4 | 5 | 6 | 7 | 8 | 9 | 10 | 11 | 12 | 13 | 14 |

104b ▶ 15 Composing Letter Formatting Features

Read the questions at the right. Compose a complete sentence answer for each. If needed, refer to Letter Formatting Guide on p. 76. Number your answers as you key them. SS the lines of answers; DS between answers. X-out or strike over keyboarding errors you may make as you compose.

1. How many words may be in the body of an average-length letter?
2. How wide (in inches) should the left margin be for a long letter?
3. How wide (in pica spaces) should the left margin be for a short letter?
4. On what line should the date be keyed for a short letter?
5. What punctuation style uses a colon after the salutation?
6. What letter part follows the last line of the letter body?
7. What salutation is used if the letter is addressed to a company?
8. How many lines below the dateline should the letter address be keyed?
9. What letter part follows the writer's title?
10. How wide (in elite spaces) should the left margin be for an average-length letter?

104c ▶ 15 Format Short Letters

plain full sheets

Letter 1--Block format, open punctuation; do not correct errors; use proofreader's marks to identify errors.

Letter 2--Modified block format; mixed punctuation; do not correct errors; use proofreader's marks to identify errors.

Letter 3--Prepare a copy of Letter 1 from the rough-draft copy. Correct all errors.

words

February 10, 19--|Ms. Jane Z. Cawlfield|Sales Representative|Micro-World, 15
Inc.|89 - 54th Street, SW|Grand Rapids, MI   49508-5699|Dear Ms. Cawlfield 29

The business teachers at South High are pleased that you will speak at a 44
school-wide assembly on March 3, 19--, from 1:30 to 2:30 p.m. 56

Your presentation on how computers are used in local business and industry 71
will be of great benefit. Further, more students may see the wisdom of de- 86
veloping keyboarding and computer application skills after listening to what 102
you say. 104

Sincerely|Miss Thelma C. Scott|Department Head|xx 113

LL: 70 spaces; LS: DS
PI: 5 spaces

1. Take two 3' writings on ¶s 1-2 combined; find *gwam;* circle errors.

2. If time permits, take a 1' writing on each ¶ to build skill.

all letters used | A | 1.5 si | 5.7 awl | 80% hfw

gwam 3' | 5'

. 2 . 4 . 6 . 8 . 10 . 12
In excess of a hundred different makes and models of personal com- | 4 | 3
14 . 16 . 18 . 20 . 22 . 24 . 26 .
puters are now on the market. An amazing number of software packages | 9 | 5
28 . 30 . 32 . 34 . 36 . 38 . 40 .
are available to use in them. Each software package has its own com- | 14 | 8
42 . 44 . 46 . 48 . 50 . 52 . 54 .
mands to make an operating system work. Commands that are given in one | 18 | 11
56 . 58 . 60 . 62 . 64
package often do not work for another program. | 22 | 13

. 2 . 4 . 6 . 8 . 10 . 12 .
An operation guide usually is prepared for each disk package. The | 26 | 16
14 . 16 . 18 . 20 . 22 . 24 . 26 . 28
guide shows you how to power up and power down the system, how to format | 31 | 19
. 30 . 32 . 34 . 36 . 38 . 40 . 42
a disk, how to copy a disk if permissible, and how to perform various | 36 | 21
. 44 . 46 . 48 . 50 . 52 . 54 . 56
other major functions of which the program is capable. It is necessary | 40 | 24
. 58 . 60 . 62 . 64 . 66 . 68
to learn the commands required to make your program function. | 44 | 27

gwam 3' | 1 | 2 | 3 | 4 | 5
5' | 1 | 2 | 3

ENRICHMENT ACTIVITY: *Keyboarding Skill*

Skill Comparison: Straight Copy

1. Take two 1' writings on ¶ 1; find *gwam.*

2. Take two 1' writings on ¶ 2; find *gwam.*

3. Compare the better *gwam* figures of the two ¶s.

4. Take two additional 1' writings on the slower ¶; try to equal or exceed the best *gwam* achieved in Steps 1 and 2.

5. Take two 3' writings on ¶s 1-2 of 57c above; find *gwam* and circle errors on each writing.

all letters used in the two paragraphs

E | 1.2 si | 5.1 awl | 90% hfw

. 2 . 4 . 6 . 8 . 10 . 12
¶ 1 Do you think it is all right to cheat as long as you do not get
. 14 . 16 . 18 . 20 . 22 . 24 . 26 .
caught? Some people do. They think that what they get away with does
28 . 30 . 32 . 34 . 36 . 38 . 40 .
not concern anyone except themselves. If you cheat to move ahead, you
42 . 44 . 46 . 48 . 50 . 52 .
deny someone else the right to the prize, and that is wrong.

A | 1.5 si | 5.7 awl | 80% hfw

. 2 . 4 . 6 . 8 . 10 . 12 .
¶ 2 Some of the major rules by which we live have been devised to pro-
14 . 16 . 18 . 20 . 22 . 24 . 26 .
tect us from one another; that is, to prevent one person or group from
28 . 30 . 32 . 34 . 36 . 38 . 40 .
taking unfair advantage of another person or group. Equally important
42 . 44 . 46 . 48 . 50 . 52 . 54
tenets are intended to keep us from being unfair to ourselves.

103d ▶ 5 Improve Language Skills

LL: 70 spaces; SS with DS between 3-line groups

1. Read and key the **Learn** sentence (with number and period), noting how the rule has been applied.

2. Key the **Apply** sentences (with numbers and periods), using the correct punctuation.

3. If time permits, key the **Apply** lines again at a faster speed to quicken decision-making skill.

EXCLAMATION POINT

> Use an exclamation mark after emphatic exclamations and after phrases and sentences that are clearly exclamatory.

Learn 1. Kevin yelled excitedly, "Whew, what a run!"

Apply 2. As we reached the top, Kim said breathlessly, "What a pretty view."

Apply 3. At halftime, Jeffry said with enthusiasm, "What an exciting game."

QUESTION MARK

> Use a question mark at the end of a sentence that is a direct question; however, use a period after a request that appears in the form of a question.

Learn 4. Do you know how to move text within a document?

Learn 5. Will you stay after class to help me with my assignment.

Apply 6. Will you try to find the book for me by tomorrow.

Apply 7. Did you stay awake during the late movie.

103e ▶ 18 Improve Skill Transfer: Rough Draft

1. Two 1' writings on each ¶ for speed; find *gwam* on each writing.

2. One 1' writing on each ¶ for control; circle errors on each writing.

3. One 3' writing on ¶s 1-3 combined; find *gwam*; circle errors. If you finish before time is called, start over.

all letters used	A	1.5 si	5.7 awl	80% hfw

gwam 1' | 3'

Reputation is the image people have about your stan-   11 | 4

dards of conduct; your ethical and morale principals. Most   22 | 7

people think that a good reputation is needed for success to succeed in   35 | 12

any job; and it is therefore one of the most important per-   47 | 16

sonal assets you can acquire in your life.   56 | 19

A good reputation is a valued asset that requires time,   11 | 22

effort, and discipline to develop and project. A bad reputa-   24 | 26

tion can be a longterm liability established in a short time   38 | 31

period. It can be a result from just one misdeed and can be a   48 | 34

heavy burden to carry throughout life.   56 | 37

It is very important to realize that most of you have an op-   11 | 41

portunity to develope and protect the reputation you want.   22 | 45

You have many chioces to make which will destroy or enhance   34 | 49

the image you want to extned. The choices are hard; and hon-   47 | 53

esty, loyalty, and dedicatoin are most often involved.   58 | 56

gwam 1'   1 | 2 | 3 | 4 | 5 | 6 | 7 | 8 | 9 | 10 | 11 | 12
3'   1 | 2 | 3 | 4

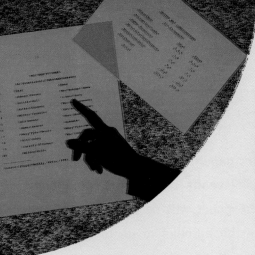

Learning Goals

1. To learn to center (format) 2- and 3-column tables.

2. To learn to align figures at the right (or at the decimal point).

3. To improve keyboarding skill on copy containing figures and symbols.

4. To improve language skills.

Format Guides

1. *Paper guide* at *0* (for typewriters).

2. LL: 70 spaces for drills and ¶s; as required for table formats.

3. LS: SS drills; DS ¶s; as required for table formats.

4. PI: 5 spaces for ¶s.

FORMATTING GUIDES: TABLES

Parts of a Simple Table

A table is a systematic arrangement of data, usually in rows and columns. Tables range in complexity from those with only two columns and a main heading to those with several columns and special features. The tables in this unit are limited to those with the following parts:

1. Main Heading (title) in ALL CAPS

2. Secondary Heading in capital and lowercase letters

3. Column Headings (blocked)

4. Body (column entries)

5. Source Note

6. Total line

The first tables to be formatted consist of only a main heading and two columns of data. The tables progress gradually in complexity so that, finally, they include three columns and several of the listed parts.

Spacing Table Parts

Short, simple tables are usually double-spaced (DS) throughout, but single-spaced (SS) column entries are acceptable. Keying all lines DS makes table processing easier, especially on computers which may require special commands to change line spacing within a document.

Horizontal/Vertical Placement of Tables

Tables are placed on the page so that the left and right margins (LM, RM) are approximately equal and the column spacing (CS), or number of spaces between columns, is exactly equal. This means that about half the characters and spaces in each line are at the left of horizontal center; about half are at the right. (Horizontal center is 42 for pica machines; 51 for elite.)

When prepared on separate sheets, tables are placed so that the top and bottom margins are approximately equal. This means that about half the lines are above vertical center; about half are below. (Vertical center of a full sheet is at line 33.) Tables that are placed slightly above vertical center (sometimes called the "reading position") are considered to look more

appealing than those that are placed at or below exact vertical center.

Aligning Data in Columns

Words in columns are aligned at the left. Figures, however, are usually aligned at the right or at the decimal point. On typewriters, alignment is done by spacing forward or backward from the tab stops. With some computer software, aligning is done automatically; for other software, it is necessary to set tabs at the leftmost figure of the columns and space forward for the shorter entries. (See User's Guide for appropriate procedure.)

Note to computer users
If your printer has only full-sheet continuous-feed paper, center half-sheet tables vertically on the upper half of a full sheet (the top 33 lines). Alternatively, center all tables on full sheets (66 lines).

103a ▶ 5
Conditioning Practice

each line twice SS (slowly, then faster); DS between 2-line groups; if time permits, rekey selected lines

alphabet	1	Jerry met his quota for seventy new wax paper and zip-lock bag orders.
figures	2	I had sold 48 hot dogs, 35 hamburgers, 72 candy bars, and 1,960 sodas.
adjacent keys	3	I hope the new report on the point of the poem will be done next week.
speed	4	The girls in the sorority dorms pay for the autobus to go to the town.

| 1 | 2 | 3 | 4 | 5 | 6 | 7 | 8 | 9 | 10 | 11 | 12 | 13 | 14 |

103b ▶ 8 Improve Keyboarding Skill: Guided Writings

1. Two 1' writings; find *gwam*.

2. Add 4 words to better rate; determine 15" goals.

3. Two 30" writings; try to reach your 15" goals.

4. Two 1' writings; try to reach your 15" goals for the entire minute.

all letters used A | 1.5 si | 5.7 awl | 80% hfw

Most codes of ethics require workers to sign an itemized statement each year to certify they are handling business in an ethical and just way. The statement usually deals with conflicts of interest which may arise when, for example, a worker accepts an unjust cash payment, favor, or present from someone who is doing or wishes to do business with the company.

103c ▶ 14 Measure Keyboarding Skill: Straight Copy

1. Two 3' writings; find *gwam*, circle errors on each writing.

2. One 5' writing; find *gwam*, circle errors.
Goal: To maintain 3' rate for 5'.

3. Record better 3' rate and the 5' rate.

4. Compare these rates with those you recorded in 101d.

all letters used A | 1.5 si | 5.7 awl | 80% hfw

	gwam 3'	5'
Appearance, which is often defined as the outward aspect of someone	5	3	43
or something, is quite important to most of us and affects just about	9	6	46
every day of our lives. We like to be around people who and things which	14	8	48
we consider attractive. Because of this preference, appearance is a	19	11	51
factor in almost every decision we make.	22	13	53
Appearance often affects our selection of food, the place in which	26	16	56
we live, the clothes we purchase, the car we drive, and the vacations we	31	19	59
schedule. For example, we usually do not eat foods which are not visu-	36	21	61
ally appealing or buy clothing that we realize will be unattractive to	40	24	64
others who are important to us.	43	26	66
Appearance is important in business. People in charge of hiring	47	28	68
almost always stress the importance of a good appearance. Your progress	52	31	71
in a job or career can be affected by how others judge your appearance.	57	34	74
It is not uncommon for those who see but do not know you to evaluate	61	37	77
your abilities and character on the basis of your personal appearance.	66	40	80

gwam 3' | 1 | 2 | 3 | 4 | 5 |
5' | 1 | 2 | 3 |

58a ▶ 6
Conditioning Practice

each line twice SS (slowly, then faster); if time permits, rekey lines 2 and 4

alphabet 1 Tex just received quite a sizable rebate check from the wagon company.

figures 2 On June 23 she served 461 hamburgers, 597 sodas, and 80 bags of chips.

fig/sym 3 Invoice #14729 was paid by Byron & Gibb's check (#6058) on January 13.

speed 4 Did the chair signal the man to name the auditor of the downtown firm?

| 1 | 2 | 3 | 4 | 5 | 6 | 7 | 8 | 9 | 10 | 11 | 12 | 13 | 14 |

58b ▶ 9 Review
Horizontal Centering

1. Set a tab stop at the horizontal center point of the paper.
2. Beginning a QS below your warm-up lines, center each line of Drill 1 horizontally, DS.
3. Center Drill 2 in the same way, a QS below Drill 1.

Drill 1

SCHOLASTIC AWARD WINNERS

David Crum

Flora Fuentes

Suzi Kwan

Christopher Leis

Drill 2

CENTERING CONCEPTS

Horizontal: side to side

Vertical: top to bottom

Horizontal center: half left; half right

Vertical center: half top; half bottom

58c ▶ 35
Learn to Format a Two-Column Table

half sheet (long edge at top); DS all lines

Automatic formatting
If your equipment has automatic centering and table formatting features, refer to your User's Guide to learn to format tables. Otherwise, follow steps at right.

1. Study the guides for vertical and horizontal centering given at right.
2. Using the model table on page 107, set LM to begin Column 1; set a tab stop for Column 2 with 10 spaces between columns (CS: 10).
3. Determine the line on which to place the heading of the DS table.
4. Format/key the model.
5. Proofread and check the formatting of your completed table; mark corrections; prepare a final copy with all errors corrected.

Vertical Centering (VC) of Tables
1. Count the lines to be keyed and the blank line spaces to be left between lines (1 blank line space between DS lines).
2. Subtract *lines needed* from *total lines available* (33 for half sheet; 66 for full sheet).
3. Divide the remainder by 2 to determine top margin. If the number that results ends in a fraction, *drop the fraction*. If an odd number results, *use the next lower even number*.

Example: lines available = 33
                 total lines needed = 13
                 $\frac{20}{2} = 10$

place heading on line 10

Horizontal Centering (HC) of Columns
1. Move margin stops to ends of scale.
2. Clear all tabulator stops.
3. Move printing point to horizontal center of paper, which is 42 for pica (10-pitch) machines and 51 for elite (12-pitch) machines.
4. If column spacing (CS) is not specified, decide how many spaces to leave between columns (preferably an even number).

5. Set left margin stop:
a. From horizontal center point, backspace once for each 2 characters and spaces in longest line of each column and once for each 2 spaces to be left between columns. If longest line in one column has an odd number of strokes, combine extra stroke with first stroke in next column, as in **check####proofread**.

◀ 1   1   1   1   1   1   1   1   1
ch|ec|kp|ro|of|re|ad|##|##

If you have 1 stroke left over after backspacing for all columnar items, disregard the extra stroke.
b. Set LM at point where all backspacing ends.
6. Set tabulator stop(s):
a. From LM, space forward once for each character and space in longest line of first column and once for each space to be left between first and second columns.
b. Set tab stop at this point for second column.
c. When there is a third column, continue spacing forward in the same way to set a tab stop for it.

102c ▶ 5 Improve Language Skills: Semicolon

LL: 70 spaces; SS with DS between 3-line groups

1. Read and key the **Learn** sentence (with number and period), noting how the rule has been applied.

2. Key the **Apply** sentences (with numbers and periods), using the correct punctuation.

3. If time permits, key the **Apply** lines again at a faster speed to quicken decision-making skill.

SEMICOLON

> Use a semicolon to separate a series of phrases or clauses (especially if they contain commas) that are introduced by a colon.

Learn 1. The dates are as follows: May 1, 1982; May 5, 1987; and May 6, 1991.
Apply 2. The cities are as follows: Ada, OH Muncie, IN and Tampa, FL.
Apply 3. The teams include the following: Reds, Area I and Lions, Area II.

> Place the semicolon *outside* the closing quotation mark; the period and comma, *inside* the closing quotation mark.

Learn 4. Miss Enders said, "Begin right away"; Ms. King said, "Wait a minute."
Apply 5. Mrs. Hart said, "Print your answers;" I said, "I need a pencil."
Apply 6. Kathy's topic was "It All Starts Here;" Sandy's was "I Can Do It".

102d ▶ 20 Improve Skill Transfer: Script Copy

1. Two 1' writings on each ¶ for speed; find *gwam* on each writing.

2. One 1' writing on each ¶ for control; circle errors on each writing.

3. One 3' writing on ¶s 1-3 combined; find *gwam*; circle errors. If you finish before time is called, start over.

all letters used | A | 1.5 si | 5.7 awl | 80% hfw

	gwam 1'	3'
Ethical conduct is a subject which has received a great	11	4
deal of attention in recent years. Many businesses have de-	23	8
veloped written codes and have taken steps to ensure that em-	36	12
ployees of the business and the public are aware of these	47	16
codes. Making people aware of the codes is a company's way	59	20
of renewing its commitment to ethical practice.	69	23
A major purpose of a code of ethics is to relay a com-	11	27
pany's values and business standards to all its workers. Each	24	31
worker must realize he or she is required to apply these stan-	36	35
dards in all relations with co-workers, potential and current	49	39
customers and suppliers, and the public at large.	59	43
Employees must be able to combine personal standards with	12	47
those of the business to adhere to the code. This mixture is	24	51
important because each job has an ethical aspect and each em-	36	55
ployee has a responsibility to carry out the functions of the	49	59
job in an ethical and proper manner.	56	61

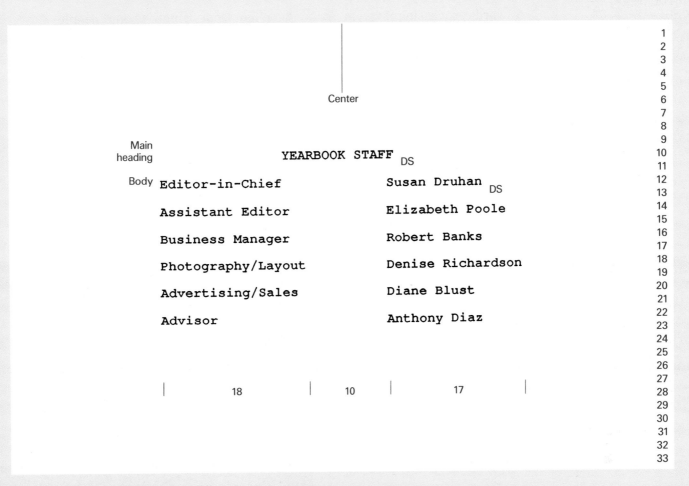

		Center	1
			2
			3
			4
			5
			6
			7
			8
Main heading		YEARBOOK STAFF ᴅˢ	9 / 10 / 11
Body	Editor-in-Chief	Susan Druhan ᴅˢ	12 / 13
	Assistant Editor	Elizabeth Poole	14 / 15
	Business Manager	Robert Banks	16 / 17
	Photography/Layout	Denise Richardson	18 / 19
	Advertising/Sales	Diane Blust	20 / 21
	Advisor	Anthony Diaz	22 / 23

18   10   17

Two-Column Table Centered Vertically and Horizontally

59a ▶ 6
Conditioning Practice

each line twice SS
(slowly, then faster);
if time permits, rekey
lines 2 and 4

alphabet 1 Fine cooks brought piquant flavor to exotic foods with zesty marjoram.

figures 2 I reviewed 50 magazines, 127 books, 189 pamphlets, and 364 newspapers.

fig/sym 3 Items marked * (as PC-478* and WP-360*) were reduced 15% May 26, 1991.

speed 4 The panel may then work with the problems of the eight downtown firms.

| 1 | 2 | 3 | 4 | 5 | 6 | 7 | 8 | 9 | 10 | 11 | 12 | 13 | 14 |

59b ▶ 9 Review Procedures for Vertical/Horizontal Centering

half sheet (long edge at top);
DS all lines

Using the model table above, see how quickly you can format and key the copy.

1. Review vertical/horizontal centering steps on page 106, if necessary.

2. Leave 12 spaces between columns (CS: 12).

3. Check work for proper placement. Is the heading on line 10? Are the LM and RM about the same width? Are there 12 spaces between columns?

101d ▶ 30
Assess/Improve Keyboarding Speed/Accuracy

1. A 1' writing on each ¶ for speed; find *gwam* on each writing.

2. A 1' writing on each ¶ for control; circle errors on each writing.

3. A 3' writing on ¶s 1-3 combined; find *gwam*, circle errors.

4. Record your 3' *gwam* to compare with your 3' *gwam* in 103c.

Skill Building

1. Set a goal of greater speed or fewer errors; if you made 6 or more errors on the 3' writing, work for control; otherwise, work for speed.

2. Take two 1' writings on each of the 3 ¶s trying to increase speed or reduce errors, according to your goal.

3. Take a 3' writing on ¶s 1-3 combined; find *gwam*, circle errors.

4. Record your 5' *gwam* to compare with your *gwam* in 103c.

all letters used	A	1.5 si	5.7 awl	80% hfw

	gwam 3'	5'
A word processing system is an excellent tool which young people	4	3	43
can use to develop their writing skills. When young people use such a	9	5	45
system to prepare papers for school or other purposes, the final copy	14	8	48
produced is likely to reflect their finest efforts because of the amazing	19	11	51
ease with which draft copies can be altered time after time.	23	14	54
Two basic functions of word processing systems that make it quite	27	16	56
easy to change writing are called insert and delete. These functions	32	19	59
permit the operator to add or take out a single space or character or an	37	22	62
entire word, sentence, paragraph, or document within a short period of	41	25	65
time with a great deal of ease.	44	26	66
When large amounts of material are moved from one place to another,	48	29	69
copied to another place, or deleted from the document, the word processor	53	32	72
often just marks the beginning and ending of the text to be moved, cop-	58	35	75
ied, or deleted. To do this, the person operating the system may use a	63	38	78
special function key to mark the material at the proper points.	67	40	80

gwam 3' | 1 | 2 | 3 | 4 | 5 |
5' | 1 | 2 | 3 |

Lesson 102 — Keyboarding/Language Skills

102a ▶ 5
Conditioning Practice

each line twice SS (slowly, then faster); DS between 2-line groups; if time permits, rekey selected lines

alphabet	1	Buffi was told to try to keep singing until her next major vocal quiz.
fig/sym	2	Tony Mason had 702 points, 451 rebounds, and 436 assists from '88-'91.
adjacent keys	3	Sam has to avoid a higher rent policy if he hopes to have more action.
speed	4	Their proficient robot with a giant hand and eye can fix the problems.

| 1 | 2 | 3 | 4 | 5 | 6 | 7 | 8 | 9 | 10 | 11 | 12 | 13 | 14 |

102b ▶ 20 Improve Keyboarding Skill: Timed Writing

1. Two 1' writings on each ¶ in 101d, above; find *gwam* on each writing.

2. A 3' writing on ¶s 1-3 combined; try to equal your best 1' rate in Step 1.

3. A 5' writing on ¶s 1-3 combined; find *gwam*, circle errors.

59c ▶ 35 Format Two-Column Tables with Main Headings

2 half sheets (long edge at top), 1 full sheet; DS all headings and column entries

Table 1
Center table vertically on a half sheet; center horizontally with 10 spaces between columns (CS: 10).

PERSONNEL RECORD		3
Employee Name	Jorge L. Ortega	9
Street Address	1624 Melody Drive	16
City	Midwest City	20
State	OK	21
ZIP Code	73110-2856	25
Telephone	733-1958	29

Table 2
Center table vertically on a half sheet; center horizontally with 12 spaces between columns (CS: 12).

COMMONLY MISSPELLED WORDS		5
accommodate	corporate	10
adequate	customer	13
appropriate	electrical	18
categories	eligible	22
committee	employees	26
compliance	immediately	30
compliment	implemented	35
correspondence	international	41

Table 3
Reformat Table 2 on a full sheet with 14 spaces between columns (CS: 14). Correct all errors you make as you key. Keep the list and master the spelling of the words.

Lesson 60 — Simple Two-Column Tables

LL: 70
LS: SS

60a ▶ 6 Conditioning Practice

each line twice SS (slowly, then faster); if time permits, two 1' writings on line 4

alphabet	1	A judge will quiz expert witnesses before he makes any vital decision.
figures	2	Please order 1,520 pencils, 894 pens, 350 file boxes, and 76 dividers.
fig/sym	3	Order #5-207 (May 24) from Kline & Co. totals $98.56, less 2/10, n/30.
speed	4	It is a civic duty to handle their problem with proficiency and vigor.

| 1 | 2 | 3 | 4 | 5 | 6 | 7 | 8 | 9 | 10 | 11 | 12 | 13 | 14 |

60b ▶ 10 Learn to Align Figures

QS below your drill lines in 60a; then key the drill at right twice SS, with 12 spaces between columns (CS: 12).

Computer users
Set a tab stop for the longest item in each column (after Column 1). To align the figures, space forward as necessary. (See your User's Guide for alternative procedures).

Typewriter users
Set a tab stop for the digit in each column (after Column 1) that requires the least forward and backward spacing to align the figures at the right. To align the figures, space forward ▶ or backward ◀ as necessary.

margin

492 —tab→ 1640 —tab→		2288
63	930	826
110	4610	1049
374	475	638
85	928	1177
211	2017	405

KEY | 3 | 12 | 4 | 12 | 4 |

Extend Keyboarding and Language Skills

Learning Goals

1. Improve and assess keyboarding techniques.

2. Improve and assess keyboarding speed and control (accuracy).

3. Improve language skills.

Format Guides

1. Paper guide at *0* (for typewriters).

2. LL: 70 spaces.

3. LS: SS word and sentence drills; DS ¶s; or space as directed within an activity.

4. PI: 5 spaces for ¶s.

Lesson 101 | *Keyboarding/Language Skills*

101a ▶ 5
Conditioning Practice

each line twice SS (slowly, then faster); DS between 2-line groups; if time permits, rekey selected lines

alphabet	1	Vera quickly justified the six itemized party food bills while dining.
figures	2	He flew 3,250 miles on Monday, 1,896 on Tuesday, and 475 on Wednesday.
adjacent keys	3	The loud voices from Drew's radio in the atrium were from a new opera.
speed	4	An off-duty ensign got sick with the toxic virus and was to go to bed.

| 1 | 2 | 3 | 4 | 5 | 6 | 7 | 8 | 9 | 10 | 11 | 12 | 13 | 14 |

101b ▶ 5 Improve Language Skills: Semicolon

LL: 70 spaces; SS with DS between 3-line groups

1. Read and key the **Learn** sentence (with number and period), noting how the rule has been applied.

2. Key the **Apply** sentences (with numbers and periods), using the correct punctuation.

3. If time permits, key the **Apply** lines again at a faster speed to quicken decision-making skill.

SEMICOLON

> Use a semicolon to separate two or more independent clauses in a compound sentence when the conjunction is omitted.

Learn 1. Eve Harris must enjoy dancing; she goes to every dance at South High.
Apply 2. Tom was worried about the engine noise he went to see his mechanic.
Apply 3. Joe is an excellent student he reads every chance he gets.

> Use a semicolon to separate independent clauses when they are joined by a conjunctive adverb (however, therefore, consequently, etc.)

Learn 4. We waited in line for an hour; however, the movie was worth the wait.
Apply 5. Al is a good speaker therefore, he receives invitations to speak.
Apply 6. Ed will not be president furthermore, he will not accept any office.

101c ▶ 10 Improve Response Patterns

Key each line twice SS; DS between 2-line groups; then 1' writings as time permits on lines 2, 4, and 6.

Adjacent keys

words	1	same suit cure spot sale foil other prior worthy fields opened quickly
sentences	2	Open bidding on truck tires will suit the clerk's priority quite well.

Direct reaches

words	3	much race cent fund worthy music union checks fifty zebra great length
sentences	4	Eight special loans in the large green manuals depend on mutual funds.

One-hand words

words	5	race upon sage yolk refer union vases zebra wages tested uphill veered
sentences	6	Ted's greatest starts in regatta races were based on a steadfast crew.

| 1 | 2 | 3 | 4 | 5 | 6 | 7 | 8 | 9 | 10 | 11 | 12 | 13 | 14 |

60c ▶ 34 Format Two-Column Tables with Secondary Headings

2 half sheets (long edge at top), 1 full sheet

Table 1
Center table vertically on a half sheet; center horizontally with 8 spaces between columns (CS: 8). DS all headings and column entries.

BASIC UNITS OF METRIC MEASURE		words
BASIC UNITS OF METRIC MEASURE		6
Units and Names		9
Unit of length	meter (m)	14
Unit of mass (weight)	kilogram (kg)	21
Unit of temperature	kelvin (K)	28
Unit of time	second (s)	32
Unit of electrical current	ampere (A)	40
Unit of luminous intensity	candela (cd)	48
Unit of substance	mole (mol)	54

Table 2

1. Center table vertically on a half sheet; center horizontally with 8 spaces between columns (CS: 8).

2. Set line spacing to SS the column entries; strike *return/ enter* key twice to DS below the headings and between classes of information.

3. Align figures at decimals.

> **Note**
> Because the figure "1" and the letter "l" are so similar, "L" is often used as the abbreviation for "liter."

Table 3
Reformat Table 2 on a full sheet with 10 spaces between columns (CS: 10). Correct all errors you make as you key.

COMMON U.S./METRIC EQUIVALENTS		words
COMMON U.S./METRIC EQUIVALENTS		6
Approximate Values		10
1 inch	25.4 millimeters (mm)	16
1 inch	2.54 centimeters (cm)	22
1 foot	0.305 meter (m)	26
1 yard	0.91 meter (m)	31
1 mile	1.61 kilometers (km)	36
1 pint	0.47 liter (l or L)	42
1 quart	0.95 liter (l or L)	47
1 gallon	3.785 liters (l or L)	54
1 ounce	28.35 grams (g)	59
1 pound	0.45 kilogram (kg)	64

Lesson 61	*Three-Column Tables*	LL: 70 LS: SS

61a ▶ 6 Conditioning Practice

each line twice SS (slowly, then faster); if time permits, rekey lines 2 and 4

alphabet	1	Peter may quit cutting flax when jet black clouds cover the azure sky.
figures	2	I ordered 36 desks, 49 chairs, 15 tables, 80 lamps, and 72 file trays.
fig/sym	3	Su paid a $72.48 premium on a $5,000 insurance policy (dated 6/13/91).
speed	4	Eighty of the city firms may form a panel to handle the fuel problems.

| 1 | 2 | 3 | 4 | 5 | 6 | 7 | 8 | 9 | 10 | 11 | 12 | 13 | 14 |

61b ▶ 9 Build Skill in Formatting Tables

full sheet; CS: 10; DS all lines

Using Table 1 above, see how quickly you can format and key the copy.

1. Review vertical/horizontal centering steps on page 106 if necessary.

2. Check work for proper placement. Is the heading on line 24? Are the LM and RM about the same width? Are there 10 spaces between columns?

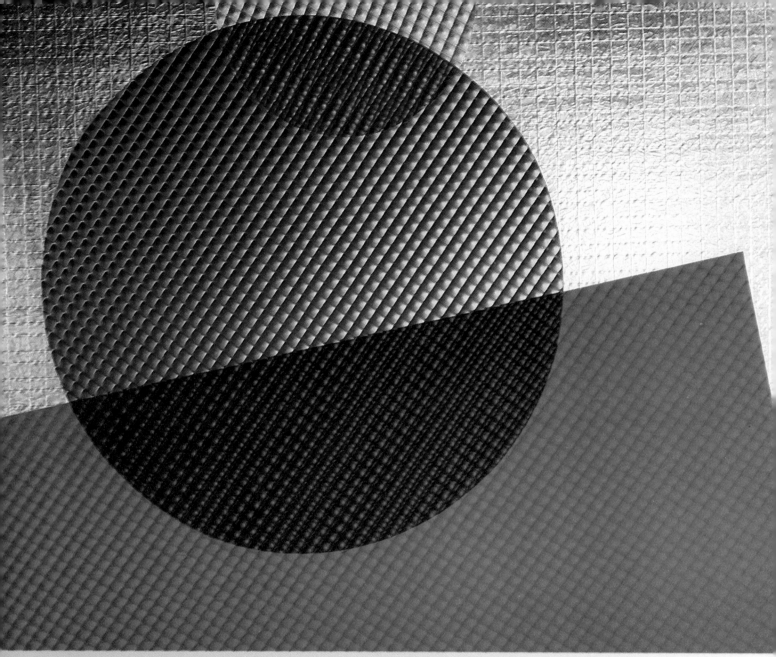

PHASE 5

EXTEND DOCUMENT PROCESSING SKILLS

Phase 5 continues the emphasis on improving keyboarding and document processing skills. The lessons are designed to help you:

1. Further refine keyboarding techniques as you apply your keyboarding skill.

2. Improve and extend document formatting skills on simple and complex tables, reports containing footnotes or endnotes, and letters in block and modified block formats.

3. Increase language-skill competency.

4. Increase keyboarding speed and control.

5. Improve proofreading competency.

6. Improve skill in keying from rough-draft and script copy.

61c ▶ 35 Format Three-Column Tables

2 half sheets, 1 full sheet
DS all lines; block column headings

Table 1
Three-Column Table with Total Line
half sheet; CS: 6

Note: Do not count $ as part of a column.

Keying _Total_ Lines

1. Underline the last figures in the columns so that the underlines extend over the _Total_ figures.

2. DS below the underlined figures.

3. Indent the word "Total" 5 spaces; key the totals; align figures at decimals.

Table 2
Three-Column Table with Source Note
half sheet; CS: 8

DS above and below the 1½" rule above the source note (15 underline spaces, pica; 18 underline spaces, elite).

Table 3
Reformat Table 1 on a full sheet with CS: 10. Correct all errors you make as you key.

UNITED WAY CONTRIBUTIONS			5
(In Thousands)			8
Department	Goal	Final	16
Accounting/Credit	$ 4.5	$ 5.0	23
Human Resources	3.8	3.9	28
Manufacturing/Shipping	5.6	7.1	34
Marketing/Sales	9.4	10.2	39
Purchasing	2.0	2.7	45
Total	$25.3	$28.9	49

HEISMAN TROPHY WINNERS			5
(Best College Football Player of the Year)			13
Year	Player	College	21
1984	Doug Flutie	Boston College	27
1985	Bo Jackson	Auburn	32
1986	Vinny Testaverde	Miami (Fla.)	39
1987	Tim Brown	Notre Dame	44
1988	Barry Sanders	Oklahoma State	51
1989	Andre Ware	Univ. of Houston	57
			61
Source: The World Almanac, 1990.			71

Lesson 62 | Two- and Three-Column Tables | LL: 70
LS: SS

62a ▶ 6 Conditioning Practice

each line twice SS (slowly, then faster); if time permits, two 1' writings on line 4

alphabet	1	Zoya picked a bouquet of vivid flowers growing next to the jungle gym.
figures	2	Order 196 was for 38 vests, 72 jackets, 40 skirts, and 25 plaid suits.
fig/sym	3	I said, "The quiz covering pages 35-149 and 168-270 will be on May 5."
speed	4	She is to pay the six firms for all the bodywork they do on the autos.

| 1 | 2 | 3 | 4 | 5 | 6 | 7 | 8 | 9 | 10 | 11 | 12 | 13 | 14 |

62b ▶ 9 Build Skill in Formatting Tables

full sheet; CS: 10
DS all lines

Using Table 2 above, see how quickly you can format and key the copy.

1. Review vertical/horizontal centering steps on page 106 if necessary.

2. Check work for proper placement. Is the heading on line 22? Are the LM and RM about the same width? Are there 10 spaces between columns?

Time Schedule
Plan and prepare .... 4'
Document processing ...... 25'
Proofread; compute
  n-pram .... 6'

3 plain full sheets

Document 1
Unbound Report
Format and key the material given at the right as an unbound report. Correct any errors you make as you key. Before removing each page from the machine or screen, proofread and correct any remaining errors.

Document 2
Reference Page
Prepare a reference page for the report using the following information.

Cherrington, David J. The Work Ethic. New York: AMACOM Division of the American Management Association, 1980.

Manning, George, and Kent Curtis. Morale: Quality of Work Life. Cincinnati: South-Western Publishing Co., 1988.

Document 3
Title Page
Prepare a title page for the report using your **name, school,** and **current date.**

words

WORK--TODAY AND YESTERDAY _QS_

5

Even though there are those who question the degree of

16

existence of the american work ethic, most americans still

28

believe it exists in the (U.S.) today. Included as part of

41

this work ethic is the belief that:

49

1. Workers should take pride in their work and do
their jobs well.

59
63

2. Employees should have feelings of commitment and
loyalty to their profession, their company, and their work
group.

73
85
87

3. People should acquire wealth through honest labor
and retain it through thrift and wise investments (Cherrington, 1980, 20).

97
108

Regard less of whether the American Work Ethic has or
has not changed over the years, work and how it is viewed
have changed. Because of technology, jobs are less physical
and more mental than ever before. Worker expectations of
jobs have also changed. Jobs are no longer viewed as simply
a means of putting food on the table. Such things as job
satisfaction and employee morale are now extremely important
to employees as well as employers.

118
130
142
154
166
178
190
197

Job Satisfaction
Today's employees are more concerned about job satis-

204
214

faction than ever before. The emphasis following the
depression which was during and following the depression placed on income and job security, has

222
237

been replaced by an emphasis on job satisfaction. This is

249

directly related to an affluent society with many well-paying jobs

262

available. As a result, qualified workers can now be more selective

276

in choosing jobs that offer intrinsic rewards. personal fulfillment

286
292

Employee Morale
With research indicating a direct relationship between

303

job performance and employee morale, employers are continually evaluating taking a long look
ways in which employee to determine how morale can be increased. Manning and Curtis

318
332

(1988, 71) believe morale energizes people and brings out

343

the best in their job performance. They define morale as

355

being a person's attitude toward the work experience. The

376

job itself, the work group, management practices, and econom-

388

ic rewards are included as part of this work experience.

390

62c ▶ 35 Build Skill in Formatting Tables
2 half sheets, 1 full sheet

Table 1
Two-Column Table
with Source Note
half sheet, DS; CS: 14

Remember to DS above and below the 1½″ rule above the source note.

PLAYS MOST OFTEN STAGED BY HIGH SCHOOLS		8
(Times Produced by Schools Surveyed)		15
You Can't Take It with You	42	21
Bye Bye Birdie	35	25
Arsenic and Old Lace	31	30
Guys and Dolls	27	33
The Music Man	24	37
_____		41
Source: International Thespian Society.		49

Table 2
Three-Column Table
with Column Headings
and Source Note

1. Center table on a half sheet with CS: 8.

2. Set line spacing to SS the column entries; strike *return/enter* key twice to DS above and below the headings and divider rule.

Table 3
Reformat Table 2 on a full sheet, but DS the entries and use CS: 10. Correct all errors you make as you key.

JOHN R. WOODEN AWARD WINNERS			6
(Best College Basketball Player of the Year)			15
Year	Player	College	22
1984	Michael Jordan	North Carolina	30
1985	Chris Mullin	St. John's	37
1986	Walter Berry	St. John's	43
1987	David Robinson	Navy	49
1988	Danny Manning	Kansas	55
1989	Sean Elliott	Arizona	61
_____			65
Source: The World Almanac, 1990.			75

Lesson 63	Prepare for Measurement	LL: 70 LS: SS

63a ▶ 6
Conditioning Practice
each line twice SS (slowly, then faster); if time permits, rekey lines 2 and 4

alphabet	1	Chan just dropped a queer pink vase we got on sale for my next bazaar.
figures	2	What is the sum of 16 3/8 and 27 4/5 and 49 1/2 and 10 2/3 and 17 1/6?
fig/sym	3	There is a credit (on 3/9) of $481.23 and a debit (on 3/25) of $70.62.
speed	4	He may go with us to a small town by the lake to do the work for them.

| 1 | 2 | 3 | 4 | 5 | 6 | 7 | 8 | 9 | 10 | 11 | 12 | 13 | 14 |

63b ▶ 44 Prepare for Measurement
2 half sheets, 1 full sheet; correction supplies

correct errors

To prepare for measurement in Lesson 64, format and key each of the tables on p. 112 according to the directions given with the problems.

Refer to the centering guides on p. 106 as needed.

If you finish all the tables before time is called, start over

with Table 1. Use a full sheet and DS all the lines.

100a ▶ 5
Conditioning
Practice

each line twice SS
(slowly, then faster);
DS between 2-line
groups; if time permits,
rekey selected lines

alphabet 1 Judy quickly spent all her extra money on a new puzzle before leaving.

figures 2 Order No. 78966 was for 140 disks, 30 printer ribbons, and 25 manuals.

fig/sym 3 March sales ($366,680) were 24% higher than February sales ($295,700).

speed 4 The big social for their neighbor may also be held in the city chapel.

| 1 | 2 | 3 | 4 | 5 | 6 | 7 | 8 | 9 | 10 | 11 | 12 | 13 | 14 |

100b ▶ 10
Evaluate Keyboarding
Skills: Straight Copy

1. A 3' writing on ¶s 1-3
combined; find *gwam*, circle
errors.

2. A 1' writing on ¶ 1; then
a 1' writing on ¶ 2; find
gwam and circle errors
on each.

3. Another 3' writing on
¶s 1-3 combined; find
gwam, circle errors.

4. Record on LP p. 3
your best 3' *gwam*.

all letters used | A | 1.5 si | 5.7 awl | 80% hfw

gwam 3' | 5'

Firms that plan to operate at a profit must employ people who are   4 | 3
willing to work as a team to achieve goals. Various management styles   9 | 5
have been used in the past to achieve company goals. These range from an   14 | 8
autocratic style where decisions are made by one person to a democratic   19 | 11
style where decisions are made by a group of employees. The team method   24 | 14
of decision making has become more accepted by many firms.   28 | 17

One of the more democratic forms of management that is becoming   32 | 19
quite popular is the quality circles concept. Employees are invited to   37 | 22
participate as part of a team to make decisions and deal with the problems   42 | 25
related to their jobs. The idea behind quality circles is to have the   47 | 28
workers who are most familiar with the job make all of the decisions   51 | 31
directly related to it rather than those who are further removed.   56 | 33

Research shows that employees who feel they are a valuable part of   60 | 36
a company team are more satisfied with their jobs. The end result of   65 | 39
job satisfaction is a higher level of achievement. Of course, a higher   70 | 42
achievement level means more profit for a firm and more benefits to the   74 | 45
worker. Because of the recent success of quality circles, more firms are   79 | 48
using this approach to help maximize employee output.   83 | 50

gwam 3' | 1 | 2 | 3 | 4 | 5 |
5' | 1 | 2 | 3 |

63b (continued)

Table 1
Two-Column Table
with Main Heading
half sheet; CS: 12; SS column
entries with DS below heading

		words
OTHER OFTEN MISSPELLED WORDS		6
installation	previously	11
judgment	prior	14
monitoring	pursuant	18
opportunity	received	22
permanent	recommendation	27
personnel	reference	31
participants	similar	35
patient	successful	39
possibility	sufficient	43

Table 2
Two-Column Table
with Main, Secondary,
and Column Headings
and Source Note
half sheet; CS: 8;
DS all lines

∧	insert	
sp	spell out	
∿	transpose	

		TEMPORARY	words
sp	MOST WANTED WORKERS		6
	% of Companies Hiring		12
Job Clasification		%	20
Clerical/receptionist		87	25
Secretarial/word processing		75	31
Accounting/finacial		52	36
Data procesing		30	39
Engineering		14	42
			46
Source: USA Today, April 24 1989.			55

Table 3
Three-Column Table
with Multiple Headings
and Source Note
full sheet; CS: 8;
DS all lines

			words
TOP TEN TV STARS			3
At Television's 50th Anniversary			10
No.	Star	Show	15
1	Johnny Carson	The Tonight Show	22
2	Lucille Ball	I Love Lucy	27
3	Jackie Gleason	The Honeymooners	34
4	Walter Cronkite	CBS Evening News	41
5	Sid Caesar	Your Show of Shows	47
6	James Arness	Gunsmoke	52
7	Mary Tyler Moore	Mary Tyler Moore Show	60
8	Bill Cosby	The Cosby Show	66
9	Carroll O'Connor	All in the Family	73
10	Milton Berle	Texaco Star Theater	81
			84
Source: People Weekly, Extra, 1989.			92

Document 2
Simplified Memo

plain full sheet

Format and key the memo in simplified style.

words

April 21, 19-- | Mark McGinnis | INFORMATION MANAGEMENT SALARIES   12

Attached is the information you requested on salaries for   24

various fields in the Information Management area. I have   36

listed the job titles as well as the geographic locations of the firms ad-   50

vertising the positions. This information was gathered from   63

the careers section of Computer Focus.   73

The salary range was $21,200 to $48,500. This range should give you some   88

idea of the salary level you will need to offer for the the   99

two new positions in our information management department.   112

Let me know if there is further information that I can pro-   123

vide to assist in filling these positions.   132

Courtney Williams | Attachment | xx   138

Document 3
Table

Format and key the table on a full sheet. Center column headings and leave 8 spaces between columns.

Document 4
Rekey Document 1. Address letter to:

Miss Michelle R. Gordon
Management Systems, Inc.
2845 Finch Street
Stamford, CT 06905-6384

Address an envelope.

INFORMATION MANAGEMENT SALARY Ranges   7

April 15, 19--   10

Job Title	Location	Salary	
Business Systems Analyst	Atlanta, GA	$45,000	22
Computer Systems Analyst	Brooklyn, NY	48,500	32
			41
Data Processing Manager	St. Louis, MO	32,000	50
Data Base Analyst	Houston, TX	48,000	57
Program Analyst	Raleigh, NC	37,000	64
Senior Program Analyst	New Orleans, LA	40,000	73
Software Consultants	Detroit, MI	32,760	81
Support Systems Engineer	Portland, OR	32,200	90
Systems Analyst	Los Angeles, CA	36,000	98 / 101

Source: Computer Focus, February 20, 19--.   113

64a ▶ 6
Conditioning Practice

each line twice SS
(slowly, then faster);
if time permits, two
1' writings on line 4

alphabet	1	Al criticized my six workers for having such quick tempers on the job.
figures	2	Add 14 meters 25 centimeters, 89 meters 36 centimeters, and 70 meters.
fig/sym	3	Both start today (6/7): Tina Ho at $421.89/wk.; Vic Kuo at $10.53/hr.
speed	4	It is the wish of all of us to lend a hand to the visitor to the city.

| 1 | 2 | 3 | 4 | 5 | 6 | 7 | 8 | 9 | 10 | 11 | 12 | 13 | 14 |

64b ▶ 9 Check
Keyboarding Skill: Straight Copy

1. Take a 1' writing on each ¶; find *gwam*; circle errors.

2. Take a 3' writing on the two ¶s combined; find *gwam*; circle errors.

3. If time permits, take an additional 1' writing on each ¶ to build speed.

all letters used | A | 1.5 si | 5.7 awl | 80% hfw

gwam 3' | 5'

As you build your keying power, the number of errors you make is   4 | 3

not very important because most of the errors are accidental and inci-   9 | 5

dental. Realize, however, that documents are expected to be without   14 | 8

flaw. A letter, report, or table that contains flaws is not usable   18 | 11

until it is corrected. So find and correct all of your errors.   22 | 13

The best time to detect and correct your errors is while the copy   27 | 16

remains in the machine or on a monitor. Therefore, just before you   31 | 19

remove the copy from the machine or screen, proofread it and correct   36 | 21

any errors you have made. Learn to proofread carefully and to correct   40 | 24

your errors quickly. This is the way to improve your productivity.   45 | 27

gwam 3' | 1 | 2 | 3 | 4 | 5 |
5' | 1 | 2 | 3 |

64c ▶ 35 Check
Formatting Skill: Tables

2 half sheets, 1 full sheet;
DS all lines; correct errors

Table 1
Table with Main and Secondary Headings and Source Note
half sheet; CS: 18

Tables 2 and 3 are on p. 114.

	words
ENLISTED WOMEN IN UNIFORM	5
(Percent of Each Service Branch)	12
Air Force 13.2%	15
Army 11.0%	17
Navy 9.3%	19
Marines 5.1%	22
	26
Source: Dept. of Defense, 1988.	32

UNIT 22 LESSONS 99 – 100
Evaluate Keyboarding/Document Processing Skills

Evaluation Goals

1. To measure the speed and accuracy with which you key straight-copy material.

2. To evaluate your ability to process correspondence in proper formats.

3. To evaluate your ability to process tables in proper format.

4. To evaluate your ability to process reports in proper format.

Format Guides

1. Paper guide at *0* (for typewriters).

2. LL: 70-space line for drills and ¶s; as appropriate for documents.

3. LS: SS drills; DS ¶s; as required by document formats.

4. PI: 5 spaces for ¶s; as appropriate for document formats.

Lesson 99 | Evaluate Formatting Skills: Letters, Memos, and Tables

---

99a ▶ 5
Conditioning Practice

each line twice SS (slowly, then faster); DS between 2-line groups; if time permits, rekey selected lines

alphabet	1	Their equipment manager always kept an extra five dozen jumper cables.
figures	2	The total attendance for 1992 was 87,653, about a 40 percent increase.
fig/sym	3	The desk (#28A935) and chair (#73Z146) are usually sold for over $700.
speed	4	Sue owns the wheelchair in the shanty at the end of the big cornfield.

| 1 | 2 | 3 | 4 | 5 | 6 | 7 | 8 | 9 | 10 | 11 | 12 | 13 | 14 |

99b ▶ 45
Evaluate Formatting Skills

Time Schedule

Plan and prepare .... 5'
Document processing ...... 30'
Proofread; compute
  n-pram .... 10'

2 letterheads
LP pp. 41-43
2 plain full sheets

**Document 1
Business Letter**

Format the letter in block style with open punctuation. Use the Letter Placement Guide on p. 76 to determine margins and dateline placement.

Correct any errors you make as you key; proofread and correct any remaining errors before removing the document from the machine or screen. Address an envelope.

	words
April 20, 19-- / Mr. Martin J. Pasquez / Human Resource Manager /	12
Murphy Enterprises / 2950 Freedom Drive / Charlotte, NC 28208-	24
2389 / Dear Mr. Pasquez / Subject: JUNE SEMINAR	33
¶ Here is the information on our seminar being held June 5-9.	45
The seminar on "Quality Circles" is excellent for companies that	58
are interested in involving employees in decision making.	70
¶ Companies that implement quality circles have found that em-	82
ployee morale is increased, human relations among employees	94
are improved, and employee potential is maximized. These are	106
just a few of the extra benefits derived from using quality	118
circles. The main benefit is more profits from increased productivity.	133
¶ More information about the seminar is enclosed. We always en-	145
joy working with employees from Murphy Enterprises. (122)	156
Sincerely / Ms. Jacqueline C. Bennett / Seminar Coordinator /	167
xx / Enclosure / c Mark J. Harada	173/**194**

64c (continued)

Table 2
Two-Column Table
with Multiple Headings
and Total Line
full sheet; CS: 8

Item	%	
HOW FAMILIES SPEND THEIR INCOME		6
(Showing Percent of Total)		12
Item	%	15
Housing	30.3	17
Transportation	21.2	21
Food	14.8	23
Insurance and Retirement Plans	9.4	31
Apparel, Services	5.1	35
Savings	4.3	38
Other	14.9	41
Total	100.0	44

Table 3
Three-Column Table
from Rough Draft
with Source Note
half sheet; CS: 6; recall
proofreader's marks below

WORD (SKATING CHAMPIONS) — *L FIGURE* — 6

Year	Men	Women	
1985	Aleksandr Fade~e~v, USSR	Kate~a~rina Witt, E. Germany	22
1986	Brian Boitano, USA	Debbi Thomas, USA	31
1987	Bry~i~an Orser, (Can.) *sp*	Katarina ~w~Vitt, E. Ger~m~any	41
1988	Brian Boitano, USA	Katarina Witt, E. Germany	51
1989	Kurt Browning, Canada	Midori Ito, Japan	60

64

Source: <u>The World Almanac</u> 1990. — 74

```
∧   insert

sp  spell out

ℐ   delete and close
```

ENRICHMENT ACTIVITY: Language Skills

Capitalization, Number Expression, and Word Choice

LL: 60 spaces; LS: DS

1. Read and key each line, making needed changes in capitalization, number expression, and word choice.

2. Check accuracy of work with your teacher; rekey any line that contains errors in rule applications.

1 if your going for a new goal, chose the goal with care.

2 they are do hear in an our for the banquet honoring athletes.

3 we must choose cheerleaders from only fifteen applicants.

4 i no your hear earlier then necessary; in fact, so am i.

5 mr. wojcik lead the choir in 4 of my favorite songs.

6 its their wish to live on cypress avenue in new britain?

7 your very fortunate to have mary ann for a sister.

8 if its up to me, i say let's go four the winning field goal.

9 i went to salem on monday; than on friday i went to boston.

10 we waited hear for half an our to here president bush speak.

**Message from
JESSICA SAMPSON**

*Three more clients have
accepted invitations to
the private showing.
Send a copy of the at-
tached letter using the
information provided
below.*

Mr. and Mrs. Mark O'Mara
1583 Nassau Bay Drive
Houston, TX 77058-2196

Ms. Kathy S. Ristow
1418 Rainwood Drive
Houston, TX 77079-3170

Mr. and Mrs. Juan Cruz
4573 Red Maple Drive
Houston, TX 77064-4407

*Mark Grayson will show
Mr. and Mrs. O'Mara
and Ms. Ristow the homes
on Saturday, June 6, at
7 p.m. Mathew Sparks
will show Mr. and Mrs.
Cruz the homes on Fri-
day, June 5, at 1 p.m.*

JS 5/16

May 16, 19--

Mr. and Mrs. Jason R. Walton
1825 Victoria Drive
Houston, TX 77022-1903

Dear Mr. and Mrs. Walton

We are pleased to have you take part in our private showing of the homes that will be in this year's Parade of
Homes. The eight homes you will see combine quality construction, professional decorating, and exclusive land-
scaping to make this year's show the best ever.

I have made arrangements with (AGENT'S NAME) to show you
the homes. Please meet (HIM/HER) at our office at (TIME)
on (FRIDAY/SATURDAY), June (5/6). It will take approximately two hours to visit the homes.

I am looking forward to hearing your comments about the
homes after the showing. If you have any questions prior
to the showing, please telephone me.

Sincerely

Jessica A. Sampson

Ms. Jessica A. Sampson
Branch Manager

xx

c (NAME OF AGENT)

Improve Keyboarding/Language Skills

Learning Goals

1. To improve keying technique.
2. To improve keying speed.
3. To improve keying accuracy.
4. To review/improve language skills.

Format Guides

1. *Paper guide* at *0* (for typewriters).
2. LL: 70 spaces for drills and ¶s.
3. LS: SS drills; DS ¶s.
4. PI: 5 spaces for ¶s.

| Lesson 65 | Keyboarding/Language Skills | LL: 70 LS: SS |

65a ▶ 6 Conditioning Practice

each line twice SS (slowly, then faster); if time permits, two 1' writings on line 4

alphabet 1 With quick jabs and deft parries, a young boxer amazed several people.

figures 2 Yuki keyed 51 letters, 84 envelopes, 37 tags, 92 labels, and 60 cards.

fig/sym 3 He's given me the numbers and prices: #16392, $48.30; #14593, $75.95.

speed 4 It is their duty to sign the amendment if he is to handle the problem.

| 1 | 2 | 3 | 4 | 5 | 6 | 7 | 8 | 9 | 10 | 11 | 12 | 13 | 14 |

65b ▶ 14 Improve Language Skills: Word Choice

1. Study the spelling/definitions of the words in the color block at right.

2. Key line 1 (the **Learn** line), noting the proper choice of words.

3. Key lines 2-3 (the **Apply** lines), choosing the right words to complete the lines correctly.

4. Key the remaining lines in the same way.

5. Check your accuracy; rekey lines containing word-choice errors.

to (prep/adj) used to indicate action, relation, distance, direction

too (adv) besides; also; to excessive degree

two (pron/adj) one plus one in number

sew (vb) to fasten by stitches

so (adj/conj) in the same manner or way; in order that; with the result that

sow (vb) to plant seed; scatter; disperse

Learn 1 Is it too late for the two of us to go to the two o'clock movie today?
Apply 2 I am (to, too, two) give everyone (to, too, two) cupfuls of beef soup.
Apply 3 We are going (to, too, two) the opera; Stan is going, (to, too, two).

Learn 4 He can sew the bags so that we can use them to sow the grass seed.
Apply 5 I can have them (sew, so, sow) the oats if you say (sew, so, sow).
Apply 6 The design is intricate, (sew, so, sow) I can't (sew, so, sow) it now.

65c ▶ 13 Improve Keyboarding Technique: Response Patterns

1. Key each line twice SS (slowly, then faster); DS between 6-line groups.

2. If time permits, take a 1' writing on each of lines 3, 6, and 9; find *gwam* on each; compare rates.

letter response

1 were pump edge join gave milk bear pink fact upon draw jump ever union
2 red ink | get him | draw up | bad milk | gave him | draw upon | ever join | beat him
3 As we are aware, my union drew upon a few area data in a gas tax case.

word response

4 with they them make than when also work such form then wish paid their
5 rich girl | pays half | they also | busy firm | auto fuel | turn down | city panel
6 I paid the busy girls to make the six bus signs for the big city firm.

combination response

7 the pin | big ads | aid him | for oil | got you | oak bed | tie pin | and him | pay up
8 fuel test | busy area | city cars | held fast | then join | when safe | both serve
9 John is to sign the card and join the union with the rest of the crew.

| 1 | 2 | 3 | 4 | 5 | 6 | 7 | 8 | 9 | 10 | 11 | 12 | 13 | 14 |

Job 10

LP p. 29

Message from JESSICA SAMPSON

Please send the attached letter to JS 5/15

Mr. Charles L. Atkins
1241 Warren Drive
Denver, CO 80221-7463

Job 11

Message from JESSICA SAMPSON

Please key the attached Parade of Homes schedule for Roxanne Davis.
JS 5/16

Dear Mr. Atkins

It appears as though you would fit in very nicely with the "Ritter Realty Team." Your resume looks very impressive, and your references all speak very highly of you.

As you know from speaking with John Morgan about two weeks ago at the convention in Miami, we are looking for a person from outside the area who can bring in new ideas and who has been successful in the promotion and sales area. Your background shows a strength in both of these areas.

Would you be available to spend a day with us in Houston during the week of May 26-30 to discuss the position? I will call next week to determine your availability and to make arrangements for your visit.

SCHEDULE FOR ROXANNE DAVIS

Client	June 5	Phone	Time
Mr. and Mrs. Dave Johnson		836-4877	10 a.m.
Dr. and Mrs. Reed Kurth		839-8125	
Ms. Patricia Hansen		823-1143	1 p.m.
Mr. and Mrs. Scott Jones		834-1935	
Dr. Faye Snell		839-7680	4 p.m.
Mr. and Mrs. Timothy Reedsberg		823-4676	
Mr. and Mrs. Karl Hallie		836-2908	7 p.m.
Mr. and Mrs. Gregory Haas		823-1298	

June 6

Client		Phone	Time
Mr. Jerry Sawyer		823-1095	10 a.m.
Mr. and Mrs. Jason Walton		836-6547	
Mr. Robert Todd		839-7231	1 p.m.
Miss Sandra Kurtz		836-3452	
Ms. Gretchen Kuehn		823-9876	
Mr. and Mrs. Barry Bauer		839-2349	4 p.m.
Dr. and Mrs. Ronald Baker		823-1520	7 p.m.
Miss Tami Seymour		836-4822	

Check/Improve Keyboarding Skill

1. Take a 1′ writing on ¶ 1; find *gwam*.

2. Add 2-4 *gwam* to the rate attained in Step 1, and note quarter-minute check-points from the table below.

3. Take two 1′ guided writings on ¶ 1 to increase speed.

4. Practice ¶s 2 and 3 in the same way.

5. Take a 3′ writing on ¶s 1-3 combined; find *gwam* and circle errors.

6. If time permits, take another 3′ writing.

gwam	¼′	½′	¾′	1′
24	6	12	18	24
28	7	14	21	28
32	8	16	24	32
36	9	18	27	36
40	10	20	30	40
44	11	22	33	44
48	12	24	36	48
52	13	26	39	52
56	14	28	42	56

all letters used | A | 1.5 si | 5.7 awl | 80% hfw

	gwam 3′	5′

What is a job? In its larger sense, a job is a regular duty, role, · · · · · · · 5 | 3

or function that one performs for pay. Therefore, when you apply for · · · · · · · 9 | 6

and accept a job, you accept responsibility for completing a series of · · · · · · · 14 | 8

specified tasks such as record keeping, word processing, and data entry. 19 | 11

What is a career? A career is a broad field in business, profes- 23 | 14

sional, or public life that permits one to progress in successive steps 28 | 17

up the job ladder. Whatever the tasks performed, one may have a career 33 | 20

in law, in health services, in education, or in business, for example. 37 | 22

It should be very clear that a career may include many jobs, each 42 | 25

with different ability requirements. Realize, however, that many of the 47 | 28

jobs leading to increasing success in most careers are better done with 51 | 31

greater ease by people who have built a high level of keying skill. 56 | 34

gwam 3′ | 1 | 2 | 3 | 4 | 5 |
5′ | 1 | 2 | 3 |

| Lesson 66 | Keyboarding/Language Skills | LL: 70 LS: SS |

66a ▶ 6
Conditioning Practice

each line twice SS (slowly, then faster); if time permits, two 1′ writings on line 4

alphabet 1 Jan was very quick to fix many broken zippers for the bright children.

figures 2 The shipment included 162 sofas, 179 lamps, 104 desks, and 385 chairs.

fig/sym 3 Order the roll-top desks (57″ × 26″ × 48″) from Hermann's for $391.50.

speed 4 Rick may wish to go downtown by bus to pay a visit to a busy rug firm.

| 1 | 2 | 3 | 4 | 5 | 6 | 7 | 8 | 9 | 10 | 11 | 12 | 13 | 14 |

66b ▶ 14 Improve Language Skills: Word Choice

1. Study the spelling/definitions of the words in the color block.

2. Key the **Learn** lines as shown; key the **Apply** lines using the proper words to complete them correctly.

3. Check your accuracy; rekey lines containing word-choice errors.

buy (n/vb) a bargain; to purchase; to acquire
by (prep/adv) close to; via; according to; close at hand; at/in another's home

vary (vb) change; make different; diverge
very (adj/adv) real; mere; truly; to a high degree

Learn 1 She stopped by a new shop on the square to buy the new CD album.
Apply 2 We are to go (buy, by) bus to the ski lodge to (buy, by) ski togs.
Apply 3 Did you (buy, by) the new novel (buy, by) Margaret Atwood?

Learn 4 Marquis said it is very important that we vary our attack.
Apply 5 The (vary, very) nature of skill is to (vary, very) the response.
Apply 6 As you (vary, very) input, you get (vary, very) different results.

Job 7

Location	Builder	Price
3885 Wimbledon Lane	Brock Construction	$ 133,000
3892 Glencliffe Lane	Murphy Homes Inc.	95,000
115 Fernbrook Lane	J & P Construction	215,000
803 Ashmore Drive	Berry & Sons Construction	149,000
5574 Blue Hills Road	Homes by Makely	99,000
4348 Mossridge Drive	Valleyview Home Builders	105,000
3872 Glencliffe Lane	Dalton & James Realty	91,000
120 Fernbrook Lane	Your Home Builders	175,000

Job 8

*19-- Parade of Homes
June 7-21
Monday — Friday 5 p.m. to 9 p.m.
Saturday & Sunday 10 a.m. to 6 p.m.
Featuring homes built by
(List the eight homebuilders in alphabetical order)
Sponsored by Ritter Realty Company*

Job 9

LP p. 27

Dear Mr. and Mrs. Taylor:

¶ Rebecca Smithson, personnel manager of Tyson Production Company, informed me that you have accepted a position with them and will be moving to Houston the first part of July. I know you will enjoy living in this area.

¶ A copy of the "Movers Guide" published by our real estate company is enclosed. It is designed to give helpful hints on making the move as painless as possible. We hope you will find it useful as you organize for the move to Texas.

¶ If we can be of assistance to you in locating a place to rent or a home to purchase, please telephone our office.

Sincerely,

1. Key each line twice SS; DS between 2-line groups.

2. Take a 1′ writing on each of lines 2, 4, 6, 8, and 10.

Space bar (quick down-and-in thumb motion)

1 All the men on the quay may go by bus to the town on the lake to work.
2 Jan may do key work for the six men on the audit of the big city firm.

Shift keys (finger reaches to shift keys)

3 Spiro and Jacki left with Epson and Lana for a trip to Padua and Rome.
4 Mars leaves for Bora Bora in March; Nancy goes to Lake Worth in April.

Adjacent-key reaches (fingers curved and upright)

5 Luis was the last guy to be weighed in before stadium practice opened.
6 We are to open a shop by the stadium to offer the best sporting goods.

Long direct reaches with same finger (quiet hands and arms)

7 Myra broke my gym record to receive a bronze medal at the county meet.
8 Eunice brought a recorder to music hall to record my recital of hymns.

Balanced-hand sentences (word response)

9 Both of them may also wish to make a formal bid for the big auto firm.
10 I wish to do the work so the girls may go with them to make the signs.

| 1 | 2 | 3 | 4 | 5 | 6 | 7 | 8 | 9 | 10 | 11 | 12 | 13 | 14 |

66d ▶ 17 *Check/Improve Keyboarding Skill*

1. Take a 1′ writing on ¶ 1; find *gwam*.

2. Add 2-4 *gwam* to the rate attained in Step 1, and note quarter-minute check points from the table below.

3. Take two 1′ guided writings on ¶ 1 to increase speed.

4. Practice ¶s 2 and 3 in the same way.

5. Take a 3′ writing on ¶s 1-3 combined; find *gwam* and circle errors.

6. If time permits, take another 3′ writing.

gwam	¼′	½′	¾′	1′
24	6	12	18	24
28	7	14	21	28
32	8	16	24	32
36	9	18	27	36
40	10	20	30	40
44	11	22	33	44
48	12	24	36	48
52	13	26	39	52
56	14	28	42	56

all letters used | A | 1.5 si | 5.7 awl | 80% hfw

gwam 3′ | 5′

In deciding upon a career, learn as much as possible about what   4 | 3
individuals in that career do. For each job class, there are job re-   9 | 5
quirements and qualifications that must be met. Analyze these tasks   13 | 8
very critically in terms of your personality and what you like to do. 18 | 11

A high percentage of jobs in major careers demand education or   22 | 13
training after high school. The training may be very specialized, re- 27 | 16
quiring intensive study or interning for two or more years. You must 32 | 19
decide if you are willing to expend so much time and effort.   36 | 21

After you have decided upon a career to pursue, discuss the choice 40 | 24
with parents, teachers, and others. Such people can help you design a 45 | 27
plan to guide you along the series of steps required in pursuing your 49 | 30
goal. Keep the plan flexible and change it whenever necessary.   54 | 32

gwam 3′ | 1 | 2 | 3 | 4 | 5 |
5′ | 1 | 2 | 3 |

**Message from
JESSICA SAMPSON**

*Here are the names of
three more clients that
Jeff Grayson would like
invited to the private
showing. A copy of the
original letter is at-
tached. Key a letter to
each client for me to
sign.*

Mr. and Mrs. Chi Shen
1288 Paramount Lane
Houston, TX 77067-4310

Ms. Marjorie S. Butler
3198 Rosedale Circle
Houston, TX 77004-7120

Mr. Kevin N. King
2982 Spring Field Road
Houston, TX 77062-1312

May 1, 19--

Mr. and Mrs. Jason R. Walton
1825 Victoria Drive
Houston, TX 77022-1903

Dear Mr. and Mrs. Walton

The 19-- Parade of Homes will be held June 7-21. This year
we are planning something new. A limited number of our previous home buyers from Ritter Realty are being invited to
participate in a private showing prior to the public opening
of the Parade of Homes.

The private showing will give Ritter Realty agents the time
needed to point out the many fine features of the quality
homes being shown this year and to answer any questions you
may have. With so many people taking part in the Parade of
Homes, it is difficult to give our preferred customers the
attention they deserve during the days the homes are shown
to the public.

If you are interested in this free showing, sign and return
the enclosed card. We look forward to showing you the outstanding homes built for this year's home show.

Sincerely

Jessica A. Sampson

Ms. Jessica A. Sampson
Branch Manager

xx

Enclosure

**Message from
JESSICA SAMPSON**

*Please send the attached
letter to*

Mr. Nelson C. Decker
Lakeside National Bank
2310 North Main Street
Houston, TX 77009-4612

Here is a copy of an article/which may be of interest to you⌃ *on streamlining the mortgage process*
~~from~~ *It appeared in* the April issue of <u>Mortgage Banking</u>. ~~It has~~ several
good sug̱gestions for ways of cutting the time between the ap-
plication ~~date~~ and ~~the~~ closing dates⌃. # *are presented* As I mentioned to
you last week, we have⌃ *recently* had several customers who ~~are~~ *were* quite
concerned about the length of time that ~~it is currently tak-~~ *was required*
~~ing~~ for⌃ *the* processing⌃ *of* their loans. I will be interested in
your reaction to the article. Sincerely,

67a ▶ 6
Conditioning Practice

each line twice SS (slowly, then faster); if time permits, two 1' writings on line 4

alphabet	1	The blitz vexed the famous quarterback whose game plan just went awry.
figures	2	Today we keyed 40 letters, 15 reports, 369 orders, and 278 statements.
fig/sym	3	Make finger reaches (hands quiet) to key 303#, 126.95%, and $1.475.98.
speed	4	He may hand me the clay and then go to the shelf for the die and form.

| 1 | 2 | 3 | 4 | 5 | 6 | 7 | 8 | 9 | 10 | 11 | 12 | 13 | 14 |

67b ▶ 14 Improve Language Skills: Word Choice

1. Study the spelling/definitions of the words in the color block.
2. Key the **Learn** lines as shown; key the **Apply** lines using the proper words to complete them correctly.
3. Check your accuracy; rekey lines containing word-choice errors.

passed (vb) past tense of *pass;* already occurred; gave an item to someone
past (adv/adj/prep/n) gone or elapsed; time gone by; moved by

some (n/adv) unknown or unspecified unit or thing; to a degree or extent
sum (n/vb) the whole amount; the total; to find a total; summary of points

Learn	1	In the past we passed the church before we marched past the library.
Apply	2	As we (passed, past) in our tests, we filed (passed, past) the teacher.
Apply	3	In the (passed, past) month, I have (passed, past) up two new jobs.
Learn	4	The problem was to find the sum, but some of the students couldn't.
Apply	5	"In (some, sum)," she said, "both ideas are true to (some, sum) degree."
Apply	6	I bought (some, sum) pears and apples for the (some, sum) of $2.30.

67c ▶ 13 Improve Keyboarding Speed: Skill Transfer

LL: 60 spaces; LS: DS

1. Take a 1' writing on each ¶; find *gwam* on each.
2. Compare the *gwam* figures to identify the two slower ¶s.
3. Take two more 1' writings on each of the two slower ¶s, trying to equal your *gwam* on the fastest ¶.
4. Take another 1' writing on each ¶; find *gwam* on each.

Goals
¶ 2: 80% of ¶ 1 *gwam*
¶ 3: 90% of ¶ 1 *gwam*

Each ¶ is of average difficulty. Differences in speed, therefore, should result from the form in which the copy is presented:
● straight copy
● rough-draft copy
● script copy

	gwam 1'	2'
As you prepare for your chosen career, try to talk with	11	6
as many individuals as possible who are in that career. If	23	12
you exhibit interest in the tasks these people perform on a	35	18
regular basis, they will answer questions and volunteer in-	47	24
formation that is hard to obtain in any other way. In this	59	30
continuing process, you may acquire vital job leads.	69	35
Whether you have to earn money or not make part time or	11	40
summer work apart of your carere plan. A carefully chosen	22	46
work experience can offer many chances to meet workers in	34	52
you career field and to observe directly many of the activi-	47	58
ties and fetures ofthe jobs related to that feild. You can	59	64
make work a valuable career learning experince.	70	70
Do not expect your first position to be near the top of	11	75
your chosen career ladder. Although you may not be required	23	81
to begin at the very bottom rung, realize that you have to	35	87
demonstrate your capability of performing at a higher level	47	93
before you will be placed there. To advance in your chosen	59	99
career, you must gain related experience of increasing value.	71	105

HOME MORTGAGES

Many types of creative financing for home loans are offered by financial institutions. However, the two most common types of mortgages are the fixed-rate mortgage and the adjustable-rate mortgage. } DS

Fixed-Rate Mortgage # The intrest rate of a fixed-rate mortgage remains the same for the duration of the loan. Even if ecomic conditions change, the interest rate cannot be adjusted. this can be an advantage or disadvantage, depending on whether interest rates are increasing or decreasing. The table below (Wyllie, 1988, 301) illustrates the amount of a monthly mortgage payment on a 30 year loan per $1,000 borrowed. For example, The monthly payment for a $50,000 loan for 30 years at 10 percent would be $439 ($8.78 x 50 = $439).

Insert A

One percentage point can # make a sizable difference in the amount paid each month. It is to a borrowers advantage to check with several financial institutions to find the best interest rate available. When analyzing interest rates, however, a buyer should keep in mind that there are variable closing costs attached associated with securing a loan. These costs may include the following:

Insert B

Adjustable-Rate Mortgage

Another common type of morgage offered by most financial institutions is the adjustable rate mortgage.

An adjustable-rate mortgage is a loan with an interest rate that can be adjusted up or down an agreed-upon number of times during the life of the loan. The interest rate is usually tied to changes in a monetary index, such as the interest rates on U.S. Treasury securities or the rates financial institutions must pay their depositors or investors. (Green, 1988, 441)

REFERENCES

Wyllie, Eugene D., et al. _Consumer Economics_. 11th ed. Cincinnati: South-Western Publishing Company, 1988.

Green D. Hayden. _Consumers in the Economy_. 2nd ed. Cincinnati: South-Western Publishing Co., 1988.

Message from JESSICA SAMPSON

Key the document as an unbound report. The material should answer some of the questions that first-time home buyers often ask. The two inserts are attached. Key the references on a separate page. JS 5/13

Insert A

Rate	Monthly Payment
8.0%	$ 7.34
9.0	8.05
10.0	8.78
11.0	9.53
12.0	10.29
13.0	11.07

Insert B

1. Loan origination fees
2. Mortgage insurance application fee
3. Appraisal fee
4. Credit report fee
5. Loan discount (points)

Check/Improve Keyboarding Skill

1. Take a 1' writing on ¶ 1; find *gwam*.

2. Add 2-4 *gwam* to the rate attained in Step 1, and note quarter-minute checkpoints from the table below.

3. Take two 1' guided writings on ¶ 1 to increase speed.

4. Practice ¶s 2 and 3 in the same way.

5. Take a 3' writing on ¶s 1-3 combined; find *gwam* and circle errors.

6. If time permits, take another 3' writing.

gwam	¼'	½'	¾'	1'
24	6	12	18	24
28	7	14	21	28
32	8	16	24	32
36	9	18	27	36
40	10	20	30	40
44	11	22	33	44
48	12	24	36	48
52	13	26	39	52
56	14	28	42	56

all letters used | A | 1.5 si | 5.7 awl | 80% hfw

	gwam 3'	5'
For many people in the early part of the century, staying in the	4	3
same job with a single company or institution for their entire produc-	9	5
tive lives was not too uncommon. Now it is thought that many fledgling	14	8
workers will switch jobs several times in their working lifetimes.	18	11
The pace of change in the national job arena today requires that	23	14
all people prepare themselves to move upward or outward in the same com-	27	16
pany or from firm to firm. Such moves demand widened experience and	32	19
education. Often the moves result in better pay and benefits.	36	22
So do not envision your diploma or your initial job as the end of	40	24
anything. Recognize that they are merely milestones in the ongoing	45	27
process of preparing for a richer, more responsible life. Living is a	50	30
process of becoming rather than a state of being.	53	32

gwam 3' | 1 | 2 | 3 | 4 | 5 |
5' | 1 | 2 | 3 |

ENRICHMENT ACTIVITY: Language Skills Checkup

LL: 70 spaces
LS: SS; DS between groups

1. Lines 1-7: As you key each line, select the words that correctly complete the sentence.

2. Lines 8-14: As you key each line, supply capitalization where needed.

3. Lines 15-20: As you key each line, express numbers correctly.

1 He (passed, past) the ball just as the receiver ran (passed, past) me.
2 (Its, It's) up to them to (do, due) the work required to win the prize.
3 She is (to, too, two) small (to, too, two) play on the varsity squad.
4 We (sew, so, sow) seed in the fall (sew, so, sow) we have early grass.
5 They want (vary, very) much to (buy, by) a new car (buy, by) spring.
6 More (than, then) an (hour, our) passed before the bus arrived.
7 (Choose, Chose) the right one, since (your, you're) the leader.

8 ms. barnes visited the eiffel tower in paris when she was in france.
9 the senior class will have its prom at the skirvin hotel this fall.
10 maria, frederic, and joanna comprise this year's prom committee.
11 on labor day we had a picnic in sloan park, followed by a ball game.
12 "how often," she asked, "do you watch the san diego chargers on TV?"
13 did you write the check to stephen p. kendall, d.d.s.?
14 we took wilshire boulevard to the beverly wilshire hotel yesterday.

15 15 members of the Drama Club attended the meeting; 4 did not.
16 She took the eight thirty a.m. shuttle; I met her at Gate twenty-nine.
17 Kenney Center is at One 4th Street; Keyes Tower, at 4 Kyles Lane.
18 Your article will appear on pages three and four of the next issue.
19 I answered Questions 1-10 on page nine and Questions 1-5 on page 18.
20 The committee met in Room ten at three p.m. on November fifteenth.

94a–98a ▶ 5 (daily)
Conditioning Practice

each line twice SS
(slowly, then faster);
DS between 2-line
groups

alphabet 1   Stacks of judo magazines were piled very high on the exquisite tables.

figures 2   By 6:45 p.m. on May 28 the men had branded all but 19 of the 730 cows.

double letters 3   good need meet been issue happy letter effect accept dollars committee

speed 4   Enrique may wish he had vigor when he duels with the haughty neighbor.

| 1 | 2 | 3 | 4 | 5 | 6 | 7 | 8 | 9 | 10 | 11 | 12 | 13 | 14 |

94b–98b ▶ 45 (daily)
Work Assignments
Jobs 1-3

Message from JESSICA SAMPSON

Key the attached memos.

The first memo goes to All Agents. Use PARADE OF HOMES SCHEDULE for the subject line.

The second memo goes to Mary Carlson, Sales Agent. Use REFRESHMENTS FOR PARADE OF HOMES as the subject line.

The third memo goes to John Morgan, Broker. Use ELECTRONIC MAIL as the subject line. JS 5/12

The response from former home buyers who are interested in the private showing of this year's Parade of Homes has been excellent. Meeting with past customers to determine if we can be of further assistance to them with their housing requirements is a real opportunity for us. All of the individuals invited have been in their present homes for over five years and may be ready to consider the purchase of a new home.

Michi will be coordinating schedules for the two days of the private showing. We should have your schedule ready within the next two or three days. A meeting will be held on May 20 at 8:30 a.m. to discuss specific details for the Parade of Homes.

Mary, last month when we were discussing some of the details for the Parade of Homes private showing, you indicated that you would be willing to handle the arrangements for refreshments. I would like to take you up on that offer if it still stands.

Please stop by my office sometime this week so that we can discuss a few of the specifics.

John, the information on electronic mail you brought back from the convention in Miami was intriguing. When you have a few minutes, stop by my office and let's discuss the applications that you think may be of value to our office.

Prepare for Measurement

Learning/Review Goals

1. To improve keyboarding skills.
2. To review/improve language skills.
3. To review formatting guides and procedures for letters, memos, tables, reports and outlines.
4. To demonstrate skill in formatting letters, memos, tables, reports and outlines.

Format Guides

1. *Paper guide* at *0* (for typewriters).
2. LL: 70 spaces for drills and ¶s; as required for document formats.
3. LS: SS drills; DS ¶s; as required for document formats.
4. PI: 5 spaces for ¶s and reports.

Lesson 68	Prepare for Measurement	LL: 70 LS: SS

68a ▶ 5
Conditioning Practice

each line twice SS (slowly, then faster); if time permits, rekey line 4

alphabet	1	Five excellent joggers pounded quickly along the beach in a warm haze.
figures	2	They replaced at cost 50 plates, 78 knives, 194 forks, and 362 spoons.
fig/sym	3	The Roe & Son check, dated May 17, should be $45.39 instead of $62.80.
speed	4	She may cycle to the city to go to the ancient chapel by the big lake.

| 1 | 2 | 3 | 4 | 5 | 6 | 7 | 8 | 9 | 10 | 11 | 12 | 13 | 14 |

68b ▶ 15 *Improve Language Skills: Word Choice*

1. Study the spelling/ definitions of the words in the color block at right.

2. Key line 1 (the **Learn** line), noting the proper choice of words.

3. Key lines 2-4 (the **Apply** lines), choosing the right words to complete the lines correctly.

4. Key the remaining **Learn/Apply** lines in the same way.

5. Key the **Review** lines, inserting the proper words to complete each sentence correctly.

6. Check your accuracy; rekey lines containing word-choice errors.

> **their** (pron) belonging to them
>
> **there** (adv/pron) in or at that place; word used to introduce a sentence or clause
>
> **they're** (contr) a contracted form of *they are*
>
> **raise** (vb/n) to lift up; to collect; an increase in amount, as of wages
>
> **rays** (n) beams of energy or light; lines of light from a bright object
>
> **raze** (vb) to tear down; to demolish

Learn	1	They're to be there to present their plans for the new building.
Apply	2	Were you (their, there, they're) for the fireworks display?
Apply	3	Do you think (their, there, they're) going to elect her as mayor?
Apply	4	In (their, there, they're) opinion, the decision was quite unfair.
Learn	5	The rays of the sun caused the flowers to raise their heads.
Learn	6	If we raise the price, will they raze the old building this month?
Apply	7	The (raise, rays, raze) of the sun will (raise, rays, raze) the fog.
Apply	8	After they (raise, rays, raze) the gym, work on a new arena can begin.
Review	9	(Your, You're) to (choose, chose) two of the (for, four) gifts.
Review	10	Is it (to, too, two) late for us to (vary, very) the choices?
Review	11	If you are taller (than, then) I am, why do (your, you're) clothes fit me?
Review	12	They are (do, due) in an (hour, our), and I (know, no) they'll come.

68c ▶ 30
Selective Review: Document Formats

plain full sheets

Review the formatting guides on p. 68, p. 76, and p. 105.

Letters/Memos

Make a list of the problems and page numbers given below:
pp. 69-70, 39c-40c, model
pp. 73-74, 41c-42c, model
pp. 77-78, 43c, model

Tables

List the problems and page numbers given below.
p. 106, 58b, Drill 2
pp. 106-107, 58c, model
p. 112, 63b, Table 3

Select the formats you need most to review. Review the format features given in the unit introductions. Then format and key selected documents from your list. Correct all errors.

Learning Goals

1. To experience the keyboarding activities of an executive assistant in a real estate office.

2. To improve your document processing skills by keying from unarranged, rough-draft, and script source documents.

Documents Processed

1. Simplified memorandums.
2. Letters in block format.
3. Centered announcement.
4. Tables with centered headings.
5. Report in unbound format.
6. Reference page of a report.

RITTER REALTY COMPANY
(An Office Job Simulation)

Before you begin the jobs on pages 168-173, read the copy at the right. When planning the assigned jobs, refer to the formatting guides given here to refresh your memory about the proper formatting and spacing of documents.

Work Assignment

You have been hired to work as an executive assistant for Ritter Realty Company. You will work for the Branch Manager, Ms. Jessica Sampson.

Each year Ritter Realty sponsors a Parade of Homes. The Parade of Homes is a showing open to the general public of newly constructed homes which feature the latest innovations in the housing industry. This year the company will be inviting former clients to attend a private showing prior to the Parade of Homes. Most of the documents that you will process this week will be about the Parade of Homes and the private showing. The work will include the processing of memos, tables, letters and a report.

Written instructions for each job assigned are given by Ms. Sampson. Use the date included on the instructions for all correspondence requiring a date. Ms. Sampson likes all her letters signed as follows:

Sincerely

Ms. Jessica A. Sampson
Branch Manager

Ms. Sampson has given you a copy of "A Quick Guide to Document Formats" which summarizes the basic features of formats used by Ritter Realty Company. Refer to this guide as needed when processing the various documents.

You will supply appropriate parts of documents when necessary. You will use your own initials for reference.

If Ms. Sampson's directions and the "Quick Guide" summary are not sufficiently detailed, use what you have been taught when making formatting decisions. In some cases, you are expected to correct undetected errors in grammar or punctuation that have been overlooked by Ms. Sampson.

You are expected to produce error-free documents, so proofread and correct your work carefully before presenting it for Ms. Sampson's approval.

A QUICK GUIDE TO DOCUMENT FORMATS

Use the following quick reference as a guide to formatting and spacing documents.

Memos

Stationery: plain sheets
Side margins: 1″
Format: simplified
Spacing: QS below date and last paragraph. DS below other parts of memo and between paragraphs.
Date: line 10 from top of paper
Subject: ALL CAPS

Letters

Stationery: letterheads
Side margins: short, 2″; average 1½″
Spacing: SS with DS between paragraphs
Format: block with open punctuation
Date: short, line 18; average, line 16

Tables

Stationery: plain full sheets
Placement: centered
Vertical spacing: DS throughout
Horizontal spacing: 6-10 spaces between columns (Use an even number)

Reports

Stationery: plain sheets
Format: unbound with internal citations
Side margins: 1″
Top margin: line 10, 10-pitch; 12, 12-pitch
Bottom margin: at least 1″
Spacing: DS text; SS quotations and lists
References: on separate sheet

69a ▶ 5
Conditioning Practice

each line twice SS (slowly, then faster); if time permits, rekey line 4

alphabet 1 Jacki saw five prime quail and two big foxes down by the old zoo lake.

figures 2 We had 36 work tables, 247 office chairs, and 85 office desks in 1990.

fig/sym 3 The bookcase (36" × 59" × 14½") is on sale at the Mart for $178.50.

speed 4 The busy visitor may work with usual vigor to form a key social panel.

| 1 | 2 | 3 | 4 | 5 | 6 | 7 | 8 | 9 | 10 | 11 | 12 | 13 | 14 |

69b ▶ 10 Check Keyboarding Skill: Straight Copy

1. Take two 3' writings on the 3 ¶s combined; find *gwam* and circle errors on each writing.

2. Record the *gwam* and number of errors on the better writing.

3. If time permits, take a 1' writing on each ¶ to improve speed.

all letters used | A | 1.5 si | 5.7 awl | 80% hfw

gwam 3' | 5'

A job description is a formal statement of the duties performed by   4 | 3

a worker. It may include both quality and quantity factors. The job   9 | 5

description is used to select new workers and place them in jobs that   14 | 8

best fit their abilities. A brief summary of the job description may   18 | 11

be given to people who show interest in working for a company.   23 | 14

A performance appraisal form is a formal method of assessing the   27 | 16

performance of workers. It defines each level of excellence a person   32 | 19

may reach. It then lists in major groups the duties workers in a job   36 | 22

class perform. The supervisor rates the person on each duty, using a   41 | 25

scale of one to five, with a rating of three representing the standard.   46 | 27

A job description and an appraisal form may have a section on work   50 | 30

habits: attitude on the job, working well with others, proper use of   55 | 33

time, skill in writing and speaking, and initiative. When a job is done   60 | 36

equally well by two workers, the one who shows better work habits and   64 | 39

attitudes will usually get the prized promotion or pay increase.   69 | 41

gwam 3' | 1 | 2 | 3 | 4 | 5 |
    5' | 1 | 2 | 3 |

69c ▶ 35
Selective Review: Document Formats

plain full sheets

Review the formatting guides on p. 92, p. 96, and p. 102.

Reports
Make a list of the problems and page numbers given below.
pp. 93-95, 51d, model
p. 96, 52c

Outline
Note the problem and page number given below.
p. 102, 56c, Outline 1

Select the formats you need most to review. Review the format features given in the unit introduction. Then format and key selected documents from your list. Correct all errors.

93c ▶ 35
Improve Table Formatting Skill

3 full sheets; format the tables given at the right; DS all lines; correct any errors you make as you key

Table 1
Table with Centered Column Headings
CS: 6; center column headings over columns

Table 2
Table with Centered Column Headings
CS: 8; center column headings over columns

Table 3
Reformat Table 2. Alphabetize the table by name of national park; CS: 12; use the copy you keyed for Table 2 to mark for alphabetizing.

			words
19-- SPRING RECRUITMENT *Schedule*			7
Martin Bartlet*t*			10
University	**Date**	**Area of Specialization**	27
San Diego *State* University	March 3	Marketing	36
Arizona State University	March 10	Management Information	47
University of Colorado	March 10~~7~~	Management Information	58
University of Kentucky	March 24	*Management*	67
Tennesse*e* State *University*	March 31	Accounting	76
Florida A & M	April 7	Marketi~~gn~~ng	83
Duke University	April 14	Accounting	90

			words
National Parks			3
(Established 1872-1917)			8
National Park	*State*	*Year*	18
Yellowstone	Wyoming	1872	23
Sequoia	California	1890	28
Yosemite	California	1890	33
Mount Rainier	Washington	1899	39
Crater Lake	Oregon	1902	44
Wind Cave	South Dakota	1903	49
Mesa Verde	Colorado	1906	54
Glacier	Montana	1910	58
Rocky Mountain	Colorado	1915	64
Hawaii Volcanoes	Hawaii	1916	70
Lassen Volcanic	California	1916	76
Mount McKinley	Alaska	1917	82
			85
Source: Encyclopedia Americana.			96

Measure Keyboarding/Formatting Skills

Measurement Goals

1. To demonstrate that you can key for 3′ on straight-copy material of average difficulty at an acceptable speed and within an error limit specified by your teacher.

2. To demonstrate that you can format and key letters, memos, reports, and tables according to standard formatting guides and with errors corrected.

Format Guides

1. *Paper guide* at *0* (for typewriters).

2. LL: 70 spaces for drills and ¶s; as formats require for letters, memos, reports, and tables.

3. LS: SS drills; DS ¶s; as formats require for letters, memos, reports and tables.

4. PI: 5 spaces when appropriate.

Lesson 70	Measure Letter/Memo Skills	LL: 70 LS: SS

70a ▶ 5
Conditioning Practice

each line twice SS (slowly, then faster); if time permits, a 1′ writing on line 4

alphabet 1 Barth was given a big prize for completing six quick high jumps today.

figures 2 The inventory includes 96 pamphlets, 1,827 books, and 3,450 magazines.

fig/sym 3 The #329 item is sold by Janoch & Co. for $875.46 (less 10% for cash).

speed 4 The key to proficiency is to name the right goals, then work for them.

| 1 | 2 | 3 | 4 | 5 | 6 | 7 | 8 | 9 | 10 | 11 | 12 | 13 | 14 |

70b ▶ 10 Check Keyboarding Skill: Straight Copy

1. Take two 3′ writings on ¶s 1-3 combined; calculate *gwam* and circle errors on each writing.

2. If time permits during the next unit, take additional 3′ writings on the combined ¶s to improve your skill.

all letters used | A | 1.5 si | 5.7 awl | 80% hfw

gwam 3′ | 5′

	3′	5′
Workers on the job have to plan their workdays and organize their	4	3
work so that all duties are done in a timely fashion. As a result,	9	5
much is being said about teaching students to prioritize work. The	13	8
truth is that novice office workers have only limited opportunities to	18	11
set their own priorities; rather, priorities are often set for them.	23	14
For example, in a word processing center a supervisor receives the	27	16
work from various document writers. He or she then assigns the work to	32	19
keyboard operators on the basis of their work loads and in the sequence	37	22
of immediacy of need. Even a private secretary is often told by the	41	25
"boss" which work is urgent and which may not be needed immediately.	46	28
As workers develop on the job and are given a greater variety of	50	30
tasks to perform, the need to set priorities increases. By then, how-	55	33
ever, they will have learned through their supervisors which types of	60	36
tasks take priority and which ones can be put off. Realize that pri-	64	39
orities grow out of the immediacy or timeliness of need.	68	41

gwam 3′ | 1 | 2 | 3 | 4 | 5 |
5′ | 1 | 2 | 3 |

Improve Language Skills: Punctuation

LL: 70 spaces; SS with DS between line groups

1. Read the first rule.

2. Key the **Learn** sentences below it (with number and period), noting how the rule has been applied.

3. Key the **Apply** sentences (with number and period), supplying the needed commas.

4. Read and practice the other rules in the same way.

5. If time permits, key the **Apply** sentences again to increase decision-making speed.

COMMA (continued)

> Use a comma to separate the day from the year and the city from the state.

Learn   1. On July 4, 1776, the Declaration of Independence was signed.

Learn   2. The next convention will be held in New Orleans, Louisiana.

Apply   3. Kingsborough Community College is located in Brooklyn New York.

Apply   4. Abraham Lincoln was born on February 12 1809 in Kentucky.

> Use a comma to separate two or more parallel adjectives (adjectives that could be separated by the word "and" instead of a comma).

Learn   5. The angry, discouraged teacher felt she had been betrayed.

Learn   6. Sara opened the door and found a small brown box. *(comma cannot be used)*

Apply   7. Karen purchased a large antique desk at the auction on Friday.

Apply   8. Ms. Sawyer was an industrious dedicated worker for our company.

> Use a comma to separate (a) unrelated groups of figures which come together and (b) whole numbers into groups of three digits each. Note: Policy, year, page, room, telephone, and most serial numbers are keyed without commas.

Learn   9. Before 1995, 1,500 more employees will be hired by our firm.

Learn 10. The serial number on the television in Room 1338 is Z83251.

Apply 11. The telephone number listed on Policy #39445 is 834-8822.

Apply 12. During the summer of 1990 32980 policyholders submitted claims.

Lesson 93	Centered Column Headings/Language Skills

93a ▶ 5
Conditioning Practice

each line twice SS (slowly, then faster); DS between 2-line groups; if time permits, rekey selected lines

alphabet 1 Max would ask very specific questions before analyzing the job issues.

figures 2 Test scores of 84, 93, 75, 62, and 100 gave Marcia an average of 82.8.

fig/sym 3 Jane wrote Checks #807 & #794 for $1,650.03 and $212.50, respectively.

speed 4 He owns both the antique bottle and the enamel bottle on their mantle.

| 1 | 2 | 3 | 4 | 5 | 6 | 7 | 8 | 9 | 10 | 11 | 12 | 13 | 14 |

93b ▶ 10
Improve Language Skills: Word Choice

1. Study the spelling and definition of each word.

2. Key the line number (with period), space twice, then key the **Learn** sentence; key the **Apply** sentences in the same format, selecting the correct word in parentheses to complete the sentences.

3. DS between three-line groups.

done (adj) brought to an end; through

dun (vb) to make demands for payment

seam (n) the joining of two pieces

seem (vb) to give the impression of being

Learn 1. When he is done with the big job, we can dun him for payment.

Apply 2. Carol planned to (done, dun) Tim every week until the bill was paid.

Apply 3. When you are (done, dun) with the project, please hand it in.

Learn 4. If I putty the seam using the same color, it will seem much smaller.

Apply 5. Does it (seam, seem) to be about the same size as the one we replaced?

Apply 6. The (seam, seem) should hold until we are able to buy a new connection.

70c ▶ 35 Check
Formatting Skill:
Letters/Memos

1 letterhead (LP p. 79); plain
full sheets; correction supplies

Document 1
Personal-Business Letter

Format and key the letter on a
plain full sheet. Use block format;
LL: 60 spaces; PB: line 14.
Correct errors.

2274 Cogswell Road | El Monte, CA   91732-3846 | December 3, 19-- | Mrs. Alice   14
M. Wiggins | 11300 Lower Azusa Road | El Monte, CA   91732-4725 | Dear Mrs.   28
Wiggins   30

Thanks to you and other PTA members who brought guests, our November 18   44
meeting was a tremendous success. Dr. Gibson was overwhelmed by the   58
high level of interest in computer literacy shown by parents of our students.   74

You will be pleased to know that two of the guests you brought have now reg-   89
istered to become regular PTA members. The total new-member registra-   103
tion was nine.   106

The other officers of the El Monte PTA join me in appreciation of the active   121
role you are taking this year.   128

Cordially yours | Ms. Laura J. Marsh   134

Document 2
Business Letter

Format and key the letter on a
letterhead. Use block format; use
the *Letter Placement Guide* on
p. 76 for margins and date placement. Correct errors.

December 4, 19-- | Mr. Duane R. Burk, Office Manager | Huesman & Schmidt,   14
Inc. | 662 Woodward Avenue | Detroit, MI   48226-1947 | Dear Mr. Burk   27

Miss Chun and I certainly enjoyed our discussions with you last week. We   41
are highly pleased that you have given us an opportunity to work with you to   57
maximize your office space.   63

Based upon your plan to regroup certain personnel, Miss Chun is reworking   77
her design to accommodate the changes. That work should be completed   91
next week. At that time we shall also have a firm bid to show you.   105

Would next Friday at ten o'clock be a convenient time for us to show you the   121
new plans? If not, please suggest another date and time.   132

Sincerely yours | Virgil P. Thompson | Assistant Sales Manager | xx (105)   145

Document 3
Simplified Memo

Format and key the simplified
memo on a plain full sheet.
SM: 1"; PB: line 10. Correct errors.

Date: **December 4, 19--**
Addressee: **Vicente W. Lugo**
Subject: **NEW SERVICE CONTRACT**
FOR OFFICE EQUIPMENT
Writer: **Danielle E. Bogarde**
Reference: **your initials**

opening lines 15

(¶) We have just signed a new service contract with the   25
Lee & Perin Company. Henceforth, they will clean, service,   37
and repair all our keyboarding and word processing   48
equipment.   50
(¶) L & P has asked me to notify all supervisors that only   61
L & P personnel should do internal cleaning or make repairs   72
on any typewriter, computer, or word processor. When service   85
is required, please call 521-8590 to make your request.   96
(¶) Make sure everyone under your supervision knows   106
about this change.   110

closing lines 114

Document 4

If time remains after completing
Document 3, begin rekeying
Document 1.

92a ▶ 5
Conditioning Practice

each line twice SS (slowly, then faster); DS between 2-line groups; if time permits, rekey selected lines

alphabet 1 Marquis Becks enjoyed expanding his vast knowledge of Arizona history.

figures 2 Games of 36, 28, 24, and 21 gave Brian a 1990 season average of 27.25.

fig/sym 3 Stone Realty sold the houses on Lots #3 & #6 for $87,950 and $104,200.

speed 4 The proficient man was kept busy with the problem with the city docks.

| 1 | 2 | 3 | 4 | 5 | 6 | 7 | 8 | 9 | 10 | 11 | 12 | 13 | 14 |

92b ▶ 35
Improve Table Formatting Skill

3 full sheets, format the tables given at the right; correct any errors you make as you key

Table 1
Three-Column Table with Blocked Column Headings and Total Line
CS: 8; DS table

words

MARCH SALES — 2

Sales Manager	Territory	Sales	
			14
Diane Aldredge	Connecticut	$204,500	21
Marcia Kelly	Maine	135,200	27
Ruth Peterson	Massachusetts	125,000	34
Rebecca Johnston	New Hampshire	135,800	42
Orlando Martinez	New York	172,900	48
Jonathan Akervik	Rhode Island	88,200	56
Roger McDonald	Vermont	115,200	64
Total Sales		$976,800	69

Table 2
Three-Column Table with Blocked Column Headings and Notation
CS: 8; DS table

Table 3
Three-Column Table with Centered Column Headings and Footnote
Reformat Table 2; SS; CS: 10

Learning cue: To center column headings shorter than column entries, follow these steps:
1. Determine placement of columns in usual way.
2. From column starting point, space forward once for each two strokes in longest entry. From this point, backspace once for each 2 strokes in column heading.
3. Key and underline column heading.

HAMBURG SCHOOL OF BALLET ITINERARY — 7

19-- Summer Tour* — 11

Sponsor	City	Date	
			17
Boston Ballet	Boston	June 4	24
Ballet Academy of Miami	Miami	June 11	32
Dallas Ballet Academy	Dallas	June 18	39
Ruth Page Foundation	Chicago	June 25	47
Northwest Ballet	Minneapolis	July 1	54
Colorado Ballet Center	Denver	July 8	61
Dancers' Stage Company	San Francisco	July 15	70
Pacific Northwest Ballet	Seattle	July 22	79

82

*Leave for Boston on June 1; return to Hamburg on July 27. — 94

71a ▶ 5
Conditioning Practice

each line twice SS (slowly, then faster); if time permits, a 1' writing on line 4

alphabet 1 Monkeys in the quaint park watched a fat lizard devour six juicy bugs.

figures 2 The telephone number for your 120 N. Lotus Drive location is 378-4569.

fig/sym 3 The rates varied from 15 1/2% to 17 1/4% on loans from $98 to $36,500.

speed 4 Kay may make an authentic map of the ancient city for the title firms.

| 1 | 2 | 3 | 4 | 5 | 6 | 7 | 8 | 9 | 10 | 11 | 12 | 13 | 14 |

71b ▶ 45 Check Formatting Skill: Reports

plain full sheets; correction supplies

Document 1
2-Page Unbound Report with Enumerated Items
Format and key the copy at right and on p. 125. Place the reference list on the second page. Make all changes marked in the source document and correct all errors.

Note: Before removing a page from your machine or screen, make a final check for errors and correct any that you may have overlooked.

words

CARE OF WORD PROCESSING EQUIPMENT — 7

In the ~era~ days of manual typewriters, ~typists~ keyboard operators often cleaned, — 20

oiled, adjusted, and repaired their ~own~ machines. Manufacturers of and vendors — 36

electronic keyboarding/word processing devices today recommend that — 50

only professionally trained service people attempt to make internal ad- — 64

justments and repairs (IBM Operators Guide, 1988, iii). — 80

~lc~ Because modern equipment uses sofisticated technology, ~ph~ — 91

warranties may be revoked if untrained people attempt to correct malfunc- — 105

tions. Some maintenance contracts become void if equipment damage results — 120

from attempts of owners or operators to adjust internal parts. — 137

The operator's guide that acompanies equipment usually repair, or install — 149

contains a statement about equipment care and maintenance. new — 161

Care of Typewriters. — 169

1. If a dust cover is available, cover the typewriter — 180
when it is not being used for extended periods. — 189

2. Dust the area around the typewriter once a week. at least — 202

3. Clean the printing head (daisy wheel or element) periodically using a vendor- — 218
reccommended cleaner. — 223

4. Clean the outer surfaces (housing and keyboard) of the — 234
typewriter as needed to remove fingerprints, stains, and — 246
dust. Do not use water, alcohol, or thinners; use only — 256
vendor-recommended products. — 263

5. When If equipment does not function, be sure it is properly — 275
plugged in and turned on before calling a service/main- — 286
tenance representative. Call your maintenance vendor — 297
when a bona fide malfunction occurs; do not attempt to — 308
make internal repairs yourself. — 314

(continued, p. 125)

Improve Language Skills: Punctuation

LL: 70 spaces; SS with DS between groups

1. Read the first rule.

2. Key the **Learn** sentence below it (with number and period), noting how the rule has been applied.

3. Key the **Apply** sentences (with number and period), supplying the needed commas.

4. Read and practice the other rules in the same way.

5. If time permits, key the **Apply** sentences again to increase decision-making speed.

COMMA (continued)

Use a comma before and after word(s) in apposition.

Learn | 1. Jan, the new reporter, has started working on the next newsletter.
Apply | 2. Our branch manager Carmen Jackson will be here tomorrow.
Apply | 3. The editor Jason Maxwell said several changes should be made.

Use a comma to set off words of direct address.

Learn | 4. If I can be of further assistance, Mario, please let me know.
Apply | 5. Finish this assignment Martin before you start on the next one.
Apply | 6. I would recommend Mr. Clinton that we cancel the order.

Use a comma to set off nonrestrictive clauses (not necessary to the meaning of the sentence); however, do not use commas to set off restrictive clauses (necessary to the meaning of the sentence).

Learn | 7. The manuscript, which I prepared, needs to be revised.
Learn | 8. The manuscript that presents banking alternatives is now available.
Apply | 9. The movie which was on the top ten list was very entertaining.
Apply | 10. The student who scores highest on the exam will win the scholarship.

91d ► 8
Check/Improve Keyboarding Skill: Straight Copy

1. Take a 1' writing.

2. Take another 1' writing starting at the place where you stopped after the first 1' writing.

3. Take another 1' writing starting at the place where you stopped after the second 1' writing.

4. Take a 3' writing trying to go beyond your last stopping point. Determine your *gwam*.

all letters used | A | 1.5 si | 5.7 awl | 80% hfw

gwam 3' | 5'

The value of an education has been a topic discussed many times with | 5 | 3
a great deal of zest. The value is often measured in terms of costs and | 9 | 6
benefits to the taxpayer. It is also judged in terms of changes in the | 14 | 9
individuals taking part in the educational process. Gains in the level | 19 | 11
of knowledge, the development and refinement of attitudes, and the | 24 | 14
acquiring of skills are believed to be crucial parts of an education. | 28 | 17

Education is a never-ending process. A person is exposed to formal | 33 | 20
and informal education throughout his or her life. Formal learning takes | 38 | 23
place in a structured situation such as a school or a college. Informal | 42 | 25
learning occurs from the experience gained from daily living. We are | 47 | 28
constantly educated from all the types of media with which we come in | 52 | 31
contact each day as well as by each person with whom we exchange ideas. | 57 | 34

gwam 3' | 1 | 2 | 3 | 4 | 5
5' | 1 | 2 | 3

words

2   315

DS The ∧above guides will help you attain long life and   326
satisfactory performance from electronic typewriters.   337
(foregoing)

Care of Computers   344

5 ¶ ⊐ Dusting, cleaning∧ and covering sugestions for computers   356

are the same as for typewriters. Some proceedures apply more   368

specifically to computers ∧ (Oliverio and Pasewark, 1988, 194).   380

   1. Be sure all components are properly installed, properly   392
 # ∧ interconnected, and plugged into wall outlets.   402
   2. Be sure all components are turned off before plugging   414
   them into or unplugging them from wall outlets.   423

   3. Clean disk drive ∧heads periodically by using a cleaning   435
   disk as prescribed by your vendor.   443

   4. Do not remove the housing ∧of the CPU to adjust or install chips,   456
   boards, or other electronic devices.   464

   5. Keep electronic hardware/software in a cool∧ dry place   476
   that is free of magnetic fields.   483

   6. When malfunctions occur, call your service/mainten-   493
   ance person; do not attempt to make repairs yourself.   504

                    REFERENCES   507

IBM Operator's Guide. International Business ∧Machines Corporation,   524
      1988.   526

Oliverio, Mary Ellen, and William R. Pasewark. The Office: 540
      Procedures and Technology. Cincinnati: South-Western   556
      Publishing Co., 1988.   560

Document 2
Title Page
Format and key a title page for the report on a plain full sheet. Use **your name** and **school name** and the **current date.** Correct errors.

Document 3
If time remains after completing Document 2, begin rekeying Document 1.

| Lesson 72 | Measure Centering/Table Skills | LL: 70 LS: SS |

72a ▶ 5
Conditioning Practice
each line twice SS (slowly, then faster); if time permits, a 1' writing on line 4

alphabet 1 Brave jockeys and large quarter horses whiz past farmers in box seats.
figures 2 Your Order No. 648 calls for 103 chairs, 29 typewriters, and 75 desks.
fig/sym 3 She wired them $365 on May 29 for the items ordered on Invoice #40187.
speed 4 Cy may be the right man to blame for the big fight in the penalty box.

| 1 | 2 | 3 | 4 | 5 | 6 | 7 | 8 | 9 | 10 | 11 | 12 | 13 | 14 |

91a ▶ 5
Conditioning Practice

each line twice SS (slowly, then faster); DS between 2-line groups; if time permits, rekey selected lines

alphabet	1	Making a yearly budget was a very unique experience for Jonathan Zorn.
figures	2	There were 386 blue, 274 green, and 159 yellow lights on the 10 trees.
fig/sym	3	Computer Model #364-A8 sells for $1,250; Model #364-A7 sells for $995.
speed	4	I may work with the city on their problems with the city turn signals.

| 1 | 2 | 3 | 4 | 5 | 6 | 7 | 8 | 9 | 10 | 11 | 12 | 13 | 14 |

91b ▶ 27
Recall Table Formatting

1 half sheet; 2 full sheets; DS all lines; format the tables given at the right; block column headings; correct errors

Table 1
Table with Main and Column Headings
half sheet; CS: 14

Table 2
Table with Main and Column Headings with Source Note
full sheet; CS: 18

Table 3
Table with Main, Secondary, and Column Headings with Total Line
full sheet; CS: 14

words

EXECUTIVE OFFICERS — 4

Position	Name	
		9
Chief Executive Officer	Donald Espinosa	17
Chairperson of the Board	Alice Gomory	25
Chief Financial Officer	Gregg Foster	32
Senior Vice President	Michael McCoskey	40
Vice President	Mary Whitney	45
Treasurer	Nancy Schneider	50

1983–1989 WORLD SERIES CHAMPIONS — 7

Team	Year	
		10
Baltimore (AL)	1983	14
Detroit (AL)	1984	18
Kansas City (AL)	1985	22
New York (NL)	1986	26
Minnesota (AL)	1987	30
Los Angeles (NL)	1988	34
Oakland (AL)	1989	38
		41
Source: World Almanac.		48

UNITED WAY — 2
(July Donations) — 6

Company	Amount	
		11
Gunderson Construction Company	$1,500	19
Lakeview Data Products	1,500	25
Wilkerson Automotive	1,000	30
First National Bank	500	35
Bates Photography	400	40
Krause Associates	250	45
Anderson's Home Furnishings	200	53
Total	$5,350	56

72b ▶ 10 *Check*
Language Skills
LL: 70 spaces; LS: DS
Key each line, making
needed changes in capitalization, number expression,
and word choice.

1   b. j. goodman moved from 2277 arbor lane to 910 beverly circle.

2   the cod package was received at two ten p.m. on february tenth.

3   we took the paddlewheel <u>Delta Queen</u> down the ohio to louisville.

4   after you have past st. louis, you still have a long drive to dallas.

5   dr. kenz is attending an ama convention in san juan, puerto rico.

6   the bedford bid is forty-five dollars more then the kaplan bid.

7   if their going with us to boston, they should be hear by now.

8   he asked, "is labor day always the first monday in september?"

9   she said that their was to much rain last week to sew the wheat.

10 hartwell corporation had it's sales conference in colorado springs.

11 of the twelve branch offices, only too failed to increase sales.

12 the quotation can be found in section 4, page 67, lines 14-16.

13 the new foundation will raze the floor by four and a half inches.

14 we worked 4 ours a day at markum's during the christmas rush.

15 the queen city club is the site for they're valentine's day party.

72c ▶ 35 *Check*
Formatting Skill:
Centering/Tables
plain full sheets for all tables;
correction supplies; LS: DS

Document 1
Announcement
plain full sheet; center announcement horizontally and vertically;
correct errors

words

ANNUAL PTA BAZAAR	4
Saturday, February 13, 19 – –	9
10 a.m. to 3 p.m.	13
Central High School Gymnasium	19
FLEA MARKET, FOOD, BEVERAGES, PRIZES	26
Admission $1.00	29
Proceeds Go to Senior Prom Fund	36

Documents 2, 3, and 4 are on p. 127.

words

OTHER COMMONLY MISSPELLED WORDS

6

addition	fiscal	maintenance	12
approximately	foreign	material	18
especially	implementation	means	25
expenditures	industrial	maximum	31
facilities	initial	minimum	36
faculty	limited	mortgage	41

90d ▶ 10
Improve Language Skills: Commas

LL: 70 spaces; SS with
DS between groups
1. Read the first rule.
2. Key the **Learn** sentences
below it (with number and period), noting how the rule has
been applied.
3. Key the **Apply** sentences
(with number and period), supplying the needed commas.
4. Read and practice the other
rules in the same way.
5. If time permits, key the **Apply** sentences again to increase
decision-making speed.

COMMA

> Use a comma after (a) introductory words, phrases,
> or clauses and (b) words in a series.

Learn 1. If you finish your homework, you may go to the play with Mary.
Learn 2. We will play the Tigers, Yankees, and Indians on our next home stand.
Apply 3. The next exam will cover memos simple tables and unbound reports.
Apply 4. When she came to visit Jo brought Dave Rob and Juanita with her.

> Do not use a comma to separate two items
> treated as a single unit within a series.

Learn 5. Her favorite breakfast was bacon and eggs, muffins, and juice.
Apply 6. My choices are peaches and cream brownies and strawberry shortcake.
Apply 7. She ordered macaroni and cheese ice cream and a soft drink.

> Use a comma before short, direct quotations.

Learn 8. The announcer said, "Please stand and welcome our next guest."
Apply 9. The woman asked "What time does the play begin?"
Apply 10. Sachi answered "I'll be in Chicago."

90e ▶ 5
Improve Technique: Response Patterns

Key each line twice.
Technique hints:
1. Keep fingers curved
and upright.
2. Use quick, snappy
keystroking.
3. Space quickly after
each word.

Fingers curved
and upright

Use quick, snappy
keystroking

Space quickly
after each word

letter 1 In my opinion, Dave agreed on estate taxes only after we defeated him.

word 2 She and the neighbor may go downtown to sign the form for the auditor.

combination 3 Helen started to work on the audit after they paid their estate taxes.

72c (continued)

Document 2
Two-Column Table
with Secondary Heading
plain full sheet; CS: 12; center
horizontally and vertically;
correct errors

NOISE LEVEL OF SELECTED SOUNDS		
(Measured in Decibels)		
Gun Muzzle Blast	140	
Auto Horn	115	
Chainsaw	100	
Truck Traffic	90	
Typewriter	60	
Whisper	30	

Document 3
Two-Column Table
with Columnar Headings
and Source Note
plain full sheet; CS: 12; center
horizontally and vertically;
correct errors

CELLULOID PRESIDENTS	
(Those Most Often Portrayed in Movies)	
Name	Times
Abraham Lincoln	134
Ulysses S. Grant	44
George Washington	34
Theodore Roosevelt	23
Franklin D. Roosevelt	23
Thomas Jefferson	18

Source: <u>Guinness Book of Movie Facts</u>
<u>and Figures</u>, 1988.

Document 4
Three-Column Table
with Columnar Headings
and Source Note
plain full sheet; CS: 8; center
horizontally and vertically;
correct errors

CHANGES IN WEEKLY BASE SALARIES		
(Based on 5% Increase in Cost of Living)		
Job Title	Current	New*
Clerical Assistant I	$210	$221
Clerical Assistant II	250	263
Secretary I	270	284
Secretary II	320	336
WP Specialist	295	310
Administrative Assistant	350	368

*Rounded to nearest dollar.

Improve Table Formatting Skills

Learning Goals

1. To review and improve table formatting skills.
2. To maintain and improve techniques and basic skills.
3. To improve language skills.

Format Guides

1. Paper guide at *0* (for typewriters).
2. LL: 70 spaces for drills, language skills, and timed writings.
3. LS: SS drills and language skills; DS ¶s; as directed for tables.
4. PI: 5 spaces.

Lesson 90   Two- and Three-Column Tables/Language Skills

90a ▶ 5
Conditioning Practice

each line twice SS (slowly, then faster); DS between 2-line groups; if time permits, rekey selected lines

alphabet	1	They are moving to a new development just back of the Vasquez complex.
figures	2	Between 1987 and 1992 there were 203,564 recorded births in our state.
fig/sym	3	The balance due on Account #2849 after the 10% down payment is $3,756.
speed	4	The proficient auditor was in dismay due to the problem with an audit.

| 1 | 2 | 3 | 4 | 5 | 6 | 7 | 8 | 9 | 10 | 11 | 12 | 13 | 14 |

90b ▶ 10
Recall Centering Skills

half sheet, long edge at top; correct any errors you make as you key

1. Review horizontal and vertical centering procedures on page RG 10.
2. DS copy; center problem vertically and each line horizontally.

DRUGS: FACTS OR FICTION

January 23, 19--

3:30 p.m.

High School Gymnasium

Sponsored by:

McNamara Drug Treatment Center

90c ▶ 20
Recall Table Formatting

2 half sheets; DS all lines; format the tables given at the right and on page 161, long edge at top; correct any errors you make as you key

Table 1
Two-Column Table with Main Heading
CS (column spacing): 14

COMMONLY MISSPELLED WORDS		words
		5
absence	arrangements	9
academic	audit	12
access	authorized	16
already	benefits	19
alternative	calendar	24
appreciate	commission	28

Learning Goals

1. To learn to transfer your keying, formatting, and language skills to a realistic office setting.
2. To learn to format mailing-list index cards and file-folder labels as processed in a business office.
3. To learn to process a series of related documents (errors corrected) in orderly fashion with minimum assistance.

Documents Processed

1. Mailing-List Index Cards
2. "Form" Letters with Variables
3. File-Folder Labels
4. Summary of Talk in Report Format
5. Simplified Memo with Table

KEYSTONE RECREATION CENTER (An Office Job Simulation)

Before you start to process the documents on pp. 129-131, read the *Work Assignment* and study the *Standard Formatting Guides* given at right. When planning documents, refer to the *Standard Formatting Guides* again to refresh your memory.

Work Assignment

You have been hired as a part-time office assistant at Keystone Recreation Center.

Keystone Recreation Center (KRC) is located at the edge of Woodward Park on the Arkansas River in West Tulsa, Oklahoma. KRC offers recreational and educational programs for children, teenagers, and adults of all ages.

The center is organized and operated by the following people:

Mr. Morgan W. Lindsay, Director
Mrs. Doris L. Moon, Associate Director
Ms. Elva Mae Simms, Assistant Director of Child Programs
Mr. Jason B. Appel, Assistant Director of Teenager Programs
Mrs. Joyce M. Dempsey, Assistant Director of Adult Programs

As an office assistant, you will work in the office of Mrs. Doris L. Moon. Your primary responsibility is to process letters, memos, reports, and other documents for various members of the staff. A few of the documents--index cards and file-folder labels, for example--must be completed on a typewriter rather than a word processor. In addition, you may be asked to answer the telephone, copy and file correspondence and other records, and enter data into a computer.

Your keyboarding teacher has verified that you know how to format standard documents in the basic styles used by Keystone Recreation Center: letters in block format, reports in unbound format, memos in simplified format, and announcements and tables centered on full and half sheets.

To assist you in formatting documents, Mrs. Moon gives you *Standard Formatting Guides*. When unfamiliar tasks are assigned, she will give special instructions.

Standard Formatting Guides

Letters

1. Process letters on KRC letterheads; use block format with open punctuation.
2. Use 1½″ SM.
3. Place date on line 16.
4. QS between the date and letter address and between complimentary close and keyed (printed) name of writer. DS between all other letter parts.

Memos

1. Process memos on plain paper; use simplified format.
2. Use 1″ SM.
3. Place date on line 10.
4. QS between date and name(s) of addressee(s) and between last line of message and keyed (printed) name of writer. DS between all other memo parts.

Announcements and Tables

1. Process announcements on half sheets; process tables on full sheets.
2. DS all lines of announcements and tables unless otherwise directed. Center both types of documents horizontally and vertically. An even number of spaces between columns is preferred.

Reports

1. Use unbound format for all reports:
   SM: 1″
   PB: line 10 in pica (10-pitch)
        line 12 in elite (12-pitch)
   Bottom Margin: at least 1″
2. QS between title and report body; DS between all other lines of reports, including side headings. SS enumerated items but DS between items and above and below the series.
3. Place page numbers on line 6 at the RM of all pages except the first, which is not numbered. DS and continue the report body on line 8.

89d ▶ 10
Improve Language Skills: Pronoun Agreement

LL: 70 spaces; SS with DS between line groups

1. Read the first rule.

2. Key the **Learn** sentences below it (with number and period), noting how the rule has been applied.

3. Key the **Apply** sentences (with number and period) using the correct pronoun shown in parentheses.

4. Practice the second rule in the same way.

5. If time permits, key the **Apply** lines again at a faster speed to quicken decision-making skill.

PRONOUN AGREEMENT (continued)

Pronouns agree with their antecedents in number (singular or plural).

Learn 1. Timothy bought his new car in Atlanta early last month. *(singular)*

Learn 2. The members made plans for their next convention. *(plural)*

Apply 3. The boys must finish (his, their) game before noon.

Apply 4. The dog had (its, their) chain caught on the fence.

When a pronoun's antecedent is a collective noun, the pronoun may be either singular or plural, depending on the meaning of the collective noun.

Learn 5. The Board of Directors has completed its meeting. *(acting as a unit)*

Learn 6. The Board of Directors have their own offices. *(acting individually)*

Apply 7. The Executive Committee presented (its, their) plan to the members.

Apply 8. The Executive Committee will give (its, their) reports on Friday.

89e ▶ 12
Improve/Check Keyboarding Skill

1. A 3' writing on ¶s; find *gwam*.

2. Add 3 *gwam* to the rate attained in Step 1.

3. Take a 1', 2', and 3' writing, trying to achieve the goal established in Step 2 for each writing.

all letters used	A	1.5 si	5.7 awl	80% hfw

gwam 3' | 5'

The requirements of today's secretary are changing. The ability to 5 | 3

use a computer or a word processor is a major skill now required for 9 | 5

office support personnel by a sizeable number of firms. This is a trend 14 | 8

expected to continue with an even greater emphasis on computer usage in 19 | 11

the future. This will make it more critical than ever for those pursuing 24 | 14

a position in this field to have an excellent keyboarding skill in order 29 | 17

to make the best use of the costly equipment. 32 | 19

A student deciding on a career in this field will also find that the 36 | 22

role assumed by many office support staff members is that of an assistant 41 | 25

to a person at the management level. More and more of the titles used in 46 | 28

offices of today reflect this trend. It is quite common now for a secre- 51 | 31

tarial position to have a title of an administrative assistant or an 56 | 33

executive assistant. A college degree for positions such as these, how- 60 | 36

ever, may be stipulated. 62 | 37

gwam 3' | 1 | 2 | 3 | 4 | 5
5' | 1 | 2 | 3

73a-75a ▶ 5
Machine Check

each line twice *daily* to see that equipment is working properly

alphabet 1 Jacques has asked to be given one week to reply to this tax quiz form.

figures 2 Raul must study Section 2, pages 75-190, and Section 4, pages 246-380.

fig/sym 3 The new rate on Glenn & Taylor's $2,856 note (due 4/13/97) is 10 1/2%.

speed 4 Jo may sign the usual form by proxy if they make an audit of the firm.

| 1 | 2 | 3 | 4 | 5 | 6 | 7 | 8 | 9 | 10 | 11 | 12 | 13 | 14 |

73b-75b ▶ 45 (daily)
Document Processing Work Assignments

Documents 1-2
Mailing-List Index Cards

LP p. 81

Mrs. Moon asks you to prepare mailing-list index cards for two new members, using the format guides and model index card shown at right.

Index Card Format Guides

1. On line 2, 3 spaces from left edge of card, key the name in index order (surname, first name, middle initial). Key a courtesy title (Miss, Ms., Mrs., Mr.) in parentheses after the middle initial.

2. DS; key the name (in address order) and address in USPS style.

3. DS; key the phone number.

4. DS; key the Group information.

```
Hummingbird, George C. (Mr.)                    ↓ line 2
DS
MR GEORGE C HUMMINGBIRD
4265 S PEORIA AVENUE
TULSA OK   74105-1844
DS
(918) 541-8255
DS
Group:   Senior Adult
↑
3 spaces
```

New Members

Mr. and Mrs. Jacob N. Ishimura
4510 S. Lewis Avenue
Tulsa, Oklahoma 74105-2845

(918) 541-2665

Group: Young Adult

Miss Ramona L. Ogilvie
1748 S. Harvard Avenue
Tulsa, Oklahoma 74112-3810

(918) 871-3628

Group: Upper Teenager

Documents 3-4
"Form" Letters

LP pp. 83-86

Mrs. Moon asks you to process "form" letters (copy at right) to the new members (Documents 1-2). By using the variables below, you will tailor each letter to fit its addressee(s). Use the **current date** and supply an appropriate **salutation** and **complimentary close**. Don't forget to add **reference initials** and an **enclosure notation**.

Document 3 Variables

V 1: **Ishimura address**
V 2: **young adult**
V 3: **young men and women**
V 4: **couples**
V 5: **Mrs. Joyce M. Dempsey**
　　Assistant Director

Document 4 Variables

V 1: **Ogilvie address**
V 2: **upper teenager**
V 3: **high school students**
V 4: **young people**
V 5: **Mr. Jason B. Appel**
　　Assistant Director

("Mr." on envelope only.)

(V 1)

Here is your Keystone Recreation Center (KRC) Membership Card. You should bring it along each time you visit the center. This card identifies you as a member in good standing and is your entree to all regular and special (V 2) activities.

You have joined a stimulating group of (V 3). I'm sure KRC membership will mean a lot to you, as it has to so many other (V 4). Do take full advantage of it during the coming year. Use the enclosed "Activity Schedule" to remind you of the wide variety of activities that awaits you at Keystone Recreation Center.

I hope to see you here often. Why not stop by my office the next time you come in; perhaps I can answer any questions you may have about the many programs we have planned for you.

(V 5)

Documents 5, 6, 7, and 8 are on pp. 130-131.

89a ▶ 5
Conditioning Practice

each line twice (slowly, then faster); as time permits, repeat selected lines

alphabet	1	Mozambique was the place Karen most enjoyed visiting in exotic Africa.
figures	2	South High School had 350 graduates in 1986 and 284 graduates in 1987.
fig/sym	3	Order #3845-6079 was damaged during shipment by J&B Express on May 21.
speed	4	The lame lapdog may wish to dognap on the burlap by the antique chair.

| 1 | 2 | 3 | 4 | 5 | 6 | 7 | 8 | 9 | 10 | 11 | 12 | 13 | 14 |

89b ▶ 8
Improve Techniques: Return/Tab Keys

LL: 50 spaces; set a tab 15 spaces to the right of center

1. Key the lines given at the right. Concentrate on correct techniques for return and tab keys.

2. Take two 30″ writings; work for speed.

3. Take three 1′ writings; try to increase amount keyed with each writing.

Emphasize quick return and start of new line.

gwam 1′

Yellowstone ——————— Tab ——————— Wyoming	4
Yosemite ——————— Tab ——————— California	8
Glacier ——————— Tab ——————— Montana	11
Rocky Mountain ——————— Tab ——————— Colorado	16
Grand Canyon ——————— Tab ——————— Arizona	20
Zion ——————— Tab ——————— Utah	22

89c ▶ 15
Improve Technique: Response Patterns

each line 3 times (slowly, faster, top speed); as time permits, repeat selected lines

Goal: To reduce time interval between keystrokes (read ahead to anticipate stroking pattern).

Finger reaches, quiet hands

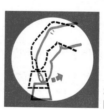
Snappy keystroking

Quick spacing

Emphasize curved, upright fingers; finger-action keystroking.

	1	my beg oil sat joy car him add ink egg inn far ill few mom set pup bed
one-hand words	2	best hymn acre join face milk draw pull edge upon wage only tact knoll
	3	onion weave union beads pupil defer holly erase imply serve jolly gate

Emphasize independent finger action; quiet hands.

	4	in my bag |at ease |be at my |bad debt |grade on my test |you better beware
one-hand phrases	5	a nylon vest |bad career start |pink kimono |average grades |minimum taxes
	6	bad start |a red taffeta dress |you deserve better |only awards |on a date

Emphasize continuity; finger-action with fingers close to keys.

	7	After a decrease in oil tax rates, we agreed on a greater oil reserve.
one-hand sentences	8	In my opinion, my award was based on my grade average on my art tests.
	9	Jim agreed on decreased cab fare rates after gas taxes were decreased.

| 1 | 2 | 3 | 4 | 5 | 6 | 7 | 8 | 9 | 10 | 11 | 12 | 13 | 14 |

Documents 5-6
File-Folder Labels

LP p. 81

Mrs. Moon asks you to prepare file-folder labels for the new members. She gives you format guides and a model to help you. Use the mailing-list index cards for information.

Label Format Guides

1. On line 1 below the rule, 3 spaces from the left edge, key the name (surname, first name, middle initial) and title in ALL CAPS, no punctuation.

2. Key the city, state, and ZIP Code on the next line; key the street address on the third line.

```
HUMMINGBIRD GEORGE C MR
Tulsa, OK  74105-1844
4265 S. Peoria Avenue
```

Document 7
Talk Summary
in Report Format

Mrs. Moon asks you to prepare for Mr. Lindsay the summary of a talk he gave at our recent seminar for adult members and their guests. Mrs. Moon suggests that you use standard unbound report format. Mr. Lindsay requested two photocopies of the final draft. Mrs. Moon asks you to watch for and correct any unmarked errors as well as the marked ones and those you make as you key.

FIVE BASIC STEPS TO PHYSICAL AND MENTAL FITNESS HEALTH

Human beings are both body and mind--flesh and spirit. Whatever our personnel definition of "soul" it is quiet clear that our minds and bodies are intricately interrelated. The health of the one effects the well-being of the other. Let us look then at some ways of "keeping body and sould together"--healthfully.

The basic steps to physical and mental fitness listed here are few and with a bit of self-discipline, not difficult to take.

1. Consume Eat the right kinds and amounts of food and drink.
2. Engage daily in appropriate forms of bodily exercise.
3. Relax the mind and body with plenty of rest, sleep.
4. Keep yourself clean, inside and out.
5. Engage in a wide variety of interests, activities.

Consume the right amounts of food and drink. Nearly all most of us eat too much of to few different kinds of food. We gorge ourselves with French fries, double-decker sandwiches, and pizza--washing them down with cola and other carbonated sugar waters. We eat more then we need and "justify" it by saying "waste not, want not." Is it better, however, for food to go to waist than to waste? Eat according to a plan, rather than according to habit: Try a new food each weak and learn to choose foods that are rich in protien, vitamins, and minerals, avoiding those that are high in fat, salt, and sugar.

Engage daily in appropriate forms of bodily exercise. Office workers are a sedentary lot. Teh only exercise many of us get during the day is the short walks we take to and from coffee breaks and lunch. Evven worse, our at home exercise often consists of little more than trips to the refrigerator and, for some, the TV and CD player controls. Most people say they can't afford a health club. The truth is, sedentary office workers can't afford not to. Unless you discipline your self to a daily exercise routine, such as those outlined in popular physical fitness books, you should discipline your pocket book to a health or recreation club membership to join.

(continued, p. 131)

88d ▶ 10
Improve Technique: Keystroking and Response Patterns
LL: 70 spaces

1. Lines 1-3: each word 3 times (slowly, faster, top speed); when bell rings, complete word, return, and continue.

2. Lines 4-6: each phrase 3 times (slowly, faster, top speed); when bell rings, complete word, return, and continue.

3. Lines 7-9: each sentence 3 times (slowly, faster, top speed).

Goal: High-speed keyboarding response (think and key each word or word group as a whole).

Emphasize fast finger reaches with hands quiet, wrists low and relaxed.

balanced-hand words

1 to end cow dog eye apt for cue ham ivy bug may men rug toe cut bus six
2 corn bush idle paid rush torn auto duty form work hair wish lamb world
3 giant field right rocks focus amend blend cycle ivory snake their girl

Emphasize high-speed phrase response.

balanced-hand phrases

4 paid for it | fix it | go to work | go with them | sign the title | their island
5 their own problems | if they go | when she paid | the right box | turn signals
6 haughty neighbor | small cubicle | bushel of corn | giant firm | to the end of

Emphasize high-speed, word-level response; quick spacing.

balanced-hand sentences

7 I paid the man by the dock for the six bushels of corn and the turkey.
8 Diana and Vivian kept the food for their fish by the antique fishbowl.
9 Did the haughty girls pay for their own gowns for the sorority social?

| 1 | 2 | 3 | 4 | 5 | 6 | 7 | 8 | 9 | 10 | 11 | 12 | 13 | 14 |

88e ▶ 15
Check/Improve Keyboarding Skill

1. A 1' writing on ¶ 1; find *gwam*.

2. Add 2-4 *gwam* to the rate attained in Step 1, and note quarter-minute checkpoints from table below.

3. Take two 1' guided writings on ¶ 1 to increase speed.

4. Practice ¶ 2 in the same way.

5. A 3' writing on ¶s 1 and 2 combined; find *gwam* and circle errors.

6. If time permits, take another 3' writing.

Quarter-Minute Checkpoints

gwam	¼'	½'	¾'	1'
32	8	16	24	32
36	9	18	27	36
40	10	20	30	40
44	11	22	33	44
48	12	24	36	48
52	13	26	39	52
56	14	28	42	56
60	15	30	45	60
64	16	32	48	64

all letters used | A | 1.5 si | 5.7 awl | 80% hfw

gwam 3' | 5'

Many options are available for people to ponder as they invest their — 5 | 3
money. Real estate, savings accounts, money market accounts, bonds, and — 9 | 6
stocks are but a few of the options that are open to those who wish to — 14 | 9
invest their extra money. Several factors will determine which type of — 19 | 11
investment a person will choose. These factors pertain to the expected — 24 | 14
rate of return, the degree of liquidity desired, and the amount of risk a — 29 | 17
person is willing to take. — 30 | 18

An investor who seeks a high rate of return and who is willing to — 35 | 21
take a high degree of risk often considers the stock market. Stock mar- — 40 | 24
kets or stock exchanges are organizations that bring investors together — 44 | 27
to buy and sell shares of stock. Stock represents a share in the owner- — 49 | 30
ship of a company. Since more risk is associated with an investment that — 54 | 33
has a high rate of return, judgment must be exercised by those thinking — 59 | 35
about the purchase of stock. — 61 | 37

gwam 3' | 1 | 2 | 3 | 4 | 5 |
5' | 1 | 2 | 3 |

Relax the mind and body with plenty of ~~rest~~. *sleep* How much *one* sleep does the average working person require? Some~~/~~ has facetiously an~~w~~serd, "Five minutes more." All people don't require the same amount of sleep, but seven to eight hours is a good rule of thumb. It is desirable, too, that they be the __same__ hours every night. And if you are one of those people who needs "five minutes more," get them by going too bed earlier instaed of getting up latter!

__Keep you~~r~~self clean--inside and out__. Cleanliness may not be next to godliness, but its close. Water, soap, shampoo, antiperspirant, dentifrice, and other toiletries are to inexpensive not to be used by every one as insurance against being personally offensive. And don't put off frequent trips to the laundry, dry cleaner, and shoe repair shop. Clothes do not make the person; but clean, well-maintained clothes reflect her or his self concern.

__Engage in a wide variety of~~interests~~__. *activities* With todays increasing leisure time, we are no longer concerned with the "all work and no play" adage. But we __are__ concerned with the __kinds__ of leisure activity in which people engage in. Too many of us have become spectators rather than participants. We over use one or two kinds of recreation: TV __or__ movies __or__ reading __or__ musical tapes/disks. Diversify your recreational activities. Develop some interests that reqiure you to take action __for__ others as well __with__ others.

These five steps, easily taken *as* will go far in helping you improve your physical and mental fitness. *a*

Document 8
Simplified Memo
with Table

Mrs. Moon asks you to process for her signature the attached memorandum. She gives you these notes:

Date: **Current**
Addressee: **All KRC Assistant Directors**
Subject: **EVENT SCHEDULE FOR MARCH**

Mrs. Moon points out that a table in an SS document should be SS. She tells you to be alert to possible unmarked errors in the rough-draft copy and asks that you make 5 photocopies.

The following *special* events are scheduled to take place during the month of March.

Senior Adult Ping Pong Tournament	March 4
Young Adult Marathon	March 8
Lower Teen Basketball Play-off Game	March 10
Upper Teen Basketball Play-off Game	March 16
Children's Arts/Crafts ~~Show~~ *Exhibit*	March 17
Young Women's Softball Opening Game	March 20
Young Men's Baseball Opening Game	March 25
Young Adult Racquet ball Tournament	March 27

Please prepare bulletin board announcements and plan a publicity campaign to promote the event(s) for which you are responsible. Keep in mind that we want to attract as many members and freinds to these events as ~~possible~~ *we can.*

Let's plan to meet next Thursday at 2 ~~a~~*p*.m. to discuss your promotion plans.

Improve Keyboarding and Language Skills

Learning Goals

1. To refine keyboarding technique and response patterns.

2. To increase speed and improve accuracy on straight copy.

3. To review/improve language skills.

Format Guides

1. Paper guide at *0* (for typewriters).

2. LL: 70 spaces for drills, language skills, and timed writings.

3. LS: SS drills and language skills; DS ¶s.

4. PI: 5 spaces.

Lesson 88 | *Keyboarding Technique/Language Skills*

88a ▶ 5
Conditioning Practice

each line twice SS (slowly, then faster); as time permits, rekey selected lines

alphabet 1 Jacob was quite puzzled when Mr. Grifey told us to take the exam over.

figures 2 There are 1,503 engineering majors; 879 are males and 624 are females.

fig/sym 3 My 1992 property tax increased by 6.75% ($241); I paid $3,580 in 1991.

speed 4 Helen owns the six foals and the lame cow in the neighbor's hay field.

| 1 | 2 | 3 | 4 | 5 | 6 | 7 | 8 | 9 | 10 | 11 | 12 | 13 | 14 |

88b ▶ 10
Improve Technique: Numbers

Beginning at the left margin, set 3 tab stops according to the key beneath the lines. Key the lines twice (slowly, then faster), tabbing from column to column.

04/15/49	(715) 809-4657	$1489.88	4:06 a.m.
11/23/63	(803) 629-9879	$ 38.27	10:25 p.m.
01/25/67	(343) 821-4546	$ 638.79	10:57 a.m.
12/17/64	(609) 459-6093	$ 6.86	7:45 p.m.
02/28/54	(302) 905-1756	$2788.25	12:29 a.m.
05/21/34	(786) 965-7489	$ 302.97	12:37 p.m.

KEY | 8 | 10 | 14 | 10 | 8 | 10 | 10 |

88c ▶ 10
Improve Language Skills: Pronoun Agreement

LL: 70 spaces; SS with DS between line groups

1. Read the first rule.

2. Key the **Learn** sentences below it (with number and period), noting how the rule has been applied.

3. Key the **Apply** sentences (with number and period) using the correct pronoun shown in parentheses.

4. Practice the second rule in the same way.

5. If time permits, key the **Apply** lines again at a faster speed to quicken decision-making skill.

PRONOUN AGREEMENT

Pronouns (I, we, you, he, she, it, their, etc.) agree with their antecedents in person (i.e., person speaking — first person; person spoken to — second person; person spoken about — third person).

Learn 1. Kay said, "I will see the play when I finish my project." *(1st person)*

Learn 2. When you are finished with your homework, turn it in. *(2d person)*

Learn 3. Janet said that she would host the party at her home. *(3d person)*

Apply 4. The executives who saw the plans said (he/she, they) were pleased.

Apply 5. After you get in shape, (one's, your) level of energy increases.

Apply 6. "(I/She) want to revise the schedule before I leave the office."

Pronouns agree with their antecedents in gender (masculine, feminine, and neuter).

Learn 7. Rebecca will recite her part after the introductions. *(feminine)*

Learn 8. The tree lost its leaves before the end of October. *(neuter)*

Apply 9. Each female will be given a rose as she receives (her, its) diploma.

Apply 10. The ball bounced strangely before (he, it) whizzed past the outfielder.

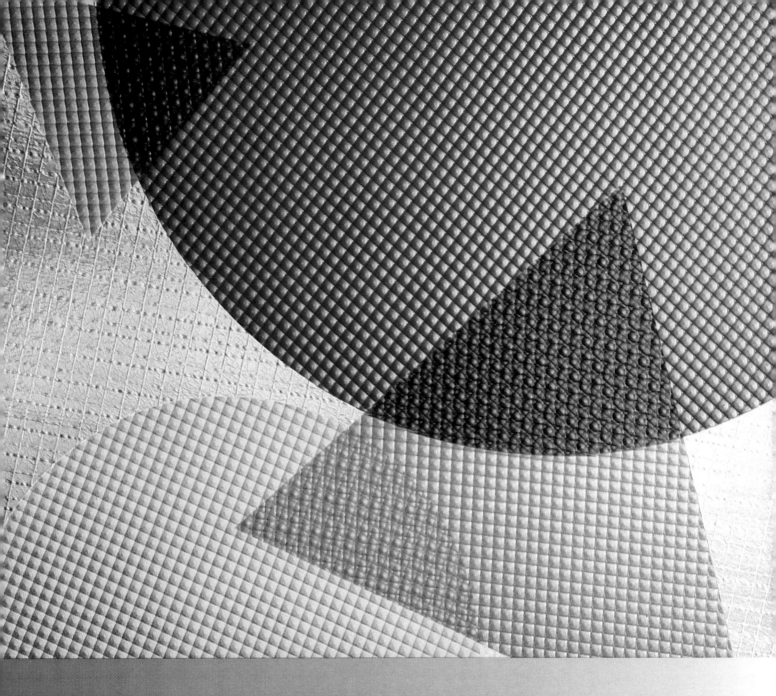

APPENDICES

87c ▶ 35
*Format and Key
an Unbound Report*
Document 1
**Unbound Report with Long
Quotation and Numbered List**

Format and key the copy as an
unbound report. Correct all errors
you make as you key.

words

TAXES

Americans are taxed in order to raise revenues to finance governmental activities. Taxation has never been popular. Much time and energy have been devoted by the legislature trying to devise a system that requires everyone to pay his/her fair share. Taxes are generally based on the benefits received and/or on the ability to pay. Two of the most common revenue raising taxes are the personal income tax and the sales tax.

Personal Income Tax

The personal income tax is the tax individuals are required to pay on their earnings. Employers deduct this tax from employees' paychecks. When employees file their income tax returns, they will either receive a refund for any excess which has been paid or they will have to pay the balance due.

Personal income taxes have been the Federal Government's largest single source of revenue and a major source of state revenues as well. On the federal level, the personal income tax is a graduated tax, which means the more you make, the higher the percentage of your income you pay in taxes (Rachman and Mescon, 1987, 529).

With the Tax Reform Act of 1986, the highest tax an individual will pay is 33 percent. The amount an individual pays changes with each tax reform. In the past, the top tax rate has been as high as 70 percent (Anrig, 1988, 56).

Sales Taxes

The sales tax is another tax with which most people are familiar. It is a tax that is added to the retail price of goods and services. Two examples of this type of tax are as follows:

1. General Sales Tax. The general sales tax is a tax levied by most states on goods and services. The amount of tax and the specific goods and services that are taxed varies by state.

2. Excise Tax (Selective Sales Tax). The excise tax is a state tax levied against specific items. Examples of items with an excise tax include tobacco, alcoholic beverages, and gasoline.

While the income tax is a tax based on the individual's ability to pay, the general sales tax and the excise tax are based on benefits received. For example, taxes collected on gasoline are used for highways. Individuals purchasing gasoline are those who benefit from the construction and maintenance of highways.

words
1
15
30
44
59
74
87
95
109
123
137
152
154
169
183
198
213
220
235
249
266
270
285
301
308
323
337
345
360
375
383
398
413
428
443
446

Document 2
Reference List

Format and key the reference list on a separate sheet. Correct any errors you make as you key.

Document 3
Title Page

If time permits, prepare a title page using your name, school, and current date.

REFERENCES

Anrig, Greg, Jr. "Making the Most of 1988's Low Tax Rate." Money, February 1988, 56-57.

Rachman, David J., and Michael H. Mescon. Business Today. New York: Random House, 1987.

2
18
21
38
42

APPENDIX A
Numeric Keypad Operation

Learning Goals

1. To learn key locations and keyboarding technique on the numeric keypad of a microcomputer.

2. To learn to enter figures rapidly and accurately by touch (without looking).

Practice Procedure

Follow directions given on an instructional diskette for learning key locations and for initial practice. Then return to this book for additional drill and practice.

Use of these activities on word processing software is not recommended.

Activity 1   4/5/6/0

1a ▶ Get Acquainted with Your Data-Entry Equipment

Figure keys 1-9 are in standard locations on numeric keypads of microcomputers (as well as on 10-key calculators).

The zero (0 or Ø) key location may vary slightly from one keyboard to another.

The illustrations at the right show the location of the figure keys on popular makes of microcomputers.

Consult your operator's manual to learn how to correct an error you detect as you enter figures.

Apple IIe numeric keypad

IBM PC

Tandy 1000

1b ▶ Take Correct Operating Position

1. Position yourself in front of the computer just as you do for entering alphabetic copy--body erect, both feet on floor for balance.

2. Place this textbook at the right of the keyboard.

3. Curve the fingers of the right hand and place them on the numeric keypad:

first (index) finger on 4
second finger on 5
third finger on 6
thumb on 0

86c ▶ 13
Improve Language Skills: Verbs

LL: 70 spaces; SS with DS between line groups.

1. Read the first rule.

2. Key the **Learn** sentences below it (with number and period), noting how the rule has been applied.

3. Key the **Apply** sentences (with number and period) using the correct word shown in parentheses.

4. Practice the other rules in the same way.

5. If time permits, key the **Apply** lines again at a faster speed to quicken decision-making skill.

> If there is confusion whether a subject is singular or plural, consult a dictionary.

Learn   1. The data presented in your report are confusing.
Learn   2. Several alumni are invited to this year's commencement activities.
Learn   3. The analyses completed by Mrs. Carter are excellent.
Apply   4. The same criteria (has, have) been used in the past.
Apply   5. The analysis (is, are) very extensive.

> When used as the subject, the pronouns *I, we, you,* and *they,* as well as plural nouns, require the plural verb *do not* or the contraction *don't.*

Learn   6. They do not want to become involved with the project.
Learn   7. The plans don't include a private office for the manager.
Apply   8. I (don't, doesn't) agree with the report you submitted.
Apply   9. The reviews (don't, doesn't) look very promising.

> When used as the subject, the pronouns *he, she, it,* as well as singular nouns, require the singular verb *does not* or the contraction *doesn't.*

Learn   10. She doesn't want the office layout changed.
Learn   11. The price does not include the software.
Apply   12. It (don't, doesn't) concern me; you take care of it.
Apply   13. The job (don't, doesn't) require shorthand.

Lesson 87 | Report with Long Quotation and Numbered List/Language Skills

87a ▶ 5
Conditioning Practice

each line twice SS (slowly, then faster); DS between 2-line groups; as time permits, rekey selected lines

alphabet   1   Everyone except Zelda Jenkins will be required to go to the math fair.
figures   2   Jo's Nursery sold 370 trees and 458 shrubs between May 29 and June 16.
fig/sym   3   The checks written on 8/4 ($81.52) and 9/3 ($68.70) were not recorded.
speed   4   The box with the emblem of the bugle is on the mantle by the fishbowl.

| 1 | 2 | 3 | 4 | 5 | 6 | 7 | 8 | 9 | 10 | 11 | 12 | 13 | 14 |

87b ▶ 10
Improve Language Skills: Word Choice

Study the definition and spelling of each word. Note how it is used in the **Learn** sentence. Key the **Learn** sentence and the **Apply** sentences (with number and period) selecting the proper word in parentheses to complete the sentence correctly.

die (vb) to pass from physical life

dye (n) a soluble or insoluble coloring matter

peace (n) a state of tranquility or quiet

piece (n) a part of a whole

Learn   1.   He will die when he sees the color of the dye they plan to use.
Apply   2.   The (die, dye) they ordered will arrive in time to meet their needs.
Apply   3.   Before I (die, dye) I want to see Austria, Germany, and Switzerland.

Learn   4.   If you want peace, Brad, you better save him a piece of your cake.
Apply   5.   She was about to give him a (peace, piece) of her mind when he hung up.
Apply   6.   He was at (peace, piece) with himself after passing his written exams.

1c ▶ Enter Data Using Home Keys: 4, 5, 6, 0

1. Turn equipment "on".

2. Curve the fingers of your right hand and place them upright on home keys:
   first (index) finger on 4
   second finger on 5
   third finger on 6
   fourth finger on + bar
   thumb on 0 or Ø (zero)

3. Using the special ENTER key to the right of the keypad, enter data in Drill 1a as follows:
   4 ENTER
   4 ENTER
   4 ENTER
   Strike ENTER

Note: Ignore any decimal (.) or comma (,) that may appear in an entry or total figure.

4. Check TOTAL figure on display screen. It should show 12 on the computer display.

5. If you do not get 12 as the total, reenter the data.

6. Enter and check columns b, c, d, e, and f in the same way.

7. Using the special ENTER key to the right of the keypad, enter data in Drill 2a as follows:
   44 ENTER
   44 ENTER
   44 ENTER
   Strike ENTER

8. Check TOTAL figure and reenter data if necessary.

9. Continue Drill 2 and complete Drills 3-5 in a similar manner.

Note: In Drills 4 and 5, strike 0 (zero) with the *side* of your right thumb.

Technique cue

Strike each key with a quick, sharp stroke with the *tip* of the finger; release the key quickly. Keep the fingers curved and upright, the wrist low, relaxed, and steady.

Drill 1

a	b	c	d	e	f
4	5	6	4	5	6
4	5	6	4	5	6
4	5	6	4	5	6
12	15	18	12	15	18

Drill 2

a	b	c	d	e	f
44	55	66	44	55	66
44	55	66	44	55	66
44	55	66	44	55	66
132	165	198	132	165	198

Drill 3

a	b	c	d	e	f
44	45	54	44	55	66
55	56	46	45	54	65
66	64	65	46	56	64
165	165	165	135	165	195

Drill 4

a	b	c	d	e	f
40	50	60	400	500	600
40	50	60	400	500	600
40	50	60	400	500	600
120	150	180	1,200	1,500	1,800

Drill 5

a	b	c	d	e	f
40	400	404	406	450	650
50	500	505	506	540	560
60	600	606	606	405	605
150	1,500	1,515	1,518	1,395	1,815

86a ▶ 5
Conditioning Practice

each line twice SS (slowly, then faster); DS between 2-line groups; if time permits, rekey selected lines

alphabet 1 Kevin justified his low quiz score by explaining his unusual problems.

figures 2 She accumulated 2,453 miles in June, 989 in July, and 1,706 in August.

shift keys 3 Ms. Nancy Slater and Mr. Robert Siverson will arrive on Monday, May 1.

speed 4 Diana and the visitor can handle the problems of the eighth amendment.

| 1 | 2 | 3 | 4 | 5 | 6 | 7 | 8 | 9 | 10 | 11 | 12 | 13 | 14 |

86b ▶ 32 Format and Key an Unbound Report with Internal Citations and References

1. Format the copy as an unbound report; correct any errors you make as you key.

2. Prepare a reference page on a separate sheet; correct all errors.

words

STUDENT ORGANIZATIONS   4

Student organizations play a vital role in the 14
educational process of students. Students who 23
participate in such organizations are given op- 32
portunities to test the concepts they were taught 42
in the formal classroom environment. Two such 52
organizations that are widely recognized in the 61
business education field are Future Business 70
Leaders of America and Business Professionals 80
of America (formerly called Office Education 89
Association). 92

Future Business Leaders 101

Future Business Leaders of America is a vo- 109
cational association that helps students bridge 119
the gap between the classroom and the business 128
world. Two of the major goals outlined in the 138
Future Business Leaders of America Handbook 147
(1985, 5) are as follows: 152

1. Develop competent, aggressive business 161
leadership. 163
2. Create more interest in and understand- 172
ing of American business enterprise. 179

Business leadership. Students have the oppor- 192
tunity to develop leadership skills by serving 201
as officers, attending conferences, working with 211
businessmen and businesswomen in the com- 219
munity, and participating in competitive events 229
sponsored by the organization. The organiza- 238
tion's strong emphasis on community service 246
provides another avenue for the development 255
of leadership skills. 260

Business enterprise. A greater understanding 273
of business enterprise is gained by students as 282
they participate in chapter projects dealing with 292
this important subject. These projects give stu- 302
dents experiences in learning more about the 311
operation of business enterprise in America. 320

Business Professionals of America 334

Business Professionals of America is another 343
vocational business and office education pro- 351
gram for students interested in developing per- 361
sonal, leadership, and office skills. According 370
to Goodman (1987, 11), the executive director 380
of the organization for 1987-88, the goal of the 389
organization has been to promote leadership 398
and professionalism among students in order 407
to prepare them for satisfying and successful 416
careers in the business world. 423

The two goals, developing business leadership 432
and understanding business enterprise, empha- 441
sized by FBLA are also emphasized by Business 450
Professionals of America. They, too, have pro- 459
grams designed to provide students with the op- 468
portunity to develop their leadership skills and 478
to foster a greater understanding of the role of 488
the entrepreneur in the free enterprise system. 498

REFERENCES   500

Future Business Leaders of America Handbook. 518
Reston, Virginia: FBLA-PBL, Incorporated, 526
1985. 528

Goodman, Dorothy M. "A New Image for Our 536
Organization," 1987-88 Chapter Handbook, 549
Columbus, Ohio: Office Education Associa- 557
tion, 1987. 559

2a ▶ Improve Home-Key Technique

Enter and check the columns of data listed at the right as directed in Steps 1-9 on p. A-3.

a	b	c	d	e	f
4	44	400	404	440	450
5	55	500	505	550	560
6	66	600	606	660	456
15	165	1,500	1,515	1,650	1,466

2b ▶ Learn New Keys: 7, 8, 9

Learn reach to 7

1. Locate 7 (above 4) on the numeric keypad.

2. Watch your index finger move up to 7 and back to 4 a few times *without striking keys*.

3. Practice striking 74 a few times as you watch the finger.

4. With eyes on copy, enter the data in Drills 1a and 1b; check the total figures; reenter data if necessary.

Learn reach to 8

1. Learn the second-finger reach to 8 (above 5) as directed in Steps 1-3 above.

2. With eyes on copy, enter the data in Drills 1c and 1d; check the total figures; reenter data if necessary.

Learn reach to 9

1. Learn the third-finger reach to 9 (above 6) as directed above.

2. With eyes on copy, enter the data in Drills 1e and 1f; check the total figures; reenter data if necessary.

Drills 2-4

Practice entering the columns of data in Drills 2-4 until you can do so accurately and quickly.

Drill 1

a	b	c	d	e	f
474	747	585	858	696	969
747	777	858	888	969	999
777	474	888	585	999	696
1,998	1,998	2,331	2,331	2,664	2,664

Drill 2

a	b	c	d	e	f
774	885	996	745	475	754
474	585	696	854	584	846
747	858	969	965	695	956
1,995	2,328	2,661	2,564	1,754	2,556

Drill 3

a	b	c	d	e	f
470	580	690	770	707	407
740	850	960	880	808	508
704	805	906	990	909	609
1,914	2,235	2,556	2,640	2,424	1,524

Drill 4

a	b	c	d	e	f
456	407	508	609	804	905
789	408	509	704	805	906
654	409	607	705	806	907
987	507	608	706	904	908
2,886	1,731	2,232	2,724	3,319	3,626

2c ▶ Learn to Enter Data with Unequal Numbers of Digits

Enter single, double, and triple digits in columns as shown, left to right. The computer will align the digits automatically.

a	b	c	d	e	f
4	90	79	4	740	860
56	87	64	56	64	70
78	68	97	78	960	900
90	54	64	60	89	67
4	6	5	98	8	80
232	305	309	296	1,861	1,977

85b (continued)

<u>Ways to Improve Listening</u> _DS_   305

    Barriers to listening can be overcome ; However, it   316

does take a conscientious effort on the part of the   326

listener. A ~~good~~ _stet_ listener will try to maintain eye contact   338

with the speaker and work to avoid tuning the speaker out. Removing as many   353

external distractins as possible is another means for   364

improving listening.   369

    Listening is also improved by directing attention to   379

the message rather than ~~on~~ _to_ the speaker. _appearance and mannerisms_ Focusing on the   396

main points being made by the speaker and taking notes, if   408

(Rader and Kurth, 1988, 417-419) appropriate, are ways of directing attention to the message.   427

Document 2
Reference Page
Review, if necessary, the arrangement of references in the model on page 148; then prepare a reference page.

Document 3
Title Page
Using your name, school, and the current date, prepare a title page for your report. Refer to page 96 for illustration.

Nixon, Judy C., and Judy _F._ West. "Listning--The New Com-   14

_SS_ petency. The Balance Sheet, January/February 1989 _;27-29_   29

Rader, M.H., and Linda A. Kurth. Business   40

Communication for the Computer Age. South-   55

Western Publishing Company, Cincinnati, 1988.   63

85c ▶ 10
Improve Language Skills: Verbs

LL: 70 spaces; SS with DS between line groups

1. Read the first rule.

2. Key the **Learn** sentences below it (with number and period), noting how the rule has been applied.

3. Key the **Apply** sentences (with number and period), using the correct word shown in parentheses.

4. Practice the next rule in the same way.

5. If time permits, key the **Apply** lines again at a faster speed to quicken decision-making skill.

PLURAL VERBS

> Use a plural verb with a plural subject (noun or pronoun).

Learn   1. The three pictures have been framed.
Learn   2. They are going to ask you to present the award.
Apply   3. The napkins (is, are) on the counter.
Apply   4. New desks (has, have) been ordered.

> Use plural verbs with compound subjects joined by *and*.

Learn   5. Tom and Sue are in charge of the program.
Learn   6. Mr. Miller and his wife have already registered to vote on Monday.
Apply   7. My dog and your cat (has, have) been digging in Mrs. Chi's garden.
Apply   8. The treasurer and the secretary (is, are) planning to attend.

3a ▶ Reinforce Reach-Strokes Learned

Enter and check the columns of data listed at the right as directed in Steps 1-9 on p. A-3.

a	b	c	d	e	f	g
44	74	740	996	704	990	477
55	85	850	885	805	880	588
66	96	960	774	906	770	699
165	255	2,550	2,655	2,415	2,640	1,764

3b ▶ Learn New Keys: 1, 2, 3

Learn reach to 1

1. Locate 1 (below 4) on the numeric keypad.

2. Watch your first finger move down to 1 and back to 4 a few times *without striking keys*.

3. Practice striking 14 a few times as you watch the finger.

4. With eyes on copy, enter the data in Drills 1a and 1b; check the total figures; reenter data if necessary.

Learn reach to 2

1. Learn the second-finger reach to 2 (below 5) as directed in Steps 1-3 above.

2. With eyes on copy, enter the data on Drills 1c and 1d; check the total figures; reenter data if necessary.

Learn reach to 3

1. Learn the third-finger reach to 3 (below 6) as directed above.

2. With eyes on copy, enter the data in Drills 1e, 1f, and 1g; check the total figures; reenter data if necessary.

Drills 2-4

Practice entering the columns of data in Drills 2-4 until you can do so accurately and quickly.

Drill 1

a	b	c	d	e	f	g
414	141	525	252	636	363	174
141	111	252	222	363	333	285
111	414	222	525	333	636	396
666	666	999	999	1,332	1,332	855

Drill 2

a	b	c	d	e	f	g
114	225	336	175	415	184	174
411	522	633	284	524	276	258
141	252	363	395	635	359	369
666	999	1,332	854	1,574	819	801

Drill 3

a	b	c	d	e	f	g
417	528	639	110	171	471	714
147	280	369	220	282	582	850
174	285	396	330	393	693	936
738	1,093	1,404	660	846	1,746	2,500

Drill 4

a	b	c	d	e	f	g
77	71	401	107	417	147	174
88	82	502	208	528	258	825
99	93	603	309	639	369	396
264	246	1,506	624	1,584	774	1,395

3c ▶ Enter Data Containing Commas

Enter the data in Columns a-g; check totals; reenter data as necessary.

Note: Even though number data often include commas to separate hundreds from thousands, do not enter them.

a	b	c	d	e	f	g
14	25	36	17	28	39	174
174	285	396	197	228	339	285
1,014	2,025	3,036	9,074	1,785	9,096	1,736
1,740	2,850	3,960	4,714	8,259	6,976	3,982
7,414	8,250	9,636	1,417	2,528	3,639	2,803
753	951	321	283	173	357	196
1,474	2,585	3,696	4,974	5,285	6,398	1,974
2,785	3,896	4,914	8,795	6,836	7,100	8,200
15,368	20,867	25,995	29,471	25,122	33,944	19,350

85b ▶ 35
Format and Key
Unbound Reports

Document 1
Unbound Report
with a Table

Format and key the copy shown at the right as an unbound report. Correct the errors marked in the copy and any you make as you key.

Learning cue: To place a table within the body of a report, follow these guidelines:

1. DS above and below the table; SS the body of the table.

2. Clear all tab stops.

3. Determine and set the tab stop for each column of the table. (The table must be centered within the margins of the report.)

4. After completing the table, reset the tab stop for paragraph indention before keying the remainder of the report.

LISTENING   2

One of the most ~~important~~ *critical* skills that an individual   12

~~possesses~~ *acquires* is the skill of communicating. Studdies indicate   24

that a person spends 70-80 percent of ~~their~~ *his/her* time communicat-   36

ing. A break down for the average individual of ~~the~~ time   *Nixon and West (1989, 28) give the following*   55

spent communicating: ~~includes (Bell, 1987, 8)~~:   60

	Writing	9%	62
SS	Reading	16%	64
	Speaking	30%	67
	listening	45%	70

Since ~~most~~ *almost half* of the time spent communicating is spent listen-   83

ing, it is important to overcome any barriers that obstruct   95

our ability to listen and to learn new ways to improve our   107

listening ability.   111

Barriers to Listening   119

Anything that interferes with our ability to listen ~~can~~ *is*   130

~~be~~ classified as a barrier to listening. Barriers that   141

obstruct our ability to listen can be divided into two basic   153

categories-external and internal barriers.   162

lc
Internal Barriers. Internal barriers are those *barriers* that   178

deal with the mental or psychological aspects of listening.   190

The perception of the importance of the message, the emo-   202

tional state, and the tuning in and out of the speaker by   213

the listener are *a few* examples of internal barriers.   224

lc
External Barriers. External barriers are barriers other   239

than those that deal *with* the mental and psychological make up of   252

the listener that tend to keep the listener from devoting *full* at-   265

tention to what is being said. Telephone interruptions,   277

uninvited visitors, noise, and the physical environment are examples   290

of external barriers.   295

(continued, p. 152)

4a ▶ Review Key Locations

Enter and check the columns of data listed at the right as directed in Steps 1-9 on p. A-3.

a	b	c	d	e	f	g
44	55	66	714	414	525	636
14	25	36	825	474	585	696
74	85	96	936	400	500	600
132	165	198	2,475	1,288	1,610	1,932

4b ▶ Improve Keyboarding Facility

Enter the data listed in each column of Drills 1-3; check each total; reenter the data in each column for which you did not get the correct total.

Drill 1

a	b	c	d	e	f	g
14	19	173	1,236	1,714	4,174	4,074
25	37	291	4,596	2,825	5,285	5,085
36	18	382	7,896	3,936	6,396	6,096
74	29	794	5,474	7,414	1,400	9,336
85	38	326	2,975	8,525	2,500	8,225
96	27	184	8,535	9,636	3,600	7,114
330	168	2,150	30,712	34,050	23,355	39,930

Drill 2

a	b	c	d	e	f	g
1	3	40	123	114	1,004	8,274
14	36	50	789	225	2,005	9,386
174	396	70	321	336	3,006	7,494
2	906	740	456	774	7,004	1,484
25	306	360	174	885	8,005	2,595
285	20	850	285	996	9,006	3,686
805	50	960	396	500	5,005	6,006
1,306	1,717	3,070	2,544	3,830	35,035	38,925

Drill 3

a	b	c	d	e	f	g
126	104	107	707	4,400	3,006	1,714
786	205	208	808	5,000	2,005	2,825
324	306	309	909	6,600	1,004	3,936
984	704	407	1,700	7,000	9,006	7,144
876	805	508	2,800	8,800	8,005	8,255
216	906	609	3,900	9,000	7,004	9,366
3,312	3,030	2,148	10,824	40,800	30,030	33,240

4c ▶ Enter Data with Decimals

Enter the data in Columns a-f, placing the decimals as shown in the copy.

a	b	c	d	e	f
1.40	17.10	47.17	174.11	1,477.01	10,704.50
2.50	28.20	58.28	285.22	2,588.02	17,815.70
3.60	39.30	69.39	396.33	3,996.03	20,808.75
4.70	74.70	17.10	417.14	4,174.07	26,909.65
5.80	85.80	28.20	528.25	5,285.08	30,906.25
6.90	96.90	39.30	639.36	6,396.06	34,259.90
24.90	342.00	259.44	2,440.41	23,916.27	141,404.75

words

2. Commercial electronic mail. (E-mail which is supplied   301
by organizations such as General Electric Information Ser-   318
vices and MCI Communication.)   324

Summary   327

Desktop publishing and electronic mail are but 2 of the   339

changes which are shaping the future of information process-   351

ing. Each year new technology enhances the ability of office per-   364

sonnel to produce quality information in less time.   374

Document 2
Reference List

Center the word REFER-
ENCES on line 10 (pica) or
line 12 (elite); key the list.

Winsor, William M. "Electronic Publishing: The Next Great   14
    Office Revolution." *The Secretary*, June/July 1987, 29-30   28

Reiss, Levi, and Edwin G. Dolan. *Using Computers: Managing*   46
    Change. Cincinnati: South-Western Publishing Company,   57
    1989.   59

84c ▶ 10
*Improve Language
Skills: Verbs*

LL: 70 spaces; SS with
DS between line groups

1. Read the first rule.

2. Key the **Learn** sentences below it (with number and period), noting how
the rule has been applied.

3. Key the **Apply**
sentences (with number
and period), using the
correct word shown in
parentheses.

4. Practice the next rule
in the same way.

5. If time permits, key
the **Apply** lines again at a
faster speed to quicken
decision-making skill.

SINGULAR VERBS (continued)

> Use singular verbs with the pronouns *all* and *some* (and with frac-
> tions and percentages) when used as subjects if their modifiers
> are singular. Use plural verbs if their modifiers are plural.

Learn 1. Some of the research is finished.
Learn 2. All of the girls were planning to attend the banquet.
Apply 3. All of the wood (is, are) stacked behind the garage.
Apply 4. Some of the clothes (was, were) purchased in Paris.

> Use a singular verb when *number* is used as the subject and is pre-
> ceded by *the,* however, use a plural verb if *number* is preceded by *a.*

Learn 5. The number of students who are passing the CPA exam has not decreased.
Learn 6. A number of women have volunteered to assist with the project.
Apply 7. A number of clients (has, have) complained about our service.
Apply 8. The number of students representing our district (is, are) excellent.

Lesson 85   *Report with a Table*

85a ▶ 5
*Conditioning
Practice*

each line twice SS
(slowly, then faster);
DS between 2-line
groups; if time permits,
rekey selected lines

alphabet 1 For the next two weeks you could save the big quilts for major prizes.
figures 2 Kane received 1,845 votes; Kennedy, 973 votes; and Mertins, 602 votes.
fig/sym 3 Their bill came to $68.19 ($47.63 for paper and $20.56 for envelopes).
speed 4 Their neighbor on the cozy island is the chair of the sorority social.

| 1 | 2 | 3 | 4 | 5 | 6 | 7 | 8 | 9 | 10 | 11 | 12 | 13 | 14 |

5a ▶ Review Key Locations

Enter and check the columns of data listed at the right.

a	b	c	d	e	f	g
477	588	707	107	41.6	141.4	936.6
417	528	808	205	52.9	252.5	825.6
717	825	909	309	63.3	393.3	719.4
1,611	1,941	2,424	621	157.8	787.2	2,481.6

5b ▶ Improve Keyboarding Facility

Enter the data listed in each column of Drills 1-4; check each total by entering the data a second time (from bottom to top).

If you get the same total twice, you can "assume" it is correct. If you get a different total the second time, reenter the data until you get two totals that match.

Drill 1

a	b	c	d	e	f	g
5	77	114	5,808	1,936	9,300	6,936
46	89	225	3,997	2,825	8,250	3,896
3	78	336	9,408	3,796	10,475	7,140
17	85	725	5,650	8,625	7,125	4,874
28	98	825	3,714	9,436	12,740	2,515
9	69	936	2,825	8,514	12,850	8,360
10	97	704	6,796	4,174	9,674	1,794

Drill 2

a	b	c	d	e	f	g
99	795	1,581	1,881	2,642	4,573	2,185
67	657	1,691	1,991	2,772	4,683	3,274
88	234	1,339	2,202	2,992	5,477	9,396
96	359	1,221	2,432	3,743	6,409	4,585
84	762	1,101	3,303	3,853	6,886	5,872
100	485	1,144	4,650	4,714	7,936	6,903

Drill 3

a	b	c	d	e	f
1,077	3,006	5,208	7,104	1,774	7,417
1,400	3,609	5,502	8,205	2,885	8,528
1,700	3,900	5,205	9,303	3,996	9,639
2,008	4,107	6,309	7,407	4,174	3,936
2,500	4,400	6,600	8,508	5,285	5,828
2,805	1,704	6,900	9,609	6,396	4,717

Drill 4

a	b	c	d	e	f
1.4	14.00	170.40	1,714.70	7,410.95	1,147.74
2.5	17.00	170.43	2,825.80	8,520.55	2,258.88
3.6	25.00	250.90	3,936.90	9,630.65	3,369.93
7.4	28.00	288.50	4,747.17	10,585.78	7,144.74
8.5	36.00	369.63	5,878.25	11,474.85	8,255.85
9.6	39.00	390.69	6,969.39	12,696.95	9,366.63

84a ▶ 5
Conditioning Practice

each line twice SS (slowly, then faster); DS between 2-line groups; if time permits, rekey selected lines

alphabet	1	Dr. Zisk told us to keep quiet just before the physics exam was given.
figures	2	Jason hit .418 in May, .257 in June, .360 in July, and .409 in August.
space bar	3	If I can find the parts for the old car, it will be quite easy to fix.
speed	4	The ornament on their oak mantle is a small antique ivory lamb or cow.

| 1 | 2 | 3 | 4 | 5 | 6 | 7 | 8 | 9 | 10 | 11 | 12 | 13 | 14 |

84b ▶ 35
Format and Key Unbound Report

Document 1
Report from Rough Draft

1. Review the formatting guides for unbound reports on page 148.

2. Format the report in unbound style. Do not correct your errors as you key.

3. When you finish, proofread your copy, mark it for correction, and prepare a final copy, all errors corrected.

Recall: Indent the quotation 5 spaces to the right of the left margin; let the line run full to the right margin. DS above and below the quotation.

words

THE CHANGING OFFICE   4

DS ¶

A secretary returning to an office job after a 25-year   15
leave of absence would have a difficult time coping with the   25
changes that have taken place during that time. Changing   37
technology would best describe the challenges facing today's   49
office worker. Two "buzzwords" which are currently being   61
used in the office are electronic desktop publishing and   72
electronic mail.   stet   76

Electronic Desktop Publishing   88

    Desktop publishing is the process of integrating text   98

and graphics by utilizing computer software to produce   109

professional-looking documents without using #8 professional ser- 122

vices. According to Winsor: 130
                     (1987, 29)

    Desktop publishing has a bright future. . . . Desktop   141
publishing enables people and businesses to develop their   153
own brochures, newsletters, and other documents at a frac-   164
tion of the cost and time expended sending the work out   175
to a professional graphics studio.   183

    Since today's firms are more concerned than ever about   194

creating the proper image, it is expected that a greater num- 206

ber of firms will turn to desktop publishing to enhance their images. 220

Electronic Mail   226

    The second "Buzz word" being used extensively in the modern 238

office is electronic mail (E-mail). E-mail is the sending,   250

storing, and delivering of written messages electronically. According 262

to Reiss and Dolan (1989, 529) identify two categories of   273

electronic mail services: 279

SS 1. In-house electronic mail. (E-mail which is run on   290
    a firm's computer system.)   295
                     DS

(continued, p. 150)

| B | C | D | F2 LAYOUT |
| | | | F3 SWITCHES |
ST QUARTER SALES - REGION 1

	QUOTA	SALES	OVER/UNDER	F4 PRINT BLK.
				F5 PRINT DOC.
$1,750,000	$2,362,500	35.00%

F6 HEADR FILE
F7 FOOTR FILE
Page: 1 Line: 12   J_SMART.LTR   F8 FMAT. FILE

F9 LINEFEED
F0 FORMFEED

Dear John:

Congratulations! You not only met your sa
you exceeded it by 35% which is tops in th
This is just a quick note to tell you how much we
appreciate your work and that you have won a trip
the Bahamas all expenses paid for a week.

I'll see you next week at the sales meeting.
will be my pleasure to present you with t
award certificate. Meanwhile, we have
quota 20% for the next quarter. Go

APPENDIX B
Automatic Features/Editing Functions of Electronic Equipment

Learning Goals

1. To learn the basic functions of electronic equipment.

2. To learn the specific commands for your particular software package.

3. To apply these functions and commands to perform the activities.

Practice Procedure

Follow the directions for each activity. Practice the drills until you feel comfortable enough to move to the next activity.

Study the software documentation and note the command for each function.

KNOW WHAT'S HAPPENING...
"For the times they are a-changin" went the words of a popular tune some years ago. And my how they've changed! A quick look at the composition of the United States labor force illustrates only one component of change. In 1920, close to 80 percent of the work force consisted of agricultural and industrial workers. The dominant sector of today's labor force, close to 90 percent, consists of information and service workers. Today's information technologies--such as electronic typewriters, personal computers, FAX machines, scanners, intelligent copiers and printers, electronic mail, and telecommunication devices--are having a major impact on workplace roles. Due to the information explosion, many of the new career opportunities in today's marketplace are based on computer technology.

The tools we work with have changed and will continue to change. For example, look what's happened to the typewriter and the world of document preparation. The user of a manual typewriter purchased an eraser to correct errors. The user of an electric may have had the luxury of correct-o-type to fix blunders. The electronic typewriter user may be able to store a few phrases or pages before printing a document. A personal computer, also called a microcomputer, makes document creation, formatting, and editing even easier when word processing software is used.

As the tools we work with continue to change, we ourselves must adapt to remain successful workers and fulfilled individuals. This section has been designed to inform you of some of the features and functions you will encounter when using an electronic typewriter and/or personal computer with word processing software to prepare documents.

KNOW THE "IN BRIEF" SECTION...
"In Brief" is designed to give you a generic description of the most commonly used word processing features. Read each one carefully. Since directions for each feature differ from program to program and not all programs contain every feature, study your software user's manual to learn the specific step-by-step instructions for your particular program. The software commands given in "In Brief" are for WordPerfect Versions 4.2 and 5.0.

KNOW YOUR SOFTWARE... Software is a program, a set of directions (instructions) that tells your computer to perform a specific task. Word processing software is a package that allows the user to create and format a document, save (store/file) it, retrieve and edit the text, and print the document. Some commonly used word processing features are insert and delete, center, move, copy, indent, columns and decimal alignment, page numbering, boldface, underline, and print. It is important to become familiar with your software package.

KNOW WHAT TO DO... (1) Read the "In Brief" feature section. (2) Study the user's manual for your equipment. (3) Study your software documentation for the specific function. (4) Read the directions for the lesson, then key the drills accordingly.

KNOW YOUR EQUIPMENT...THE KEYBOARD... For a quick review of the components of a personal computer, refer to pages viii and ix. Since many word processing functions require the user to strike a combination of keys, the keyboard arrangement of the three popular machines shown on these pages may help. Use the numbered items listed there to identify each key. If you are using a different computer, consult the instruction booklet that came with the equipment.

Improve Report Formatting Skills

Learning Goals

1. To review/improve report formatting knowledge and skills.

2. To improve keyboarding skills on straight copy, script copy, and rough-draft copy.

3. To improve language skills (verbs).

Format Guides

1. Paper guide at *0* for typewriters.

2. LL: 70 spaces for drills and ¶s; as required for documents.

3. LS: SS drills; as required for documents.

4. PI: 5 spaces.

FORMATTING GUIDES: UNBOUND REPORTS

Margins

Top	Place main heading on
First Page	line 10 (pica/10 pitch)
	line 12 (elite/12 pitch)
Second Page	line 6
Side	1″ left and right
Bottom	At least 1″ on all pages

Spacing

Reports are usually double-spaced, but may be single-spaced if desired. Whether double- or single-spaced, the paragraphs are indented five spaces.

Single-space quoted material of four or more lines. Indent the quoted material five spaces from the left margin; block the lines at that point. The right margin for quoted material remains at one inch. Double-space above and below the quoted material.

Indent enumerated items five spaces from the left margin; block the lines at that point. The right margin for enumerated items remains at one inch. Single-space individual items; DS between items as well as above and below a series of items.

Page Numbers

The first page may be numbered, but it need not be. The number, if used, is centered on line 62 from the top edge of the sheet. For the second page and subsequent ones, place the page number on line 6 from the top edge approximately even with the right margin. Leave a DS below the page number; begin the first line of the report body on line 8.

Headings and Subheadings

Main heading. Center the main heading in ALL-CAPS over the line of writing. Quadruple-space (QS) below it. A QS is 2 DS or 4 SS.

Side headings. Begin side headings at the left margin. DS above and below them. Capitalize the first letter of the first word and all other main words in each heading. Underline side headings.

Paragraph headings. Begin paragraph headings at the same point other paragraphs of the report begin. Capitalize the first letter of the first word only, underline the heading, and follow the heading with a period.

Documentation (Textual Citation)

References used to give credit for quoted or closely paraphrased material may be cited in parentheses in the report body. This form of documentation is known as a textual or internal citation. (Footnotes are presented in Phase 5.)

Textual citations should include the name(s) of the author(s), the date of the referenced publication, and the page number(s) of the material cited (Roberts, 1992, 275). When the author's name is used in the text introducing the quotation, only the year of publication and the page number(s) appear in parentheses: Roberts (1992, 275) said that . . . .

All references cited are listed alphabetically by author surnames on the last page of the text or at the end of the report (often on a separate page) under the heading REFERENCES or BIBLIOGRAPHY. The reference page has the same top and side margins as the first page of the report. Each reference is single-spaced with a double space between references. The first line of each reference begins at the left margin; all other lines are indented five spaces from the left margin.

Activity 1
Backspace Erase Feature

1. Read the "In Brief" copy at right.

2. Study software documentation to learn to use the backspace erase feature.

3. Read sentences at right.

4. Key each line twice DS using the backspace erase feature when needed.

BACKSPACE ERASE

An electronic editing tool that allows you to backspace and delete a previously keyed character (or characters).

Every time you strike the backspace erase key, the character to the left of the cursor is automatically erased (deleted).

1 Work is not only a way to make a living: It's the way to make a life!

2 The majority of new jobs will come from small, independent businesses.

3 Planning a career today requires more thought than it ever did before.

Activity 2
Cursor (Arrow) Keys

1. Read the "In Brief" copy at right.

2. Study software documentation to learn to use cursor keys.

3. Read sentences at right.

4. Key the sentences DS.

5. Using arrow keys, move the cursor to:
x in **flexibility,** line 1
v in **effectively,** line 3
d in **attitudes,** line 1
p in **compete,** line 3
m in **motivation,** line 2

CURSOR

A blinking light on the screen that identifies the position where text (copy) will be entered or edited. Arrow keys (cursor keys) used to move the cursor around the screen may be located on your computer's numeric keypad or as a separate group of keys between the main keyboard and the keypad.

LEFT/RIGHT CURSOR (ARROW) KEYS

These keys move the cursor one space at a time in a left or a right direction.

UP/DOWN CURSOR (ARROW) KEYS

These keys move the cursor up or down one line at a time.

1 Today, job seekers must possess a flexibility of skills and attitudes.

2 Getting the job you want requires motivation, energy, and preparation.

3 To compete effectively for the most attractive jobs, be well informed.

Activity 3
Strikeover, Insert, and Delete Editing Features

1. Read the "In Brief" copy at right.

2. Study software documentation to learn to use strikeover, insert, and delete features.

3. Read sentences at right.

4. Key each sentence DS as shown.

5. Make these changes (use the arrow keys to move the cursor):
Line
1, insert " after **career (career")**
1, replace 2d **e** in **seperate** with an **a**
2, delete **b** in **jobb**
2, delete **r** in **carreer (career)**
2, delete space in **it self**
3, insert **c** in **piking (picking)**
3, insert **e** in **carer (career)**
3, insert **l** in **chalenge (challenge)**
4, delete **s** in **keys**
4, replace 2d **s** in **sequense** with **c**
4, insert **c** and **s** in **aces (access)**

STRIKEOVER/REPLACEMENT MODE

Editing feature that allows you to position the cursor and key over (strikeover) characters. Existing text is automatically erased and replaced by new text.

INSERT

Editing feature that allows you to add characters without rekeying the entire document. New text is inserted and existing text is pushed to the right or down to make room for the addition.

DELETE

Editing feature that removes (erases) any character or characters, including blank spaces, identified (highlighted) by the cursor. Existing text to right moves over and text below moves up to close the space.

1 Today the two terms "career and "job" have totally seperate meanings.

2 Consider your jobb as a way to a carreer, not a career in and of it self.

3 No longer is piking a carer to get a job the chalenge workers face.

4 The keys is choosing the best sequense of jobs with aces to a career.

83c ▶ 15
Improve Keyboarding Technique

1. Key each line twice.

2. Take three 1′ writings on line 3; first for accuracy, then for speed, then again for accuracy.

3. Repeat Step 2 for lines 6 and 9.

Shift keys

1 Donald, Tom, Jan, and I all live on Park Haven Court, two blocks away.
2 We have visited Alabama, Kansas, Colorado, Maine, Florida, and Hawaii.
3 Mark Wolterman, president of Sparks Electric, lives near Jasmine Lane.

Space bar

4 Jane will go to the city next week to buy trees for our moms and dads.
5 Chi may be in town next week to see his aunt and uncle for a few days.
6 They may be able to fix only seven of the ten tires by noon on Friday.

Balanced-hand sentences

7 To the right of the dismal shanty is a small cornfield with six foals.
8 Their tutor may go with them when they go to the city for the bicycle.
9 The ivory box with the shamrock and iris is by the door of the chapel.

| 1 | 2 | 3 | 4 | 5 | 6 | 7 | 8 | 9 | 10 | 11 | 12 | 13 | 14 |

83d ▶ 10
Improve Techniques: Numbers/Tabulation

LL: 70 spaces; CS: 4

1. Key copy given at the right. Correct any errors you make as you key.

2. Take two 1′ writings.

			words
802 Crawley Road	Odessa, FL 33556-9512	(813) 920-7447	11
3173 Murphy Drive	Memphis, TN 38106-1001	(901) 454-6954	22
1049 Sunny Vale Lane	Madison, WI 53713-3358	(608) 266-6782	34
22 West 12th Street	Cincinnati, OH 45210-6904	(513) 512-5674	46
1908 Association Drive	Reston, VA 22091-1591	(703) 860-4977	58
1834 W. Southern Avenue	Mesa, AZ 85202-4867	(602) 833-3469	70

83e ▶ 10
Improve Language Skills: Verbs

LL: 70 spaces; SS with DS between line groups

1. Read the first rule.

2. Key the **Learn** sentences below it (with number and period), noting how the rule has been applied.

3. Key the **Apply** sentences using the correct verb shown in parentheses.

4. Practice the other rules in the same way.

5. If time permits, key the **Apply** lines again at a faster speed to quicken decision-making skills.

SINGULAR VERBS (continued)

> Use a singular verb with singular subjects linked by *or* or *nor*. Exception: If one subject is singular and the other is plural, the verb agrees with the closer subject.

Learn   1. Either my mother or father was invited to the opening ceremony.
Learn   2. Neither Mr. Puleo nor the word processing operators have the manual.
Apply   3. Either Eric or Marsha (has, have) the blueprints.
Apply   4. Neither the editor nor the authors (is, are) aware of the deadlines.

> Use a singular verb with a singular subject that is separated from the verb by phrases beginning with *as well as* and *in addition to*.

Learn   5. The report as well as the letters has to be finished before noon.
Apply   6. The advisor as well as the officers (is, are) going to attend the meeting.

> Use singular verbs with collective nouns (committee, team class, jury, etc.) if the collective noun acts as a unit.

Learn   7. The finance committee has the April budget.
Learn   8. The parliamentary procedure team is going to perform on Friday.
Apply   9. The board (is, are) going to discuss that issue next week.
Apply 10. The staff (wants, want) to be in charge of the banquet.

Activity 4
Margins, Tabs, and Vertical Spacing

1. Read the "In Brief" copy at right.
2. Study software documentation to learn to set a 60-space line, 5-space paragraph indent tab, and double spacing.
3. Read copy below right.
4. Key the paragraph.

RULER/FORMAT LINE

Line at the top or bottom of the screen or accessible within a document used to set the document format consisting of left and right margins, tab stops, text alignment and line-spacing.

MARGINS

The blank space on the left and right sides and at the top and bottom of a page. Left and right margins can be adjusted according to the desired line space; top and bottom margins can also be adjusted.

TABS

Stops set in the ruler/format line that allow you to indent paragraphs and lists and to align columns in tables. When you strike the TAB key, the cursor moves to the desired tab stop. If you key more than one line, the following lines align with the left margin instead of the tab stop.

SPACING

The space between lines of text. Line-spacing may be set for SS (1) or DS (2). A quadruple space is keyed by striking the return an appropriate number of times.

The average person spends 9 percent of the time writing, 16 percent reading, 30 percent speaking, and 45 percent listening. The fact that an individual is given two ears and only one mouth indicates the proper proportion of listening to speaking. Therefore, take heed of the Korean proverb: "Fools chatter; wise men listen."

Activity 5
Word Wrap and Soft and Hard Returns

1. Read the "In Brief" copy at the right.
2. Study software documentation to learn to use the word wrap and soft and hard returns.
3. Read paragraphs at right.
4. Use your program's default settings (or set a 70-space line and a 5-space paragraph indent tab).
5. Key the paragraphs DS using hard returns only between paragraphs.
6. As you key, correct any mistakes using the backspace key.
7. Proofread; make any necessary corrections using the strike-over, insert, and delete functions.
8. With the arrow keys, move the cursor to the beginning of the first ¶. Change to a 50-space line, 5-space paragraph indent tab. Then strike the down arrow repeatedly. What happened?
9. With the arrow keys, move the cursor to the beginning of the first ¶. Change to a 60-space line, 5-space paragraph indent tab. Then strike the down arrow repeatedly. What happened?

WORD WRAP

An automatic feature that determines whether the word being keyed will extend beyond the right margin. If so, the program automatically "wraps the text around" to the beginning of the next line while the user continues keying. A carriage return is necessary only when mandatory, such as at the end of a paragraph or a line of statistical copy.

SOFT RETURN

Automatically entered by the program at the end of a line of copy when text is being "wrapped around" to the next line. When you adjust the margins or insert and/or delete copy, the program automatically changes the position of the soft return.

HARD RETURN

Entered by striking the return key. Hard returns can be removed only by deleting them with backspace erase or the delete feature.

How does your word processing program know where to set the margins when you don't key the numbers? Simple. The program sets them according to the default. A default is a setting entered into a program by the designer. Paper size (8½ × 11 inches), pitch (pica--10), left and right margins, and tab settings are example of preset defaults.

Let's say your program has a default setting of 10 for the left margin and 74 for the right. Should you desire a longer or shorter line of copy, simply change the default setting. Defaults are created to appeal to the majority of users most of the time. Designers try to assume exactly what settings users will want to work with.

82d ▶ 8

Improve Technique: Numbers and Tabulator

LL: 70 spaces; CS: 4; key the drill twice (slowly, then faster); correct any errors you make as you key; if time permits, rekey lines

Concentrate on figure location; quick tab spacing; eyes on copy.

2831	4094	9018	9335	7481	3042	4402	10297	34783
7609	5961	3137	192	9366	3149	7215	41234	66552
9078	8272	463	8656	5438	476	321	79809	12676
6562	3735	6555	7051	1017	2022	8797	8458	93081

82e ▶ 12

Improve Keyboarding Skill: Straight Copy

1. A 3' writing on ¶s 1-2 combined; find *gwam*, circle errors.

2. A 1' writing on ¶ 1, then on ¶ 2; find *gwam* and circle errors on each.

3. Another 3' writing on ¶s 1-2 trying to increase your *gwam* by 2 *wam* over first 3' writing.

4. Record your best 1' and 3' writing for use in 83b.

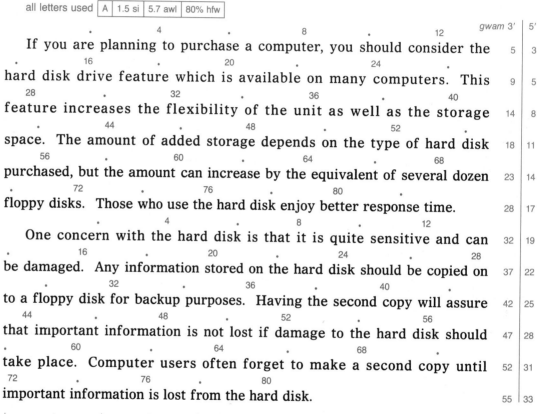

all letters used | A | 1.5 si | 5.7 awl | 80% hfw

	gwam 3'	5'
If you are planning to purchase a computer, you should consider the	5	3
hard disk drive feature which is available on many computers. This	9	5
feature increases the flexibility of the unit as well as the storage	14	8
space. The amount of added storage depends on the type of hard disk	18	11
purchased, but the amount can increase by the equivalent of several dozen	23	14
floppy disks. Those who use the hard disk enjoy better response time.	28	17
One concern with the hard disk is that it is quite sensitive and can	32	19
be damaged. Any information stored on the hard disk should be copied on	37	22
to a floppy disk for backup purposes. Having the second copy will assure	42	25
that important information is not lost if damage to the hard disk should	47	28
take place. Computer users often forget to make a second copy until	52	31
important information is lost from the hard disk.	55	33

gwam 3' / 5'

Lesson 83   Keyboarding Technique/Language Skills

83a ▶ 5

Conditioning Practice

each line twice SS (slowly, then faster); if time permits, rekey selected lines

alphabet	1	Mr. Garvey told Jay to pick up six dozen roses for the awards banquet.
figures	2	Gains of 5.09 and 6.15 the last two days put the Dow Jones at 1842.37.
one-hand	3	After I averaged my art grades, I sat defeated in my car in my garage.
speed	4	They may blame the six girls for the problem with the neighbor's auto.

| 1 | 2 | 3 | 4 | 5 | 6 | 7 | 8 | 9 | 10 | 11 | 12 | 13 | 14 |

83b ▶ 10

Improve Keyboarding Skill: Straight Copy

1. Two 1' writings on ¶1 of 82e above. Strive to increase rate recorded previously for 82e by 4 *wam*.

2. Repeat Step 1 using ¶ 2.

3. A 3' writing using both ¶s.

4. Determine 3' *gwam* and record.

Activity 6
Review Setting Margins, Tabs, Vertical Spacing, Word Wrap, Insert, Delete, and Strikeover Features

1. Read the ¶s at the right.

2. LL: 60 spaces; LS: DS; ¶ indent tab: 5 spaces.

3. Key ¶s as is; do not correct errors; use a hard return only between ¶s.

4. Make these changes:

Paragraph 1
Line
1, replace **s** in **sertain** with **c**
2, replace 2d **e** in **seperate** with **a**
2, delete space in **up scale**
2, delete space in **down scale**
3, hyphenate **not so rich**
3, change **people** to **individuals**
4, replace **there** with **their**
4, change **area** to **field**
5, insert **entertainment** after **education**
6, change 1st **you** to **yourself**
7, change **imagine** to **picture**

Paragraph 2
Line
8, delete **l** in **successfull**
9, change **they're** to **they are**
10, delete space in **any one**
10, delete space in **under stand**
11, change **&** to **and**
11, replace **T** in 2d **They** with **t**
12, delete space in **care fully**
12, delete **r** and insert **l** in **generraly (generally)**

1 Research has shown that sertain personality traits

2 seperate the up scale from the down scale, the rich from

3 the not so rich. These traits bring people success

4 regardless of there chosen area--business, sports,

5 education, or politics. One of the necessary

6 traits is the ability to envision you succeeding. If you

7 can imagine it, you can achieve it.

8   Another trait of successfull individuals is goal

9 setting. Usually they're not any more intelligent than

10 any one else. However, they set their goals, under stand

11 them, & make sure they are achieved. They don't rush; They

12 plan their actions care fully. Generraly they live by the

13 rule "plan your work, then work your plan."

Activity 7
Underline Text Automatically While Keying

1. Read the "In Brief" copy.

2. Study software documentation to learn to underline existing text and how to underline text automatically while keying.

3. LL: 70 spaces; LS: DS.

4. Read sentences at right.

5. Key sentences using automatic underscore where shown.

6. When finished, proofread your work, making any corrections using insert, delete, and strikeover features.

7. Underline these words in the existing text:
Line:
1, **listening**
2, **information, notes**
3, **listening**
4, **First**

UNDERLINE EXISTING TEXT

Position the cursor (or printwheel) at the beginning of the existing text. Hold down the left shift key and strike the hyphen key. You may have to identify the block of text by entering a specific command *(such as the Alternate and F4 keys)* and then enter the underline command *(such as the F8 key)*.

UNDERLINE TEXT AS YOU KEY (AUTOMATIC)

Turn on automatic (continuous) underlining by striking a keystroke combination *(such as Code and u)*, or strike the assigned function key *(such as F8)*. As you key, the text will be underlined. When you're finished, turn automatic underlining off by striking the same key or combination.

1 The four steps to listening are: <u>sense</u>, <u>interpret</u>, <u>evaluate</u>, <u>respond</u>.

2 <u>Active</u> <u>listening</u> involves processing the information and taking notes.

3 A <u>conversation</u> requires both listening for main ideas and <u>interacting</u>.

4 First on the list of very <u>nonproductive</u> listening habits is <u>fidgeting</u>.

5 If you fidget, you may <u>tug</u> your <u>earlobe</u>, <u>shuffle</u> your <u>feet</u>, or <u>squirm</u>.

Improve Keyboarding and Language Skills

Learning Goals

1. To improve/refine technique and response patterns.
2. To increase speed on straight copy.
3. To improve language skills.

Format Guides

1. Paper guide at *0* (for typewriters).
2. LL: 70 spaces.
3. LS: SS drills; DS ¶s.
4. PI: 5 spaces.

Lesson 82   *Keyboarding/Language Skills*

82a ▶ 5
Conditioning Practice

each line twice SS (slowly, then faster); DS between 2-line groups; if time permits, rekey selected lines

alphabet	1	The vast Cox farm was just sold by the bank at quite an amazing price.
figures	2	Their firm constructed 340 of the 560 new homes between 1987 and 1992.
fig/sym	3	Martin paid Invoice #382 ($56.79 with a 5% discount) with Check #1084.
speed	4	The girls and the maid may go downtown to pay for the six giant signs.

| 1 | 2 | 3 | 4 | 5 | 6 | 7 | 8 | 9 | 10 | 11 | 12 | 13 | 14 |

82b ▶ 15
Improve Keyboarding Skill: Skill Comparison

1. A 30″ writing on each line; find *gwam* on each.
   1′ *gwam* × 2
2. Compare rates.
3. Another 30″ writing on each line; try to increase speed.

balanced-hand	1	He is apt to make the men go to the island for the coalfish and clams.
double letters	2	Kellee saw three little rabbits hopping between rows looking for food.
3d row	3	Three of our territory reporters were told to type their trade report.
adjacent-key	4	Every owner was there to report the trade union's prior point of view.
outside reach	5	Paula Quixote won all six top prizes last season for her zealous play.
one-hand	6	Polly saw a few deserted cats on a battered crate in a vacated garage.
shift-keys	7	Janie saw Karen, Lauren, Ellen, and Claudia while she was in Columbus.
figures	8	Her phone number is 836-9572; her address is 3014 Jefferson Boulevard.

| 1 | 2 | 3 | 4 | 5 | 6 | 7 | 8 | 9 | 10 | 11 | 12 | 13 | 14 |

82c ▶ 10
Improve Language Skills: Verbs

LL: 70 spaces; SS with DS between 2-line groups

1. Read and key the **Learn** sentences (with number and period), noting how the rule has been applied.

2. Key each **Apply** sentence using the correct verb shown in parentheses.

3. If time permits, key the **Apply** lines again at a faster speed to quicken decision-making skill.

SINGULAR VERBS

Use a singular verb with a singular subject.

Learn 1. The mail carrier has not delivered today's mail.
Learn 2. She has already completed her solo.
Apply 3. An outstanding executive assistant (is, are) difficult to find.
Apply 4. He (has, have) been accepted at Harvard.

Use singular verbs with indefinite pronouns (each, every, any, either, neither, one, etc.) used as subjects.

Learn 5. Every employee is expected to attend the exquisite awards banquet.
Learn 6. Everyone has been given permission to attend the game.
Apply 7. Each person (has, have) his/her own ideas on the subject.
Apply 8. Neither one of the gymnasts (is, are) very good.

Activity 8
Bold Text

1. Read the "In Brief" copy.
2. Study software documentation to learn to bold text.
3. Set a 70-space line, DS.
4. Key the sentences using the bold feature where shown.
5. Proofread your work. Make any necessary corrections and print a copy.

BOLD TEXT

The bold feature emphasizes text by printing characters darker than others. This bold effect is created when the printer strikes each designated character twice. Turn on the bold command by striking the assigned key or keystroke combination (such as the F6 key or the Code and b keys). Key the text to be printed in bold, which may appear highlighted on the screen. Turn off the bold command by striking the same key or keystroke combination.

1 **Boom boxes** and various other background noises are **distractions** to us.

2 Your **emotions** and **personal ideas** influence your reaction to a speaker.

3 One huge roadblock we all face is an **overestimation** of our **importance**.

4 A **passive listener** simply nods in **agreement** throughout a **conversation**.

Activity 9 Center
Text Horizontally

1. Read the "In Brief" copy.
2. Study software documentation to learn to center text.
3. Set a 50-space line, SS.
4. Read the drills below.
5. Key each line of each drill using automatic centering, if offered. If not, center each drill manually. Underline and bold the text as shown.

AUTOMATIC CENTERING

To center automatically, position the cursor (or printwheel) at the left margin. Hold down the designated key combination (such as Code and c); the cursor moves to the center of the line. As you key, the cursor backs up (but does not print). To print the centered copy, strike the return key. You may have to enter the center command (such as shift and F6 keys). The cursor moves to the center of the line. As you key, the letters back up once for every two characters. Strike the return key (hard return).

Drill 1

STAND UP AND DELIVER

Express Your Opinion Concisely
Be Confident
Beware--Your Body Language is also "Speaking"
Your Tone of Voice Says it All
Pay Attention to Your Listener
Observe Body Language of Others

Drill 2

A KEY TO EFFECTIVE COMMUNICATION:
MATCHING STYLES WITH CONTENT

Small Talk--Chatty, Noncommittal
Control Talk--Take Charge
Search Talk--Analyze Problems; Possible Solutions
Straight Talk--Handle Conflicts Constructively

Drill 3

GAMESMANSHIP PROBLEMS AT WORK

Answer a Question with a Question
Discuss Others Rather than One's Self
Send Incomplete Messages
Provide Superficial Information About an Issue
Use We or They rather than I or You
Withhold Important Information

81d ▶ 25
*Document
Processing Skills:
Letters and Memos*

2 letterheads
LP pp. 11-13
or plain full sheets
Use Letter Placement Guide
on p. 76, if necessary; correct
errors.

Document 1
Business Letter

block format; open punctuation

Current date|Mrs. Jacki Babcock|1390 Wilcox Avenue|Los Angeles, CA	14
90028-4130|Dear Mrs. Babcock	20

We hope you and your family are enjoying the living room furniture you 34
purchased at Wilson's Department Store. Oakwood is an excellent line of 49
furniture that should last for many years. If, however, there is any reason 64
you are not pleased with the furniture, let us know. We will take the neces- 79
sary steps to guarantee your satisfaction. 88

Wilson's has been in business for over 100 years because of satisfied cus- 103
tomers. We are committed to keeping customer satisfaction high by offer- 117
ing quality goods and services at reasonable prices. 128

We appreciate our loyal customers and hope you will remain one of them. 142
Please let me know when we can be of further service. (133) 153

Sincerely yours\|Miss Phyllis B. Clayborn\|Furniture Consultant\|xx   166/**179**

Document 2
Business Letter

modified block format, blocked
¶s; mixed punctuation

Current date\|Ms. Beverly J. Lorenzo\|308 Paseo El Greco\|Anaheim, CA   14
92807-8030\|Dear Ms. Lorenzo: 20

Discussing your dining room furniture needs with you yesterday was enjoy- 34
able. I checked with the department manager, and the next shipment of 48
furniture should arrive within a few weeks. Eight new styles of dining room 64
sets were ordered. When the shipment arrives, I will call you. 77

In the meantime, you may be interested in looking over the brochures of 91
dining room furniture that are enclosed. If there is a set which is of particu- 107
lar interest to you, we could order it for you. About four weeks are required 123
for delivery. You would be under no obligation to buy the set if it does not 138
meet your expectations when it arrives. As I indicated, Wilson's Department 154
Store is committed to customer satisfaction. 163

I look forward to working with you to assure that you will become one of 178
Wilson's satisfied customers. If you have any questions about any of the 192
furniture you looked at yesterday, please call me at 836-4829. (183) 205

Sincerely,\|Miss Phyllis B. Clayborn\|Furniture Consultant\|xx\|Enclosures   219/**232**

Document 3
Simplified Memo

standard format and placement
(see p. 74 if necessary)

Current date\|Adrian S. Comstock\|OFFICE TECHNOLOGY SYMPOSIUM   12

Information on the "Fifth Annual Office Technology Symposium" is enclosed. 28
I attended last year's symposium and found it very beneficial. Since we 42
have been allocated money for upgrading the word processing department, I 57
plan to attend again this year. 64

There is enough money in the budget to pay the expenses for two people to 78
attend. Since you will be involved in upgrading the word processing center, 94
you may be interested in attending. If you are, please let me know before 109
the end of the month so I can make the necessary arrangements. 122

Harriet D. Steinman\|xx\|Enclosure   128/**137**

Activity 10
Required Space Feature

1. Read the "In Brief" copy at right.
2. Study software documentation to learn to use the required space feature.
3. Set a 60-space line, DS.
4. Read sentences at right.
5. Key sentences using required space feature where needed.
6. Proofread; make any necessary corrections.
7. Print a final copy.

HARD (REQUIRED) SPACE

A feature that guards against breaking a line of printed text between title and surname (Mr. Magoo), initials (B. L. Smith), month and date (December 7, 1941), and parts of a formula (a + b + c), etc. Inserting hard (required) spaces between items of text causes the printer to regard the phrase as one word. When you strike a specific key *(such as the Home key),* along with the space bar, you enter a "hard space." (A special symbol or code may appear on the screen.) The printer will print the text containing the hard space on one line.

1　A cartoon personality that won the hearts of many was Mr. Magoo.

2　The movies have brought us many stars; for example, Zsa Zsa Gabor.

3　The Declaration of Independence was signed on Thursday, July 4, 1776.

Activity 11
Review Margins, Tabs, Spacing, Required Space, Automatic Center, Underline, and Bold Features

1. Read paragraphs at right.
2. Set a 70-space line, 5-space paragraph indent tab, DS.
3. Center headings; use underline and bold where shown.
4. Key the document.
5. Proofread your work. Make any necessary corrections and print a copy.

PERSONAL STYLE
HOW TO MAKE YOURSELF SPECIAL

The basis for style--one's distinctive manner of expression--comes from within. Style is not something we're born with but rather a combination of abilities that we learn as we mature, just as we learn to speak Russian, repair leaky faucets, or drive a car. Style is a very personal achievement; it's a quality that money cannot buy. As a matter of fact, style has nothing at all to do with money.

WHAT IT TAKES...

Personal style is a mixture of six main elements. (1) Knowing what to add and when to stop is a matter of **balance** and **restraint**. (2) Paying **attention to detail** allows you to think things through to create comfort and satisfaction. (3) **Consideration** means you are alert to other people's needs and sensitivities and respond to them. (4) **Poise, grace,** and **self-confidence** come from knowing one's self without being vain. (5) The ability to **make good choices** helps you make the right decision at the right time. (6) **Individuality** is the distinctive expression of your personal preferences. (7) **Identity** means you have a point of view that marks your place in the game plan of life.

81a ▶ 5
Conditioning Practice

each line twice SS (slowly, then faster); DS between 2-line groups; if time permits, rekey selected lines

alphabet 1 Jackson believed he might maximize profits with a quality sales force.

figures 2 Jo's social security number, 504-18-2397, was recorded as 504-18-2396.

fig/sym 3 Invoice #689 (dated 10/24) for $3,575 was paid on Tuesday, November 1.

speed 4 Their neighbor may dismantle the ancient ricksha in the big cornfield.

| 1 | 2 | 3 | 4 | 5 | 6 | 7 | 8 | 9 | 10 | 11 | 12 | 13 | 14 |

81b ▶ 10 Check Keyboarding Skill: Straight Copy

1. A 3' writing on ¶s 1 and 2 combined; find *gwam*; circle errors.

2. A 1' writing on each ¶; find *gwam*; circle errors.

3. Another 3' writing on ¶s 1 and 2 combined; find *gwam*; circle errors.

4. Compare the better 3' rate with the rate recorded for 76b, page 134. How much did your rate improve?

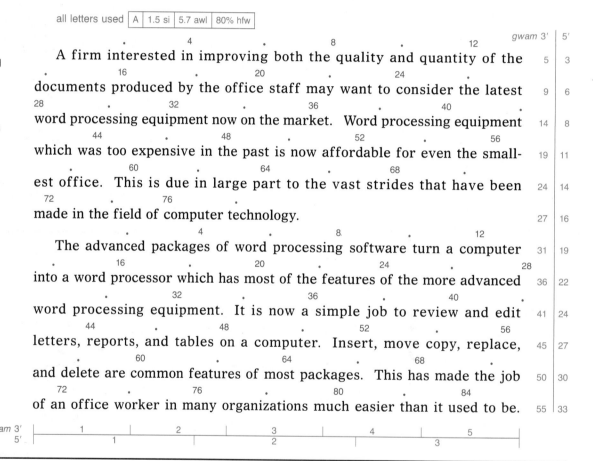

all letters used | A | 1.5 si | 5.7 awl | 80% hfw

                                                                gwam 3' | 5'

A firm interested in improving both the quality and quantity of the   5   3

documents produced by the office staff may want to consider the latest   9   6

word processing equipment now on the market. Word processing equipment   14   8

which was too expensive in the past is now affordable for even the small-   19   11

est office. This is due in large part to the vast strides that have been   24   14

made in the field of computer technology.   27   16

The advanced packages of word processing software turn a computer   31   19

into a word processor which has most of the features of the more advanced   36   22

word processing equipment. It is now a simple job to review and edit   41   24

letters, reports, and tables on a computer. Insert, move copy, replace,   45   27

and delete are common features of most packages. This has made the job   50   30

of an office worker in many organizations much easier than it used to be.   55   33

gwam 3' | 1 | 2 | 3 | 4 | 5 |
     5' | 1 | 2 | 3 |

81c ▶ 10 Improve Language Skills: Word Choice

Study the spelling and definition for each word. Read the **Learn** sentence. Key the **Learn** sentence and the **Apply** sentences (select the proper word in parentheses to complete the sentence correctly).

adapt (vb) to make fit; adjust

adept (adj) thoroughly proficient; expert

air (n) the look, appearance or bearing of a person

heir (n) one who inherits or is entitled to inherit money

Learn 1. Once he was able to adapt the form, he became adept with it.

Apply 2. Yoko will (adapt, adept) the house plans to take care of your concerns.

Apply 3. Juan was very (adapt, adept) at working with the integrated software.

Learn 4. Rebecca felt the heir to the throne possessed a certain air about him.

Apply 5. Martin always displayed an (air, heir) of importance when in public.

Apply 6. As (air, heir) to the entire fortune, she will someday be very rich.

Activity 12
Learn to Use the Hyphenation Feature

1. Read the "In Brief" copy at right.
2. Study software documentation to learn to use the hyphenation feature.
3. Read paragraph at right; identify the required, soft, and/or hard hyphen character features.
4. Set a 70-space line and a 5-space paragraph tab, then key the paragraph DS using your program's hyphenation feature.
5. When finished, proofread your work making any corrections and/or changes.
6. Print a final copy.

HARD (REQUIRED) HYPHEN

Entered when the user strikes the hyphen key. Regardless of where the hyphen appears within the paragraph, the program prints it. Hard hyphens are used in telephone numbers, a numeric range, certain phrases that should not be broken (jack-o-lantern), and compound words (self-confident). A hard hyphen can be deleted by the user.

SOFT (GHOST OR NONREQUIRED) HYPHEN

An electronic feature that allows the user to decide whether a word should be hyphenated to avoid a very ragged right margin. When the hyphenation feature is "on," the cursor stops when a word will not fit on the line. Some programs automatically insert a soft hyphen; others allow the user to make the decision. Should the location of the hyphenated word change during reformatting, the soft hyphen is deleted automatically.

HYPHEN CHARACTER

A feature used for keying dates or minus signs in formulas. The hyphen character may require the user to strike a specific key *(such as the Home key)* before striking the hyphen key. The feature prevents a minus or a dash from being separated from related characters when it occurs at the end of a line.

Most of us never realize the important role imagination plays in our lives. Imagination sets the goal "picture" upon which we act (or fail to act). Imagination is the way we are built--our automatic mechanism works on our "creative imagination." Depending on what a person imagines to be true about herself/himself and her/his environment, that individual will always act and feel and perform accordingly. Therefore, why not imagine yourself successful? If you picture yourself performing in a certain manner, it is almost the same as the actual performance. Mental practice helps to make perfect.

Activity 13
Learn About Pagination (Page Format) Features

1. Read the "In Brief" copy at right and on the next page.
2. Study software documentation to learn about pagination (page format) features.
3. Identify the features available on your software.
4. Create a checklist on "how to perform" each feature; use a step-by-step enumerated format.
5. Set a 60-space line and a 5-space indent tab for the enumerations.
6. Key each checklist, center the headings; indent each step (enumerations).
7. When finished, proofread your work making any corrections using any of the electronic features introduced thus far.

PAGE BREAK

The point (generally a given line count) at which a page ends. When the printer reaches the page break, it automatically advances a new sheet or allows the user to insert paper.

AUTOMATIC (SOFT/NONREQUIRED) PAGE BREAKS

A feature (sometimes called page format) that allows the user to select the number of lines allowed on the page (generally 54). When the program recognizes the given number of lines, it automatically inserts a soft page break. When repagination occurs (a paragraph is added or deleted, for example), all soft page breaks are deleted and new ones inserted automatically.

CONTROLLED (HARD/REQUIRED) PAGE BREAKS

A special command inserted by the user to ensure that a page remains intact during automatic pagination. When the program recognizes the special command, it breaks the page at that point. Usually hard page breaks must be deleted by the user.

HEADER/FOOTER

Text line (or lines) printed consistently in the top margin (header) or bottom margin (footer) of each page of a multiple-page document. A header/footer may include such information as the document title, page number, and date. Rarely does a single document contain both a header and a footer.

(continued, p. A-15)

80b (continued)

Memo 2
plain full sheet

1. Format and key the memo at high speed.

2. Proofread and mark copy for correction using proofreader marks.

3. Rekey the document; correct errors.

	words
November 4, 19--	3
Accounting Department	8
SELECTION OF NEW ACCOUNTING DEPARTMENT MANAGER	17

As most of you have heard by now, last week Marsha Mobley announced her 32 intent to retire at the end of this year. In keeping with company policy, 47 President Norwood prefers to have the position filled by a current employee. 62

If you are interested in applying for the position, submit an updated resume 78 and letter of application to the personnel office before November 21. It is 93 our intent to have the position filled by December 1, so that the new man- 108 ager will have the opportunity of working with Ms. Mobley for a month be- 122 fore she retires. 126

Sophia Ramirez, Personnel 131

xx 132

80c ▶ 10 Improve Language Skills: Word Choice

Study the spelling and definition for each word. Read the **Learn** sentence. Key the **Learn** sentence and the **Apply** sentences (select the proper word in parentheses to complete the sentence correctly).

lie (n) an untrue or inaccurate statement; as a verb, to rest or recline

lye (n) a strong alkaline solution

flew (vb) to move through the air

flue (n) a channel in a chimney

Learn 1. Jeffrey told a lie about how the lye stained our brand new carpet.
Apply 2. They told one (lie, lye) after another just to protect themselves.
Apply 3. Did you ask the owner how much (lie, lye) is needed in the solution?

Learn 4. The bird flew to the chimney where it made a nest in the flue.
Apply 5. The blocked (flew, flue) in the chimney was the cause of the problem.
Apply 6. The only time Mary (flew, flue) to New York, the plane was hijacked.

80d ▶ 10 Improve Keyboarding Skill: Straight Copy

1. Take a 1' writing on the ¶; find *gwam*.

2. Add 4-6 words to your *gwam*; divide the new rate by 4 to determine the number of words you must key each 15" to reach your new goal rate.

3. Note where you must be in the copy at the end of 15, 30, 45, and 60" to reach new goal.

4. Take a 15" timing, trying to achieve your goal.

5. Take a 30" timing, trying to reach your goal each 15".

6. Take a 45" timing.

7. Take a 60" timing, trying to maintain your goal rate.

8. Repeat this activity as time permits.

all letters used | A | 1.5 si | 5.7 awl | 80% hfw

Year after year employers express their desire to hire employees who have strong communication skills. Those with the ability to organize and deliver ideas in written or oral form become an asset to their firms; those who do not have this ability quickly become a liability. If you plan on entering the job market in the near future, you will want to refine these skills so that you will be an asset rather than a liability.

WIDOW/ORPHAN

The widow/orphan feature prevents the printing of the last line of a paragraph at the top of a new page (widow) and the first line of a paragraph at the bottom of a page (orphan). The widow/orphan feature "protects" documents from containing these undesirable formatting features.

Before the widow/orphan feature is turned on, the cursor must be at the beginning of the text to be protected--usually at the beginning of the document. The feature may be turned on and off within a document. Use widow/orphan protection for proper page breaks in all documents of two or more pages.

Activity 14
Applying What You've Learned About Pagination

1. Read the copy at right.

2. Set a 60-space line and 5-space paragraph tab.

3. Center the title on line 10, pica; line 12 elite; QS between title and first line of body.

4. Key this document; DS all paragraphs.

5. If available, use the soft hyphen feature as you key.

6. Use the pagination feature allowing 54 lines per page; do not allow widows and orphans.

7. Create a header on line 6 of the second page; place the title **JOB HUNT** at the left margin and the page number flush right.

8. Proofread your work; make any necessary corrections.

9. Print a copy.

SHAKING THE BUSHES--THE JOB HUNT!

Finding a job can be faster and easier--and even more enjoyable--if you chart your course in the right direction.

First and foremost, know what you want to do. You should have some idea about "what you want to be when you grow up." Be active; don't let fate control your course! Take the initiative in your job hunt. Visit many prospects. The more you interview, the more comfortable you become. Another plus: Your enthusiasm about job hunting starts to soar.

Don't be too aggressive. Coming straight out and asking for a job is an approach considered to be too direct by many employers.

Be a Sherlock Holmes. Search for those individuals who are in the position to hire you. Try information interviewing. Talk to the people you will be working for (and with) as well as those to whom you will report directly. By asking questions (How do you like your job? What do you do here? and What problems do you encounter?) you gather information about a potential career.

The lyrics from a recent Broadway play said it well: **"Who am I anyway; am I my resume?"** Absolutely! Make sure your resume relates specifically to your objective. Focus on your skills, knowledge, experiences, and activities. Today's employer is looking for a well-rounded individual who can make a contribution to the company as well as to the community.

Sell yourself. Stress your fine points, such as your ability to communicate (oral and written skills), adaptability, flexibility, ability to learn, and your willingness to be retrained if need be. Smile! It's the enthusiasm in your eyes that clinches the interview.

Follow through. Send a thank-you note to the interviewer. Call to let the person know you're genuinely interested. Remember--persistence pays off.

79c ▶ 10 Check
*Language Skills:
Number Expression*

SS sentences; DS between
groups of sentences

Key line number (with period);
space twice, then key the
sentence, supplying the correct form of number expression. If time permits, key the
sentences again to increase
decision-making speed.

1. About 2/3's of the senior class attended the last forum.
2. The bank was on the corner of 3rd Avenue and 35th Street.
3. Almost 50 of our former students passed the CPA exam last May.
4. Only 2 of the fifteen applicants applying for the job will be hired.
5. The President will address the nation on Monday, June 5, at 6:10 p.m.

6. The office of Baxter & Jones is located at Six McKinley Avenue.
7. Of Mathew's twenty hits, eight of them were for extra bases.
8. Twelve of the computers arrived on Monday; 12 arrived on Wednesday.
9. There were six seniors, 12 juniors, and 15 sophomores at the dance.
10. Rules 7-10 are presented in Chapter four; Rules 11-13 in Chapter 5.

11. The new baby was twenty-one inches long and weighed 7 lbs. 12 oz.
12. Fifteen of the delegates voted for Johnson; twenty voted for Lopez.
13. The instructor had to replace seven of the 25 computer diskettes.
14. The address of the New York Historical Society is 1 State Street.
15. The publishing company plans for Volume Two to be finished by May 5.

Lesson 80 | *Simplified Memos/Language Skills*

80a ▶ 5
*Conditioning
Practice*

each line twice SS
(slowly, then faster);
DS between 2-line
groups; if time per-
mits, rekey selected
lines

alphabet 1	Morgan Sanchez was frequently invited to exhibit her artwork in Japan.
figures 2	We purchased 3,148 of her 7,260 shares on Thursday, December 15, 1990.
fig/sym 3	Frederick & Gilbertson paid me $635,000 for the 460 acres on 12/17/89.
speed 4	She may make us visit the big chapel in the dismal city on the island.

| 1 | 2 | 3 | 4 | 5 | 6 | 7 | 8 | 9 | 10 | 11 | 12 | 13 | 14 |

80b ▶ 25 *Recall
Document Processing
Skills: Simplified Memo*

Memo 1
plain full sheet

Format and key the memo given
at the right. (See p. 74 for an example of simplified memo format.)
Correct any errors you make as
you key.

words

November 4, 19--   3

All Employees   6

PROFESSIONAL DEVELOPMENT SEMINARS   13

The company is implementing a new program for professional development   27
this year. Every employee will be given one day off to attend one of the   42
company-sponsored professional development seminars.   53

Tentative topics for this year's seminars are the value of leadership, im-   67
proving oral communication skills, integrated software applications, and   82
stress management. Indicate your preference for each of the seminars on   97
the attached form by placing #1 by your first choice, #2 by your second   111
choice, and so forth.   116

We will try to accommodate everyone's first or second choice. The more   130
popular programs will be offered twice during the year in an effort to con-   145
trol the number of participants at each seminar.   155

Sophia Ramirez, Personnel   160

xx   161

Enclosure   162

Memo 2 is on p. 142.

Activity 15
Learn to Search a Document for a Character String

1. Read the "In Brief" copy.
2. Study software documentation to learn to use the search feature.
3. Set 60-space line and 10-space paragraph tab.
4. Read paragraph at right, then key it DS as is.
5. Position cursor at beginning of text; search for character string **halo effect.** How many occurrences?
6. Return to beginning of document; search for the string **psychologists.** How many?

SEARCH

A *string* is a group of characters. A group of letters (hugs), numbers (394,823,315), symbols ("@&%!@#+*), or alphanumeric characters (A34C23Z9884TI) are all regarded as a string. A search feature allows you to search forward (and sometimes backward) through the document to locate a character string or a code (tab, hard return, etc.).

When you enter the proper command *(such as striking the F4 key),* the program prompts (asks) you to enter the word to search for. When you strike the same key (or the return key), the program begins searching the document. Every time the designated string is found, the program highlights it or positions the cursor on it.

Research has shown that most employers make up their minds about job applicants in the first 30 seconds of an interview. These findings are based on what many psychologists refer to as the halo effect. The term halo effect refers to the first impression a person makes. A good first impression is called by psychologists a positive halo effect. A not-so-good first impression is called a negative halo effect. The point is that the first impression lingers--like a halo--causing it to become a lasting impression.

Activity 16
Learn to Use the Search and Replace Feature

1. Read the "In Brief" copy.
2. Study software documentation to learn to use the search and replace feature.
3. Set a 70-space line and a 10-space paragraph tab.
4. Read paragraph at right, then key it DS as is.
5. Move cursor to the beginning of text.
6. Search for every occurrence of **affect** and replace it with **effect.**
7. Move cursor to the beginning of document again.
8. Search for every occurrence of **hula** and replace it with **halo.**

SEARCH AND REPLACE

A feature that searches forward (or backward) through a document until it finds the designated character string or code and then replaces it with a new string that the user designates. Some programs also allow you to delete a string using the replace feature. A *discretionary replace* (sometimes called *selective search* or *search with confirmation*) allows you to replace character strings selectively. A

global replace will automatically replace every occurrence of the designated character string. By entering the proper command, the program prompts you with special directions such as "Search For:" and "Replace With:". When the command is executed, the program locates each occurrence of the character string and replaces it with the new string.

Regardless of whether the hula affect is negative or positive, it radiates in all directions from the first affect or impression. People with a positive hula affect project a positive self-image, have a firm handshake, maintain eye contact, and smile. Generally, individuals who do not paint a confident and competent image have a cold, clammy handshake, do not maintain eye contact, and, therefore, radiate a negative hula affect.

79b ▶ 35
Format Letters in Modified Block Style
3 plain sheets; correct errors

Letter 1
Business Letter

modified block, open punctuation; blocked ¶s

Date: March 1, 19--
Address letter to:

Mr. Morris E. Young
904 Beatrice Street
Titusville, FL 32780-8192

Salutation: Dear Mr. Young

Learn to "make" an exclamation mark (!)
If your machine has an exclamation mark key, the left little finger is used to strike it. To "make" the !:

Strike ' (apostrophe); backspace and strike . (period).

Letter 2
Business Letter

modified block, mixed punctuation; indented ¶s

Learning cue: To place a table within the body of a letter, follow these guidelines.

1. DS above and below the table; SS the body of the table.

2. Clear all tab stops.

3. Determine and set the tab stop for each column of the table. (The table must be centered within the margins of the letter.)

Letter 3
Business Letter

Reformat Letter 2 to:

Miss Michelle L. Mistle
2840 Ardwick Drive
Rockville, MD 20852-4127

Change the certificate number to B-2995 and the value of the certificate to $2,646.16 on the letter to Miss Mistle.

---

opening lines 19

Walstrom Industries has informed us that you have accepted a position in their accounting department and soon will be moving to Rockville. Congratulations and best wishes. | 29 / 39 / 49 / 54

Our bank has designed a packet of information to help new citizens in the community become acquainted with the local area. The packet includes a map of the city, housing and rental guides, and a brochure that highlights upcoming cultural and civic events. This material will provide you with information that will make relocating a little easier. | 65 / 75 / 88 / 100 / 112 / 124

Once you arrive in Rockville, we would appreciate having the opportunity to discuss ways that the First National Bank of Rockville can accommodate your banking needs. (139) | 135 / 147 / 157

Sincerely / Ms. Marge L. Bowman / Customer Service / xx / Enclosures | 169

March 1, 19-- | Mr. Cody G. Sykes | 625 Pacific Avenue | Rockville, MD 20853-3107 | Dear Mr. Sykes: | 14 / 19

How quickly time passes! It seems like only yesterday that you renewed your 24-month certificate of deposit (B-2987) with our bank. On March 15 it will again mature. | 33 / 49 / 53

For your convenience we processed the certificate so that it would be renewed automatically for the same time period at the current market rate. If we do not hear from you prior to the maturity date, your certificate will be renewed at 7.5 percent for the next two years. The value of your certificate as of March 15 will be $1,323.08. | 67 / 83 / 98 / 114 / 121

Should you wish to have the certificate renewed for a longer period of time at a higher interest rate, we can also do that. The time periods and current interest rates are as follows: | 135 / 151 / 158

36-month certificate	7.8 percent	165
48-month certificate	8.1 percent	172
60-month certificate	8.4 percent	178

Call or stop in if you decide to go with a longer period for your certificate. We appreciate your patronage and look forward to assisting with your banking needs in the future. (193) | 194 / 209 / 214

Sincerely, | Mrs. Eiko R. Kimura | Investments | xx | 223

Activity 17
Learn to Copy a Block of Text

1. Read the "In Brief" copy.
2. Study software documentation to learn to copy a text block.
3. Set a 60-space line and 5-space paragraph tab.
4. Read paragraph at right, then key it DS. Center the title using the bold feature.
5. Since the paragraph does not flow very well, it is your asignment to edit it.
6. Instead of trying to rewrite the original paragraph, copy it below its present location.
7. Use all the editing features you have learned until the paragraph is exactly as you want it.
8. Delete the original paragraph.
9. Print a copy.

COPY

Editing feature that allows you to define a block of text (word, phrase, sentence, paragraph, page, or document) in one location of a document and copy (repeat) it in another location of the same document or in a different document. The original block remains intact. First you identify the copy command by striking a specific keystroke combination *(such as the shift and F4 keys)*. Next you identify the block to be copied (word, phrase, etc.). Then you position the cursor in the location where the copied text will appear. To complete the copy function, strike the return key or a special function key as directed in your documentation.

THE RIGHT STUFF

Are you "cut out" to be an entrepreneur? Do you have the "right stuff" to launch a successful business? Some say success depends on education. Others base it on business savvy. Many still call it luck--being in the right place at the right time! What about an individual's personality? Clearly there is no single set of experiences from which today's entrepreneur emerges. What are your goals? Do you have a burning desire to be your own boss? If not, perhaps your goal is to start a business that grows rapidly and helps you amass a fortune. Depending on your goal, personality may be the key in determining your success and happiness.

Activity 18
Learn to Move a Block of Text

1. Read the "In Brief" copy.
2. Study software documentation to learn to move a text block.
3. Set a 70-space line and a 5-space paragraph tab.
4. Read paragraphs at right, then key SS as shown.
5. Using the move feature, make the following changes:

Line
1, move **today** after **loosely**
3, move **simply** after **it**; switch **tear** and **wear**
4, move **people** after **often**
10, move **television** after **viewing**
13 and 14, switch position of lines

6. Use the move feature to move second paragraph to end of the document.
7. Print a copy.

MOVE

Editing feature commonly called "cut and paste" that allows you to remove (cut) a block of text from one location in a document and place (paste) it in a different location within the same document. The original block is removed. First you identify the move command by striking a specific keystroke combination. Next you identify the block to be moved (cut out). Then you position the cursor in the location where the moved text will be retrieved (pasted). Finally, strike the return key or a special function key.

1	Stress today is a term used very loosely. Even though stress is
2	something we are all aware of, we may find the term very difficult to
3	define. To simply put it, stress is the rate of tear and wear within
4	the body. People often report events as stressful when in reality
5	these events turn out to be only symptoms. Some of the more fre-
6	quently reported stressful events include the following:
7	
8	Unfortunately, a common mistake we all make is to respond to
9	stressful situations by avoiding them! A pizza binge, a night of
10	television viewing for eight hours straight, or sleeping the weekend
11	away produces nothing but guilt.
12	
13	* Disagreements and conflict with friends and family.
14	* Too heavy a workload with never-ending deadlines.
15	* Demands being made by everyone around you.
16	* Social activities that are much more pressure than fun.

78c (continued)

Letter 3
Business Letter

plain paper; modified block format; blocked ¶s; open punctuation; correct errors

Address letter to:

Mr. Jonathan R. Coggins
FBLA President
Lincoln High School
5987 Plymouth Drive
Princeton, NJ 07065-8172

Date the letter February 26 and supply an appropriate salutation.

words
opening lines 28

¶ Thank you for your invitation. Jones & Bartells Asso- 39
ciates would be delighted to take part in the career 49
day being sponsored by your FBLA Chapter. 58

¶ This time of year is very busy for accounting firms. 69
However, we will be able to have one of our partners attend 81
during the morning and another in the afternoon. Miss 92
Kathleen Cruz will be there from 9 a.m. to 1 p.m. and Mr. Jay 104
Lorentz will be there for the remainder of the day. 115

¶ Please call Miss Cruz and Mr. Lorentz to finalize 125
the arrangements. Their business cards are enclosed. (110) 135
Sincerely / Seth J. Johnson, CPA / Partner in Charge / xx / 146
Enclosures / c Kathleen A. Cruz / Jay P. Lorentz 155

78d ▶ 10 Improve Language Skills: Word Choice

1. Study the spelling and definition of each word.

2. Key the line number (with period), space twice, then key the **Learn** sentence; key the **Apply** sentences in the same format, selecting the correct word in parentheses to complete the sentences.

3. DS between three-line groups.

want (vb) need, desire; as a noun, lacking a required amount	**peak** (n) pointed end; top of a mountain
won't (vb) will not	**peek** (vb) to glance or look at for a brief time

Learn 1. If they want additional supplies, won't Dr. Greenawalt contact us?
Apply 2. Each (want, won't) was evaluated in terms of the actual cost involved.
Apply 3. If you (want, won't) be leaving until Sunday, you can go to the game.

Learn 4. If you peek around the corner, you will see the mountain peak.
Apply 5. The (peak, peek) of the iceberg was about to disappear from view.
Apply 6. The instructor told the students not to (peak, peek) at the keyboard.

Lesson 79	*Modified Block Letters/Language Skills*

79a ▶ 5
Conditioning Practice

each line twice SS (slowly, then faster); DS between 2-line groups; if time permits, rekey selected lines

alphabet 1 Robert kept examining the size and quality of the very choice jewelry.
figures 2 He scored 94, 75, 82, 64, and 100 on the quizzes for an average of 83.
shift keys 3 Why are Mary and Kathy going to Chicago on Labor Day for eight months?
speed 4 The eight giant signs are downtown by the city chapel by the big lake.

| 1 | 2 | 3 | 4 | 5 | 6 | 7 | 8 | 9 | 10 | 11 | 12 | 13 | 14 |

1. Read the "In Brief" copy.
2. Study software documentation to learn to use the indent feature.
3. Set a 60-space line and 5-space paragraph tab stop.
4. Read the copy at right.
5. Key the copy; DS paragraphs, SS indented text, underline and bold where indicated.
6. Proofread and correct your work; then print a copy.

INDENT

A tab stop set in the ruler/format line to mark the position where every line of text (paragraph or column) will begin from the left margin. When word wrap is on, strike a specific key *(such as F4)* and the indent feature remains in effect until the return key is struck.

THE LIFE OF THE PARTY?

Experts assure us that we're all boring people every now and then. Being judged boring makes most people more upset than being judged incompetent! Since boring people are often rejected because of their conversational style, don't let it happen to you. Be aware of these helpful tips:

1. **Behavior that is tedious.** A boring conversationalist drags a two-minute story into a fifteen-minute event.

2. **Preoccupation with one's self.** Often the most boring individual is the one who wants to talk only about herself/himself.

3. **Out to impress others.** Boring people work too hard to be funny and nice. They're always out to impress others. Often they lack a sense of humor resulting in a conversation that is always "serious."

To avoid being a "yawner" who puts others to sleep at a social gathering, give these tips a try:

1. **Help other people get involved.** Always try to involve other persons in conversation by making clear to each of them that they are as valuable as you.

2. **Ask questions.** To find out what another individual wants to talk about, ask questions. How else can you find a topic that interests her or him?

3. **Gain insight into the other person's feelings.** Ask the other person what he or she thinks about a specific topic. Then talk about that person's ideas and thoughts.

4. **Be natural; always be yourself.** Don't attempt to be witty or clever unless you <u>are</u> witty or clever.

5. **Smile!** A smile is the light in your window that tells people you're a caring individual--someone they'll like a lot.

78a ▶ 5
Conditioning Practice

each line twice SS (slowly, then faster); DS between 2-line groups; if time permits, rekey selected lines

alphabet 1   Pamela Jaworski inquired about the exact size of the very large house.

figures 2   Flight 687 from Boston will arrive at 10:45 a.m. on May 29 at Gate 13.

fig/sym 3   The 5% sales tax on Order #394 is $16.80; for Order #202 it is $17.50.

speed 4   The haughty man may signal with a giant emblem or with the usual sign.

| 1 | 2 | 3 | 4 | 5 | 6 | 7 | 8 | 9 | 10 | 11 | 12 | 13 | 14 |

78b ▶ 7
Formatting Drill: Modified Block Letter

plain paper; 1½" SM

1. Two 1' writings in modified block format on opening lines (date through ¶ 1) of letter on p. 137. Concentrate on correct placement of letter parts.

2. Two 1' writings in modified letter format on closing lines (¶ 3 through copy notation) of letter on p. 137. If you finish before

time is called, DS and begin again. Stress correct placement of letter parts.

78c ▶ 28 *Format Letters in Modified Block Format*

Letter 1 -- Business Letter

plain paper; modified block format, blocked ¶s; open punctuation; correct errors

words

February 21, 19--   4

Mr. Seth J. Johnson   8
Jones & Bartells   11
Accounting Associates   15
2893 Frederick Avenue   20
Princeton, NJ   07067-3093   25

Dear Mr. Johnson   28

Is your company interested in participating in   38
our high school's chapter of Future Business   47
Leaders of America Career Day? It will be held   56
on Friday, March 22, from 9 a.m. to 3 p.m.   65

The purpose of Career Day is to provide a forum   75
for chapter members to become acquainted with   84
occupations they are interested in pursuing.   93
Many members are interested in the field of   102
accounting. It would be great to have Jones &   112
Bartells Accounting Associates be one of the   121
firms representing this dynamic area.   128

If you are interested, please let me know by   137
March 1. One of our members will telephone   146
you with the details of the day's activities. (128)   155

Sincerely   157

Jonathan R. Coggins   161
President   163

xx   164

c Ms. Charla G. Oaks, Advisor   170

Letter 2 -- Personal-Business Letter

plain paper; modified block format, indented ¶s; mixed punctuation; 60-space line; correct errors

words

3988 Bancroft Court   4
Roswell, GA   30075-9082   9
July 2, 19--   11

Attention Software Manager   16
Fehr Computer Products   21
829 Silverwood Drive   26
Atlanta, GA   30349-4217   30

Ladies and Gentlemen: 35

   "QUALITY SYSTEM" WP SOFTWARE

   Last week when I was in Atlanta, I purchased
the "Quality System" word processing software
package from your store. Today when I tried   68
to use the software, I found that there was no   77
user's manual included.   82

   Please send me a copy of the manual as soon   91
as possible so that I will be able to install the   101
software and start using it. I've enclosed a copy   111
of the receipt which contains the identification   121
numbers for the software. (84)   126

Sincerely yours,   130

Mrs. Carla A. Cerone   134

Enclosure   136

Letter 3 is on p. 139.

Activity 20
Learn to Use the Hanging Indent Feature

1. Read the "In Brief" copy.

2. Study software documentation to learn to use the hanging indent feature.

3. Set a 60-space line and 5- and 10-space tab stops.

4. Read the drill at right.

5. Key the drill; DS paragraphs, SS hanging indented text; bold where indicated.

6. Proofread and correct your work; then print a copy.

HANGING INDENT

When you enter a specific command *(such as striking the F4 key then holding down on the shift key and striking Tab),* **this feature positions the first line of a paragraph** at the left margin and the remaining lines indented at a specific tab stop from the left margin. Hanging indent remains until the return key is struck.

GETTING YOUR ACT TOGETHER

Are you involved in the drama club, student council, band, or sports? Have you acquired new interests during the past year? Is your head swimming with new projects? If so, you've probably been asking yourself the same question over and over: "How can I make sure I'll have time to fit everything into my busy schedule?"

The answer: A crash course in time management. Time management skills help you to make the most of each day and to meet your goals almost effortlessly. Consider the following tips for time management.

DAILY TO DOs. Take 10 minutes each morning (when you're fresh and alert) to make a daily "to do" list. Put everything on the list, from feeding the fish and paying a bill to meeting friends for dinner and studying for a test.

"A" AND "B" LISTS. Divide your list into two categories: the "A" items, things that are a must for today; and the "B" items, things that you can put off until tomorrow. When you've completed the lists, rank each item according to its importance, such as A1, A2, B1, B2, etc. This ranking helps you eliminate nonessential, time-consuming tasks from your schedule.

HAVE A MEETING--WITH YOURSELF. Do you let interruptions and distractions get in the way of accomplishing your goals? When the phone rings or a friend stops over to visit, do you stop what you're doing? If that behavior continues, you'll never achieve your objectives. Start setting aside an hour or an hour and a half each day for yourself. Turn off the radio and don't allow interruptions to distract you. Choose a time when your creativity is generally at its peak. Soon you'll find that scheduling a meeting with yourself allows you to accomplish many of your goals.

GET ORGANIZED! Stop spreading yourself thin. If you're like most people, you probably keep information in separate places: a calendar, a phone book, a schedule of appointments, and a datebook. Then you can't find the information when you need it. Purchase a pocket-sized reference folder (the handy, go-anywhere kind) and put all of your information in it. That way you're sure to have what you need when you need it.

DOCUMENT PROCESSING SPECIALISTS
6652 Remington Street
New Haven, CT 06517-1498
(203) 266-8215

		words in parts	total words
Dateline	April 16, 19-- Line 16	3	3
	QS; operate return 4 times to quadruple-space (3 blank lines)		
Letter address	Miss Linda S. LaValley	8	8
	Vermillion Paper Products	13	13
	5067 Blackstone Lane	17	17
	Hartford, CT 06108-4913 DS	22	22
Salutation	Dear Miss LaValley: DS	26	26
Subject line	MODIFIED BLOCK LETTER FORMAT/BLOCKED PARAGRAPHS DS	10	36

This letter is arranged in modified block format with
blocked paragraphs. The only difference between this
letter format and the block format is that the dateline and the closing lines (complimentary close, keyed
name of the originator, and his or her title) begin at
the horizontal center point. DS

20	46
31	57
41	67
52	78
63	89
69	95

Mixed punctuation (a colon after the salutation and a
comma after the complimentary close) is used in this letter. If an enclosure is mentioned in the body of the
letter, the word Enclosure is keyed a double space below
the reference notation, flush with the left margin. Copy
notations are placed a double space below the enclosure
notation or below the reference notation if no enclosure
has been indicated. DS

80	106
91	117
102	128
114	140
125	151
136	163
148	174
152	178

A copy of the block format letter is enclosed so that
you can compare the different formats. As you can see,
either format presents an attractive appearance. DS

163	189
174	200
184	210

Sincerely yours, QS   3   213

Jeffrey R. McKinley

Jeffrey R. McKinley   7   217
Word Processing Consultant DS   13   223

ph DS   13   223

Enclosure DS   15   225

c William L. Gray DS   19   229

Body of letter
Complimentary close
Keyed name
Official title
Reference notation
Enclosure notation
Copy notation

Shown in pica type
1½" side margins
camera reduced

Modified Block with Blocked Paragraphs and Mixed Punctuation

Activity 21
Learn to Set Column Tabs

1. Read the "In Brief" copy.
2. Study software documentation to learn to set column tabs.
3. Format the table SS; DS below the main heading.
4. Proofread and correct your work; then print the table.

COLUMN TABS

1. Identify the longest item in each column and determine the number of spaces to be placed between columns.
2. Use the automatic centering feature: key these items and spaces (Step 1) on the line.
3. Move the cursor to the beginning of the first column; note (write down) the cursor position.

4. Repeat Step 3 for each remaining column.
5. Clear all tabs in the ruler line.
6. Set tabs in the ruler line at the positions noted in Steps 3 and 4.
7. Delete the line keyed in Step 2.
8. Key the table.

SPELLING WORDS FOR WEEK OF 01/02/--

accommodate	committee	industrial	participation
appreciate	correspondence	interest	personnel
appropriate	customer	maintenance	possibility
categories	eligible	monitoring	recommend
commitment	immediately	necessary	services

Activity 22
Learn to Set Right Alignment Tabs

1. Read the "In Brief" copy.
2. Study software documentation to learn to set right alignment tabs.
3. Format Drill 1 DS.
4. Proofread and correct your work; then print the table.
5. Repeat Steps 3 and 4 for Drill 2.

RIGHT ALIGNMENT TAB

A tab position set in the ruler line to align a column of text on the right (called "flush right" or "right justified"). A right alignment tab is set in the last position of the longest line in the column.

Often a right alignment tab is set by striking R, which then may display on the ruler line. Copy that is keyed at that tab will "back up" from the tab, ending where the tab is set.

Follow the usual procedure for determining and setting the left margin and for noting (writing down) the position, EXCEPT place right tabs at the <u>end</u> of the column.

Drill 1

WOMEN'S TEAM CAPTAINS

Basketball	Diana Lindsay
Gymnastics	Lili Wong
Soccer	Adia Lopez
Softball	Nancy Brand
Volleyball	Glenda Ford

Drill 2

MEN'S TEAM CAPTAINS

Baseball	Ken Morrison
Basketball	Cy Briggs
Football	Joe Hererra
Gymnastics	Kevin Kwan
Soccer	Bo Simpson

Activity 23
Learn to Set Decimal Tabs

1. Read the "In Brief" copy.
2. Study software documentation to learn to set decimal tabs.
3. Format the table SS.
4. Proofread and correct the table; then print it.

DECIMAL TAB

A tab position set in the ruler line to align numbers at the decimal point. Follow the usual procedure for determining and setting the left margin and for determining tab positions, EXCEPT place decimal tabs at the decimal position, not at the beginning of the column. A decimal tab often is indicated by striking D, which then may display in the ruler line.

Figures entered at a decimal tab "back up" from the tab until the decimal key (.) is struck; then the figures appear aligned at the decimal point. Whole numbers are treated by the decimal tab feature as though a decimal point follows the last figure.

TEST SCORES/AVERAGE SCORE--UNITS 1-3

Adams, R.	75	89.5	82.75	82.42
Ellis, L.	89.25	94	96.25	93.17
Jenkins, Z.	68.75	75.25	71	71.67
Oblinger, S.	85	89	93.5	89.17
Trabel, D.	71.5	68.25	75	71.58
Worrell, K.	82.75	89	75.5	82.42

77a ▶ 5
Conditioning
Practice

each line twice SS
(slowly, then faster);
DS between 2-line
groups; if time permits,
rekey selected lines

alphabet 1   Jack answered many questions about the exact value of each topaz ring.

figures 2   On Monday, November 14, 1988 I bought pattern numbers 32A57 and 60B94.

fig/sym 3   The 1987 cost ($414) was 15 percent greater than the 1982 cost ($360).

speed 4   The neighbor's dog was with the girl by the big sign in the cornfield.

| 1 | 2 | 3 | 4 | 5 | 6 | 7 | 8 | 9 | 10 | 11 | 12 | 13 | 14 |

77b ▶ 35 Learn to Format Letters in Modified Block Format

plain full sheet; correct errors

1. Read the information at the right and study the model letter on page 137 illustrating modified block format (blocked paragraphs) with mixed punctuation.

2. Key the model letter using the Letter Placement Guide on page 76 to determine correct side margins and placement. The body of the letter contains 173 standard 5-stroke words.

3. Key letter again, but address it to

**Mr. Karl M. Bedford
Berwick Drilling Co.
1088 Windsor Avenue
Waco, TX 76708-9316**

4. Indent the subject line and ¶s and change "blocked" to "indented" in the subject line.

5. For the first two lines, substitute the following:

Modified Block Letter Format

"Modified Block" simply means that the block format has been *modified*; that is, the date and the closing lines (complimentary close, writer's name, and writer's job title or department) start at the horizontal center of the paper instead of at the left margin. Modified block format may have either blocked (p. 137) or indented (see model at right) paragraphs.

Open and Mixed Punctuation

A letter in modified block format may be keyed with either open or mixed punctuation. In *open punctuation,* no punctuation follows the salutation or the complimentary close. In *mixed punctuation,* a colon follows the salutation and a comma follows the complimentary close.

```
This letter is arranged in modified block format
with indented subject line and paragraphs. Another
difference (continue lines) .
```

77c ▶ 10 Check Language Skills: Capitalization

SS sentences; DS between 5-line groups

1. Key line number (with period); space twice, then key the sentence, supplying the needed capital letters.

2. If time permits, key the sentences again to increase decision-making speed.

1. sacred heart hospital is located on madison or monroe street.
2. reno, las vegas, and sparks are the largest cities in nevada.
3. is your dental appointment with dr. hall in november or december?
4. the next phi beta lambda meeting will be wednesday, september 12.
5. my favorite holidays are thanksgiving day and the fourth of july.

6. mr. jay told us to key lines 7, 8, and 9 on page 20 of lesson 9.
7. aaa must be the abbreviation for american automobile association.
8. the next commencement address will be given by president miller.
9. is mt. rushmore located in south dakota or in north dakota?
10. alex and damion both live in mead hall on lincoln boulevard.

11. mary will arrive this wednesday at noon on american airlines.
12. the california angels beat the new york yankees on friday night.
13. the secretary for future business leaders of america is oki saga.
14. the steam engine played a major part in the industrial revolution.
15. yellowstone lake and jackson lake are both located in wyoming.

Begin all tables on line 10 or as directed by your teacher. Clear all preset tabs from the ruler line before setting tabs for a table.

Activity 24
Two-Column Table with Right Alignment Tab

1. Format the table at the right DS. Use the centering feature to center the main and secondary headings; use a right alignment tab for the right-hand column.

2. Proofread and correct errors; then print the table.

Activity 25
Three-Column Table with Column and Right Alignment Tabs

1. Format the table at the right SS. Use the centering feature to center the main and secondary headings; use the bold feature for the main heading. Block the column heads as shown.

2. Use the underline feature to key a line a DS below the table; then DS to the source note. (If your equipment will not display or print the line, insert the line with a pen on the printed table.)

Activity 26
Multi-Column Table with Decimal Tab

1. Format the table at the right DS. Use the centering feature to center the main and secondary headings. To determine the left margin (center the table), use the column heading if it is the longest line in the column. Key the column headings before setting decimal tabs.

2. Use the underline feature to key a line between the table and source note or use a pen to insert the line on the printed table.

3. Proofread and correct the table; then print.

Riverfront Dinner Show

Week of March 12-16

Dinner Music	Lou Springer
Emcee	Eric Simpson
Dance Demo	Valley School of Dance
Music and Humor	Halcyon Days
Comedy	Fred Hines
Dance Band	Halcyon Days

MOTION PICTURE ACADEMY AWARDS (OSCARS)

1980 - 1989

Year	Movie Title	Studio
1980	Ordinary People	Paramount
1981	Chariots of Fire	Warner Bros
1982	Gandhi	Columbia
1983	Terms of Endearment	Paramount
1984	Amadeus	Orion Pictures
1985	Out of Africa	Universal
1986	Platoon	Orion Pictures
1987	The Last Emperor	Columbia
1988	Rain Man	United Artists
1989	Driving Miss Daisy	Warner Bros.

Source: <u>Information Please Almanac</u>, 1990.

Temperature of Selected Metropolitan Areas

Average Monthly Fahrenheit Degrees

Metro Area	January	April	July	October
Chicago	21.4	48.8	73	53.5
Dallas-Fort Worth	44	65.9	86.3	67.9
Detroit	23.4	47.3	71.9	51.9
Houston	51.4	68.7	83.1	69.7
Los Angeles	56	59.5	69	66.3
New York	31.8	51.9	76.4	57.5
Washington	35.2	56.7	78.9	59.3

Source: <u>Information Please Almanac</u>, 1990.

76c ▶ 35
Review Document Formatting Skill: Letters

3 plain full sheets

Letter 1
Personal-Business Letter

Format and key in block style the letter shown at the right. Use a 60-space line; place date on line 16. (See p. 70 for model.) Correct any errors you make as you key.

3716 Rangely Drive | Raleigh, NC 27609-4115 | October 14, 19-- | Mr. Robert C.   15
Johnson | Wayler Insurance Company | 206 Polk Street | Raleigh, NC 27604-   28
4120 | Dear Mr. Johnson | Subject: INFORMATION ON CAREER OPPORTUNITIES   40

Please send me information on career opportunities available with Wayler   55
Insurance Company in the administrative services area. As part of a class   70
assignment, I will be giving an oral report on a company for which I would   85
be interested in working. Wayler Insurance is an impressive company, and   99
I would like to do the report on career opportunities with your firm.   114

The report needs to address job titles, job requirements, educational require-   129
ments, salary, and opportunities for advancement. Any information that you   144
are able to provide on these areas will be greatly appreciated.   157

Sincerely | Richard B. Lyons | xx   163

Placement Note

Use the Letter Placement Guide on page 76 to determine margins and dateline placement for business letters in this unit. The number of words in the body is indicated by the number in parentheses at the end of each letter.

Letter 2
Business Letter

Format in block style with open punctuation the letter shown at the right. Correct any errors you make as you key.

October 20, 19-- | Mr. Richard B. Lyons | 3716 Rangely Drive | Raleigh, NC   14
27609-4115 | Dear Mr. Lyons   19

Wayler Insurance Company is always interested in potential employees. We   34
hope that you will consider us once you are graduated.   45

As you will see from reading the information which is enclosed, we have   59
different levels of administrative support positions in our company. Job ti-   75
tles, job requirements, educational requirements, and starting salaries are   90
included for each level. Our company philosophy is to reward loyal employees;   106
therefore, we like to promote from within when qualified employees are avail-   121
able. We also reimburse employees for additional job-related schooling   135
completed during their employment.   142

If you need further information or would like one of our administrative sup-   157
port supervisors to talk with your class, please call us. (words in body: 149)   169

Sincerely yours | Robert C. Johnson | Customer Relations Director | xx | Enclosure   184

Letter 3
Business Letter

Format in block style with open punctuation the letter shown at the right. Use the address and date given in Letter 2. Use an appropriate salutation. Correct any errors you make as you key.

opening lines 19

Robert Johnson, our director of customer relations, indicated that you are   34
interested in career opportunities with Wayler Insurance Company in the   48
administrative support services division. He asked me to provide you with   63
additional information.   69

As word processing supervisor, I have the opportunity to interview and test   84
many applicants. We are looking for applicants with excellent communi-   98
cation and keyboarding skills. Both are extremely important skills for indi-   113
viduals to possess in order to be an asset to our organization. Any course you   129
take to enhance these skills will increase your marketability.   142

If you would like to visit our word processing center before giving your re-   157
port, please let me know. You can telephone me at 833-7291. (149)   169

Sincerely yours | Mrs. Mary A. Worthington | Word Processing Supervisor | 183
xx | c Robert C. Johnson   187

Begin all tables on line 10 or as directed by your teacher. Clear all preset tabs from the ruler line before setting tabs for a table.

Activity 27
Three-Column Table with Right, Column, and Decimal Tab

1. Format the table at the right DS, setting the appropriate tab for each column. Block the column headings as shown. Key the column headings before setting tabs.

2. Proofread; correct errors; print the table.

Activity 28
Four-Column Table with Varied Tabs

1. Format the table at the right DS, using the appropriate tab for each column. Note (write down) the positions where columns begin and end; on a separate list note the position for each tab.

2. To center column headings, add the numbers representing the beginning and ending positions of the column; divide by 2. (The result is the center of the column.) Count the spaces in the column heading; divide by 2. Subtract the result from the center position. (Begin the column heading in this position.)

3. Proofread your work, checking for format errors as well as misstrokes. Make necessary corrections; then print the table.

Activity 29
Four-Column Table with Decimal and Right Alignment Tabs

1. Format the table at the right SS, using the appropriate tab for each column. Center the column headings (See Step 2, Activity 28).

2. Use the underline feature as you key the last number in each amount column. (If necessary, insert the underlines on the printed table with a pen.)

3. Proofread carefully before printing the table.

PRICE QUOTATION FOR MORTON ASSOCIATES INC.

Item No.	Description	Unit Price
PC-4001A	Microprocessor	$2,895
PC-4031A	Input/Output Units	589
PC-4041A	Dual Disk Drive	416
4050NM	Color Monitor	325
4054M	B/W Monitor	195
840X	Glare Guard	94.95
PC-4024A	Dot Matrix Printer	325
7210X	Printer Stand	194.95
704X	Power Surge Strips	69.95

CLIENT CONTACTS MADE BY SHEILA SANDERS
Week Ending February 2, 19--

Client	Date	Hours	Site
Swatzky	January 28	1.5	His Office
Grossmane	January 29	.17	Telephone
Schlosser	January 29	.42	Telephone
Wagner	January 30	2	Their Office
Cook	January 30	2.25	Their Office
Washburn	January 31	1.75	Their Office
Murphy	January 31	1	My Office
O'Connor	February 1	.75	Telephone
Daniels	February 1	1.5	Their Office
Miller	February 2	2.5	Their Office

Regional Sales (In Millions)

Region	This Year	Last Year	% Change
Central	$3.0	$2.8	7% inc.
Northeast	.6	.5	20% inc.
Northwest	2.1	2.0	5% inc.
Southeast	1.8	1.8	0% none
Southwest	1.6	1.4	14% inc.
Total	$9.1	$8.5	

Improve Letter/Memo Formatting Skills

Learning Goals

1. To review/improve letter and memo formatting skills.
2. To learn to format business letters in modified block style.
3. To check/improve language skills.

Format Guides

1. Paper guide at *0* (for typewriters).
2. LL (line length): 70 spaces for drills and ¶s; as specified in placement table for letters, p. 76; 1″ margins for memos.
3. LS (line spacing): SS drills, letters, and memos; DS ¶s.
4. PI (paragraph indention): 5 when appropriate.

| Lesson 76 | Keyboarding Skills/Letters |

76a ▶ 5
Conditioning Practice

each line twice SS (slowly, then faster); DS between 2-line groups; as time permits, rekey selected lines

alphabet 1 Mr. Zahn will ask very specific questions before judging the exhibits.

figures 2 Only 32 of the 64 computers were replaced in 1990 with the B758 model.

space bar 3 It may not be too late for him to bake the cake in time for the party.

speed 4 The formal social for the visitor is to be held in the ancient chapel.

| 1 | 2 | 3 | 4 | 5 | 6 | 7 | 8 | 9 | 10 | 11 | 12 | 13 | 14 |

76b ▶ 10 Check Keyboarding Skill: Straight Copy

1. A 3′ writing on ¶s 1-3 combined; find *gwam*, circle errors.

2. A 1′ writing on each ¶; find *gwam*, circle errors.

3. Another 3′ writing on ¶s 1-3 combined, find *gwam*, circle errors.

4. Record your better 3′ rate for comparison in 81b, page 143.

Additional Skill Building

As time permits during the unit

1. Take a series of 1′ *guided* writings on each of the 3 ¶s using the plan given on p. 38.

2. Take additional 3′ writings to check skill increases.

all letters used | A | 1.5 si | 5.7 awl | 80% hfw |

gwam 3′ | 5′

People in business are concerned about what is communicated by the — 4 | 3

written word. As they write memos, letters, and reports, they may plan — 9 | 6

for the content but may not plan for the image of the message. Experts, — 14 | 8

however, realize that neglecting the way a document looks can be costly. — 19 | 11

Many times a written piece of correspondence is the only basis on — 23 | 14

which a person can form an impression of the writer. Judgments based on — 28 | 17

a first impression that may be formed by the reader about the writer — 33 | 20

should always be considered before mailing a document. — 36 | 22

The way a document looks can communicate as much as what it says. — 41 | 25

Margins, spacing, and placement are all important features to consider — 46 | 27

when you key a document. A quality document is one that will bring the — 50 | 30

interest of the reader to the message rather than to the way it appears. — 55 | 33

gwam 3′ | 1 | 2 | 3 | 4 | 5 |
5′ | 1 | 2 | 3 |

Activity 30
Learn About Boilerplate Documents, the Merge Feature, and Stop Codes

1. Read the "In Brief" copy.

2. Study software documentation to learn which specific features are offered by your program.

3. Format the memo (60-space line) at the right below on plain paper. Set a right alignment tab for the colon sequence and a tab for the text in the memo headings. DS between memo headings.

4. Key the document using your program's stop code (or merge code) wherever the @1, @2, @3, etc., symbol appears.

5. Save the document.

6. Print the document three times; insert the following variables in the first printout.

@1 Olivian DeSouza
@2 (yesterday's date)
@3 Ms. DeSouza
@4 crepe hangers
@5 "It won't work"
@6 downers
@7 Ms. DeSouza
@8 Thursday morning

The second document variables:

@1 Maurizio Chuidioni
@2 (today's date)
@3 Mr. Chuidioni
@4 ones with their chins on their shoes
@5 "It's no use trying"
@6 pessimists
@7 Mr. Chuidioni
@8 Wednesday afternoon

The third document variables:

@1 Miyoki Kojima
@2 (tomorrow's date)
@3 Dr. Kojima
@4 ones who think nothing ever goes their way and
@5 "Are you serious?"
@6 negativists
@7 Dr. Kojima
@8 Tuesday afternoon

BOILERPLATE DOCUMENT

A document, such as a form letter or sales contract that is used again and again, in which most of the text remains the same each time. Only names and certain details, such as amounts and dates, are changed here and there within the document.

CONSTANT

The text in a boilerplate document that remains the same for each use of the document.

VARIABLE

The text (names, phrases, dates, etc.) in a boilerplate document that is changed to "personalize" the document.

STOP CODES

A command (or symbol) embedded within a boilerplate document. While printing a document, the printer stops when it recognizes the "stop" command allowing the user to key variable (personalized) information. The user then must strike a designated key to reactivate the printer until the next stop code is recognized.

PRIMARY DOCUMENT

A word processing document made up of the constant and embedded codes.

SECONDARY DOCUMENT

A word processing document consisting only of the variables.

MERGE

Word processing feature that allows the user to combine a primary document and secondary documents to print "personalized" documents.

```
        TO:  @1
      FROM:  Dan Henderson
   SUBJECT:  Positively! Seminars
      DATE:  @2
```

Although they're often reasonably competent people, negativists can unnerve, devitalize, exhaust, and fatigue the best of us. I'm certain, @3 that you've met at least one or two of them. They're the @4 who respond to anyone else's productive suggestion with @5 or "Forget it, we tried that last year" or "Why waste your time; they'll never let you do it."

What is needed to get the best from @6 in the workplace? An upbeat attitude, that's what! Have you checked yours lately? We all have the potential for being dragged down into despair. @7, is your attitude showing?

This question and many others will be answered for you in the Positively! seminars next week. The seminar presenter, Adele Cook, a nationally known speaker/trainer/consultant, will conduct sessions in Conference Room D.

Sessions are scheduled from 1 to 4 on Monday through Thursday and from 9 to 12 on Tuesday through Friday. The people in your area are to attend the @8 session.

This seminar will pick up where Ms. Cook's sessions ended last year. Distribute the attached materials, please.

Attachments

IMPROVE KEYBOARDING, FORMATTING, AND LANGUAGE SKILLS

In the 25 lessons of Phase 4, you will:

1. Refine technique patterns.

2. Improve basic keyboarding and language skills.

3. Improve skill on rough-draft and script copy.

4. Improve formatting and production skill on memos, letters, reports, and tables.

5. Learn to format in modified block style.

6. Apply formatting skills to process a series of documents for a simulated real estate office.

7. Measure and evaluate document processing skills.

Format the copy at the right as an unbound report, employing the word processing features you have learned.

1. Use the automatic centering and bold text features for the main heading; and, the automatic underline feature for the side headings.

2. For the enumerated items and items at the end of the report, use the hang indent feature.

3. If a widow/orphan feature is available on your software, use it to prevent widows and orphans.

4. After keying the document, turn on the hyphenation feature, if the feature is available on your software, and use it to divide words properly at line endings.

5. Use the page format (automatic page breaks) feature to assure a bottom margin of 1 inch.

6. Using the header/footer feature, create a header on line 6 of the second page; key **TIME MANAGEMENT** at the left margin and the page number flush right.

7. Proofread the document on the screen. Make necessary corrections and format changes; then print the document.

TIME MANAGEMENT: PLAN FOR ATTACK

Do you have time management problems? If so, you belong to a large group with a growing membership. Why should you care about managing your time? Because time is life and when you waste your time, you're wasting your life! Time management revolves around the principle of effectiveness over efficiency. Efficiency refers to how well something is done; effectiveness refers to whether something should be done at all. Effectiveness means making the right choice from all the tasks available and doing it the best way possible. Efficiency is a good trait, but effectiveness should become one of your most important goals.

The Culprits Attack

Culprits surround us every minute of the day. If you look carefully, you'll be able to identify several culprits undermining your efforts toward the best use of your time:

1. Time is a limited, unique commodity. Unfortunately, most people excel at squandering it.

2. It's easy to establish broad goals such as wanting to be healthy, wealthy, and wise, but very rarely do people establish specific goals.

3. Everyone wants some of your time. But if you're busy taking care of everybody else's needs and desires, there's little time left for planning your own time.

4. Does a crisis turn you into an adrenaline junkie? Do you rely on the excuse: "I work best under pressure"?

5. Fear! Regardless of the kind (fear of success, fear of failure, fear of alienating others, etc.), fear often immobilizes a person.

Counterattack

To fight back against these culprits, an individual must devise a plan of action. The following tips serve as a battle plan in the counterattack.

Time is money; therefore, place a dollar value on your time. You're less likely to give up something that costs money.

Determine realistic objectives for yourself. Write them down and specify a date of accomplishment. When you write down your goals, you're less likely to daydream.

Since all objectives are not of equal value, establish priorities. Base your priorities on what is important to you now, not on the ease or your liking for the task.

Learn to say "no." "No" must become a part of a person's vocabulary. Otherwise, time is frittered away at someone else's request.

Set aside a block of time for yourself each day. Use this time to think and plan for immediate and long-range goals.

Skill Comparison: Sentences

LL: 70 spaces;
LS: SS; DS between groups

1. Key lines 1, 3, 5, 7, and 9 at your own pace to master keystroking patterns.

2. Key a 1' writing on line 2 to establish a goal rate.

3. Key a 1' writing on each of lines 4, 6, 8, and 10; calculate *gwam* on each.

4. Compare rates on the 5 timed writings.

5. Key additional 1' writings on each of the slower lines.

balanced-hand words	1	if he but own held firm sign visit girls profit height entitle visible
	2	The men may visit the ancient town by the lake when he signs the form.
double-letter words	3	all too off zoo good food door hall keep small issue sorry allow shall
	4	All seem to meet my new speed goal; few will keep within three errors.
combination response	5	six you the joy for are also best such only form wear work union title
	6	Only six of them serve on the wage panel for the oil union in my town.
adjacent-key words	7	as buy saw top try pod fort post ruin owes coin dare glass opens moist
	8	We are going to post top scores at the regional meet and at the state.
long-reach words	9	my sun ice mug sum gym sect nice curb bran must cent under bring curve
	10	Myra served a number of guests a mug of iced punch after the gym meet.

| 1 | 2 | 3 | 4 | 5 | 6 | 7 | 8 | 9 | 10 | 11 | 12 | 13 | 14 |

Timed Writing: Paragraphs

1. Take a 1' writing on ¶ 1; calculate *gwam*. Add 2-4 words to set a new goal rate.

2. Take two 1' writings on ¶ 1 at your new goal rate, guided by a ¼' call of the guide.

3. Key ¶ 2 in the same way.

4. Key a 3' or a 5' writing on ¶s 1-2 combined; calculate *gwam*; circle errors.

5. If time permits, key additional 1' writings on each ¶ for speed or for control, according to your needs.

all letters used | A | 1.5 si | 5.7 awl | 80% hfw

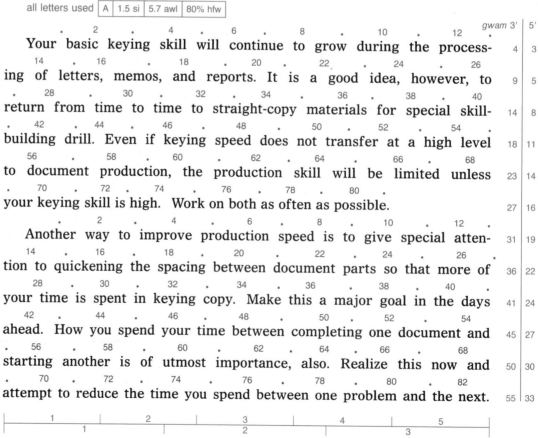

	gwam 3'	5'
Your basic keying skill will continue to grow during the process-	4	3
ing of letters, memos, and reports. It is a good idea, however, to	9	5
return from time to time to straight-copy materials for special skill-	14	8
building drill. Even if keying speed does not transfer at a high level	18	11
to document production, the production skill will be limited unless	23	14
your keying skill is high. Work on both as often as possible.	27	16
Another way to improve production speed is to give special atten-	31	19
tion to quickening the spacing between document parts so that more of	36	22
your time is spent in keying copy. Make this a major goal in the days	41	24
ahead. How you spend your time between completing one document and	45	27
starting another is of utmost importance, also. Realize this now and	50	30
attempt to reduce the time you spend between one problem and the next.	55	33

gwam 3' | 1 | 2 | 3 | 4 | 5 |
5' | 1 | 2 | 3 |

CAPITALIZATION GUIDES

■ Capitalize

1 The first word of every sentence and the first word of every complete direct quotation. Do not capitalize (a) fragments of quotations or (b) a quotation resumed within a sentence.

She said, "Hard work is necessary for success."
He stressed the importance of "a sense of values."
"When all else fails," he said, "follow directions."

2 The first word after a colon if that word begins a complete sentence.

Remember this: Work with good techniques.
We carry these sizes: small, medium, and large.

3 First, last, and all other words in titles of books, articles, periodicals, headings, and plays, except words of four or fewer letters used as articles, conjunctions, or prepositions.

Century 21 Keyboarding   "How to Buy a House"
Saturday Review   "The Sound of Music"

4 An official title when it precedes a name or when used elsewhere if it is a title of distinction.

President Lincoln   She is the Prime Minister.
The doctor is in.   He is the class treasurer.

5 Personal titles and names of people and places.

Miss Franks   Dr. Jose F. Ortez   San Diego

6 All proper nouns and their derivatives.

Canada   Canadian Festival   France   French food

7 Days of the week, months of the year, holidays, periods of history, and historic events.

Sunday   Labor Day   New Year's Day
June   Middle Ages   Civil War

8 Geographic regions, localities, and names.

the North   Upstate New York   Mississippi River

9 Street, avenue, company, etc., when used with a proper noun.

Fifth Avenue   Avenue of the Stars   Armour & Co.

10 Names of organizations, clubs, and buildings.

Girl Scouts   4-H Club   Carew Tower

11 A noun preceding a figure except for common nouns such as *line, page,* and *sentence,* which may be keyed with or without a capital.

Style 143   Catalog 6   page 247   line 10

12 Seasons of the year only when they are personified.

icy fingers of Winter   the soft kiss of Spring

NUMBER EXPRESSION GUIDES

■ Use words for

1 Numbers from one to ten except when used with numbers above ten, which are keyed as figures. Note: Common business practice is to use figures for all numbers except those which begin a sentence.

Was the order for four or eight books?
Order 8 shorthand books and 15 English books.

2 A number beginning a sentence.

Fifteen persons are here; 12 are at home sick.

3 The shorter of two numbers used together.

ten 50-gallon drums   350 five-gallon drums

4 Isolated fractions or indefinite amounts in a sentence.

Nearly two thirds of the students are here.
About twenty-five people came to the meeting.

5 Names of small-numbered streets and avenues (ten and under).

1020 Sixth Street   Tenth Avenue

■ Use figures for

1 Dates and time, except in very formal writing.

May 9, 1982   10:15 a.m.
ninth of May   four o'clock

2 A series of fractions.

Key 1/2, 1/4, 5/6, and 7 3/4.

3 Numbers following nouns.

Rule 12   page 179   Room 1208   Chapter 15

4 Measures, weights, and dimensions.

6 ft. 9 in. tall   5 lbs. 4 oz.   8 1/2″ × 11″

5 Definite numbers used with the percent sign (%); but use *percent* (spelled) with approximations in formal writing.

The rate is 15 1/2%.
About 50 percent of the work is done.

6 House numbers except house number One.

1915-42d Street   One Jefferson Avenue

7 Sums of money except when spelled for extra emphasis. Even sums may be keyed without the decimal.

$10.75   25 cents $300
seven hundred dollars ($700)

■ Use an apostrophe

1 As a symbol for *feet* in billings or tabulations or as a symbol for *minutes.* (The quotation mark may be used as a symbol for *seconds* and *inches.*)

12' × 16'	3' 54"	8'6" × 10'8"

2 As a symbol to indicate the omission of letters or figures (as in contractions).

can't	wouldn't	Spirit of '76

3 To form the plural of most figures, letters, and words used as words rather than for their meaning. Add the apostrophe and *s.* In market quotations, form the plural of figures by the addition of *s* only.

6's	A's	five's	ABC's	Century Fund 4s

4 To show possession: Add the apostrophe and *s* to (a) a singular noun and (b) a plural noun which does not end in *s.*

a man's watch	women's shoes	boy's bicycle

Add the apostrophe and *s* to a proper name of one syllable which ends in *s.*

Bess's Cafeteria	Jones's bill

Add the apostrophe only after (a) plural nouns ending in *s* and (b) a proper name of more than one syllable which ends in *s* or *z.*

boys' camp	Adams' home	Melendez' report

Add the apostrophe after the last noun in a series to indicate joint or common possession of two or more persons; however, add the possessive to each of the nouns to show separate possession of two or more persons.

Lewis and Clark's expedition
the manager's and the treasurer's reports

■ Use a colon

1 To introduce an enumeration or a listing.

These are my favorite poets: Shelley, Keats, and Frost.

2 To introduce a question or a long direct quotation.

This is the question: Did you study for the test?

3 Between hours and minutes expressed in figures.

10:15 a.m.	12:00	4:30 p.m.

■ Use a comma (or commas)

1 After (a) introductory words, phrases, or clauses and (b) words in a series.

If you can, try to visit Chicago, St. Louis, and Dallas.

2 To set off short direct quotations.

She said, "If you try, you can reach your goal."

3 Before and after (a) words which come together and refer to the same person, thing, or idea and (b) words of direct address.

Clarissa, our class president, will give the report.
I was glad to see you, Terrence, at the meeting.

4 To set off nonrestrictive clauses (not necessary to the meaning of the sentence), but not restrictive clauses (necessary to the meaning).

Your report, which deals with the issue, is great.
The girl who just left is my sister.

5 To separate the day from the year and the city from the state.

July 4, 1986	New Haven, Connecticut

6 To separate two or more parallel adjectives (adjectives that could be separated by the word "and" instead of the comma).

a group of young, old, and middle-aged persons

Do not use commas to separate adjectives so closely related that they appear to form a single element with the noun they modify.

a dozen large red roses	a small square box

7 To separate (a) unrelated groups of figures which come together and (b) whole numbers into groups of three digits each (however, *policy, year, page, room, telephone,* and most *serial numbers* are shown without commas).

During 1991, 1,750 cars were insured under Policy 806423.

page 1042	Room 1184	(213) 825-2626

■ Use a dash

1 For emphasis.

The icy road--slippery as a fish--was a hazard.

2 To indicate a change of thought.

We may tour the Orient--but I'm getting ahead of my story.

3 To introduce the name of an author when it follows a direct quotation.

"Hitting the wrong key is like hitting me."--Armour

4 For certain special purposes.

"Well--er--ah," he stammered.
"Jay, don't get too close to the --." It was too late.

■ Use an exclamation mark

1 After emphatic interjections.

Wow!   Hey there!   What a day!

2 After sentences that are clearly exclamatory.

"I won't go!" she said with determination.
How good it was to see you in New Orleans last
  week!

■ Use a hyphen

1 To join compound numbers from twenty-one to ninety-nine that are keyed as words.

forty-six   fifty-eight   over seventy-six

2 To join compound adjectives before a noun which they modify as a unit.

well-laid plans six-year period two-thirds majority

3 After each word or figure in a series of words or figures that modify the same noun (suspended hyphenation).

first-, second-, and third-class reservations

4 To spell out a word or name.

s-e-p-a-r-a-t-e   G-a-e-l-i-c

5 To form certain compound nouns.

WLW-TV   teacher-counselor   AFL-CIO

■ Use parentheses

1 To enclose parenthetical or explanatory matter and added information.

The amendments (Exhibit A) are enclosed.

2 To enclose identifying letters or figures in lists.

Check these factors: (1) period of time, (2) rate of
  pay, and (3) nature of duties.

3 To enclose figures that follow spelled-out amounts to give added clarity or emphasis.

The total award is five hundred dollars ($500).

■ Use a question mark

At the end of a sentence that is a direct question; however, use a period after a request in the form of a question.

What day do you plan to leave for Honolulu?
Will you mail this letter for me, please.

■ Use quotation marks

1 To enclose direct quotations.

He said, "I'll be there at eight o'clock."

2 To enclose titles of articles and other parts of complete publications, short poems, song titles, television programs, and unpublished works like theses and dissertations.

"Sesame Street"   "Chicago" by Sandburg
"Laura's Theme"   "Murder She Wrote"

3 To enclose special words or phrases, or coined words.

"power up" procedure   "Murphy's Law"

■ Use a semicolon

1 To separate two or more independent clauses in a compound sentence when the conjunction is omitted.

Being critical is easy; being constructive is not
  so easy.

2 To separate independent clauses when they are joined by a conjunctive adverb (*however, consequently*, etc.).

I can go; however, I must get excused.

3 To separate a series of phrases or clauses (especially if they contain commas) that are introduced by a colon.

These officers were elected: Lu Ming, President;
  Lisa Stein, vice president; Juan Ramos, secretary.

4 To precede an abbreviation or word that introduces an explanatory statement.

She organized her work; for example, putting work
  to be done in folders of different colors to indicate
  degrees of urgency.

■ Use an underline

1 With titles of complete works such as books, magazines, and newspapers. (Such titles may also be keyed in ALL CAPS without the underline.)

SuperWrite   The New York Times   TV Guide

2 To call attention to special words or phrases (or you may use quotation marks). **Note:** Use a continuous underline unless each word is to be considered separately.

Stop keying when time is called.
Spell these words: steel, occur, separate.

■ **Use a singular verb**

1 With a singular subject.

The weather is clear but cold.

2 With an indefinite pronoun used as a subject (each, every, any, either, neither, one, etc.).

Each of you is to bring a pen and paper.
Neither of us is likely to be picked.

3 With singular subjects linked by *or* or *nor*. If, however, one subject is singular and the other is plural, the verb should agree with the closer subject.

Either Jan or Fred is to make the presentation.
Neither the principal nor the teachers are here.

4 With a collective noun (*committee, team, class, jury,* etc.) if the collective noun acts as a unit.

The jury has returned to the courtroom.
The committee has filed its report.

5 With the pronouns *all* and *some* (as well as fractions and percentages) when used as subjects *if* their modifiers are singular. Use a plural verb *if* their modifiers are plural.

All of the books have been classified.
Some of the gas is being pumped into the tank.

6 When *number* is used as the subject and is preceded by *the*; however, use a plural verb if *number* is preceded by a.

The number of voters has increased this year.
A number of workers are on vacation.

■ **Use a plural verb**

1 With a plural subject.

The blossoms are losing their petals.

2 With a compound subject joined by *and*.

My mother and my father are the same age.

■ **Negative forms of verbs**

1 Use the plural verb *do not* (or the contraction *don't*) when the pronoun *I, we, you,* or *they,* as well as a plural noun, is used as the subject.

You don't have a leg to stand on in this case.
The scissors do not cut properly.
I don't believe that answer is correct.

2 Use the singular verb *does not* (or the contraction *doesn't*) when the pronoun *he, she,* or *it,* as well as a singular noun, is used as the subject.

She doesn't want to attend the meeting.
It does not seem possible that winter's here.

■ **Pronoun agreement with antecedents**

1 Pronouns (*I, we, she, he, it, their,* etc.) agree with their antecedent *in person*--person speaking, first person; person spoken to, second person; person spoken about, third person.

We said we would go when we complete our work.
When you enter, present your invitation.
All who saw the show found that they were moved.

2 Pronouns agree with their antecedents *in gender* (feminine, masculine, and neuter).

Each of the women has her favorite hobby.
Adam will wear his favorite sweater.
The tree lost its leaves early this fall.

3 Pronouns agree with their antecedents *in number* (singular or plural).

A verb must agree with its subject.
Pronouns must agree with their antecedents.
Brian is to give his recital at 2 p.m.
Joan and Carla have lost their homework.

4 When a pronoun's antecedent is a collective noun, the pronoun may be either singular or plural depending on whether the noun acts individually or as a unit.

The committee met to cast their ballots.
The class planned its graduation program.

■ **Commonly confused pronoun sound-alikes**

it's (contraction): it is; it has
its (possessive adjective): possessive form of it
It's good to see you; it's been a long time.
The puppy wagged its tail in welcome.

their (pronoun): possessive form of they
there (adverb/pronoun): at or in that place/used to introduce a clause
they're (contraction): they are
The hikers all wore their parkas.
Will he be there during our presentation?
They're likely to be late because of the snow.

who's (contraction): who is; who has
whose (pronoun): possessive form of who
Who's been to the movie? Who's going now?
I chose the one whose skills are best.

■ Word-division guides

1 Divide words between syllables only; therefore, do not divide one-syllable words. **Note:** When in doubt, consult a dictionary or a word-division manual.

through-out	pref-er-ence	em-ploy-ees
reached	toward	thought

2 Do not divide words of five or fewer letters even if they have two or more syllables.

into   also   about   union   radio   ideas

3 Do not separate a one-letter syllable at the beginning of a word or a one- or two-letter syllable at the end of a word.

across   enough   steady   highly   ended

4 Usually, you may divide a word between double consonants; but, when adding a syllable to a word that ends in double letters, divide after the double letters of the root word.

writ-ten	sum-mer	expres-sion	excel-lence
will-ing	win-ner	process-ing	fulfill-ment

5 When the final consonant is doubled in adding a suffix, divide between the double letters.

run-ning   begin-ning   fit-ting   submit-ted

6 Divide after a one-letter syllable within a word; but when two single-letter syllables occur together, divide between them.

sepa-rate   regu-late   gradu-ation   evalu-ation

7 When the single-letter syllable *a, i,* or *u* is followed by the ending *ly, ble, bly, cle,* or *cal,* divide before the single-letter syllable.

stead-ily	siz-able	vis-ible	mir-acle
cler-ical	but	musi-cal	practi-cal

8 Divide only between the two words that make up a hyphenated word.

self-contained   well-developed

9 Do not divide a contraction or a single group of figures.

doesn't $350,000   Policy F238975

10 Try to avoid dividing proper names and dates. If necessary, divide as follows.

Mary J./Pembroke	not	Mary J. Pem-/broke
November 15,/1995	not	November/15, 1995

■ Letter-placement points

Paper-guide placement

Check the placement of the paper guide for accurate horizontal centering of the letter.

Margins and date placement

Use the following guide:

5-Stroke Words In Letter Body	Side Margins	Date-line
Up to 100	2″	18
101-200	1½″	16
Over 200	1″	14

Letters containing many special features may require changes in these settings. Horizontal placement of date varies according to the letter style.

Address

The address begins on the fourth line (3 blank line spaces) below the date. A personal title, such as Mr., Mrs., Miss, or Ms., should precede the name of an individual. An official title, when used, may be placed on the first or the second line of the address, whichever gives better balance.

Two-page letters

If a letter is too long for one page, at least 2 lines of the body of the letter should be carried to the second page. The second page of a letter, or any additional pages, requires a proper heading. Use the block form shown below, beginning on line 6. Single-space the heading, and double-space below it.

Second-Page Heading

Dr. Ronald L. Spitz
Page 2
June 5, 19--

Attention line

An attention line, when used, is placed on the first line of the letter address.

Subject line

A subject line, when used, is placed on the second line (a double space) below the salutation. It is usually keyed at the left margin but may be centered in the modified block letter format. A subject line is required in the Simplified Block format; it is placed on the second line below the letter address.

Company name

Occasionally the company name is shown in the closing lines. When this is done, it is shown in ALL-CAPS 2 lines (a double space) below the complimentary close. Modern practice is to omit the company name in the closing lines if a letterhead is used.

Keyed/Printed name/official title

The name of the person who originated the letter and his/her official title are placed a quadruple space (3 blank line spaces) below the complimentary close, or a quadruple space below the company name when it is used. When both the name and official title are used, they may be placed on the same line, or the title may be placed on the next line below the keyed/printed name.

In the Simplified Block format, the name and official title of the originator are placed a quadruple space below the body of the letter.

■ 2-Letter State Abbreviations

Alabama .... AL	Guam .... GU	Massachusetts .... MA	New York .... NY	Tennessee .... TN
Alaska .... AK	Hawaii .... HI	Michigan .... MI	North Carolina .... NC	Texas .... TX
Arizona .... AZ	Idaho .... ID	Minnesota .... MN	North Dakota .... ND	Utah .... UT
Arkansas .... AR	Illinois IL	Mississippi .... MS	Ohio .... OH	Vermont .... VT
California .... CA	Indiana .... IN	Missouri .... MO	Oklahoma .... OK	Virgin Islands VI
Colorado .... CO	Iowa .... IA	Montana .... MT	Oregon .... OR	Virginia .... VA
Connecticut .... CT	Kansas .... KS	Nebraska .... NE	Pennsylvania .... PA	Washington .... WA
Delaware .... DE	Kentucky .... KY	Nevada .... NV	Puerto Rico .... PR	West Virginia .... WV
District of Columbia ..... DC	Louisiana .... LA	New Hampshire ...... NH	Rhode Island .... RI	Wisconsin .... WI
Florida .... FL	Maine .... ME	New Jersey .... NJ	South Carolina .... SC	Wyoming .... WY
Georgia .... GA	Maryland .... MD	New Mexico .... NM	South Dakota .... SD	

1   Block, open

MERKEL-EVANS, Inc.
1321 Commerce Street • Dallas, TX 75202-1648 • Tel. (214) 871-4400

November 10, 19--   QS (space down
4 blank lines)

Mrs. Evelyn M. McNeil
4582 Campus Drive
Fort Worth, TX 76119-1835
DS
Dear Mrs. McNeil
DS
The new holiday season is just around the corner, and we invite you to beat the rush and visit our exciting gallery of gifts. Gift-giving can be a snap this year because of our vast array of gifts "for kids from one to ninety-two."
DS
What's more, many of our gifts are prewrapped for presentation. All can be packaged and shipped right here at the store.
DS
A catalog of our hottest gift items and a schedule of special hours for special charge-card customers are enclosed. Please stop in and let us help you select that special gift, or call us if you wish to shop by phone.
DS
We wish you happy holidays and hope to see you soon.
QS
Cordially yours
DS
Ms. Carol J. Suess, Manager
DS
rj
DS
Enclosures

2   Modified block, open

ASSOCIATION OF OFFICE MANAGERS
518 JUNIPER CIRCLE • GOLDEN, CO 80403-6249 • (303) 930-7749

September 26, 19--   QS (space down
4 blank lines)

Mr. Frank P. Dalton
90 Spring Street
Portland, ME 04101-7430
DS
Dear Mr. Dalton
DS
It has come to my attention that several of the publications you ordered in August may not have arrived as yet. According to the enclosed copy of your order, Items 3765A, 4890B, and 5021X have not yet been shipped.
DS
Normally, orders received by the Association of Office Managers are processed within 10 days of receipt. Because of a computer problem, however, it appears that some orders in August may not have been completed.
DS
A copy of Item 3765A is enclosed. Copies of 4890B and 5021X will be sent priority mail within the next few days by Mrs. Carla F. Fernandez, chief of special orders.
DS
We appreciate your interest in our publications and thank you for your patronage.
DS
Sincerely yours
DS
ASSOCIATION OF OFFICE MANAGERS
QS
Brian E. Miller
Director of Publications
DS
xx
DS
Enclosures
Item 3765A
Order
DS
c Mrs. Carla F. Fernandez
DS
If you have received these publications previously, please accept these copies with our compliments.

3   Simplified block

Communication Concepts Inc.
178 S. Prospect Avenue • San Bernardino, CA 92410-4567 • (714) 586-7934

September 15, 19--
QS
MISS MICHELLE T LAWSON
DEL AMO SECRETARIAL SERVICE
21200 HAWTHORNE AVE
LOS ANGELES CA 90058-2820
DS
SIMPLIFIED BLOCK LETTER FORMAT
DS
This letter illustrates the features that distinguish the simplified block letter format from the standard block format.
DS
1. The date is placed on line 12 so that the letter address will show through the window of a window envelope when used.
DS
2. The letter address is keyed in the style recommended by the U. S. Postal Service for OCR processing: ALL-CAP letters with no punctuation. Cap-and-lowercase letters with punctuation may be used if that is the format of the addresses stored in an electronic address file. Personal titles may be omitted.
DS
3. A subject line replaces the traditional salutation which some people find objectionable. The subject line may be keyed in ALL-CAP or cap-and-lowercase letters. A double space is left above and below it.
DS
4. The complimentary close, which some people view as a needless appendage, is omitted.
DS
5. The writer's name is placed on the fourth line space below the body of the letter. The writer's title or department name may appear on the line with the writer's name or on the next line below it. The signature block may be keyed in ALL-CAP or cap-and-lowercase letters.
DS
6. A standard-length line is used for all letters. A six-inch line is a common length (60 pica or 10-pitch spaces; 72 elite or 12-pitch spaces).
DS
The features listed and illustrated here are designed to bring efficiency to the electronic processing of mail.
QS
MRS. MARIA T. LOPEZ, DIRECTOR
DS
tms

4   Simplified memorandum

henderson associates
6623 Mitchell Avenue, Tallahassee, FL 32303-4429

INTEROFFICE MEMORANDUM

June 12, 19--
QS
Martin F. Jensen, Chief Financial Officer
DS
OFFICE RENOVATION
DS
All of the furniture ordered for your office has arrived except for the computer table. It is back ordered, and it should arrive within the next week.

Arrangements have been made for your new carpet to be installed on Saturday, June 26. Since your old furniture will be left in the hallway during the weekend, we will need to take the necessary security precautions. Mike Jackson has agreed to let you store your file cabinets in his office over the weekend. Please let me know by Friday if there are other things you would like stored along with the files, and I will make the necessary arrangements.
QS
Karl L. Hayward, Facilities Manager
DS
xx

ENVELOPES: ADDRESSING, FOLDING, AND INSERTING

■ Addressing procedure

Envelope address

Set a tab stop (or margin stop if a number of envelopes are to be addressed) 10 spaces left of center for a small envelope or 5 spaces for a large envelope. Start the address here on Line 12 from the top edge of a small envelope and on Line 14 of a large one.

Style

Key the address in *block style*, SS. Use ALL CAPS and omit punctuation. Key the city name, state abbreviation, and ZIP Code on the last address line. The ZIP Code is keyed 2 spaces after the state abbreviation.

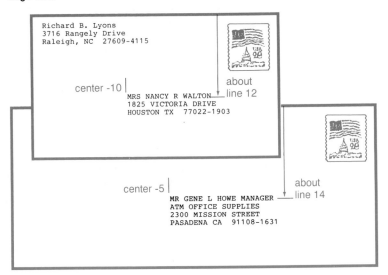

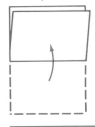

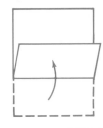

Addressee notations

Key addressee notations, such as HOLD FOR ARRIVAL, PLEASE FORWARD, or PERSONAL, a double space below the return address and about 3 spaces from the left edge of the envelope. Key these notations in ALL CAPS.

If an *attention line* is used, key it as the first line of the envelope address.

Mailing notations

Key mailing notations, such as SPECIAL DELIVERY and REGISTERED, below the stamp and at least 3 line spaces above the envelope address. Key these notations in ALL CAPS.

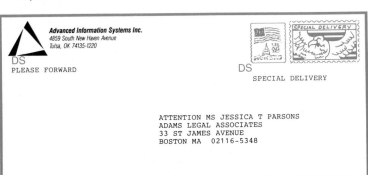

■ Folding and inserting procedure

Small envelopes (No. 6¾, 6¼)

Step 1 With letter face up, fold bottom up to ½ inch from top.
Step 2 Fold right third to left.
Step 3 Fold left third to ½ inch from last crease.
Step 4 Insert last creased edge first.

Large envelopes (No. 10, 9, 7¾)

Step 1 With letter face up, fold slightly less than ⅓ of sheet up toward top.
Step 2 Fold down top of sheet to within ½ inch of bottom fold.
Step 3 Insert letter into envelope with last crease toward bottom of envelope.

Window envelopes (letter)

Step 1 With sheet face down, top toward you, fold upper third down.
Step 2 Fold lower third up so address is showing.
Step 3 Insert sheet into envelope with last crease at bottom.

1 Unbound, page 1

Main
head

line 10 pica; line 12 elite

THE CHANGING OFFICE
QS

1"

A secretary returning to an office job after a 25-year absence
would have a difficult time coping with the changes that have taken
place during that time. Changing technology would best describe
the challenges facing today's office worker. Two "buzzwords" which
are currently being used in the office are electronic desktop publishing and electronic mail. DS

Side
head

Electronic Desktop Publishing DS

Desktop publishing is the process of integrating text and
graphics by utilizing computer software to produce professional-
looking documents without using professional services. According
to Winsor (1987, 29) DS

Desktop publishing has a bright future. . . . Desktop publishing enables people and businesses to develop their own brochures, newsletters, and other documents at a fraction of the
cost and time expended sending the work out to a professional
graphics studio. DS

Since today's firms are more concerned than ever about creating
the proper image, it is expected that a greater number of firms will
turn to desktop publishing to enhance their images. DS

Electronic Mail DS

The second "buzzword" being used extensively in the modern office is electronic mail (E-mail). E-mail is the sending, storing,
and delivering of written messages electronically. Reiss and Dolan
(1989, 529) identify two categories of electronic mail services: DS

1. In-house electronic mail. (E-mail which is run on a firm's
computer system.)

at least 1"

2 Unbound, page 2

line 8   2 line 6

2. Commercial electronic mail. (E-mail which is supplied by
organizations such as General Electric Information Services
and MCI Communication.)

Summary

Desktop publishing and electronic mail are but two of the
changes which are shaping the future of information processing.
Each year new technology enhances the ability of office personnel
to produce quality information in less time. QS

REFERENCES
QS

Reiss, Levi and Edwin G. Dolan. Using Computers: Managing Change.
Cincinnati: South-Western Publishing Co., 1989. DS

Winsor, William M. "Electronic Publishing: The Next Great Office
Revolution." The Secretary, June/July 1987.

1"   1"

3 Leftbound, page 1

Main
head

line 10 pica; line 12 elite

CAREER PLANNING
QS

1½"

Career planning is an important, ongoing process. It is
important because the career you choose will affect the quality of your life and will help determine the respect and recognition you receive. Throughout your lifetime you are likely
to make three or four career changes.[1] DS

Establish a Career Objective DS

One early, important step in the career planning process
is to define your career objective.

The career objective may indicate your area of interest
(such as finance or sales), the sort of organization you
would like to work for (such as banking or manufacturing), and the level of the position you want.[2]

Complete a Personal Inventory

Another useful step in career planning is to develop a
personal profile of your skills, interests, and values.

Skills. An analysis of your skills is likely to reveal
that you have many different kinds.

1. Functional skills that determine how well you manage time, communicate, motivate people, write, etc.

2. Adaptive skills that determine how well you will
fit into a specific work environment. These skills include personal traits such as flexibility, reliability,
efficiency, thoroughness, and enthusiasm for the job.

DS
DS

[1]Susan Bernard, Getting the Right Job, AT&T's College
Series (Elizabeth, NJ: AT&T College Market, 1988), p. 6.

DS

[2]William H. Cunningham, Ramon J. Aldag, and Christopher
M. Swift, Introduction to Business, 2d ed. (Cincinnati:
South-Western Publishing Co., 1989), p. 620.

at least 1"

4 Leftbound, page 2

line 8   2 line 6

3. Technical or work content skills that are required
to perform a specific job. These skills may include
such things as keyboarding, accounting, computer operation, and language usage skills.[3]

Interests. "Interests refer to the things that you like
or dislike."[4] By listing and analyzing them you should be
able to identify a desirable work environment. For example,
your list is likely to reveal if you like to work with things
or people, work alone or with others, lead or follow others,
or indoors or outdoors.

1½"   1"

Values. Values are your priorities in life, and you
should identify them early so that you can pursue a career
which will improve your chances to acquire them. Some of the
more obvious values include the importance you place on family, security, wealth, prestige, creativity, power, independence, and glamour.[5]

DS
DS

[3]Adele Scheele, "Deciding What You Want To Do," Business
Week Careers, 1988 ed., p. 7.

DS

[4]Bernard, Getting the Right Job, pp. 1-2.

[5]Cunningham, Introduction to Business, p. 617.

5 Leftbound, contents page

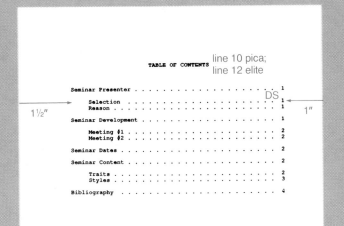

TABLE OF CONTENTS line 10 pica; line 12 elite

Seminar Presenter	1
Selection	1
Reason	1
Seminar Development	1
Meeting #1	2
Meeting #2	2
Seminar Dates	2
Seminar Content	2
Traits	2
Styles	3
Bibliography	4

DS

1½"   1"

6 Leftbound, bibliography (references)

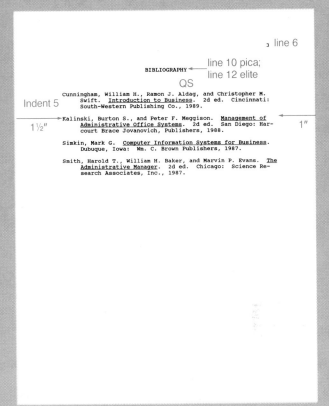

₃ line 6

BIBLIOGRAPHY line 10 pica; line 12 elite

QS

Cunningham, William H., Ramon J. Aldag, and Christopher M. Swift. _Introduction to Business_. 2d ed. Cincinnati: South-Western Publishing Co., 1989.

Kalinski, Burton S., and Peter F. Meggison. _Management of Administrative Office Systems_. 2d ed. San Diego: Harcourt Brace Jovanovich, Publishers, 1988.

Simkin, Mark G. _Computer Information Systems for Business_. Dubuque, Iowa: Wm. C. Brown Publishers, 1987.

Smith, Harold T., William H. Baker, and Marvin P. Evans. _The Administrative Manager_. 2d ed. Chicago: Science Research Associates, Inc., 1987.

Indent 5   1½"   1"

7 Topbound, page 1

Main head

FINDLEY HIGH SCHOOL BUSINESS CLUB ACTIVITIES line 12 pica; line 14 elite

QS

The members of the Findley High School Business Club met last week and decided to conduct the projects listed below. Please consider this document as the club's request for permission to organize and conduct these projects during this school year. The proposed projects will publicize the business education program to students, parents, and other members of the community that Findley High School serves. In addition, they will bring recognition to current business education students.

Fall Semester Projects

The following projects have been suggested for the fall semester. These projects will help to draw students' attention to the business education program early in the school year.

Poster contest. The club will sponsor a poster contest in late September to recruit new members into the Business Club. The posters will be displayed throughout the high school building and the winner will receive a coupon good for two dinners at George's Family Restaurant.

Open house. Club members will participate in the Business Education Department's Fourth Annual Open House. The members will

1. Greet the guests at the main entrance.

2. Escort the guests to the Business Education Department where the program will be held.

3. Demonstrate the computer hardware and software that is used in the business classes.

1"   1"   at least 1"

8 Formal memorandum

EAGLE & SONS

2299 Seward Highway ▪ Anchorage, Alaska ▪ 99503-4100   INTEROFFICE MEMORANDUM

TO: Warren E. Latouch, Director of Administration

FROM: Carla M. Boniface, Chief of Personnel

DATE: May 2, 19--

SUBJECT: Employee Evaluation Program DS

As the company continues to expand, it is desirable that we establish an effective program for evaluating the performance of all our employees. A sound evaluation program offers many advantages to both the company and our employees, including the following:

1. Assists employees in judging their own value and accomplishments. Ratings should include strong points as well as shortcomings, with suggestions for improvement. DS

2. Provides managers with information which they may use to determine promotions or lateral reassignments in order to make the most effective use of each employee's abilities.

3. Provides a basis for determining increases in compensation or for bonus payments to reward the most efficient employees.

4. Requires supervisors to analyze the work done by their subordinates and to recognize the contribution they make in the accomplishment of their mutual objectives.

5. Promotes an atmosphere of mutual respect and teamwork among supervisors and employees.

6. Provides an evaluation of the effectiveness of other personnel programs such as recruitment, selection, orientation, and training.

It is essential that clear-cut policies be established for this new evaluation program. To insure success, the objectives of the program must be clearly established, thoroughly understood, and fully accepted by all concerned. A recommended plan of action to accomplish these objectives is attached.

As a matter of priority, I recommend that the establishment of a program to evaluate employee performance be placed on the agenda of the executive committee for consideration at the earliest possible date.

xx

Attachment

1"   1"

Reference Guide: Report Formats

CORRECTION SYMBOLS

■ Proofreader's marks

Sometimes keyed or printed copy may be corrected with proofreader's marks. The keyboard operator must be able to interpret these marks correctly in rekeying the corrected copy or *rough draft* as it may be called. The most commonly used proofreader's marks are shown below.

⬆ or ≡	Capitalize
◡	Close up
	Delete
∨	Insert
	Insert comma
# or #/	Insert space
	Insert apostrophe
	Insert quotation marks
	Move right
	Move left
	Move down; lower
	Move up; raise
/ or lc	Set in lowercase
¶	Paragraph
no ¶	No new paragraph
‖	Set flush; align type
	Spell out
	Let it stand; ignore correction
or tr	Transpose
_____	Underline or italics

CENTERING PROCEDURES

1 Horizontal centering

1. Move margin stops to extreme ends of scale.
2. Clear tab stops; then set a tab stop at center of paper.
3. Tabulate to center of paper.
4. From center, backspace once for each 2 letters, spaces, figures, or punctuation marks in the line.
5. Do not backspace for an odd or leftover stroke at the end of the line.
6. Begin to key where backspacing ends.

Formula for finding horizontal center of paper

Example

Scale reading at left edge of paper   0
+ Scale reading at right edge of paper   102

    102

Total ÷ 2 = Center Point   102 ÷ 2 = 51

2 Horizontal centering for machines with automatic center

1. Insert paper with the left edge at 0.
2. Set margins at the extreme right and left edges of the paper.
3. Strike **Return** to move the carrier to the left margin; then press the **Center** key. (if you are using a microcomputer/word processor, refer to your software user's guide for centering.)
4. Key the first line. (Characters will not print as you key the line, but the carrier will move to the left for each character keyed.)
5. Strike **Return** to print the line.
6. Repeat Steps 3-5 to center each line.

3 Vertical centering

Mathematical method

1. Count lines and blank line spaces needed to key problem.
2. Subtract *lines to be used* from *lines available* (66 for full sheet and 33 for half sheet).
3. Divide by 2 to get top and bottom margins. If a fraction results, disregard it.
4. If an even number results, space down that number of times from top of sheet and key the first line. If an odd number results, use the next lower number.

Dropping fractions and using even numbers usually places copy a line or two above exact center-- in what is often called *reading position.*

Formula for vertical mathematical placement

$$\frac{\text{Lines available} - \text{lines used}}{2} = \text{top margin}$$

Backspace-from-center method

Basic rule

From vertical center of paper, roll platen (cylinder) back once for each 2 lines, 2 blank line spaces, or line and blank line space. Ignore odd or leftover line.

Steps to follow:

1. To move paper to vertical center, start spacing down from top edge of paper.

   a half sheet
     down 8 DS (double spaces)
     + 1 SS (Line 17)

   b full sheet
     down 17 DS (Line 34)

2. From vertical center

   a half sheet, SS or DS; follow basic rule, back 1 for 2 lines

   b full sheet, SS or DS; follow basic rule, back 1 for 2; then back 2 SS for reading position.

Prepare

1 Insert and align paper (typewriter).

2 Clear margin stops by moving them to extreme ends of line-of-writing scale. On electronic equipment, set margins as near as possible to the edges of the paper (so that automatic centering may be used for horizontal placement).

3 Clear all tabulator stops.

4 Move element carrier (carriage) or cursor to center of paper or line-of-writing scale.

5 Decide the number of spaces to be left between columns (for intercolumns)--preferably an even number (4, 6, 8, 10, etc.).

1 Plan vertical placement

Follow either of the vertical centering procedures explained on page RG 10.

Spacing headings. Double-space (count 1 blank line space) between main and secondary headings, when both are used. Double-space between the last table heading (either main or secondary) and the first horizontal line of column items or column headings. Double-space between column headings (when used) and the first line of the column entries. On electronic equipment, use the automatic center feature (see RG 10) to center the *key* line (line made up of the longest item in each column plus the number of spaces between columns). Set a tab stop at the beginning of each column; then discard or delete the *key* line.

Spacing above totals and source notes. Double-space between the total rule and the total figures. Double-space between the last line of the table and the 1½″ rule above the source note. Double-space between the 1½″ rule and the source note.

2 Plan horizontal placement

On an electronic typewriter, backspace from center of paper (or line-of-writing scale) 1 space for each 2 letters, figures, symbols, and spaces in *longest* item of each column in the table. Then backspace once for each 2 spaces to be left between columns (intercolumns). Set left margin stop where backspacing ends.

If an odd or leftover space occurs at the end of the longest item of a column when backspacing by 2's, carry it forward to the next column. Do not backspace for an odd or leftover character at the end of the last column. (See illustration below.)

Set tab stops. From the left margin, space forward 1 space for each letter, figure, symbol, and space in the longest item in the first column and for each space to be left between Cols. 1 and 2. Set a tab stop at this point for the second column. Follow this procedure for each additional column of the table.

Note: If a column heading is longer than the longest item in the column, it *may* be treated as the longest item in the column in determining placement. The longest columnar entry must then be centered under the heading and the tab stop set accordingly.

3 Center column headings (optional)

Backspace-from-column-center method

From point at which column begins (tab or margin stop), space forward once for each 2 letters, figures, or spaces in the longest item in the column. This leads to the column center point; from it, backspace once for each 2 spaces in column heading. Ignore an odd or leftover space. Key the heading at this point; it will be centered over the column.

Mathematical methods

1 To the number on the cylinder (platen) or line-of-writing scale immediately under the first letter, figure, or symbol of the longest item of the column, add the number shown under the space following the last stroke of the item. Divide this sum by 2; the result will be the center point of the column. From this point on the scale, backspace (1 for 2) to center the column heading.

2 From the number of spaces in the longest item, subtract the number of spaces in the heading. Divide this number by 2; ignore fractions. Space forward this number from the tab or margin stop and key the heading.

4 Horizontal rulings

To make horizontal rulings in tables, depress shift lock and strike the underline key.

Single-space above and double-space below horizontal rulings.

5 Vertical rulings

On a typewriter, operate the automatic line finder. Place a pencil or pen point through the cardholder (or the typebar guide above the ribbon or carrier). Roll the paper up until you have a line of the desired length. Remove the pencil or pen and reset the line finder.

On a computer-generated table, use a ruler and pen or pencil to draw the vertical rulings.

```
                    MAIN HEADING

                 Secondary Heading

    These        Are        Column        Heads

    xxxxxx      longest      xxxx         xxxxx
    xxxx        item         longest      xxx
    xxxxx       xxxxx        item         longest
    longest     xxxxxx       xxxxx        item
    item        xxxx         xxx          xxx

    longest 1234 longest 1234 longest 1234 longest
```

1 Electronic correction

Electronic typewriters, word processors, and computers vary in the way keystroking errors may be corrected. All, however, have a correction key that removes errors from the electronic window/screen and/or paper. Use the User's Manual for your machine to learn the steps for making corrections electronically.

2 Lift-off tape

1 Strike the special backspace/lift-off key to move the printing element (or carrier) to the point of the error.
2 Rekey the error exactly as you made it. In this step, the lift-off tape actually lifts the error off the page. The printing element stays in place.
3 Key the correction.

3 Correction fluid

1 Turn the paper up a few spaces to ease the correction procedure.
2 Shake the bottle; remove the applicator; daub excess fluid on inside of bottle opening.
3 Brush fluid sparingly over the entire error by a light touching action.
4 Return applicator to bottle and tighten cap; blow on the error to speed the drying process.

4 Correction paper

1 Backspace to the beginning of the error.
2 Insert the correction tape or paper strip behind the ribbon and in front of the error, coated side toward the copy.
3 Rekey the error exactly as you made it. In this step, powder from the correction paper is pressed by force into the type of the error, thus masking it.
4 Remove the correction paper; backspace to the point where the correction begins and key the correction.

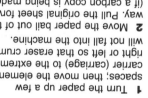

5 Rubber eraser

1 Turn the paper up a few spaces; then move the element carrier (carriage) to the extreme right or left so that eraser crumbs will not fall into the machine.
2 Move the paper bail out of the way. Pull the original sheet forward (if a carbon copy is being made) and place a card (5" × 3" or slightly larger) in front of, not behind, the first carbon sheet to protect the carbon copy from smudges.
3 Flip the original sheet back and make the erasure with a hard eraser. Brush or blow the eraser crumbs off the paper.
4 Move the protective card to a position in front of the second carbon sheet if more than one carbon copy is being made. Erase the error on the first carbon copy with a soft eraser.
5 Remove the card and key the correction.

6 Correcting errors by squeezing/spreading

Letter omitted in a word
1 Remove the word with the omitted letter.
2 Move printing element to second space after preceding word.
3 Pull half-space lever forward (or use electronic incremental backspacer) to move printing element a half space to the left.
4 Hold lever in place as you key the corrected word with the other hand.
5 Release the lever and continue keying.

Error   an omitte letter
Correction   an omitted letter

Letter added in a word
1 Remove the word with the added letter.
2 Move printing element to third space after preceding word.
3 Pull half-space lever forward (or use electronic incremental backspacer) to move printing element a half space to the left.
4 Hold lever in place as you key the corrected word with the other hand.
5 Release the lever and continue keying.

Error   a letter within
Correction   a letter within

7 Carbon-Pack Assembly

1 Assemble letterhead, carbon sheets (uncarboned side up), and second sheets as illustrated above. Use one carbon and one second sheet for each copy desired.

2 Grasp the carbon pack at the sides, turn it so that the letterhead faces away from you, the carbon side of the carbon paper is toward you, and the top edge of the pack is face down. Tap the sheets gently on the desk to straighten.
3 Hold the sheets firmly to prevent slipping; insert pack into typewriter. Hold pack with one hand; turn platen with the other.
4 To keep the carbon pack straight when feeding it into the typewriter, place the pack in the fold of a plain sheet of paper (paper trough) or under the flap of an envelope. Remove trough or envelope when the pack is in place.

Photocopier

Offset Printer

Reprographics refers to the making of multiple copies of all kinds of materials. Numerous items should be considered when planning and organizing material for duplication. One important factor is cost. The objective is to select a duplication process that will provide the material at the lowest possible cost per copy. The appearance of the copy in terms of clarity, attractiveness, format, and size must also be considered. Since time available to do the work may affect quality and cost, time is also an important factor.

The four processes used most often in schools, churches, and business offices are photocopier duplication, offset duplication, spirit duplication, and stencil duplication. Each of these processes is described briefly here.

Photocopier Duplication

Photocopiers have virtually replaced spirit and stencil duplication in the business office. The photocopy process, which produces copies directly from an original electronically, is easier, cleaner, quicker, and even less costly when only a few copies are needed, than the other processes described here.

Copiers are often classified by the kind of paper they require and the number of copies they are designed to produce. Plain-paper copiers, which use the regular paper found in the office, are most popular. Coated-paper copiers require the use of more expensive chemically-treated paper.

Copiers also may be classified by volume of copies produced. Low-volume copiers (which will produce about 20 copies per minute) are designed for no more than 20,000 copies per month. Mid-volume copiers (which produce 40-60 copies per minute) are designed to generate 20,000 to 50,000 copies per month. High-volume copiers (which produce up to 120 copies per minute) are designed to produce more than 50,000 copies per month.

Copiers, especially in the mid- and high-volume range, are available with a variety of special features. These include image reduction/enlargement, color duplication, duplex (two-sided) printing, collating/stapling, and automatic feed. All these features improve the usefulness and efficiency of copiers, but also add to their cost.

Offset Printing

Offset printing (which is done from plates made from camera-ready masters) is primarily a commercial printing process used to make thousands of copies of items containing limited numbers of pages. More sophisticated photocopiers have largely replaced offset printers for within-the-office duplication.

Preparing Master Copies for Photocopying and Offset Printing

Because photocopying and offset printing utilize a photographic process, each method begins with the preparation of a master or model copy of each page. The model or master copy can be generated on a standard or an electronic typewriter, on a computer, or on a word processor. The following steps will result in camera-ready copy usable for either photocopying or offset printing.

1. Be sure that the printing element (type, "ball," or daisy wheel) is clean and free of debris (ink, white-out, etc.).

2. Plan margins, spacing, and space to be left for illustrations (if any) before preparing a rough draft of the model.

3. Prepare a rough-draft model on the same size paper to be used for final printing (unless the copy is to be enlarged or reduced).

4. Proofread and correct the rough-draft copy before keying the final copy.

5. Prepare the final (camera-ready) copy on a smooth-finish paper so that the images are clear and sharp.

6. Correct all errors neatly. Use lift-off tape on typewriters so equipped. On other typewriters, use white-out or cover-up paper strips. On equipment with a display, correct errors on screen before printing a hard copy.

7. Give the master copy a final check to be sure it is error-free and free of smudges, wrinkles, tears, or other blemishes that could be picked up by a camera.

(continued, p. RG 14)

Spirit Duplication

The spirit duplicator, sometimes called a "Ditto" (a trade name), is the least expensive way to reproduce up to several hundred copies. The primary print color used is purple, although pale shades of red, blue, green, and black are also available. These copies are not usually as clear and attractive as those produced by other duplicators. This machine is used primarily by churches, schools, and small business firms.

The spirit master set consists of two basic parts: the master sheet and a sheet of special carbon that can be used only once. A backing sheet also may be used to improve the consistency of the print. If a specially prepared master is not available, simply place the carbon paper between the master sheet and the backing sheet, with the glossy side of the carbon toward you. When you key the copy, the carbon copy will be on the back of the master sheet.

Follow these directions for better masters.

1. Prepare a model copy of the material to be duplicated. Leave at least a one-half inch margin at the top of the master. Proofread the model copy; correct it if necessary.

2. If you do not have a carbon ribbon, you can avoid "fuzzy" type and filled-in characters by preparing the copy with the ribbon indicator in the "stencil" position. This procedure makes it difficult to proofread the copy, however.

3. Insert the open end of the spirit master into the machine first so that you can make corrections easily (see illustration at left). If you make an error, scrape off with a razor blade or knife the incorrect letter or word on the reverse side of the master sheet. Before correcting the error, tear off an unused portion of the carbon sheet and slip it under the part to be corrected. Correct the error and remove the torn portion of carbon as soon as you have done so.

4. On electric and electronic machines, which provide even pressure automatically, key as usual. Use a firm, even stroke to key the master on a nonelectric machine; key capitals a little heavier than usual and punctuation marks a little lighter.

5. Proofread the copy and correct any errors you may have missed before you remove the master from the machine.

6. "Run" the number of copies needed by following the User's Manual that accompanies your spirit duplicator.

Stencil Duplication

Thousands of copies of programs, bulletins, newsletters, and other publications can be reproduced in a short time through the use of the stencil duplication process.

A stencil consists of three basic parts: the stencil sheet, the backing sheet, and the cushion sheet. When a key strikes the stencil sheet, it "cuts" an impression in the shape of the type. Note: Only a machine having type bars is capable of "cutting" a stencil adequately. A printing element or wheel may not actually "cut" the stencil sheet. A cushion sheet is placed between the stencil and the backing sheet to absorb the impact of the type bar. A film sheet may be placed over the stencil sheet if darker print is desired. This film also protects the stencil sheet from letter cutout when the type face is extremely sharp.

Before "cutting" the stencil, follow these steps.

1. Prepare a model copy of the material to be reproduced. Check it for accuracy of format and keying; correct it if necessary. Be certain that you place the copy on the page so that it will be within the stencil guide marks (see illustration at left).

2. If your machine has a cloth ribbon, clean the printing element thoroughly, paying close attention to the letters where ink tends to accumulate, such as the o and the e. Adjust the ribbon lever to "stencil" position.

3. Insert the cushion sheet between the stencil sheet and the backing sheet. Place the top edge of the model copy at the corner marks of the stencil to see where to position the first line. The scales at the top and sides of the stencil will help you place the copy correctly.

4. Insert the stencil assembly into the machine. On electric and electronic machines, which provide even pressure automatically, key with the usual force. If you are using a nonelectric typewriter, use a firm, uniform touch. Some keys that are completely closed such as d and p must be struck more lightly. Capitals and letters such as m and u must be struck with greater force.

5. If you make an error, it can be corrected easily with stencil correction fluid. If there is a film over the stencil, this must be detached until you resume keying. Use a smooth paper clip to rub the surface of the error on the stencil sheet. Place a pencil between the stencil sheet and the cushion sheet and apply a light coat of correction fluid over the error. Let the fluid dry; then make the correction, using a light touch.

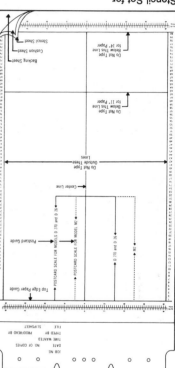

Stencil Set for Stencil Duplication

Master Set for Spirit Duplication

Regular typewriter ribbon · Master sheet · Backing sheet · Carboned surface toward master